RISING CHINA
and New Chinese Migrants in Southeast Asia

The **ISEAS – Yusof Ishak Institute** (formerly Institute of Southeast Asian Studies) is an autonomous organization established in 1968. It is a regional centre dedicated to the study of socio-political, security, and economic trends and developments in Southeast Asia and its wider geostrategic and economic environment. The Institute's research programmes are grouped under Regional Economic Studies (RES), Regional Strategic and Political Studies (RSPS), and Regional Social and Cultural Studies (RSCS). The Institute is also home to the ASEAN Studies Centre (ASC), the Singapore APEC Study Centre and the Temasek History Research Centre (THRC).

ISEAS Publishing, an established academic press, has issued more than 2,000 books and journals. It is the largest scholarly publisher of research about Southeast Asia from within the region. ISEAS Publishing works with many other academic and trade publishers and distributors to disseminate important research and analyses from and about Southeast Asia to the rest of the world.

Edited by
Leo Suryadinata and Benjamin Loh

RISING CHINA
and New Chinese Migrants in Southeast Asia

ISEAS YUSOF ISHAK INSTITUTE

First published in Singapore in 2022 by
ISEAS Publishing
30 Heng Mui Keng Terrace
Singapore 119614
E-mail: publish@iseas.edu.sg
Website: http://bookshop.iseas.edu.sg

All rights reserved. No part of this publication may be reproduced, stored in a retrieval system, or transmitted in any form or by any means, electronic, mechanical, photocopying, recording or otherwise, without the prior permission of the ISEAS – Yusof Ishak Institute.

© 2022 ISEAS – Yusof Ishak Institute, Singapore

The responsibility for facts and opinions in this publication rests exclusively with the authors and their interpretations do not necessarily reflect the views or the policy of the publisher or its supporters.

This publication is made possible with the support of Konrad-Adenauer-Stiftung.

ISEAS Library Cataloguing-in-Publication Data

Name(s): Suryadinata, Leo, editor. | Loh, Benjamin C.H., editor.
Title: Rising China and new Chinese migrants in Southeast Asia / edited by Leo Suryadinata & Benjamin Loh.
Description: Singapore : ISEAS – Yusof Ishak Institute, 2022. | Includes index.
Identifiers: ISBN 9789815011586 (paperback) | ISBN 9789815011593 (PDF) | ISBN 9789815011807 (epub)
Subjects: LCSH: Chinese–Southeast Asia. | Southeast Asia–Emigration and immigration. | China–Emigration and immigration.
Classification: LCC DS732 R59

Typeset by Superskill Graphics Pte Ltd
Printed in Singapore by Mainland Press Pte Ltd

Contents

About the Contributors ... ix

Introduction: Rising China and New Chinese Migrants in Southeast Asia ... 1
Leo Suryadinata and Benjamin Loh

PART I: General Overviews on Rising China and *Xin Yimin*

1. Rising China, New Migrants and Ethnic Chinese Identity in Southeast Asia ... 17
   Leo Suryadinata

2. Contemporary Chinese Immigration into Mainland Southeast Asia ... 31
   Terence Chong

PART II: China's Soft Power, *Xin Yimin* and Local Communities

3. Confucius Institutes in Southeast Asia: An Overview ... 49
   Neo Peng Fu

4. Cambodian Perceptions of China: A Chinese Learners' Perspective ... 68
   Chheang Vannarith

5. China's Soft Power and the Chinese Overseas: Case Study of Xiamen University and the Confucius Institute in Malaysia ... 91
   Peter T.C. Chang

6. China Dream and Singapore Heart: A Comparison between the China Cultural Centre (CCC) and the Singapore Chinese Cultural Centre (SCCC)   107
Ho Yi Kai

PART III: New Chinese Migrants and Local Communities

7. "Old" and "New" Chinese Communities in Laos: Internal Diversity and External Influence   127
Bien Chiang and Jean Chihyin Cheng

8. *Xin Yimin* in the Philippines: Challenges and Perspectives   141
Teresita Ang-See

9. New Transnational Chinese Migrants in an Evolving Malaysia   162
Danny Wong Tze Ken

10. *Xin Yimin* in Indonesia: A Growing Community That Faces New Challenges   183
Leo Suryadinata

11. Indonesian Elites' Perceptions of New Chinese Migrants during the Joko Widodo Presidency   194
Johanes Herlijanto

PART IV: New Chinese Migrants and Local Economies

12. Vietnam-China Economic Ties and New Chinese Migrants in Vietnam   213
Nguyen van Chinh

13. Chinese Engagement in Laos: Past, Present, and Uncertain Future   242
Danielle Tan

14. Casino Capitalism, Chinese Special Economic Zone and the Making of a Neoliberal Border in Northern Laos   270
Pinkaew Laungaramsri

15. 'Old' and 'New' Chinese Business in Cambodia's Capital   293
    Michiel Verver

16. Entrepreneurial Excursions: Short-Hop Chinese Migration at
    the Peripheries of Myanmar   322
    Andrew Ong

Index   339

About the Contributors

Teresita Ang-See has conducted research on the lives of Chinese in the Philippines and has presented and published papers in international conferences and journals. She published five volumes of *The Chinese in the Philippines – Problems and Perspectives*. She was formerly the President of the International Society for the Study of Chinese Overseas (ISSCO) and served as its Secretary-Treasurer for a decade.

Peter T.C. Chang, PhD, is Deputy Director of the Institute of China Studies, University of Malaya. Trained in comparative philosophy and religion, he is currently researching China's rise from the perspective of the impact of Chinese soft power on Malaysia and the wider world.

Jean Chihyin Cheng is with Banqiao Community University, Taiwan. She received her MA degree from National Tsinghua University in Taiwan.

Chheang Vannarith, PhD, is a public policy analyst with over a decade of research and practical experience in geopolitical and political economic analysis, focusing on Southeast Asia. A former visiting fellow at the ISEAS – Yusof Ishak Institute, he is President of the Asian Vision Institute, an independent think tank based in Phnom Penh, Cambodia. He received his BA in International Relations from the Diplomatic Academy of Vietnam, his MA in International Relations from the International University of Japan, Leadership Certificate from the East-West Center, and his PhD in Asia Pacific Studies from Ritsumeikan Asia Pacific University in Japan.

Bien Chiang, PhD, is Associate Professor of the Department of Public and Cultural Affairs, National Taitung University in Taiwan and Director of the Center of Austronesian Culture at the same university. He received his PhD in Anthropology from the University of Pennsylvania. His research interests include kinship, social hierarchy and ritual of the Austronesian communities.

Terence Chong, PhD, is Deputy Chief Executive Officer and Director, Research Division, of the ISEAS – Yusof Ishak Institute. He has a BA (First Class) in History from the University of Leeds and a PhD in Sociology from the University of Warwick. His research interests include heritage, arts and cultural policies, and politics in Singapore; new Chinese immigrants in CLMV countries; and Christianity in Southeast Asia.

Johanes Herlijanto received a joint PhD in Anthropology from Macquarie University and Vrije Universiteit Amsterdam. He teaches at the Department of Communication, Pelita Harapan University, Jakarta. From 2016 to 2017, Johanes was visiting fellow at the ISEAS – Yusof Ishak Institute, where he researched on the perception of China, and of Chinese Indonesians, among the 'Pribumi' Indonesian elites.

Ho Yi Kai, PhD, was Assistant Director, Confucius Institute, Nanyang Technological University, Singapore. He obtained his BA in Chinese Language and Literature from Peking University as a Public Service Commission Scholar, and his MA and PhD in the same field from Nanjing University. His research interests are in Chinese Classical Studies and in Overseas Chinese.

Pinkaew Laungaramsri, PhD, is Associate Professor, Department of Sociology and Anthropology, Faculty of Social Sciences, Chiang Mai University. She was a visiting scholar at Harvard-Yenching Institute in 2015. She received her BA from Chulalongkorn University, her MA from both Thammasat University and Washington University, and her PhD in Anthropology from Washington University. Her research interests include politics of ethnicity, women and the nation, focussing mainly on mainland Southeast Asia.

Benjamin Loh, PhD, was Senior Fellow and Coordinator of the Regional Social and Cultural Studies Programme, ISEAS – Yusof Ishak Institute.

He is currently Head of ASEAN Socio-Cultural Community Monitoring Division at the ASEAN Secretariat. He received his PhD from the University of Cambridge, MA from the University of Warwick, and BSocSci from the National University of Singapore.

Neo Peng Fu, PhD, is Director, Confucius Institute, Nanyang Technological University, Singapore, and senior lecturer at the National Institute of Education (Singapore). He was an assistant professor at the National University of Singapore from 2000 to 2009. A historian by training, he publishes in two main areas: Chinese classics and language-in-education policy (with special reference to Chinese language teaching and learning in Singapore).

Nguyen Van Chinh, PhD, is Associate Professor and Head of the Department of Development Anthropology, College of Social Sciences and Humanities, Vietnam National University in Hanoi. He received his PhD from Amsterdam University, the Netherlands.

Andrew Ong, PhD, is a political anthropologist whose work examines insurgent autonomy, political economy, and Chinese migrants in Myanmar. He received his PhD in Social Anthropology from Harvard University, where his dissertation explored the stalemate between the Myanmar state and the country's largest armed group, the United Wa State Army. He is working on a project amongst Chinese business communities in Myanmar.

Leo Suryadinata, PhD, is Visiting Senior Fellow at the Regional Social and Cultural Studies Programme, ISEAS – Yusof Ishak Institute. He was Director, Chinese Heritage Centre, Nanyang Technological University, and Professor, Department of Political Science, National University of Singapore. He has published extensively on Southeast Asian Politics, ethnic Chinese in Southeast Asia, and China-ASEAN relations.

Danielle Tan, PhD, is a consultant and independent researcher. She was formerly Assistant Professor at Sciences Po Lyon and Research Associate at the Research Institute on Contemporary Southeast Asia (IRASEC, Bangkok). She received her PhD in Political Science from Sciences Po, Paris.

Michiel Verver, PhD, is an Assistant Professor at the Department of Organization Sciences, Vrije Universiteit Amsterdam. His research focuses on the interface of Phnom Penh's private sector and ethnic Chinese minority in the context of Cambodia's political economy. More broadly, he is interested in the anthropology of entrepreneurship, including the comparative study of migrant entrepreneurship, social entrepreneurship, and family businesses in Southeast Asia and beyond. He publishes in the fields of entrepreneurship studies and Asian studies.

Danny Wong Tze Ken, PhD, is Dean of the Faculty of Arts and Social Sciences, University of Malaya. He is Professor of History and former Director of the Institute of China Studies at the same university. His research interests include the Chinese in Malaysia, China's relations with Southeast Asia, and the history of Sabah.

Introduction: Rising China and New Chinese Migrants in Southeast Asia

Leo Suryadinata and Benjamin Loh

Since the period of rapid development in the People's Republic of China (PRC) after the reforms initiated by Deng Xiaoping in the late 1970s, the world is experiencing a new wave of Chinese migration. Loosely defined as Chinese people who are outside of China to conduct business, work, study or join their family overseas, these new Chinese migrants—also known as *xin yimin* 新移民—have had a profound impact on their host countries. Their influence on local societies, economies and politics has been complicated by Beijing's dynamic policy towards the Chinese overseas in general and towards the *xin yimin* in particular.

Before we proceed further, it is important for us to put Chinese migrants in a proper historical context.

A Brief Outline of Chinese Migration[1]

The earliest contact between China and Southeast Asia can be traced back to the Han dynasty. However, significant migration to this region started during the Song dynasty of the twelfth century. The first period was from the Song dynasty in the twelfth century until the first half of the sixteenth century of the Ming dynasty. It lasted for about 400 years. During this period, the feudal economy in China was at its peak and the number of Chinese abroad also increased. This coincided with the period that Admiral Zheng He (Cheng Ho 郑和) embarked upon his seven expeditions to the West Ocean (later known as Nanyang 南洋). Groups of Chinese merchants and sailors ventured overseas and some of them remained in various sites from their voyages. Those who stayed long married local women; the number of the Chinese overseas in Southeast Asia during this period was between 150,000 and 200,000.

The second period started in the second half of the sixteenth century when there was a sea embargo for the ethnic Chinese until the eruption of the Opium Wars. This period lasted about 300 years. During this period, China experienced the rise of capitalistic elements, and the West began to colonize Southeast Asia. More Chinese left China for Southeast Asia. According to one study, there were about a million Chinese in Southeast Asia. The majority lived in urban areas and retained their Chinese heritage and cultural identity.

The third period started in 1840 and ended in 1949 when the PRC was established. It lasted for 109 years. This was the period when China became a "half feudal and half colonial" society. There was poverty and high unemployment in China. The number of poor Chinese increased and many were forced to come to Southeast Asia as labourers. This was also the period when Chinese nationalism emerged among the Chinese overseas. During this period, fresh groups of migrants poured into Southeast Asia, and their numbers increased exponentially. In 1930, for instance, there were about 3.7 million Chinese in Southeast Asia.

The fourth period began in 1949 and continues to the present. The establishment of the PRC temporarily arrested the exodus of the Chinese from the mainland to Southeast Asia. Independent Southeast Asia restricted the new Chinese migrants as the nation-building process began in the region. China's economic development was still behind Southeast Asia and especially the West at this time. Chinese mass migration reoccurred when China started to introduce their open door policy, which ushered high economic growth into the 1980s. While the migration was more to the West rather than to Southeast Asia, the new Chinese migration in Southeast Asia is still significant in this fourth iteration of Chinese migration.

Beyond "Settling" and "Sojourning"

When we examine the history of Chinese migration from the Song dynasty—which coincided with an increase in Chinese maritime activity and trade in Southeast Asia and up to the Indian Ocean—until today, we can identify a few factors that may explain the reasons for Chinese migrations over this long period of time. There was the presence of push factors from

China, including political upheaval, overpopulation and poverty. On the other hand, there was a pull factor in Southeast Asia: local development provided economic and other opportunities for Chinese migrants. Even after the establishment of the PRC, some of the push and pull factors that we mentioned continued to be present. However, the patterns of migration after the rise of China in the 1990s are quite different from the early migration, and we will return to this point later.

A question can be posed here on whether the Chinese have the concept of migration or immigration in the sense of 'planning to settle in other countries permanently'. Such an understanding will need to be grounded in China's historical reality, or context, of the nature of its movements of people. For instance, Professor Wang Gungwu argued that such a concept did not exist in traditional China. The term *yimin*, which is often used to mean 'migration' or 'immigration' today, in fact refers to "the action of the state to move people from one area to another within the territory of China",[2] and it was often mobilized to strengthen defences on the border or to respond to natural disasters. A large part of Imperial Chinese history (and even earlier) also attributed movements of people to the system of the feudal economy (*fengjian jingji zhidu* 封建经济制度), which saw emperors offering official ranks and land to vassals and allowing them to establish a state on the land.[3]

The original Chinese term that is equivalent to the Western concept of 'immigration' is *qiaoju* 侨居, which can be roughly translated as 'sojourning'.[4] In this conception, the Chinese did not intend to settle overseas but to return to the homeland once they had made enough money, or other secondary motivations such as the gaining of knowledge, experience and/or connections. However, we would maintain that the first-generation Chinese might have such an intention but, in reality, many did not return to China. For subsequent generations, especially for those who were offspring of inter-marriages, their chances of 'returning' to their ancestral land became even more remote as they are no longer 'pure' Chinese in their cultural and ethnic identity. The Minh Huong in Vietnam,[5] the Lukchin in Thailand,[6] the (Chinese) Mestizo in the Philippines,[7] and the Peranakan Chinese in the Malay Archipelago[8] are cases in point. Even during the Great Depression of the 1930s, many of the migrant Chinese—who were often called 'birds of season'—in reality stayed on and did not return to mainland China.

The dualistic binary of 'settling' and 'sojourning' have preoccupied much writing on migration in general, and not only on Chinese migration.

While the notion of settling down for the migrant Chinese in general, and first-generation Chinese in particular, took place as nation-states emerged after the end of World War II, the original intention not to settle down does not solely apply to the ethnic Chinese but also to other Asian 'immigrants'. The Indians, for instance, were also temporary 'migrants', and it was only later that they decided to settle down. In this sense, the ethnic Chinese are not unique.

Southeast Asian governments that were newly established wanted to integrate the ethnic Chinese populations by introducing nation-building policies. Some are more rigid than others. Usually, ethnic Chinese were able to retain their cultural identity through four Chinese cultural pillars; namely, Chinese organizations, Chinese mass media, Chinese-medium schools and 'Chinese' religions. Some countries imposed restrictions on these ethnic Chinese institutions, but others eventually eradicated them. The extreme 'complete assimilation' policy was introduced in the Khmer Rouge's Kampuchea and Suharto's Indonesia.

Southeast Asian Chinese in general over the last century have been subjected to integrationist policies and to a certain extent have been 'Southeast-Asianized'. This process was helped by the restrictions on new Chinese migration to Southeast Asian states before the rise of China. However, with the end of the Cold War, economic globalization and the rise of China, we witness the recurrence of mass new Chinese migration.

New Chinese Migration and Its Characteristics

The modernization reform and open-door policy introduced by Deng Xiaoping in the late 1970s succeeded in transforming China into an industrialized country within a short few decades. China has become the world's factory, which has needed to look for huge markets for its products. It also requires raw materials, and it exports surplus capital and surplus manpower. 'To go out' (走出去) has become China's new policy. This also coincides with Xi Jinping's Belt and Road Initiative (BRI; earlier known as One Belt One Road).[9] Chinese companies have been encouraged to go overseas. Many mainland Chinese also wanted to migrate overseas for a better economic future. All of these serve as the push factors. The outside world, including Southeast Asia, which is rich with natural resources, needs cheap Chinese products and Chinese investments. Developing countries need Chinese technology. Both developed and developing countries also require Chinese students who are now able to pay their fees to receive tertiary education. All of these serve as pull factors for new Chinese migrants.

These new Chinese migrants include businessmen, professionals, technical workers, teachers, students and those who badly need to have jobs. One major characteristic that was absent in the past is the export of Chinese labourers accompanying large overseas projects. This is because in the past most Western countries did not have enough manpower to be exported to work on overseas projects, especially manual work.

Unlike in the last century and earlier, the focus of Chinese migration is no longer on the 'underdeveloped' Southeast Asia but on the 'developed' West, which includes the United States, Canada, the European Union (including the United Kingdom) and Australia. Approximately eighty per cent of new migrants went to these developed countries, and only about twenty per cent came to Southeast Asia. Moreover, the origins of new migrants are not only from the southern provinces of China but also from the whole of China, Taiwan and Hong Kong.[10]

These migrants are also more educated than earlier migrants. Many are also much wealthier than the previous migrants. Last but not least, unlike the old migrants, who tended to settle down and be assimilated, these new migrants are more mobile and are 'rootless'.[11] The last point is worth elaborating on.

In the past, the pattern of Chinese migrants was either 'returning to original roots' (Luoye guigen, 落叶归根), or 'taking local roots' (Luodi shenggen 落地生根). The new Chinese migrants are a different kettle of fish. They are in a different era and are more mobile and hence they have different sets of mentality. Zhuang Guotu of Xiamen University describes this new phenomenon: they are neither *luoye guigen* nor *luodi shenggen* but searching for a better place all the time.[12] The new migrants tend to have the pattern of 'without roots'—they remain as transnational migrants without any strong commitments to the land they reside in. There is no more full integration or assimilation into local society. Are the new Chinese migrants really completely different from their forefathers in Southeast Asia? This is one of the points we would like to investigate.

Contents of the Book and General Overview

Our book that is in your hands now is on rising China and new Chinese migrants in Southeast Asia. It is based on two ISEAS projects that were sponsored by the Konrad Adenauer Stiftung under the Regional Programme

Political Dialogue Asia. The first project was on new Chinese migrants in mainland Southeast Asia, while the second one covered the whole of Southeast Asia. The papers from these two projects are categorized into four parts in this volume: 1. General overviews; 2. China's soft power, new migrants and local Chinese; 3. New Chinese migrants and local communities; and 4. New Chinese migrants and local economy.

Part One provides an overview of the thematic priorities of the edited volume. The first chapter, written by Leo Suryadinata, addresses the issue of rising China and its new policy towards the Chinese overseas. It argues that Beijing is abandoning *luodi shenggen* and adopting a *luoye guigen* policy, and this policy change coincides with a new wave of *xin yimin* that is branching out to Southeast Asia and the world. The new policy is a call to the Chinese overseas—regardless of citizenship—to orient towards China and to serve (or consider) Beijing's interests. *Huaqiao* and *huaren*, especially people in business, were called upon to help China support the Beijing Olympics, the Belt and Road Initiative, and to return and develop closer links with China. Leo Suryadinata notes that responses from the ethnic Chinese in Indonesia, Malaysia, the Philippines, Singapore and Thailand have largely been muted, as they have been localized and their identities are shaped by local politics. The chapter concludes that while ties are constantly being built between China and countries in Southeast Asia, China's new policy can problematize ethnic Chinese identities in Southeast Asia, produce ethnic tensions that can undermine domestic political and economic stability, and make it more challenging for new Chinese immigrants to Southeast Asia to integrate into local society.

The second chapter, by Terence Chong, studies the 'satellite Chinese' who had their formative years in China and came to the CLMV (Cambodia, Laos, Myanmar and Vietnam) countries from the 2000s onwards. Chong argues that these new satellite Chinese must be understood against the flow of Chinese economic aid through infrastructure development projects that have caused concern over scant benefits for CLMV countries in the extraction of their raw materials and the worry that China's unrestricted lending will undermine international efforts to fight corruption in these countries. While China's economic aid has been accompanied by a policy of non-interference in the affairs of these countries, Chong argues that it has been a crucial political lubricant to ease the flow of sometimes unwanted Chinese labour and presence into the aid-receiving countries. This chapter concludes with observations on how the satellite Chinese and the flow of Chinese capital have impacted host countries in a variety of ways, including rising property prices and the cost of living, village displacement and environmental degradation, and anxieties over Chinese identity.

China's Soft Power and Local Communities

Part Two deals with China's soft power in Southeast Asia, new Chinese migrants and local communities. It begins with the chapter written by Neo Peng Fu that discusses the presence of the over forty Confucius Institutes in Southeast Asia as a recent phenomenon that has expanded the function and social dynamics of Mandarin teaching in the region. While previously established Chinese schools—such as national or independent schools—catered primarily for ethnic Chinese students, the chapter notes that these Confucius Institutes have been providing language training, teacher training and vocational training for Southeast Asians regardless of ethnicity. The chapter offers detailed examples of the partnerships between local and Chinese universities, overseen by the Confucius Institute headquarters in China, to meet the rising demand for Chinese language classes. The chapter acknowledges that these institutes enhance China's predominance in Southeast Asia by nurturing a pool of Mandarin speakers who will facilitate China's entry into the region. And while the initiative has received some negative attention from several countries, the chapter highlights the positive contributions of these Confucius Institutes such as offering scholarships as an opportunity to pursue further studies overseas, a privilege still beyond the reach of many in the region.

The next chapter by, Vannarith Chheang, explores Cambodian views on China and the Chinese language. The chapter argues that language has been a key tool of China's soft power in the country. Based on his survey conducted on Cambodians who have learned the Chinese language through the Confucius Institutes, the chapter found that the driving forces of learning Chinese were familial relations, personal interest, and the usefulness of the language for employment and business opportunities. The survey respondents' perceptions of new Chinese migration were both positive and negative. Contribution to the local economy and prospects for economic investments were motivating factors. However, there are also negative local perceptions of new Chinese migrants, which include ignorance and lack of interest in Cambodian culture, and concern over the adverse social and environmental impacts that Chinese investments bring through the gambling industry and the resource-extractive sector. The chapter also shares other results from the survey regarding respondents' perceptions towards the Chinese government and the state of bilateral relations between China and Cambodia.

The establishment of the first Xiamen University overseas campus receives Peter Chang's attention in his chapter on the exemplars of China's expanding soft power in Malaysia and its impacts on the Chinese overseas. It notes that the establishment of Confucius Institutes in Malaysia is much more symbolic of the relationship between Malaysia and China than the promotion of the Chinese language, especially as the country already has an existing vernacular Chinese school system. In particular, the establishment of Xiamen University in Malaysia represents not just China's endeavour in opening up to the world (for example, by accepting international students in its universities) but, more importantly, stepping out to the world by shaping young minds beyond its national borders. The chapter also maintains that Xiamen University should not be understood as a conduit for China's soft power, but as a two-way bridge that strengthens China–Malaysia relations. This could be evinced from the development of Malaysia-oriented courses in Xiamen University, such as the Malaysia Studies Programme that allows Chinese students at Xiamen University Malaysia to learn more about Malaysia. Apart from promoting bilateral ties between China and Malaysia, the chapter also suggests that Xiamen University has potential to strengthen multilateral ties between China, Malaysia and the West, given the rising exposure to higher education in the West among Chinese Malaysian students.

The last chapter in Part Two is on "China Dream and Singapore Heart" written by Ho Yi Kai, which focuses on the setting up and the work of the China Cultural Centre (CCC) in Singapore and the locally established Singapore Chinese Cultural Centre (SCCC). The chapter discusses how the introduction of the two centres into the island state has raised broader questions surrounding 'Singaporean Chinese identity' in relation to 'Chinese identity'. Nevertheless, the chapter notes that the former was meant to reflect the 'China Dream', which meant promoting China's soft power, while the latter reflected 'Singapore Heart', which aimed to build local Chinese culture and cultivate bonds between Chinese and non-Chinese in Singapore. Comparing the activities of these two centres, the chapter observes that while there were some similarities between the work of the two centres, there were more differences because the centres had different objectives. Nevertheless, the chapter concludes that rather than seeing the CCC and the SCCC in competition, these centres exist in complementation as they are significant in catalysing critical questions about *xin yimin* and Chinese identity in Singapore.

New Chinese Migrants and Local Communities

Let us look at Part Three, which deals with New Chinese Migrants and local communities. It starts with the chapter on 'new' and 'old' Chinese communities in Laos jointly written by Bien Chiang and Jean Chihyin Cheng. The chapter argues that the Chinese in the Lao PDR can be divided into two broad categories: those whose families came before the end of World War II and have Laos citizenship (old Chinese); and those who came after the 1990s under the 'Open and Reform' policy and who are mostly Chinese nationals (new Chinese). They are different from the old migrants in life experience, education, business mentality, citizenship and social life. The chapter observes that there is a general perception that the first generation of immigrants usually arrive without the backing of China and are generally better integrated into the local community, which is commonly the case for Chinese arriving in insular Southeast Asian countries in the eighteenth or nineteenth centuries. This is in contrast to the late comers, who focus more on moneymaking and paying less attention to the need to integrate. This chapter argues that, while it is true that the new Chinese community has little interest in participating in the social production and reproduction of the old Chinese community through ritual practices, the Chinese government has taken a keen interest in the syllabus, administration and operations of Chinese schools in Laos. It remains to be seen, however, the extent to which the Chinese government would prevail in its United Front strategy over education in Laos, and under what circumstances the old Laotian Chinese communities would assert their interests over this traditional Chinese institution.

The second chapter in Part Three is on "*Xin yimin* in the Philippines: Challenges and Opportunities" by Teresita Ang-See. The chapter examines the issue of the influx of new Chinese migrants to the Philippines, which has received negative attention over the last two decades. While improvements in relations between Beijing and Manila brought much welcome increase in investments and infrastructure development, the presidency of Rodrigo

Duterte also saw the influx of Philippine offshore gaming operation (POGO) workers. The chapter argues that the substantial increase in the number of POGO and blue-collar workers in construction and small-time retail-trade businessmen has produced negative sentiments and some negative impacts. The chapter also examines the new norm of social networking and connecting with government agencies by Chinese businessmen and investors, who established different organizations for these purposes. Many hometown associations likewise organized new chambers of commerce in response to China's directive to organize such formations under the Belt and Road Initiative. Teresita Ang-See suggests that the coexistence of these new organizations with the well-established local Chinese associations has created dualism in Philippine Chinese society.

The third chapter in Part Three is Danny Wong's essay on the political economy of transnational new Chinese migrants who arrived in Malaysia following the rise of China and global migration. The chapter explores the various types of new Chinese migrants and argues that most of these migrants do not stay long in Malaysia and, hence, do not intend to integrate into local society. They set up their own organizations and businesses, and the Malaysian government particularly welcomes the Uighur and Hui Chinese, who are Muslims. Like many Chinese new migrants in Southeast Asia, there are also groups of new migrants who are involved in illegal activities. The chapter examines the issue of crime syndicates created by these migrants in Malaysia, which caused concern to the government and which has smeared the reputation of new Chinese migrants.

The fourth chapter is by Leo Suryadinata on the new Chinese migrants who came to Indonesia since the beginning of the twenty-first century. Some came as investors but the majority arrived as migrant workers, mainly working for Chinese companies. According to official figures, in Indonesia alone there are about 35,000 such migrant workers, but many believe that the actual number is much larger. More than 1,000 mainland Chinese companies operate in Indonesia today; some are state-linked enterprises, while others are owned by individuals. About fifty per cent of these companies are located in Java, while the rest can be found in the outer islands. They are mainly in the construction, mining and electronics sectors. The chapter also observes that mainland Chinese students studying in Indonesia have been a source of labour supply for these Chinese companies. The added advantage of these graduates lies in them being familiar with the local environment and in their ability to speak Indonesian.

Introduction

The relationship between *xin yimin* and Chinese Indonesians are generally not close, especially since the younger generation of Chinese Indonesians have lost an active command of Mandarin. The chapter argues that there is, therefore, a new Chinese migrant community emerging in Indonesia that may come into conflict with Chinese Indonesians who consider these new migrants as competitors. *Xin yimin* may also become an issue for the indigenous population who see them as foreign exploiters.

The last chapter in Part Three is on the elites' perceptions of new Chinese migrants in Indonesia written by Johanes Herlijanto. During President Susilo Bambang Yudhoyono's term from 2004 to 2014, Indonesia saw enhanced bilateral relations with China, the signing of strategic partnerships, an increase in Chinese economic investments, and also an increase in cultural exchange through the setting up of Confucius Institutes. The chapter notes that negative attitudes towards the new Chinese migrants began after the launch of the Belt and Road Initiative in 2013, which saw an increase in the number of migrants who worked for Chinese companies. These new migrants were perceived as competitors for Indonesian workers. The chapter points out that Indonesian elites harboured suspicions that the new migrants were military personnel seeking to infiltrate Indonesia. Additionally, there were concerns about potential demographic changes with the rise in the number of new migrants. The chapter further argues that the stance of the government has taken on reassurance overtones—that the new Chinese migrants were not a threat to the Indonesian economy or sovereignty. Johanes Herlijanto concludes with an analysis of the perception of new Chinese migrants among Indonesian elites (and the public to an extent) which has become far more negative during President Joko Widodo's term compared to President Yudhoyono's term.

New Chinese Migrants and the Local Economy

Part Four deals with the participation and issues of New Chinese migrants in local economic activities. It focuses on China's close neighbours such as the CLMV countries which see increasing people-to-people exchanges and flows across its shared borders and due to their geographical proximity. It begins with a chapter written by Nguyen Van Chinh on Vietnam–China economic ties and the *xin yimin*. The chapter argues that the restoration of China–Vietnam ties and improvements in economic relations since 1991 have contributed to the large number of new Chinese migrants in

Vietnam. In addition to the business conditions created through China's capital flow of investment, trade and economic aid, Vietnam and Southeast Asia have become ideal destinations for the *xin yimin* as they are able to take advantage of the ready social networks created by the local ethnic Chinese. These new migrants are mainly in the following three categories: contract labourers, traders, and Traditional Chinese Medicine practitioners. Over time, the profile and motivations of new Chinese immigrants have become more diverse and complex. Nguyen Van Chinh argues that while Vietnam has benefitted from the presence of these migrants, their presence has also generated socio-economic problems for, and pressures on, the local economy. The chapter concludes that the Vietnamese government has been reluctant to deal with the migrant problem harshly as it fears this would harm the Vietnamese economy.

The next chapter, by Danielle Tan, examines the history of Chinese business activities in the landlocked Lao PDR and its current developments. Ethnic Chinese communities almost disappeared after the communist forces seized power in Laos in 1975, but they survived due to the thriving caravan trade between Yunnan, China and mainland Southeast Asia. The Greater Mekong Subregion programme, launched by the Asian Development Bank, revitalized these historical trade routes and resulted in thousands of new Chinese migrants pouring on to the new roads of Laos, channelled through the North–South Economic Corridor linking Kunming to Bangkok. While many consider contemporary Laos as a Chinese "shadow state", this chapter argues that China's growing presence is far from eroding the power of the Lao communist regime. Instead, Chinese engagement has allowed the Lao state to cope with the challenges of globalization *and* to maintain its power at the same time. The chapter also highlights Chinese engagement in Laos throughout history by emphasizing recurrent patterns of intermediation. It describes how Chinese networks have become key partners of the Lao state's development policies. However, rising uncertainties over the neighbouring communist ally's economic potential may push China to revise its development strategy in Laos.

Pinkaew Laungaramsri's chapter on "Casino Capitalism, Chinese Special Economic Zone and the making of Neoliberal Border in Northern Laos" examines the case of the Golden Triangle Special Economic Zone (GT SEZ) to elucidate the politics of development in post-Socialist Laos. It analyses the collaboration between the Lao state and Chinese developers

Introduction

to transform the agricultural borderland of Ton Phueng into a new Chinese urban zone using casino capitalism and other shadow economies as the key economic engine. The chapter argues that foreign intervention as carried out by transnational casino capitalists and authorized by the Lao state represents another peculiar mode of government-driven and authoritarian form of neoliberalism. To facilitate economic development, the chapter argues that the Lao state has lent its sovereignty to foreign business counterparts. Chinese enterprises have claimed that they have created employment opportunities, enhanced economic competitiveness, and advanced labour skills to raise the living standards of border communities. However, this chapter shows that such rhetoric legitimizes the appropriation of local resources with unfair compensation while allowing developers to shun their responsibility to local groups.

The next chapter, written by Michiel Verver, examines Old and New Chinese Business in Cambodia's Capital. The chapter argues that China's influence over economic and political affairs in Cambodia is undisputed. China is the biggest investor in Cambodia. Recent Chinese investments and migrants have reinforced Cambodia's established politico-economic order, which is characterized by ethnic Chinese economic dominance as well as a divide between the business-state elite and the general population. Through field work and secondary data, the chapter explores the relationship between the local business community in Phnom Penh—which is historically dominated by old Chinese immigrants and their descendants—and new Chinese migration, business and investments. This chapter also provides a history of the business activities and societal position of old Chinese migrants in Cambodia, while the ensuing empirical sections examine how new Chinese migration and capital have affected the business endeavours of the old Chinese. The chapter concludes with a discussion on the implications of new Chinese migration for Phnom Penh's ethnic Chinese and Cambodian society.

The final chapter is on "Entrepreneurial Excursion: Short-Hop Chinese Migration at the Peripheries of Myanmar" by Andrew Ong. This chapter looks away from the Chinese influx to Myanmar's big cities and turns its attention to entrepreneurial excursions, a lesser-known short-hop migration of Chinese citizens to autonomous zones at the peripheries of Myanmar. Such movement, the chapter argues, is characterized by three migratory factors: low barriers to entry, ambivalence about the permanence of stay, and the prospects for further movement onward into lower Myanmar. The chapter lays out four different waves of Chinese migration into Myanmar, along with the historical complexities of the Chinese communities in Myanmar. The short-hop Chinese migration is one subgroup of this wider milieu. The chapter briefly describes the different autonomous zones then explores the nature of this short-hop migration—the ease of movement due to alternative legal regimes, the benefits of remaining close to the Chinese border through a 'short-hop', and the networks that give rise to potential further movement into Myanmar. Finally, the chapter concludes with the implications of this form of *xin yimin* to Myanmar, primarily the ambivalent role that their opportunism has in either fragmenting or consolidating Myanmar's national sovereignty and impacting its nation-building processes.

Concluding Remarks

New Chinese migration is a recent development and it has just entered an initial phase. An overarching theme and conclusion across the chapters in this volume is that China policy towards Chinese migrants changes from period to period, and it is still too early for us to see if Beijing will continue to pursue the policy of *luoye guigen* or will return to *luodi shenggen*. The various chapter contributions also show that the profile, motivations and outlook of *xin yimin* have become more diverse, while local reactions to these new migrants have become less accommodating with increasing nationalism.

While Chinese migration is unlikely to cease with the escalation of the rivalry between China and the United States, the new Chinese migrants in Southeast Asia might face new challenges. Perhaps many of them can no longer afford to be transnational. They may have to adjust to the international political developments in order to live in peace and comfort. The relationship between new Chinese migrants and ethnic Chinese who have settled down in Southeast Asia is expected to widen even further, resulting in greater economic and cultural tensions between these two groups and affecting the nation-building process. It can also make it more challenging for new Chinese immigrants to Southeast Asia to integrate locally.

The new Chinese migration is still progressing, and China's emerging policy towards Chinese migrants will require us to continue to study and seek a fuller understanding of the socio-dynamics and political economy of a rising China and the impacts of new Chinese migration. However, the one constant is that Beijing's policy trajectory has always taken a long-term view. When it comes to strengthening its influence, China has proved that it is both patient and persistent.

Notes

1. The periodization of Chinese migration history is based on the outline given by Chen Bisheng (陈碧笙), *Shijie Huaqiao huaren jianshi* (世界华侨华人简史), Xiamen: Xianmendaxue chubanshe (厦门：厦门大学出版社, 1991, pp. 19–21. However, the details are developed by Leo Suryadinata. See his "Chinese Migration in Southeast Asia: Past and Present", *CHC Bulletin* (华裔馆通讯) 9 (May 2007): 1–2.
2. Wang Gungwu, "Sojourning: The Chinese Experience", in *Don't Leave Home: Migration and the Chinese,* by Wang Gungwu (Singapore: Times Academic Press, 2001), p. 56.
3. Feng Tianyu (冯天瑜), "Society of Imperial Power: Reinterpreting China's "Feudal Society", *Journal of Chinese Humanities* 1 (2015): 25–50.
4. Wang Gungwu, *Don't Leave Home: Migration and the Chinese* (Singapore: Times Academic Press, 2001), pp. 54–57.
5. Jian Anzhi (简安志), You 'mingxiang' dao 'mingxiang' kan 17 shiji yuenan 'mingxiang/mingxiang' de luodi shenggen", ("由'明香'到'明乡'看17世纪越南·明香/明乡'的落地生根"), Taiwan dongnanya yanjiu 2012 niandu yantaohui lunwen (台湾东南亚研究 2012 年度研讨会论文), Jinan Daxue (暨南大学), 2–3 May 2012.
6. See Kenneth P. Landon, "The Chinese in Thailand: A Report in the International Research Series of the Institute of Pacific Relations", issued under the auspices of the Secretariat, first published in 1941, reissued by Russel & Russell, 1973, p. 26; Richard Coughlin, *Double Identity: The Chinese in Modern Thailand* (Hong Kong: Hong Kong University Press, 1961), p. 86.
7. Edgar Wickberg, "The Chinese in Philippine History", *Asia* 18 (Spring 1970): 1–13.
8. Leo Suryadinata, ed., *Peranakan Chinese in the Era of Globalization* (Singapore: CHC and Baba House, 2010), pp. 41–49.
9. For a brief discussion on BRI and Chinese overseas, see Leo Suryadinata, *The Rise of China and the Chinese Overseas: A Study of Beijing's Changing Policy in Southeast Asia and Beyond* (Singapore: ISEAS – Yusof Ishak Institute, 2017), pp. 167–81.
10. Wang Gungwu, "New Migrants: How New? Why New?", *Asian Culture* 26 (June 2002): 1–12.

11. Wang Gungwu argues that the concept of 'assimilation' for these new migrants is no longer relevant as they are very mobile. Ibid.
12. Zhuang Guotu (庄国土), Zhongguo xin yimin yu dongnanya huaren wenhua (中国新移民与东南亚华人文化), *CHC Bulletin* (华裔馆通讯), 9 (May 2007): 10.

PART I

General Overviews on Rising China and *Xin Yimin*

1

Rising China, New Migrants and Ethnic Chinese Identity in Southeast Asia

Leo Suryadinata

Since Deng Xiaoping introduced his four modernization programmes in 1978, China has risen, and its impact on Southeast Asia has also been strongly felt. This chapter briefly examines the impact of the programmes on the nation-building process in Southeast Asia. It will begin with a general observation of the ethnic Chinese position in Southeast Asian multi-ethnic nations, followed by a discussion about *xin yimin* or new Chinese migrants in the region and beyond, and finally an explication of Beijing's new approach towards Chinese living in five Southeast Asian countries and its impact. These countries were chosen based on the availability of information on *xin yimin* to the author.

Southeast Asian countries with majority indigenous populations regard their ethnic Chinese as 'migrants' or 'descendants of migrants'. Therefore, they are expected to be integrated, even assimilated, into the indigenous population. However, some are more integrated into their host society than others. In other words, all have adopted different degrees of local elements—which have made them different from mainland Chinese. The factors that have contributed to the intensive localization of ethnic Chinese in Southeast Asia are complex. Apart from Southeast Asian government policies, Beijing's initial policy of encouraging localization was undoubtedly relevant.

Shift in Beijing's Policy on Chinese Overseas

The policy of the People's Republic of China initially followed the Kuomintang (KMT) position, treating all overseas Chinese as Chinese nationals. But at the 1955 Afro-Asian Conference in Bandung (also known as the Bandung Conference), Chinese Premier Zhou Enlai introduced a new policy later known as *luodi shenggen* (settle down and take local roots) to ease cooperation with the newly independent states in Southeast Asia and beyond. He encouraged overseas Chinese to take up local citizenship and integrate into local society.[1] The majority of these ethnic Chinese have since become localized. In 1980, Deng Xiaoping issued the first nationality law based on single citizenship, which further encouraged Chinese overseas to localize and adopt local citizenship.[2]

The rise of the Chinese following the success of Deng Xiaoping's reform programme saw a new wave of migrants leaving China. Consequently, Beijing began adjusting its overseas Chinese policy. While the 1980 nationality law remains unchanged, in 2000 Beijing started to blur the distinction between *huaqiao* (Chinese citizens overseas) and *huaren* (foreigners of Chinese descent). The practice has been intensified since Xi Jinping assumed the Presidency toward the end of 2012.[3]

Beijing began to advocate the concept of 'Chinese Nation' (*Zhonghua Minzu*), and exhibited this at events such as the World Federation of Huaqiao and Huaren Associations, and the Beijing Olympics. The 'China Dream' notion was also promoted to mobilize Chinese overseas regardless of citizenship to serve the interest of China.[4] This policy can be characterized as 'luoye guigen' (return to original roots). It appears that the policy aims to halt both the localization of Chinese new migrants and further localization of ethnic Chinese as a whole.

New Chinese Migrants in Southeast Asia and the West

It should be noted that these new migrants differ from the earlier migrants in a number of ways. The new migrants are better educated than the earlier ones; some of these migrants have large amounts of capital and special skills and hence are more mobile.[5] They are often considered as "transnational Chinese" and may not settle in the country.[6] It is particularly the case with those who come to Southeast Asia. Those with capital and the required skills often use it as a stepping stone to go to the more developed countries when opportunities arise.

The new Chinese migrants include businessmen, professionals, students, family reunion members, refugees, workers and illegal migrants.[7] In Southeast Asia, migrant workers, who are often called foreign workers or guest workers, are legally not allowed to settle permanently in the country where they work. They are required to return to their country of origin, in this case China, once the projects are completed. In reality, some of these workers can become settlers due to weak legal systems and rampant corruption in some Southeast Asian countries.

The number of Chinese migrants leaving China since its rise is estimated to be five to six million, with about eighty per cent of these now living in developed countries (especially the West). The rest—about twenty per cent—went to Southeast Asia.[8] The former group has resulted in the emergence of new migrant Chinese societies in the West. In Southeast Asia, the number of new migrants in proportion to local ethnic Chinese is small and has not transformed local Chinese communities. The number of ethnic Chinese in Southeast Asian countries are as follows, based on 2010 estimates.

As shown in Table 1.1, the number of ethnic Chinese in Southeast Asia is huge compared to new migrants. The highest number of new migrants is probably in Singapore (seventeen per cent when compared to local ethnic Chinese), while the lowest number is found in Indonesia and Malaysia (lower than two per cent). In all these cases, the local Chinese are clearly dominant. This is not the case in countries such as the United States, Canada, Australia and New Zealand, where new Chinese migrants outnumber the local Chinese population (as indicated in Table 1.2).

Based on the above information, the problem of Chinese new migrants in Southeast Asia should not be serious as they are only a small fraction within the local ethnic Chinese community, whereas Beijing's new overseas Chinese policy would have a greater impact on the identities of ethnic Chinese, potentially undermining sociopolitical stability in Southeast Asia. Nevertheless, due to racial/ethnic prejudices and negative local perceptions of Beijing, Chinese new migrants have often become a political issue and hence have had a significant impact.

TABLE 1.1
Number of "Chinese Overseas" in Southeast Asia and *xin yimin* (2010)

Country	Ethnic Chinese (excluding new migrants)	New Chinese Migrants
Thailand	7,000,000	77,000
Malaysia	6,720,000	12,000
Indonesia	4,860,000	76,000
Singapore	2,960,000	426,000
Philippines	1,500,000	38,000
Myanmar	1,000,000	35,000
Vietnam	960,000	3,000
Laos	300,000	14,000
Cambodia	600,000	2,000
Brunei Darussalam	46,400	2,000
Total	25,946,400	1,350,000

Source: The figures from the above table, with the exception of three countries (Malaysia, Singapore and Brunei Darussalam), are based on either estimates or educated guesses stated in various publications in Chinese and English. Nevertheless, the Indonesian population census of 2020 shows that the Chinese constitute 1.2 per cent of the Indonesian population (3,301,465). As the census was based on self-identification, many Chinese Indonesians therefore were not included in the census as "Chinese". The research team and I argue that the Chinese may constitute 1.8 per cent of the Indonesian population. See Leo Suryadinata, Evi Nurvidya Arifin and Aris Ananta, *Indonesia's Population: Ethnicity and Religions in the Changing Political Landscape*, Singapore: Institute of Southeast Asian Studies, 2003, chapter on ethnic Chinese.

TABLE 1.2
Total Number of Ethnic Chinese in the West, Including New Migrants

Country	1970/71	2006
Canada	124,600	1,487,585
USA	435,062	2,565,458
New Zealand	14,860	140,570
Australia	36,638	669,890

Note: Based on tables published in Leo Suryadinata, "New Chinese Migrants in Developed 'Migrant States': Five Case Studies", *CHC Bulletin* 16 & 17 (November 2010 & May 2011): 2–5.

Impact on Southeast Asian Chinese in Five Countries

Indonesia

The Chinese in Indonesia are divided into the Peranakan Chinese (Indonesian-speaking Chinese) and *totok* Chinese (Chinese-speaking Chinese). The thirty-two years of Suharto's rule, which experienced his assimilation policy and the elimination of the three Chinese cultural pillars,[9] have turned the majority of Chinese Indonesians into Peranakan by definition. In other words, most Chinese in Indonesia have lost active command of the Chinese language and often use Indonesian or some local language for communication. About twenty-four per cent still use Chinese as their home language, but these are mostly of the older generation.[10] Many successful businessmen are still able to speak Chinese.

Chinese Embassy officials are able to maintain close ties with some Chinese-speaking groups,[11] but not Chinese Indonesians in general. When prominent Indonesian Chinese businessmen were invited to China to attend Huaqiao Huaren businessmen gatherings, few participated. Some chose to avoid such gatherings.[12] During the 2008 Beijing Olympics torch relay in Jakarta, very few old Chinese Indonesian businessmen participated. The majority stayed away. It is also worth noting that only a small number of Chinese Indonesians served in the Beijing Olympics as volunteers.[13]

In 2012, the chairman of the Overseas Chinese Affairs Office (OCAO), Li Yinze, visited Jakarta and spoke at the Chinese Chamber of Commerce. He was quoted to have urged young Chinese Indonesians to learn the Han language (Hanyu) so that they could identify themselves with the Chinese nation. He even said that Chinese Indonesians should not be afraid as they had an assertive China as the backer. Some local Chinese criticized his speech, and he was told that as a guest he should know how to behave.[14] In 2015, a Quanzhou local government contacted the most affluent Chinese Indonesian family, the Oey family, congratulating them on the success of their business, and informing them that their ancestral house had been identified. The family was welcomed to Quanzhou to develop it into an ancestral memorial home. In response, however, the Oey family called for a press conference at which they announced that they did not have any ancestral house in Quanzhou.[15]

It is also important to note that the so-called Mandarin fever did not establish fully fledged Chinese-medium schools in Indonesia. Mandarin is only studied in Indonesia as a foreign language, and many non-Chinese have also studied the language.[16] Unlike in the past, anti-Chinese groups in Indonesia focused their recent opposition and attacks on local Chinese tycoons and mainland Chinese workers, whom they claim have stolen Indonesian jobs.[17]

According to the Indonesian Manpower Ministry, in 2020 there were only 35,781 Chinese workers in Indonesia, constituting 36.18 per cent of the total foreign workers.[18] They worked in mainland Chinese companies that engaged in various projects, from mining to industrial parks. They were supposed to cover gaps in expertise unavailable in Indonesia, but opposition politicians and Indonesian workers federations have insisted that the majority of mainland Chinese workers were ordinary workers whose work could have been undertaken by Indonesians.[19]

There are also hundreds of mainland Chinese students and teachers in Indonesia as well as many mainland Chinese businessmen present in various parts of Indonesia. China's chambers of commerce have also been established in Indonesia.[20] Their presence has been felt by the local population.

Malaysia

Malaysians of Chinese origin tend to possess a much stronger Chinese cultural identity. Most of them, except for the Peranakans, are still able to speak Chinese dialects.[21] Where identity is concerned, they tend to be locally oriented, and those who feel an orientation towards China are very few, and of advanced age.

In 2015, Chinese Ambassador Huang Huikang visited Chinatown in Kuala Lumpur and encouraged Chinese Malaysians to stand up against racism; in another speech, he mixed the terms *huaqiao* and *huaren* and said China was their "maternal home".[22] Many intellectuals criticized Huang for being insensitive and Malay youths expressed anger over his statement.

Malaysia has in place a successful retirement and residence scheme for foreigners, which attracts, among others, mainland Chinese.[23] It is worth noting that a mainland China university branch was established in West Malaysia in 2015. This was arranged when Najib Razak was prime minister.[24] It is interesting to note that the presence of this university and mainland Chinese students in the country was not made into an issue by the UMNO youth and other radicals.

Nevertheless, the Belt and Road Initiative (BRI) projects became a political issue during the 2018 General Election. During the election campaign, for instance, Mahathir Mohamad criticized the Forest City project, saying it "will leech money and jobs to foreign companies while bringing in hundreds of thousands of immigrants."[25] After Mahathir re-emerged as the new prime minister, some of the BRI projects were renegotiated.[26] The topic of China and new immigrants can easily be made into an issue in Malaysia.

Singapore

Singapore is unique for being a migrant state, and ethnic Chinese make up the majority. Like the examples of the two countries above, the ethnic Chinese in Singapore are also divided. The Peranakan Chinese community is small in number, and the Chinese-speaking group is large. Nevertheless, because of the national education system, the working language in Singapore is English.

Singapore was officially established in 1965, and initially, the concept of the nation was based on the melting pot. But since 1995, Lee Hsien Loong, then deputy prime minister, adopted the "salad bowl" idea and stressed the importance of shared values for Singaporeans.[27]

China's soft power is thought to be influential in Singapore. However, the Singapore government is eager to promote its own culture. Even in the promotion of Chinese language and culture, the emphasis has been its local characteristics. The Singapore Chinese Cultural Centre was established to develop a local form of Chinese culture.[28] Singapore's political identity has also grown strong, and young Singaporeans have a much stronger sense of national identity than their forefathers.

The number of new migrants in Singapore was estimated by Beijing to be between 500,000 and 600,000.[29] Some of them have become Singapore's permanent residents and new citizens. During the past few General Elections, migration was a hot election issue.[30] This resulted in the government tightening up its migration policy whilst continuing to recognize that new migrants are needed for Singapore's continuous prosperity and development.

As the relations between *xin yimin* and Chinese Singaporeans are sometimes less cordial, the government has emphasized multi-cultural education for Singaporeans and created mechanisms to facilitate the integration of new migrants into the mainstreams of Singapore society.

The Philippines

The Chinese in the Philippines are diverse, with some being well-integrated and even assimilated. This community is known as Chinese mestizos. These are offspring of a Chinese male and a Filipino female, quite like the Peranakan Chinese. But while Peranakan Chinese in Malaysia and Indonesia are still considered as a separate group from the indigenous population, Chinese mestizos are regarded as Filipinos.[31] Former President Cory Cojuangco Aquino and the late Manila Archbishop Cardinal Sin Jaime are Chinese mestizos. Most Philippine Chinese are colloquially referred to as Tsinoy,[32] and many have embraced Catholicism, just like most Filipinos.

In the twenty-first century, however, the Chinese Embassy established close ties with the Philippine Chinese community, especially those who still speak Chinese.[33] Although rising China attracts those who have business links with China, most Tsinoys still identify with the local population.

The number of new Chinese migrants in the Philippines is estimated at around 250,000 to 300,000. A considerable number of the new Chinese migrants, the *xin yimin*, are mainly businessmen and workers in certain commercial sectors, especially in the gaming industry.[34] This gaming industry contributed significantly to the Philippine economy. Nevertheless, it also gave ample opportunities for crime syndicates to operate. While many *xin yimin* have high economic status and often display their wealth, there has also been an increase in illegal new migrants, their presence often giving rise to ethnic tension in society. This tension could be found not only between the *xin yimin* with indigenous Filipinos, but also between *xin yimin* and Tsinoys who complain that these Chinese new migrants have spoiled the good relationship between Tsinoys and Filipinos.[35] The *xin yimin* issue is further complicated with the South China Sea dispute, which often impacted Chinese-Filipino relations.

Thailand

Ethnic Chinese in Thailand are the most assimilated in the region, and it has been argued that Buddhism is a key factor in this process. The number of new Chinese migrants in Thailand is estimated at between 350,000 and 400,000.[36] They live separately, mainly in so-called new Chinatowns. They are better educated than the older Chinese migrants, with many holding a university degree. Many others are students as it is generally easier to get into Thai universities than those in China.[37] Overseas Chinese Affairs Office officials have also visited Bangkok to promote overseas Chinese collaboration with China.[38] They encourage Thai Chinese to learn Chinese. In fact, there are numerous Confucius Institutes in Thailand.

But since ethnic assimilation of people of Chinese origin is very high in Thailand, the government is convinced that these Thais would not become China-oriented. The Thai authorities also believe that these new migrants would eventually be assimilated into Thai society.

However, some scholars do not think that it would be the case. One scholar noted that there was no need to assimilate the new Chinese migrants but to make them have a sense of belonging to Thailand.[39] How to make these new migrants have a sense of belonging to their adopted land in a globalizing world remains a big challenge.

Conclusion

Beijing's policy towards Chinese living overseas, and ethnic Chinese populations in other countries, has recently changed. After China's rise, although maintaining a single nationality is still upheld, China is attempting to blur the distinction between *huaqiao* and *huaren*, urging Chinese overseas to be oriented towards China, and increasingly disregarding their difficult position in Southeast Asia. Beijing might not be fully aware that Southeast Asian ethno-nationalism remains strong and ethnic Chinese are facing these pressures.

Inter-ethnic tensions in Southeast Asia between ethnic Chinese communities and the indigenous majorities are a reality. China's new policy may inadvertently affect ethnic Chinese identities in the region and create tensions, undermining political and economic stability. Moreover, the presence of *xin yimin* has also complicated the local socio-political landscape. China's new policy may slow down the integration of *xin yimin* into local communities. If this was the intention of the new policy towards the *xin yimin*, then Beijing may have achieved its objectives.

Notes

1. Stephen Fitzgerald, *China and the Overseas Chinese: A Study of Peking's Changing Policy 1949–1970* (Cambridge: Cambridge University Press, 1972), p. 134.
2. Leo Suryadinata, "China's Citizenship Law and the Chinese in Southeast Asia", in *Law and the Chinese in Southeast Asia*, edited by M. Barry Hooker (Singapore: Institute of Southeast Asian Studies, 2002), pp. 169–202 (particularly p. 182).
3. Leo Suryadinata, "Blurring the Distinction between *Huaqiao* and *Huaren*: China's Changing Policy towards the Chinese Overseas", in *Southeast Asian Affairs 2017*, edited by Daljit Singh and Malcolm Cook (Singapore: ISEAS – Yusof Ishak Institute, 2017), pp. 101–13.
4. For a detailed discussion on these points, see Leo Suryadinata, *The Rise of China and the Chinese Overseas: A Study of Beijing's changing Policy in*

Southeast Asia and Beyond (Singapore: ISEAS – Yusof Ishak Institute, 2017), pp. 3–20, 143–51, 154–79.
5. For a discussion on these new migrants, see Liao Jianyu (廖建裕), "Quanqiuhua zhong de zhonghua yimin yu huaqiao huaren yanjiu" (全球化中的中华移民与华侨华人研究), *Huaqiao huaren lishi yanjiu* 华侨华人历史研究, no. 1 (2012): 1–17; Leo Suryadinata, "Chinese Migration in Southeast Asia: Past and Present", *CHC Bulletin* 9 (May 2007): 1–7.
6. Liao Jianyu (廖建裕), "Xian dangdai de zhonghua yimin ji qihouyi: guigen, shenggen, shigen yu wugen" (现、当代的中华移民及其后裔：归根、生根、失根与无根), *Asian Culture* 亚洲文化, no. 39 (August 2015): 45–60.
7. Liao Jianyu (廖建裕), "Quanqiuhua zhong de zhonghua yimin", p. 15.
8. Zhuang Guotu, 庄国土, "Zhongguo xinyimin yu dongnanya wenhua" (中国新移民与东南亚文化), *CHC Bulletin* 9 (May 2007): 10.
9. This usually refers to Chinese-medium schools, Chinese mass media and Chinese organizations.
10. Aris Ananta et al., *Demography of Indonesia's Ethnicity* (Singapore: Institute of Southeast Asian Studies, 2015).
11. Benny G. Setiono. "Beberapa catatan mengenai perkembangan organisasi-organisasi Tionghoa di Indonesia", *Yinni Jiaodian* 印尼焦点 (Indonesia Focus) HKSIS (July 2008): 74–77.
12. For instance, the Djarum Group and the Lippo Group were not present at the World Huaqiao Huaren Entrepreneurs Conference held on 6–7 July 2015 in Beijing.
13. To my knowledge, from Jakarta, only the president of Yinhua Writers Association served as a volunteer.
14. Beijing shi qiaoban zhuren Li Yinze fang yinni jianghua yinqi qiaojie buman 北京市侨办主任李印泽访印尼讲话引起侨界不满。Guoji Ribao 国际日报, 21 April 2012.
15. Fei Teli (费特利), ZhenJi shouxi yunying zhang Huang Zhi Sheng chengqing, Huang Jia Quanzhou wu zuwu 針記首席運營長黃志勝澄清·黃家泉州無祖屋, Qiandao Ribao 签到日报, 9 May 2016.
16. Aimee Dawis, "Chinese Education in Indonesia: Developments in the Post–1998 Era", in *Ethnic Chinese in Contemporary Indonesia*, edited by Leo Suryadinata (Singapore: Institute of Southeast Asian Studies, 2008), pp. 75–96; Personal observation.
17. Leo Suryadinata, "Anti-Ethnic Chinese Groups in Indonesia Likely to Strike Again", *ISEAS Perspective*, no. 2020/8, 3 February 2020; Leo Suryadinata, "Tensions in Indonesia over Chinese Foreign Workers during Covid-19 Pandemic", *ISEAS Perspective*, no. 2020/73, 6 July 2020).
18. Jumlah tenaga kerja asing di Indonesia 98.902, TKA China terbesar, p. 2 (kontan.co.id) (13 May 2021).

19. This may not be true. Nevertheless, until recently, many trade union leaders still hold this view. See Rachel Chaterine, "TKA China Masuk Indonesia Saat Pandemi Covid-19, KSPI: Ironi, Pemerintah Harusnya Berpihak Buruh Nasional", *Kompas*, 11 May 2021, https://nasional.kompas.com/read/2021/05/11/12292611/tka-china-masuk-indonesia-saat-pandemi-covid-19-kspi-ironi-pemerintah?page=all (accessed 20 May 2021).
20. Leo Suryadinata, "New Chinese Migrants in Indonesia: An Emerging Community that Faces New Challenge", *ISEAS Perspective*, no. 2020/61, 11 June 2020.
21. In Malaysia, Chinese-medium schools have never been banned. A large number of Chinese Malaysians still go to these schools, and hence are able to speak and write Chinese.
22. For a discussion on this event, see Leo Suryadinata, *The Rise of China and the Chinese Overseas: A Study of Beijing's Changing Policy in Southeast Asia and Beyond* (Singapore: ISEAS – Yusof Ishak Insitute, 2017), pp. 111–20.
23. Danny Wong Tze Ken, "The Xinyimin Presence in Malaysia: A New Transnational Experience", ISEAS – Yusof Ishak Institute webinar, 8 December 2020. Why there was no strong opposition from the Malays is a question that requires further investigation.
24. Peter T.C. Chang, "China's Soft Power and the Overseas Chinese, Case Study: Xiamen University in Malaysia". ISEAS – Yusof Ishak Institute webinar, 8 December 2020.
25. For more details, see *Today Online*, "Malaysia Gains Nothing but Trouble from Forest City: Dr M", https://www.todayonline.com/world/asia/look-east-policy-not-about-selling-land-foreigners-dr-mahathir-tells-sultan.
26. Joseph Sipalan, "China, Malaysia Restart Massive 'Belt and Road' Project after Hiccups", *Reuters*, https://www.reuters.com/article/us-china-silkroad-malaysia-idUSKCN1UK0DG (accessed 15 May 2021).
27. "No Melting Pot, Singapore", 29 January 1995. Reported by the Associated Press. Both *melting pot* and *salad bowl* are metaphors used in the United States. The former refers to "cultural assimilation", i.e., an American Culture without cultural diversity, while the latter refers to an American culture with cultural diversity, i.e., cultural pluralism. However, Lee Hsien Loong used the term "pluralism" to describe the "new" policy.
28. Ho Yi Kai, "China Cultural Centre and Singapore Chinese Cultural Centre: A Comparison", ISEAS – Yusof Ishak Institute webinar, 8 December 2020.
29. This figure cannot be verified. See Wang Wangbo (王望波) and Zhuang Guotu (庄国土), 2009 nian haiwai huaqiao huaren gaishu (2009年 海外华侨华人概述), Beijing: shijie zhishi chubanshe 世界知识出版社, 2011, p. 23.
30. In most of the general elections from 2011 to 2020, migration has always been an issue. It should be noted that it was not confined to Chinese new

migrants, but as the Chinese were the largest in number, the impact was most significant. In the last general election, the issue still prevailed. See Low Fhoong, "Singapore GE2020: Jobs, Immigration, Cost of Living Are Key Issues in Party Political Broadcast, Politics News & Top Stories", *Straits Times*, https://www.straitstimes.com/politics/singapore-ge2020-jobs-immigration-cost-of-living-are-key-issues-in-party-political (accessed 20 May 2021).

31. Edgar Wickberg, "The Chinese in the Philippine History", *Asia* 18 (Spring 1970): 1–15.
32. Teresita Ang See and Carmelea Ang See, "The Rise of China, New Immigrants and Changing Policies on Chinese Overseas: Impact on the Philippines", in *Southeast Asian Affairs 2019*, edited by Daljit Singh and Malcolm Cook (Singapore: ISEAS – Yusof Ishak Institute, 2019), pp. 275–76.
33. Interview with a Philippine researcher on the ethnic Chinese, Guangzhou, 12 November 2019.
34. Teresita Ang See, "Xinyimin in the Philippines: Issues and Challenges", ISEAS – Yusof Ishak Institute webinar, 7 December 2020.
35. Ibid.
36. Jon Fernquest, "New Wave of Chinese Coming to Live in Thailand", *Bangkok Post*, 23 September 2016, https://www.bangkokpost.com/learning/advanced/1093148/new-wave-of-chinese-coming-to-live-in-thailand (accessed 20 January 2021).
37. Ibid.
38. "Guowuyuan Qiaoban fuzhuren Tan Tianxing zoufang taiguo qiaotuan zuotan" 国务院侨办副主任谭天星走访泰国侨团座谈。www.gqb.gov.cn/news/2016/1123/41229.shtml (accessed 20 January 2021).
39. Yos Santasombat holds this view. See Jon Fernquest, "New Wave of Chinese Coming to Live in Thailand", *Bangkok Post*, 23 September 2016, https://www.bangkokpost.com/learning/advanced/1093148/new-wave-of-chinese-coming-to-live-in-thailand (accessed 20 January 2021).

2

Contemporary Chinese Immigration into Mainland Southeast Asia

Terence Chong

The character of immigration is often shaped by the conditions of departure. Why and how people leave their country, as well as the state of the country they leave behind, influence their attitudes and the relations they share with host societies. In the case of Southeast Asia, Chinese immigration over the centuries has been characterized by different levels of settlement and integration. There have generally been four waves of Chinese immigration into the region. The first wave saw scattered flows of Chinese merchants and traders between the tenth and fifteenth centuries into parts of Southeast Asia such as Sumatra, Cambodia and Campa, and later, Malacca from the fifteenth century. Many of these merchants and traders settled down to marry local women and integrated into local communities.

The second wave was triggered by conflict, wars, starvation, and corruption in the hinterland from the nineteenth century to 1949. This wave, also known as the "coolie pattern", was made up of "large numbers of coolie labour, normally men of peasant origin, landless labourers and the urban poor" (Wang 1991, p. 8). During this wave, many migrants spread to different parts of the globe, including the United States, Canada,

Latin America, Australia, Malaya and Indonesia, less as traders and merchants but more as indentured slaves and coolies to provide menial labour. Again, like the previous wave, many did not return to China but instead settled down in their destination countries and, in the case of Southeast Asia, to engage in the struggle to be recognized as members of newly formed nations. These waves of Chinese immigration came at a time when China was not the power it is today. Centuries of economic insulation and the '100 years of humiliation' during which China was subjugated to Western powers, together with famines and war, had shaped the character of Chinese immigration and the way immigrants engaged and settled in host societies.

China's 1978 open-door policy kick-started the third wave in Chinese immigration. Seen by some as the 'New Chinese Migration' (Wong 2012), this wave differed in scope and character from the previous two waves. Instead of traders or coolies, this wave swept towards developed societies in the West and was comprised primarily of students, scholars, and later, professionals to learn from these societies as part of Deng Xiaoping's Four Modernizations project. For the first time, it may be argued that Chinese immigration became infused with a nascent form of national consciousness and national development. The Chinese government was keen to tap the "Overseas Chinese wealth" and the "new Chinese emigrants" during this period (Zhuang 2000, p. 45). Its stance on Chinese immigration was a pragmatic one believing that the journey towards modernization and economic development would be accelerated with greater links to the Chinese diaspora and its overseas capital. The Chinese government's positive outlook was also an admission that the overseas Chinese from previous immigration waves were unlikely to return to China permanently, "at least without having established a social space abroad to which to return in the future" (Nyiri 2002, p. 221). Chinese immigration was considered desirable by the Chinese government instead of being viewed, as it had previously, as defection.

By the late 1980s and early 1990s, the so-called 'fourth wave of Chinese immigration' emerged at the tail-end of the 'New Chinese Migration' phase (Zhuang and Wang 2010). The fourth wave of Chinese immigrants coincided with the economic rise of China, making it qualitatively different from previous waves. The market reforms and export-oriented model that Deng Xiaoping introduced from the late 1970s were bearing fruit, resulting in significant poverty reduction and greater purchasing power of a growing middle class. Greater numbers of Chinese immigrants were found heading towards developing regions like Southeast Asia, Latin America and South Africa in light of "China's overseas economic expansion and friendly political relationships with these areas" (Zhuang and Wang 2010, p. 175). More specifically, this fourth wave immigration shift towards Southeast Asia in the last two decades has come about because Beijing began developing diplomatic ties and economic partnerships with ASEAN (Association of Southeast Asian Nations) and individual member states. Unlike previous phases, the fourth wave Chinese comprised those with capital and skills, and thus demonstrated greater mobility in their movement to and from China. China gradually abandoned a communist-driven foreign policy and pursued a 'good neighbourliness' policy for domestic economic development, thus paving the way for new Chinese immigrants mainly from Yunnan, the east Guangdong Province, and south Fujian Province into Cambodia, Laos, Myanmar and Vietnam (Zhuang and Wang 2010, p. 179).

The fourth wave Chinese include professionals, students, petty traders, entrepreneurs, and both semi-skilled and unskilled labour. The outflow of entrepreneurs and petty traders had been prompted by the oversupply of certain goods in China such as textiles, clothes, footwear, kitchen utensils and electric appliances, as well as intense domestic competition (Tan 2010), while semi-skilled and unskilled contract labourers often came with Chinese contractors and state-owned enterprises (SOEs) to the procurement, engineering and construction sectors of mainland Southeast Asia (Nguyen 2013). Students and professionals tend to gather in Singapore and Malaysia, while entrepreneurs and petty traders are mostly found in mainland Southeast Asia.

Today, China is an economic global power. As one, it has begun to exert its economic, diplomatic and even military influence over various issues to advance its interests. Deng's dictum to "hide your strength and bide your time" to describe China's philosophy of incremental and non-assertive rise has been replaced by Xi Jinping's triumphant observation that "It is time for us to take centre stage in the world and to make a greater contribution to humankind" while "standing tall and firm in the east" (Clover 2017). China is neither opening up to the world nor a country on the rise but an alternative economic and political model for parts of the developing world. The new ways in which China sees itself and its engagement with the rest of the world cannot help but shape the worldview of its outgoing immigrants and their relationships with societies they venture to.

Post-2000 Chinese Immigration into Mainland Southeast Asia

China's entry into the World Trade Organization (WTO) in 2001 marked its official inclusion in the global economy. The country's international profile was given a major boost when Beijing hosted the 2008 Olympic Games, and again two years later in 2010 when it surpassed Japan to become the second-largest economy in the world. Xi Jinping succeeded Hu Jintao in 2013 and promptly announced the ambitious Belt and Road Initiative (BRI) in September the same year in Kazakhstan. At its height, the BRI stretched to Europe, central Asia and Southeast Asia, and prioritized policy coordination, infrastructure connectivity, and financial integration. In the meantime, Beijing's assertions over the South China Sea based on what it perceives to be its historical rights signifies a growing nationalist sentiment within the country (Hayton 2014). Such nationalist sentiments reflect the desire to claim China's rightful place as a global power on the international stage. These sentiments are infused with the memories of historic trauma and humiliation by foreign forces, resulting in a growing and often an aggressive sense of nationalism among the Chinese, especially its youth (Cabestan 2005; Zhao 2004; Li 2017). Perhaps more interesting is the strong sense of nationalism among the millennial Chinese. This post-1990 generation is growing up with little memory of major events such as the Great Famine of the early 1960s, the violent Cultural Revolution in 1966–76, or the 1989 Tiananmen crackdown. The combination of China's rise and the newfound economic empowerment of individuals has produced an outward and entrepreneurial perspective that is laced with patriotism and national pride.

The post-2000 wave of Chinese immigration, sometimes referred to as *xin yimin* (new immigrants), are Chinese who are venturing out at a time when China is flexing its economic, military and political muscles. They should not be confused with the 'overseas Chinese', which refers only to Chinese nationals outside China, or 'Chinese overseas', which refers to *all* ethnic Chinese outside China (except Hong Kong, Macao and Taiwan) (Wang 1991; Suryadinata 2017). Like many immigrants from the 1980s and 1990s, post-2000 Chinese immigrants continue to be traders, businessmen, professionals, contractors or entrepreneurs seeking their fortunes in the developing markets of mainland Southeast Asia. They are unlikely to be illegal immigrants or students, but are more likely to have personal capital to start a business. And while culturally flexible enough for superficial integration in order to do business, their identity as Yunnanese, Guangdonger or whatever province they come from remains firm.

Unlike historical overseas Chinese, post-2000 Chinese immigrants have no plans to fully integrate into their host country. They may learn basic Vietnamese, Burmese, Lao or Khmer to do business or make contacts but retain Mandarin as their root language. They may spend long periods in their host country but are also prone to frequent travel, preferring to make the routine cross-border commute between mainland Southeast Asia and China. Like satellites transmitting signals, they transmit their cultures and practices into foreign lands. The exact numbers of Chinese immigrants are difficult to ascertain for various reasons. The long porous border makes immigration control extremely challenging. The border between Yunnan and Myanmar, Laos and Vietnam spans nearly three thousand kilometres and has numerous entry and exit points, many of which may not be heavily supervised. The mismatch of data is also an obstacle. It is not uncommon for provincial and national governments to engage in separate data collection exercises, resulting in different statistics on immigrants. Meanwhile, many post-2000 Chinese immigrants, like the waves before them, are mobile and transient. Identities are also unstable. For example, those who start businesses may adopt a local name. They do this not only to integrate into local culture but also to circumvent local regulations over foreign businesses. Zhuang and Wang (2010) estimate that there are about 2.5 million new Chinese immigrants in ASEAN, although the figure is believed to be many times higher in light of illegal migration, bribery and poor border controls.

There are a few characteristics that help us understand post-2000 Chinese immigrants. Firstly, they are absent from the "imagined community" of their host countries (Anderson 1983). They are relative newcomers to their host countries. Unlike Chinese overseas who have sunk deep roots in their respective Southeast Asian countries over a longer historic period through inter-marriage and children, and thus have little or no attachment to China, post-2000 Chinese immigrants have stronger memories and first-hand experience of China. Many would have neither the collective memory of struggling for independence nor made the sacrifices by Chinese overseas during the early nation-building years. Without this collective memory and historical sacrifice, the attachment of new Chinese to their adopted countries differs fundamentally from Chinese overseas. Nevertheless, these post-2000 Chinese immigrants are relatively comfortable living outside China for long periods of time.

Secondly, they maintain strong links with China. Many who work in neighbouring Vietnam, Myanmar, Laos or Cambodia keep in touch with the happenings in their home provinces by reading Chinese media and following Chinese national politics and popular culture through their smartphones and other devices. Workers and small traders would also get together to share information and gossip in order to stay in touch with the homeland, thus creating a series of Chinese community bubbles for networking, affirmation of identity and culture, as well as companionship. During my fieldwork in Lao Cai in North Vietnam, for example, it was not uncommon to see Chinese contract workers sitting on plastic stools on sidewalks smoking, gambling and chatting away. Such forms of socialization allow for the sustenance of emotive connectivity to China.

Thirdly, because they are profit-driven, post-2000 Chinese immigrants are not only mobile but also extremely sensitive to economic opportunities elsewhere. This combination of mobility and sensitivity has given rise to perceptions of them as resourceful, self-interested and acquisitive. They are consequently less rooted to their host country than ethnic Chinese who have lived there for generations. This, in turn, has triggered occasional tension between these ethnic Chinese and themselves. On one hand, many ethnic Chinese take pains to distinguish themselves from the newcomers while, on the other hand, the post-2000 Chinese immigrants are identified by their poorer fluency in the local language.

Finally, there is a lingering air of political suspicion around newer Chinese immigrants. Local communities may be wary of how Beijing's interests are often championed by overseas Chinese through a variety of ways. Or, as Minxin Pei observes, "China is not shy about using overseas Chinese communities to advance its interests abroad" (Levin 2016). Meanwhile, Chinese students in Australia are becoming more active in seeking to influence the government's stance on the South China Sea (Uhlmann 2016). Chinese business and cultural associations in Australia are also attempting to shape the country's foreign policy on China (Wen 2016). The presence of new immigrants, together with China's overtures towards ethnic Chinese in Southeast Asian societies, have given rise to uncertainty. This is especially when there is a blurring of the lines between Chinese nationals overseas and Southeast Asian citizens of ethnic Chinese descent (Qin 2018).

Impact of Chinese Capital and Immigrants

Unlike historic waves of immigration into mainland Southeast Asia, the flow of post-2000 Chinese immigrants has been accompanied by an unprecedented flow of Chinese capital into the region. Chinese capital flows into mainland Southeast Asia, however, is not a new phenomenon. China's economic aid to mainland Southeast Asia underwent three stages (Hao 2008). The first stage—1950s to early 1980s—was devoted primarily to the ideological desire to build stronger foreign relations with other developing socialist countries. The second stage—1980s to mid-1990s—focused on small and medium-sized projects in developing countries to meet Chinese needs and demands. The third stage—1995 to the present—is in sharp contrast to the first stage, where economic and commercial interests now reign supreme. In addition, economic aid is meant to function partly as an instrument of foreign policy to foster closer political relations between Beijing and other countries. Or, as Hao (2008, p. 184) explains, "In the long term, China hopes that the overture will not only give Chinese companies an edge in the competition for local business, but also tighten the political relations with those recipient countries."

In some pre-BRI estimates, Cambodia, Laos, Myanmar and Vietnam received at least half a billion US dollars each between 2004 and 2008 (Zhu 2009). Other sources note that Chinese-sponsored investment to broader Southeast Asia amounted to US$7.4 billion, while concessional loans amounted to US$7.1 billion between 2002 and 2007 (Lum et al. 2009). Nevertheless, to put these figures into context, Southeast Asia lags behind other regions as a recipient of Chinese economic aid. From 2002 to 2007, Africa received 44 per cent of all Chinese aid in the form of loans, infrastructure projects and other economic assistance, while Latin America received 36 per cent, and finally Southeast Asia received 20 per cent (Lum et al. 2009).

Nevertheless, Chinese investments had begun to gain momentum in Southeast Asia from the 1990s onwards, even seeing an upswing during the 2008 global financial crisis (Goh and Nan 2021). It has been estimated that over US$500 billion has been invested into Cambodia,

Indonesia, Malaysia, Singapore and Vietnam in just the first five years of the BRI's establishment in 2013 (Freeman and Ōba 2019). Perhaps except for Singapore, these investments have led to the materialization of infrastructures such as roads, highways, stadiums, bridges, office buildings and ports across the region. Consequently, this has paved the way for the Chinese to increase their stakes in areas such as port management and construction, such as the Cambodian port of Sihanoukville on the Gulf of Thailand, Melaka Gateway in Malaysia, and the port of Kyaukpyu in Myanmar. Naturally, these investments have not been without controversy, especially in areas such as resource and energy extraction. Examples such as the Myitsone Dam episode demonstrate the dilemma faced by local governments that have to reconcile Chinese capital and local interests. Malaysia also cancelled several Chinese-financed projects in 2018 under the second term of Prime Minister Mahathir because they were deemed disadvantageous to Malaysia.

Nonetheless, Chinese capital remains attractive for a variety of reasons. First, it offers a relatively quick and easy economic model for developing countries. Chinese capital brings cheap infrastructure and connectivity, traders and small businesses, local employment opportunities, and demand for local goods. Across mainland Southeast Asia, these patterns of activity offer cookie-cutter economic models that require little long-term planning or intellectual exertion from local policymakers. Second, Chinese capital has geopolitical strategic value. For a country like Cambodia, Chinese capital is akin to developmental steroids as it seeks to keep up with its more advanced neighbours of Thailand and Vietnam. This overreliance on Chinese capital has turned Cambodia into a Chinese proxy in the eyes of many, including ASEAN. But as Hun Sen has observed tersely, "If I don't rely on China, who will I rely on? If I don't ask China, who am I to ask?" (*Nikkei Asia*, 20 May 2021). Finally, and related to the previous point, Beijing rarely interferes in the domestic politics of recipient countries. Issues such as human rights, freedom of expression, oppression of minorities, authoritarian or illiberal politics are not pre-conditions for Chinese investments because "The western approach of imposing its values and political system on other countries is not acceptable to China" (Hao 2008, p. 186). Again, in the case of Cambodia, "Cambodian officials often stress their appreciation for Chinese non-interference" (Ciorciari 2013, p. 22). However, this narrative of Chinese non-interference must be taken with a pinch of salt. After all, in 2015 the Chinese ambassador in Malaysia took it upon himself to campaign for the Malaysian Chinese

Association during the country's general elections at a time when racial relations between Malaysian Chinese and Malays were fraught with tension. Meanwhile, the integration of the Overseas Chinese Affairs Department into the Chinese Communist Party's United Front Work Department in 2018 signals Beijing's increasing deployment of ethnic identity and cultural affinity as a means to appeal to ethnic Chinese populations in Southeast Asia to favour the interests of their "motherland" (Hsiao 2019).

Along with Chinese investments come human capital. Post-2000 Chinese immigrants have served as social conduits for the inflow of BRI capital such as managers and supervisors of state-owned enterprises (SOEs), construction workers (deemed more skilled than local workers) and entrepreneurs. Naturally, the influx of Chinese capital and immigrants have had several sociocultural ramifications. Rising property prices and the cost of living has been a major area of concern for locals. Take Myanmar, for example. China–Myanmar bilateral trade and Chinese direct investment amount to US$4.44 billion (68.8 per cent up from 2008) and US$1.95 billion, respectively (Tan 2012). New Chinese immigrants have had a profound impact on the price of real estate and business ownership, especially in Upper Myanmar. It has been reported that the inflated cost of living and property prices have driven many ethnic Burmese out of increasingly expensive cities like Mandalay to nearby towns. "Residents recall a 1984 fire that gutted downtown Mandalay and was followed by a government order to rebuild quickly using more expensive materials. Many had lost everything, even as Chinese citizens from neighbouring Yunnan province appeared with ready cash" (Magnier 2013). It has been estimated that over a million such relocations have taken place, with some observers noting that "the Chinese takeover of Mandalay and northern Burma replicates the economic consequences of the British colonization of Burma, which included a massive importation of Indian and, to a lesser extent, Chinese manpower and capital" (Mansfield 1999). Beyond the purging of locals from the city, it has also been suggested that the rising cost of living and property prices yields social consequences such as the rising number of singles who cannot afford to marry (Kyaw and Aung 2012).

Displacement and environmental degradation are the other major problems in light of mega projects like dams, power plants, mines and railroads. One example is the That Luang Marsh in Laos. Over a hundred families living in a part of the Lao capital slated for a Chinese-invested US$1.6 billion development project are refusing to relocate, saying compensation offered for their land is too low. Locals say the compensation offered is ten times less than the market value of their land (Radio Free Asia 2013). Another instance is the fast-speed rail from Kunming to Vientiane. Despite objections from NGOs and environmental groups, the project is expected to go ahead because the Lao government recognizes the benefit of infrastructural development, while the Chinese government sees the railway as an important way to pull Southeast Asia more tightly into its orbit under the BRI rhetoric.

According to some sources, at least sixty-nine Chinese corporations are investing in over ninety hydropower, mining, and oil and natural gas projects in Myanmar (Earth Rights International 2008). The extraction of natural resources also entails the displacement of rural people. Many villages have had to be resettled to make way for hydropower dams, mining plants and oil extraction factories. In 2010, Kachin villagers protested against the Myitsone Dam on the Irrawaddy River, built by the state-owned Chinese Power Investments Company, responsible for the relocation of up to 15,000 people. "Imagine your home has been bulldozed for a dam construction project, your farm, which is your livelihood, has been seized without compensation, and you and your family are forcibly relocated", said Ko Ko Thett, a commentator for *The Irrawaddy*. "Then the Chinese immigrants come to work the land where your farm used to exist. This is the source of tensions" (Birke 2010).

Chinese immigrants have also heightened competition for market share and posed acute entrepreneurial challenges for local traders and small businesses in areas where they are concentrated. Take the Morning Market at Talat Sao, in Laos, for example. Located at the junction of Lan Xang Road and Khu Vieng Road in Vientiane, opposite the busy Vientiane bus station, the Morning Market is now dominated by Chinese traders and shopkeepers who sell daily necessities and electrical appliances (Lim 2009). Chinese traders are also winning a bigger market share of mall shopping, thus distinguishing themselves from local traders. A new four-storey Talat Sao Mall in Vientiane was recently built by the Singapore-based Excalibur Group Pte Ltd and is now seventy per cent occupied and operated by new Chinese immigrants such that "Some of the storekeepers speak only Mandarin or very poor Laotian and rarely communicate with the locals" (Lim 2009, p. 10). Local traders and entrepreneurs have had to understand and adapt to the changing business environment. In particular, they have to realize that the new supply chains of goods and products from China have altered the marketplace. As such they have to "either acquire supplies themselves or learn how to sell the products they do have as value-added items" (Southiseng 2012, p. 11). In return, cheaper Chinese plastic and electronic goods flood local markets to alleviate oversupply in China while boosting local consumption across countries like Laos, Cambodia, Myanmar and Vietnam.

Finally, Chinese immigration and capital have impacted Chinese identity and cultural awareness in different ways. In Cambodia, for example, Chinese identity has become a way to bridge the Cambodian People's Party and China. Here the long-settled "Cambodia's ethnic Chinese are celebrated as conduits of economic and political ties between two friendly nations, to both of which they owe a certain allegiance" (Nyiri 2012, p. 105). There are practical ways in which this is done. Chinese investors and businessmen coming to Cambodia will have to look for a local backer (*kaoshan*), usually in the form of an *oknha* (sometimes translated into English as "lord"), a title granted by the king. This title, held by Chinese Cambodians, offers official tax privileges and informal authority. "Such *oknha* are in great demand by investors from China, particularly those who wish to acquire land concessions, since such concessions, by law, require a majority stake of a Cambodian company" (Nyiri 2012, p. 99). Such forms of politics and informal economies help raise awareness of Chinese identity among the Cambodian Chinese.

Conversely, there is resistance to Chinese identity and culture in other cases. Sino-Burmese have been known to distance themselves from new Chinese immigrants. Seen as materialistic, crass and having no desire to integrate into Myanmar society, these Chinese newcomers may be deemed alien to local ways of life. Than Htay, an ethnic Chinese-Burmese citizen and bookshop owner, said the newcomers don't fit in. "We are quite different from them in cultural traditions. Previous settlers paid respect to the native citizens. They lived modestly, not in a grandiose lifestyle. But now the new settlers don't care about the native people." Than Htay is himself of Chinese origin but he uses the pronoun 'they' in referring to the new Chinese settlers. There is a gap between the old and the new (Puak 2011).

Such distinctions go beyond the sociocultural. There is a clear sense of economic exclusivity. Locals complain that the Chinese newcomers live in mansions and villas in the downtown area, apart from the local community. "Some appear to live above the law. When the local authorities inspect houses for overnight guests staying in the area, they only check Burmese houses.... They dare not knock on the doors of these villas and mansions. Even if they knocked on their doors, they didn't receive an answer" (ibid.).

Conclusion

The historical waves of Chinese immigration into mainland Southeast Asia have been characterized by different levels of integration and engagement with host societies. The character and nature of these immigrant flows have been shaped by the socioeconomic and political conditions that these immigrants left behind. China's status as a global economic power, as well as its ambitious plans to build connectivity and trade through its BRI, has made contemporary immigrant flows substantially different from historical waves. China's entry into the WTO in 2001 is a convenient marker of its arrival on the international stage, paving the way for a series of milestone events such as the 2008 Beijing Olympics, its position as the world's second-largest economy in 2010, and the emergence of Xi Jinping and his BRI in 2013, all of which solidified its global presence. In the meanwhile, the realignment of global supply chains and the increased outflow of Chinese capital into the region served to entrench China in the imaginations of Southeast Asians.

On the one hand, post-2000 Chinese immigrants travel to mainland Southeast Asia with vastly different expectations and perspectives from their predecessors. No longer driven out by famine, war or the need to modernize, these new immigrants will engage with communities across mainland Southeast Asia with more confidence and perhaps with greater anticipation of deference. On the other, local communities will continue to negotiate the challenges that these newer Chinese immigrants, increased competition, and the decisions of their respective governments will bring. It is unclear how such negotiations will unfold. But what is clear is that relations between the newcomers and locals will be fraught with tension as China seeks to assert itself in the region and beyond.

References

Anderson, Benedict. 1983. *Imagined Communities: Reflections on the Origin and Spread of Nationalism.* London and New York: Verso.

Birke, Sarah. 2010. "Ethnic Tensions Grow in Myanmar". *The National*, 3 July 2010. http://www.thenational.ae/news/world/asia-pacific/ethnic-tensions-grow-in-myanmar.

Cabestan, Jean-Pierre. 2005. "The Many Facets of Chinese Nationalism". *China Perspectives* 59: 1–20.

Ciorciari, John D. 2013. "China and Cambodia: Patron and Client?" International Policy Center Working Paper no. 121. Gerald R. Ford School of Public Policy, University of Michigan.

Clover, Charles, 2017. "Xi Jinping Signals Departure from Low-profile Policy". *Financial Times*, 20 October 2017. https://www.ft.com/content/05cd86a6-b552-11e7-a398-73d59db9e399.

Earth Rights International. 2008. "China in Burma". http://www.earthrights.org/sites/default/files/publications/China-in-Burma-update-2008-English.pdf (accessed 5 May 2013).

Freeman, Carla P., and Mie Ōba. 2019. *Bridging the Belt and Road Divide*. Alliance Policy Coordination Brief, 10 October 2019. Carnegie Endowment for International Peace.

Goh, Evelyn, and Liu Nan. 2021. "Chinese Investments in Southeast Asia, 2005–2019: Patterns and Significance". *New Mandala*, 11 August 2021. https://www.newmandala.org/chinese-investment-in-southeast-asia-2005-2019-patterns-and-significance/.

Hao, Hongmei. 2008. "China's Trade and Economic Relations with CLMV". *Developing Strategy for CLMV in the Age of Economic Integration*, edited by Chap Sotharith. ERIA Research Report 2007–4. ERIA.

Hayton, Bill. 2014. *The South China Sea: The Struggle for Power in Asia*. New Haven: Yale University Press.

Hsiao, Russell. 2019. "A Preliminary Survey of CCP Influence Operations in Singapore". *China Brief* 19, no. 13: 12–17.

Kyaw, Ei Thinzar, and Aung Htwe San. 2013. "More Singles in Myanmar due to Rising Cost of Living". Asia News Network, 27 July 2012. http://burmadigest.info/2012/07/28/burma-related-news-july-27-2012/.

Levin, Dan. 2016. "Chinese-Canadians Fear China's Rising Clout is Muzzling Them". *New York Times*, 20 August 2016. https://www.nytimes.com/2016/08/28/world/americas/chinese-canadians-china-speech.html?_r=0.

Li, Audrey Jiajia. 2017. "Why China's Millennials are High on Ultra-Nationalism". *TODAY*, 28 April 2017. http://www.todayonline.com/chinaindia/china/why-chinas-millennials-are-high-ultra-nationalism.

Lim, Boon Hock. 2009. "China and the Chinese Migrants in Laos: Recent Developments". *Chinese Heritage Centre Bulletin* 13 & 14 (May & November): 7–11.

Lum, Thomas, Hannah Fischer, Julissa Gomez-Granger, and Anne Leland. 2009.

"China's Foreign Aid Activities in Africa, Latin America, and Southeast Asia". Congressional Research Service: Report for Congress. http://www.fas.org/sgp/crs/row/R40361.pdf (accessed 10 June 2013).

Magnier, Mark. 2013. "Myanmar Pivots Uneasily away from China". *Los Angeles Times*, 24 March 2013. http://articles.latimes.com/2013/mar/24/world/la-fg-myanmar-china-20130324.

Mansfield, Stephen. 1999. "Myanmar's Chinese Connection". *Japan Times*, 13 May 1995. http://www.japantimes.co.jp/life/1999/05/13/life/myanmars-chinese-connection/#.UYh-WLX2Pct.

Nikkei Asia. 2021. "Cambodia's Hun Sen: 'If I Don't Rely on China, Who Will I Rely On?'". 20 May 2021. https://asia.nikkei.com/Spotlight/The-Future-of-Asia/The-Future-of-Asia-2021/Cambodia-s-Hun-Sen-If-I-don-t-rely-on-China-who-will-I-rely-on.

Nguyen, Van Chinh. 2013. "Recent Chinese Migration to Vietnam". *Asian and Pacific Migration Journal* 22, no. 1: 7–30.

Nyiri, Pal. 2002. "From Class Enemies to Patriots: Overseas Chinese and Emigration Policy and Discourse in the People's Republic of China". In *Globalising Chinese Migration: Trends in Europe and Asia*, edited by Pal Nyiri and Igor Saveliev. Ashgate: Hampshire.

Puak, Ko. 2011. "Chinese on the Road to Mandalay". *Mizzima*, 5 July 2011. http://www.mizzima.com/edop/features/5545-chinese-on-the-road-to-mandalay.html.

Qin, Amy. 2018. "Worries Grow in Singapore Over China's Calls to Help 'Motherland'". *New York Times*, 5 August 2018. https://www.nytimes.com/2018/08/05/world/asia/singapore-china.html.

Radio Free Asia. 2013. "That Luang Marsh Residents Refuse to Move". 22 February 2013. http://www.rfa.org/english/news/laos/that-luang-02222013173942.html.

Southiseng, Nittania. 2012. "SME Development in the CLMV Region". *SIU Journal of Management* 2, no. 2: 6–25.

Suryadinata, Leo. 2017. *The Rise of China and the Chinese Overseas: A Study of Beijing's Changing Policy in Southeast Asia and Beyond*. Singapore: ISEAS – Yusof Ishak Institute.

Uhlmann, Chris. 2016. "Chinese Influence 'Challenging Fundamentals' of Australia, Says Stephen FitzGerald". ABC News, 28 September 2016. https://www.abc.net.au/news/2016-09-28/former-australia-ambassador-to-china-warns-government-of-beijing/7885140.

Wang, Gungwu. 1991. *China and the Chinese Overseas*. Singapore: Times Academic Press.

Wen, Phillip. 2016. "China's Patriots among Us: Beijing Pulls New Lever of Influence in Australia". *Sydney Morning Herald*, 13 April 2016. http://www.smh.com.au/world/chinas-patriots-among-us-beijing-pulls-new-lever-of-influence-in-australia-20160412-go4vv0.html.

Wong, Diana. 2013. "Introduction: The New Chinese Migration to Southeast Asia". Special Issue, *Asian and Pacific Migration Journal* 22, no. 1: 1–6.

Zhao, Suisheng. 2004. *A Nation-State by Construction: Dynamics of Modern Chinese Nationalism*. California: Stanford University Press.

Zhu, Zhenming. 2009. "China's Economic Aid to CLMV and Its Economic Cooperation with Them". Institute of Developing Economies, BRC Report No. 1. IDE-JETRO: Japan.

Zhuang, Guotu. 2000. "Policies of the Chinese Government towards Overseas Chinese since 1978". *Asia-Pacific World and China: Human Development: China Area Studies*, no. 10: 45–52.

Zhuang, Guotu, and Wang Wangbo. 2010. "Migration and Trade: The Role of Overseas Chinese in Economic Relations between China and Southeast Asia". *International Journal of China Studies* 1, no. 1: 174–93.

PART II
China's Soft Power, *Xin Yimin* and Local Communities

3

Confucius Institutes in Southeast Asia: An Overview

Neo Peng Fu

A Confucius Institute (CI), essentially, is a language school that teaches Mandarin (the standard form of modern Chinese) and operates outside China. It functions as a partnership between a Chinese university and a host university of the country (or administrative district) in which it operates. The former will provide teaching materials and instructors as well as an administrator known as the Chinese Director. Whereas the latter supports the running of the institute by providing infrastructure such as teaching facilities and local connections as well as an administrator known as the Foreign Director, who usually is a faculty of the host university and whose duty is to ensure the institute complies with the academic, administrative and fiscal statutes and regulations of the university.

The effort in establishing CIs worldwide was initiated by the government of the People's Republic of China (PRC) to assist the international community to develop a capacity for teaching Chinese language and culture in their own nations, a facility which was very much non-existent or scarce in most of the countries in the world. In the early 2000s, the Chinese government set up a bureau called *Hanyu Guoji Tuiguang Xiaozu Bangongshi* (汉语国际推广小组办公室), or Office of Chinese Language Council International, to realize this initiative. This office, located in Beijing, was to become the central agency overseeing the CIs that had proliferated rapidly over the globe in the one and a half decades since 2004. It was more widely known by its acronym 'Hanban' (汉办), or the Confucius Institute Headquarters.[1]

The first CI in the world was established in Seoul, the capital city of South Korea, in 2004. Ten years later, 475 CIs were operating in 126 countries.[2] By 2018, the number had further increased to 548 CIs in 154 countries.[3] The phenomenal growth of CIs, coupled with the rising economic power of China, however, is viewed by some as alarming. These institutes, entrusted with the primary duty of teaching Chinese language and culture, have come to be seen as a platform for the PRC to exercise its 'soft power'.[4] Nevertheless, there have also been voices that argue that this (perceived or real) endeavour (by the Chinese government) in using CIs to increase China's soft power has not really achieved its intended goal. It is contended that the participants of the courses, programmes and events of CIs indeed would not be easily swayed by the 'strategic narratives' deliberately propagated by Hanban to project a favourable image of China. In fact, the various stakeholders of the institutes—students, parents, teachers, university administrators and community participants—would actively negotiate for space and power while participating in the CI project, and have their very own needs and aspirations fulfilled.[5]

These findings, no doubt, have enabled us to achieve a more sophisticated understanding of CIs. Nonetheless, the current literature on CIs is predominantly based on studies conducted on those that operate in North America and European universities. How would these observations corroborate or contrast with those of the CIs in Southeast Asia (SEA)? This paper aims to present a preliminary survey on the topic by addressing the following questions:

1. Where are the Confucius Institutes in Southeast Asia?
2. When did CIs appear in SEA?
3. What are their roles?
4. Whose interest do they serve?

It will conclude by evaluating the significance of these institutes, as entities that offer an institutionalized form of Chinese language teaching and learning, against the greater historical context of the region.

Where Are the Confucius Institutes in Southeast Asia?

According to Hanban's official figures, there are now 541 Confucius Institutes in 162 countries (or administrative districts), of which 135 are in Asia, 61 in Africa, 187 in Europe, 138 in North and South America, and 20 in Oceania.[6] Southeast Asia has about a 7.4 per cent share of these global CIs.[7] Specifically, there are a total of 40 Confucius Institutes in the eight Southeast Asian states of Cambodia, Indonesia, Laos, Malaysia, Singapore, Thailand, the Philippines and Vietnam.[8] In terms of numbers, Thailand has the largest share of the CIs in Southeast Asia—16 in total. Indonesia has 8 and Malaysia and the Philippines have 5 each. Cambodia and Laos each have 2, and Singapore and Vietnam each have 1.

If seen by geographical distribution, amongst the 40 CIs in SEA, 21 of them are located in the Indochina peninsula, 3 in the Malay peninsula, 1 in Sabah, 1 in Sarawak, 1 in Singapore, 5 in Java, 1 in Sumatra, 1 in Kalimantan, 1 in Sulawesi, 4 in Luzon and 1 in Mindanao. It thus appears that these CIs are rather squarely distributed in the region, with the numbers more or less evenly split between those located in Indochina and maritime SEA. There is at least a CI in most of the major cities of SEA, with a higher concentration in the metropolitan areas (such as Bangkok and Manila).

When Did the Confucius Institutes Appear in SEA?

About two thirds of these 40 CIs, or 25 of them, were founded during the six-year period between 2005 and 2010.[9] The remaining third, or 15 of them, were founded during the seven-year period between 2013 and 2019.[10] No CIs were established in the region in the consecutive two-year period between 2011 and 2012. These numbers seem to suggest that the Southeast Asian states, in general, supported China's initiative to set up CIs during the inaugurating period of the global project. Although the momentum of building CIs in SEA stalled for a short period after 2010, it resumed again since 2013 despite the fact that the institutes were then beginning to

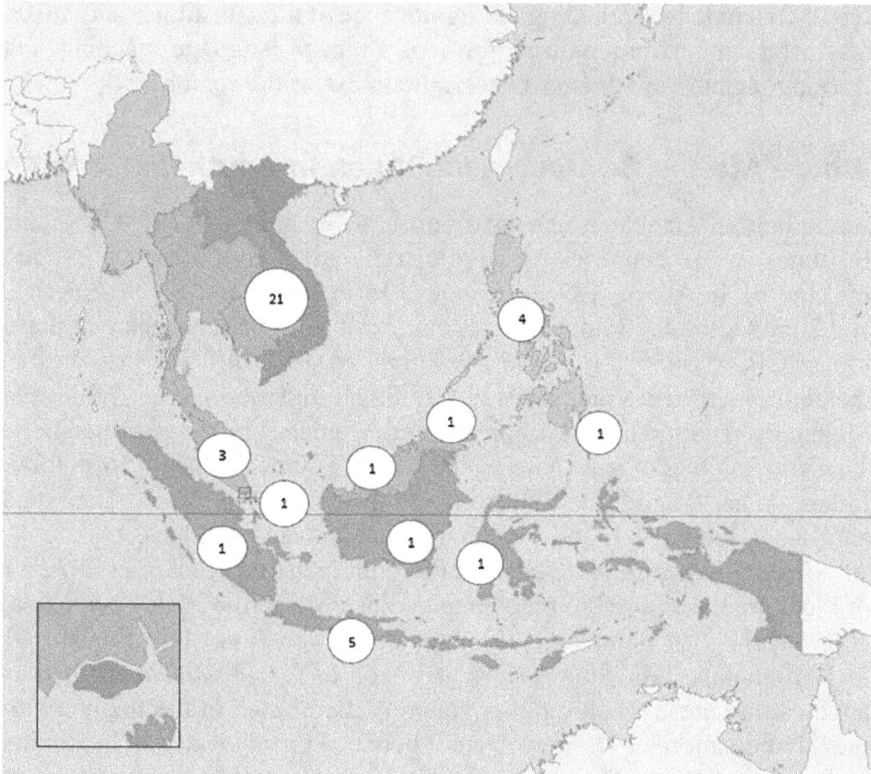

FIGURE 3.1 Number of Confucius Institutes in Southeast Asia by Geographical Distribution

attract quite a great deal of negative attention in some Western countries. This may indicate that there is perhaps a genuine demand for resourceful support to develop or enhance the capacity of teaching Chinese language in the region in order to meet the needs of the local people.

What Are the Roles of the Confucius Institutes?

In general, the CIs in Southeast Asia, as elsewhere, provide three main types of educational services: language teaching, teacher training and vocational training. They also serve as a platform for building a connection between the host universities and their Chinese partner universities.

Language Teaching

The Chinese language classes run by CIs cater to three main groups of individuals: school and university students, businessmen and professionals, and government officials. The last group of CI registered course participants is especially noteworthy because they are institutional (rather than private) participants. Their participation in CI programmes show that these institutes receive government patronage from the host countries. It appears that the Chinese classes for this group of CI students are mostly customized courses for officers of a particular government agency, which could be seen from the following examples:

- The Confucius Institute at the University of the Philippines conducts Mandarin classes for officers working in the Presidential Office, Ministry of Foreign Affairs, Immigration Department, port authority (the Subic Bay Metropolitan Authority), and the 120 trade and industry associations in the nation.[11]
- The Pusat Bahasa Mandarin at University of Al Azhar Indonesia runs Mandarin courses for the personnel of Indonesia's Ministry of Defence, Ministry of Trade, Police Headquarters and airport authority.[12]
- The Kong Zi Institute for the Teaching of Chinese Language at University of Malaya conducts customized Mandarin courses for the staff of Malaysian air and sea customs department.[13]
- In January 2018, the Confucius Institute at Kasetsart University worked with the Secretariat of the Senate to launch a Chinese Training Workshop for Members of the National Assembly of Thailand, which had attracted 20 participants. It subsequently extended the programme for Members of the Senate of Thailand in November 2019, which had 46 senators sign up for the course.[14] This CI also conducts Chinese courses for senior officials who serve in the defence, commerce, audit, comptroller general, and prime minister's departments of Thailand.[15]
- The Confucius Institute at the Royal Academy of Cambodia set up a Mandarin Center at the Cambodian Ministry of National Defence in July 2017 to help the military personnel of the Cambodian Ministry of National Defence to learn Chinese.[16]
- The Confucius Institute at the National University of Laos, in May 2019, launched an inaugural Chinese course for officials of the municipal government of Vientiane.[17]

Teacher Training

The language instructors at CIs, by and large, are expatriate teachers from the Chinese partner universities, comprising qualified and volunteer language tutors. The former usually are faculty members, whereas the latter are graduate students on internship or practicum. Nevertheless, China and the Southeast Asian host countries do see that in the long run there is a need to nurture a corps of native teachers to relieve and ultimately take over the jobs of the teachers from China.

As such, a number of the CIs in Southeast Asia have also engaged in running teacher training programmes. These programmes, as a whole, are categorized into short- and long-term courses. The former are usually in-service training for local teachers, whereas the latter are mostly in the form of degree-awarding pre-service training programmes. For example, in December 2019, the Philippine Ministry of Education signed an agreement with Hanban to run a master's degree programme at the Confucius Institute at Angeles University Foundation, which aims to groom 300 graduates in five years' time. Trainees of the programme will attend classes in both the host university and its Chinese partner university, the Fujian Normal University. They will be posted to the Philippine high schools as qualified Chinese language teachers after successfully completing their training.[18] There is good reason for the Philippine authority to do so. Beginning in 2011, the country listed Chinese as an elective foreign language subject for the students of public high schools. By 2019, some 11,000 students in the nation studying at 93 public high schools had opted to do the subject.[19] Understandably, with a student size of this magnitude, the country could no longer rely on expatriate teachers from China (and elsewhere) to meet the growing need for Chinese language instruction. There is therefore a real and urgent need for the country to nurture a sufficient pool of native Filipinos to become Chinese language teachers to cope with the demand. Another example would be the "Agreement on Cultivating Indonesian Chinese Language Teachers" signed by Hanban and the Indonesian Ministry of Education and Culture in April 2012. The collaboration aimed to groom 100 Chinese language teachers for Indonesia in three years' time. The first batch of 30 trainees for the joint project, who were full-time Chinese language teachers at Indonesian secondary schools, left for a six-month training programme on 21 June 2012 at Fujian Normal University.[20] Similar teacher training programmes are also being offered in other SEA CIs, such as the Confucius Institute at the University of Battambang in Cambodia.[21]

Vocational Training

Several CIs in Southeast Asia have moved beyond providing basic language teaching by embedding vocational training in their Chinese courses. These programmes, called "Hanyu jia" (汉语 +) or "Mandarin +", are essentially customized Chinese language curriculum closely related to imparting specialized vocational skills. There are a variety of these "Mandarin plus vocational training" programmes, which include the following:

- The Confucius Institute at the National University of Laos links up with the Kunming railway authority in China to run Mandarin courses geared towards teaching professional knowledge and skills on railway management.[22]
- The Confucius Institute at Khon Kaen University in Thailand has a link-up with the Chongqing Vocational Institute of Engineering in China. It also facilitates a tie-up between the Banphai Industrial and Community Education College in Khon Kaen province and China's Wuhan Railway Vocational and Technical College to offer a Mandarin programme called "High-Speed Rails China-Thailand Chinese Language Training Programme", which aims to groom a corps of technicians and specialists capable of managing the high-speed rail project (a joint venture between China and Thailand) slated to take place in Thailand.[23]
- The Kong Zi Institute for the Teaching of Chinese Language at the University of Malaya offers courses on "Mandarin + law enforcement", "Mandarin + legal services", "Mandarin + commerce", and "Mandarin for air & sea customs".

Network Building

Although the basic function of a Confucius Institute is to run Chinese language and culture programmes, it is also tasked with deepening the linkup between the two partner universities. It does so by supporting students and scholars of the host universities, as well as members of the local community, to undergo study trips, cultural immersions, scholarly exchanges, or further studies programmes at their Chinese partner universities. These activities are made possible through substantial financial supports from Hanban in the form of grants and scholarships. As a result, it promotes interactions that contribute to enhancing the relationships between the universities in the region and those in China.

The CI network essentially links a total of 40 universities in the region with 34 universities in China. It is interesting to note that among these Chinese universities 10 of them are located in northern China,[24] 11 in central China,[25] and the remaining 13 in southern China.[26] There seems to be a balanced distribution in the regional division of the Chinese universities assigned by Hanban to collaborate with the host universities in SEA. Albeit taking into consideration that six of the Chinese universities are allocated to run more than one CI in the region,[27] the grid for connecting the former to the latter appears to be extensive and comprehensive in design. Such a pattern of distribution may be a result of strategic planning meant to maximize the intended impact of the linkup between the Chinese universities and their counterparts in SEA via the CI network.

Whose Interest Do They Serve?

Language competency could be a skill with high market value. China is making her presence felt in the region by becoming the largest trading partner of most, if not all, of the Southeast Asian states. In fact, it has been reported that ASEAN "has replaced the European Union to emerge as China's largest trading partner in the first two months of 2020".[28] Naturally, mastering the Chinese language through studying at CIs would present the locals with enormous opportunities for gainful employment. But, of course, one could argue that by helping to groom a pool of native Southeast Asians conversant in Chinese, who could then become an intermediary between Chinese and local interests, CIs may also be playing a role in facilitating China's economic expansion in SEA. That is to say, the process works both ways. Hence, it should not be simplistically regarded as a development unilaterally favourable to either China or the individual SEA states.

If the CIs are making an impact on the region, this chapter intends to highlight an aspect of this development that, though still less noticeable, may create a profound and lasting influence on SEA society; namely, the CI scholarships for local students to pursue degree programmes in China. The Chinese partner universities have been providing undergraduate and postgraduate scholarships via their respective CIs to SEA students. The number of scholarships to be given out by each CI is about twenty in a year. These scholarships are highly sought after by local students in many SEA countries. This is not difficult to understand because these academic

TABLE 3.1
Host Universities of the CIs in SEA and their Chinese Partner Universities

	Name of CI and its Host University	Home Country	Home City	Name of Chinese Partner University	Year Founded*
1	Confucius Institute of Royal Academy of Cambodia	Cambodia	Phnom Penh	Jiujiang University	August 2009
2	Confucius Institute at University of Battambang	Cambodia	Battambang	Guilin University of Electronic Technology	December 2018
3	Pusat Bahasa Mandarin at University of Al Azhar Indonesia	Indonesia	Jakarta	Fujian Normal University	June 2010
4	Pusat Bahasa Mandarin at Malang State University	Indonesia	Malang	Guangxi Normal University	June 2010
5	Pusat Bahasa Mandarin at Maranatha Christian University	Indonesia	Bandung	Hebei Normal University	June 2010
6	Pusat Bahasa Mandarin at Universitas Negeri Surabaya	Indonesia	Surabaya	Central China Normal University	June 2010
7	Pusat Bahasa Mandarin at Tanjungpura University	Indonesia	Pontianak	Guangxi University for Nationalities	June 2010
8	Pusat Bahasa Mandarin at Hasanuddin University	Indonesia	Makassar	Nanchang University	June 2010
9	Confucius Institute at Universitas Sebelas Maret	Indonesia	Surakarta	Xihua University	July 2018
10	Tourism Confucius Institute at Udayana University	Indonesia	Padang	Nanchang University and Nanchang Normal University	December 2019

continued on next page

TABLE 3.1 – cont'd

	Name of CI and its Host University	Home Country	Home City	Name of Chinese Partner University	Year Founded*
11	Confucius Institute at National University of Laos	Laos	Vientiane	Guangxi University for Nationalities	September 2009
12	Confucius Institute at Souphanouvong University	Laos	Luang Prabang	Kunming University of Science and Technology	November 2017
13	Kong Zi Institute for the Teaching of Chinese Language at University of Malaya	Malaysia	Kuala Lumpur	Beijing Foreign Studies University	July 2009
14	Confucius Institute at SEGI University	Malaysia	Kuala Lumpur	Hainan Normal University	July 2014
15	Confucius Institute at Universiti Malaysia Pahang	Malaysia	Gambang, Pahang	Hebei University	November 2018
16	Confucius Institute at University College of Technology Sarawak	Malaysia	Sibu, Sarawak	North China University of Water Resources and Electric Power	October 2019
17	Confucius Institute at Universiti Malaysia Sabah	Malaysia	Kota Kinabalu, Sabah	Changsha University of Science and Technology	November 2018
18	Confucius Institute at Nanyang Technological University	Singapore	Singapore	Shandong University	June 2005
19	Confucius Institute at Chulalongkorn University	Thailand	Bangkok	Peking University	August 2006
20	Confucius Institute at Kasetsart University	Thailand	Bangkok	Huaqiao University	March 2005

Confucius Institutes in Southeast Asia

21	Confucius Institute at Khon Kaen University	Thailand	Khon Kean	Southwest University	March 2006
22	Confucius Institute at Mae Fah Luang University	Thailand	Chiang Rai	Xiamen University	December 2005
23	Confucius Institute at Chiang Mai University	Thailand	Chiang Mai	Yunnan Normal University	July 2005
24	Confucius Institute at Prince of Songkla University	Thailand	Songkla	Guangxi Normal University	February 2006
25	Confucius Institute at Mahasarakham University	Thailand	Maha Saraham	Guangxi University for Nationalities	February 2006
26	Confucius Institute at Bansomdejchaopraya Rajabhat University	Thailand	Bangkok	Tianjin Normal University	November 2006
27	Confucius Institute of Suan Dusit Rajabhat University at Suphanburi	Thailand	Suphan	Guangxi University	June 2006
28	Confucius Institute at Phuket, Prince of Songkla University	Thailand	Phuket	Shanghai University	March 2006
29	Confucius Institute of Betong Municipality	Thailand	Betong	Chongqing University	February 2006
30	Confucius Institute at Burapha University	Thailand	Chonburi	Wenzhou University and Wenzhou Medical University	November 2006
31	Confucius Institute at Assumption University	Thailand	Bangkok	Tianjin University of Science and Technology	September 2014

continued on next page

TABLE 3.1 – cont'd

	Name of CI and its Host University	Home Country	Home City	Name of Chinese Partner University	Year Founded*
32	Maritime Silk Road Confucius Institute	Thailand	Bangkok	Tianjin Normal University	April 2015
33	Confucius Institute for Traditional Chinese Medicine at Huachiew Chalermprakiet	Thailand	Bangkok	Tianjin University of Traditional Chinese Medicine	November 2015
34	Maritime Silk Road Confucius Institute at Phranakhon Rajabhat University	Thailand	Bangkok	Dali University	December 2017
35	Confucius Institute at Ateneo de Manila University	The Philippines	Manila	Sun Yat-Sen University	October 2006
36	Confucius Institute at Bulacan State University	The Philippines	Malolos	Northwest University	July 2007
37	Confucius Institute at Angeles University Foundation, the Philippines	The Philippines	Angeles	Fujian Normal University	October 2009
38	Confucius Institute at the University of the Philippines	The Philippines	Quezon City	Xiamen University	December 2014
39	Confucius Institute at Ateneo de Davao University	The Philippines	Davao	Huaqiao University	December 2019
40	Confucius Institute at Hanoi University	Vietnam	Hanoi	Guangxi Normal University	October 2013

Note: *This is the date the host university signed an agreement with Hanban and its Chinese partner university to set up a CI. It may take another one to two years for the CI to be fully operational.
Source: Compiled from data on Hanban's website.

grants are a prized opportunity for aspiring SEA students to go overseas for further studies, which is still a privilege beyond the reach of many local families. For example, from 2008 to 2018, the Confucius Institute at Chulalongkorn University alone awarded scholarships for more than 200 Thai students to study at the prestigious Peking University.[29] In 2020, close to 500 students from Thailand were studying in Peking University. They constituted about seven per cent of the total number of international students in Beida and had enrolled in undergraduate and postgraduate programmes across a wide range of disciplines.[30]

The opportunity for the youth to receive tertiary education in China undoubtedly contributes to promoting social mobility in SEA. But one must also see that it, correspondingly, helps the universities in China to become more internationalized by having more students from the region enrolled in their programmes. One must understand that it could be quite challenging for many of the non-elite universities in China to otherwise enrol international students. As such, the scholarship scheme through CIs serves as a systemic and reliable way of supplying the universities in China with a steady stream of international students, whose participation in campus life could contribute to changing the outlook of Chinese academia. Nonetheless, the significance of this CI scholarships scheme lies in the fact that, over the years, it will nurture a group of native Southeast Asians who are to become a class of new elites of their societies by the means of receiving higher education in China. They may have an outlook significantly different from that of their peers who have studied in the West. How the impact of this development would play out in SEA is perhaps something worth paying careful attention to.

Conclusion

Frederic Mason, a professor of education at the University of Malaya, writes in a book he published in 1954:

> Chinese schools are to be found everywhere, in town and country. In Singapore one can find them in imposing buildings like the Chinese High School, or climb up the stairs in a shop house to find eighty children crowded together into two classes in one room, or wander off the main road down a laterite road into a village where the school is a rickety wooden building with an atap roof and earth floors. In the

Federation of Malaya the range is as great, some being in the new villages (resettlement areas), and others in the great centres of Chinese population like Penang.[31]

While what he described was the scene in British Malaya, the sight was quite alike in other parts of Southeast Asia. The Chinese schools that Professor Mason talked about offered a system of modern education by using vernacular Chinese as a medium of instruction, and they had developed alongside the growth of the Chinese immigrant community in SEA since the late nineteenth century. The purpose of these schools was to enable the group to preserve their heritage language and culture, besides imparting skills and knowledge. Naturally, the students who enrolled in these schools were predominantly Chinese, perhaps with only an extremely small number of non-Chinese children. That is to say, although Chinese schools had scattered in the rural and urban areas of Southeast Asia, they did not contribute to the proliferation of the Chinese language in the region because their impact was largely confined to the Chinese community. Nevertheless, these Chinese schools (together with other vernacular schools) began to disappear in the postcolonial period when the newly independent states in Southeast Asia started to promote national language(s) as an instrument of nation-building.[32] As a result, by the 1980s, institutionalized forms of Chinese language teaching and learning were virtually non-existent in SEA, except in Malaysia and Singapore.

This historical background is important for one to see the significance of the Confucius Institutes in Southeast Asia. To begin with, CIs revitalize the institutionalized form of Chinese language teaching and learning that had once thrived in the region but had disappeared in past decades. But, more meaningfully, CIs make the teaching and learning of the Chinese language an enterprise that cuts across ethnic boundaries. In short, compared with the Chinese schools in the past that catered mainly to the Chinese community, CIs are meant to fulfil the needs and aspirations of "mainstream society".[33] That is to say, CIs may have contributed in transforming the Chinese language from being the heritage language of a particular ethnic group of the local society to an international, or business, language widely learned by the various communities of SEA.

The analysis of this chapter also indicates that if the Confucius Institutes project is indeed a scheme for China to exercise its soft power, as some have argued, it appears that the Southeast Asian states have also been able to have their national interests and local needs fulfilled by willingly participating in the power play.

Notes

1. There was a report mentioning that China's "Ministry of Education said the Confucius Institute Headquarters, or Hanban, had changed its name to the Ministry of Education Centre for Language Education and Cooperation" (Zhuang 2020). This may not be accurate. In a letter dated 11 June 2020 and signed by the Deputy Chief Executive of the Confucius Institute Headquarters, Professor Ma Jianfei, Hanban informs the foreign universities hosting a Confucius Institute on their campus that there is a plan to set up "a non-governmental foundation" named the Chinese International Education Foundation. The letter mentions that once the foundation is established, the headquarters "will be deregistered", and the "operation of the brands of Confucius Institute and Confucius Classroom" will be "transferred" from the latter to the former. In a follow-up letter dated 23 July 2020, co-signed by Ma Jianfei and Prof. Yang Wei, President of the Chinese International Education Foundation, it informs the foreign universities hosting a CI that "the Foundation was officially established on 19 June and has begun its operations". It also mentions in the letter that the "primary tasks" of the foundation, "a non-governmental international educational charitable organization registered in China", "are related to the support of Confucius Institutes and Confucius Classrooms, including the development, along with you as a contributing partner, of the strategies, vision, standards, and branding of CIs, as well as evaluating and improving the performance of the CIs". The letter specifically indicates that "The Foundation and the Headquarters have agreed to transfer to the Foundation the operation of the brands of Confucius Institute and Confucius Classrooms".
2. *Confucius Institute Annual Development Report 2014*, p. 2.
3. *Confucius Institute Annual Development Report 2018*, p. 8.
4. See, for examples, the works by Ding and Saunders 2006; Paradise 2009; Gil 2008, 2009; and Yang 2010.
5. See the recent works by Stambach 2014; Hartig 2015; and Hubbert 2019.
6. See Hanban's website, http://www.hanban.org/confuciousinstitutes/node_10961.htm (accessed 24 November 2020).
7. It may be interesting to note that, intentionally or coincidentally, the figure appears to be rather close to the proportion of SEA's population in the total population of the world.
8. To date, no CI has been established in Brunei, Myanmar and Timor-Leste.

9. Among these 25 CIs, 4 were founded in 2005, 10 in 2006, 1 in 2007, 4 in 2009, and 6 in 2010.
10. The first of these 15 CIs was founded in 2013. Subsequently, 3 were founded in 2014, 2 in 2015, 2 in 2017, 4 in 2018, and 3 in 2019.
11. See Hanban's website, http://www.hanban.org/article/2019-04/15/content_769340.htm (accessed 6 December 2020).
12. See Hanban's website, http://www.hanban.org/article/2018-04/24/content_727933.htm, and http://english.hanban.org/article/2013-05/29/content_498605.htm (accessed 6 December 2020).
13. See Hanban's website, http://www.hanban.org/article/2019-12/13/content_796178.htm (accessed 6 December 2020).
14. See Hanban's website, http://www.hanban.org/article/2018-01/24/content_716424.htm, http://www.hanban.org/article/2018-01/31/content_717051.htm, http://www.hanban.org/article/2018-07/18/content_739847.htm, http://english.hanban.org/article/2019-11/19/content_793486.htm, http://english.hanban.org/article/2018-02/05/content_717392.htm (accessed 6 December 2020).
15. See Hanban's website, http://www.hanban.org/article/2018-03/26/content_723660.htm (accessed 6 December 2020).
16. See Hanban's website, http://www.hanban.org/article/2018-10/11/content_746739.htm, and http://english.hanban.org/article/2017-07/28/content_694897.htm (accessed 6 December 2020).
17. See Hanban's website, http://www.hanban.org/2019-05/29/content_775303.htm (accessed 6 December 2020).
18. See Hanban's website, http://www.hanban.org/article/2019-12/05/content_795096.htm and CI-AUF's website http://confucius.auf.edu.ph/courses.php (accessed 26 November 2020).
19. Ibid.
20. See Hanban's website, http://english.hanban.org/article/2012-07/25/content_450449.htm (accessed 6 December 2020).
21. See Hanban's website, http://www.hanban.org/article/2020-10/27/content_813511.htm (accessed 6 December 2020).
22. See Hanban's website, http://www.hanban.org/article/2020-10/20/content_813263.htm and http://www.hanban.org/article/2020-07/10/content_810603.htm (accessed 6 December 2020).
23. See Hanban's website, http://www.hanban.org/article/2019-11/20/content_793661.htm, http://www.hanban.org/article/2019-03/14/content_766098.htm, http://www.hanban.org/article/2018-04/18/content_726930.htm, http://english.hanban.org/article/2019-11/27/content_794267.htm, http://english.hanban.org/article/2018-05/03/content_729568.htm, and http://english.hanban.org/article/2017-04/14/content_681021.htm (accessed 6 December 2020).
24. They are Beijing Foreign Studies University (北京外国语大学), Hebei University

(河北大学), Hebei Normal University (河北师范大学), North China University of Water Resources and Electric Power (河北水利水电大学), Northwest University (西北大学), Peking University (北京大学), Shandong University (山东大学), Tianjin Normal University (天津师范大学), Tianjin University of Science & Technology (天津科技大学), and Tianjin University of Traditional Chinese Medicine (天津中医药大学).

25. They are Central China Normal University (华中师范大学), Changsha University of Science and Technology (长沙理工大学), Chongqing University (重庆大学), Jiujiang University (江西九江学院), Nanchang University (南昌大学), Nanchang Normal University (南昌师范大学), Shanghai University (上海大学), Southwest University (西南大学), Wenzhou University (温州大学), Wenzhou Medical University (温州医科大学), and Xihua University (西华大学).

26. They are Dali University (大理大学), Fujian Normal University (福建师范大学), Guangxi University (广西大学), Guangxi University for Nationalities (广西民族大学), Guangxi Normal University (广西师范大学), Guilin University of Electronic Technology (桂林电子科技大学), Hainan Normal University (海南师范大学), Huaqiao University (华侨大学), Kunming University of Science and Technology (昆明理工大学), Southwest University (西南大学), Sun Yat-Sen University (中山大学), Xiamen University (厦门大学), and Yunnan Normal University (云南师范大学).

27. They include the Fujian Normal University, which runs 2 CIs (in Malaysia and the Philippines); Guangxi Normal University, with 3 CIs (in Indonesia, Thailand and Vietnam); Guangxi University for Nationalities, with 3 CIs (in Indonesia, Laos and Thailand); Huaqiao University, with 2 CIs (in Thailand and the Philippines); Tianjin Normal University, with 2 CIs (both in Thailand); and Xiamen University, with 2 CIs (in Thailand and the Philippines).

28. As reported by China's *Global Times*. See https://www.globaltimes.cn/content/1181864 (accessed 25 November 2020).

29. See Hanban's website, http://www.hanban.org/article/2018-03/27/content_723743.htm (accessed 12 January 2021).

30. See Hanban's website, http://www.hanban.org/article/2020-02/17/content_802268.htm (accessed 12 January 2021).

31. Frederic Mason, *The Schools of Malaya* (Singapore: Donald Moore, 1957), p. 11.

32. For an overview of this development, see Lee Hock Guan and Leo Suryadinata, eds. *Language, Nation and Development in Southeast Asia* (Singapore: Institute of Southeast Asian Studies, 2007).

33. See, for example, the website of the Confucius Institute at Ateneo de Manila University: http://www.ateneoconfucius.com/the-institute (accessed 25 October 2020).

References

American Association of University Professors. 2014. "On Partnerships with Foreign Governments: The Case of Confucius Institutes". https://www.aaup.org/report/confucius-institutes (accessed 16 January 2021).

Ding, Sheng, and Robert Saunders. 2006. "Talking Up China: An Analysis of China's Rising Cultural Power and Global Promotion of the Chinese Language". *East Asia* 23, no. 2: 3–33.

Gil, Jeffrey. 2008. "The Promotion of Chinese Language Learning and China's Soft Power". *Asian Social Science* 4, no. 10: 115–22.

———. 2009. "China's Confucius Institute Project: Language and Soft Power in World Politics". *Global Studies Journal* 2, no. 1: 59–72.

Hanban. 2014. *Confucius Institute Annual Development Report 2014*. Beijing: Confucius Institute Headquarters.

———. 2018. *Confucius Institute Annual Development Report 2018*. Beijing: Confucius Institute Headquarters.

Hartig, Falk. 2015. "Communicating China to the World: Confucius Institutes and China's Strategic Narratives". *Politics* 35, nos. 3–4: 245–58.

Hubbert, Jennifer. 2014. "Ambiguous States: Confucius Institutes and Chinese Soft Power in the U.S. Classroom". *PoLAR: Political and Legal Anthropology Review* 37, no. 2: 329–49.

———. 2019. *China in the World: An Anthropology of Confucius Institutes, Soft Power, and Globalization*. Honolulu, HI: University of Hawai'i Press.

Kramsch, Claire. 2014. "Teaching Foreign Languages in an Era of Globalization: Introduction". *Modern Language Journal* 98, no. 1: 296–311.

Lee, Hock Guan, and Leo Suryadinata, eds. 2007. *Language, Nation and Development in Southeast Asia*. Singapore: Institute of Southeast Asian Studies.

Paradise, James. 2009. "China and International Harmony: The Role of Confucius Institutes in Bolstering Beijing's Soft Power". *Asian Survey* 49, no. 4: 647–69.

Sahlins, Marshall, and James Turk. 2014. "Confucius Institutes", *Anthropology Today* 30, no. 1: 27–28.

Sahlins, Marshall. 2013. "China U.". *The Nation* 297, no. 20: 36–43.

Schmidt, Heather. 2013. "China's Confucius Institutes and the 'Necessary White Body'". *Canadian Journey of Sociology* 38, no. 4: 647–68.

Stambach, Amy. 2014. *Confucius and Crisis in American Universities: Culture, Capital, and Diplomacy in U.S. Public Higher Education*. New York: Routledge.

Starr, Don. 2009. "Chinese Language Education in Europe: The Confucian Institutes". *European Journal of Education* 44, no. 1: 65–82.

Wang, Danping, and Adamson Bob. 2015. "War and Peace: Perceptions of

Confucius Institutes in China and USA". *Asia-Pacific Education Researcher* 24, no. 1: 225–34.

Wheeler, Anita. 2014. "Cultural Diplomacy, Language Planning, and the Case of the University of Nairobi Confucius Institute". *Journal of Asian and African Studies* 49, no. 1: 49–63.

Yang, Rui. 2010. "Soft Power and Higher Education: An Examination of China's Confucius Institutes". *Globalization, Societies and Education* 8, no. 2: 235–45.

Zhuang Pinghui, "China's Confucius Institutes Rebrand after Overseas Propaganda Rows", 4 July 2020, Yahoo News. https://sg.news.yahoo.com/china-confucius-institutes-rebrand-overseas-121508830.html.

4

Cambodian Perceptions of China: A Chinese Learners' Perspective

Chheang Vannarith

The Chinese language has become one of the most attractive foreign languages—it ranks only second to English in Cambodia. The demand for the Chinese language is driven by the influx of Chinese tourists and investments, especially after 2010 when Cambodia and China signed their comprehensive strategic partnership. China has invested a significant amount of resources in promoting the Chinese language in Cambodia, especially under the cooperation framework of the Confucius Institute, intending to enhance people-to-people ties and project a positive image of China. The Chinese language has become a critical source of China's public diplomacy and soft power projection.

This chapter discusses the supply and demand of the Chinese language in Cambodia and the relationship between language education and acquisition with the political and social values of the learners. The chapter seeks to understand how language education and acquisition affect Cambodian learners' perception of China. The research does not aim to provide a comprehensive Cambodian perception towards China—it only targets those who learn the Chinese language. There are two assumptions here. First, there is a relationship between the acquisition of the Chinese language and the learners' perception of China. Second, the learners play an important role in promoting bilateral ties, especially under social and cultural cooperation. The chapter has three main parts: supply-side analysis, demand-side analysis and learners' perception analysis.

Research Method

The study uses a mixed research method and data collection to understand the perception of Cambodian learners of the Chinese language towards China, including desk review, semi-structured interviews and an online survey. The online questionnaire includes questions relating to learners' perceptions of the New Chinese, Chinese investments, the Chinese government, and China in general. The semi-structured interviews also focus on the informants' perception of these issues. The informants are also Chinese language learners, but they did not participate in the online survey. The online survey and interviews were administered from 1 November 2020 to 10 December 2020.

Concerning the online survey, 250 online questionnaires were sent out to Chinese learners in Cambodia using the snowballing approach. As a result, 87 survey responses were collected. The respondents are both *Kaun Chao Chen* and indigenous Khmer. In terms of gender, 55 per cent are female respondents and 47 per cent are males. In terms of education level, 74.7 per cent of the respondents had received or were about to receive bachelor degrees. In terms of occupation, 36.1 per cent of them are university students, 25.3 per cent from the private sector, 18.1 per cent from government agencies and 8.4 per cent from NGOs. As the survey data is small, this data should be treated as preliminary research into the topic and does not claim to make broad generalizations.

Supply-Side Analysis

China's soft power projection has gained momentum and international traction since 2007 after President Hu Jintao announced at the Seventeenth National Congress that the great rejuvenation of China goes along with "the thriving of Chinese culture".[1] In 2014, President Xi Jinping gave more impetus to China's soft power. He said, "We should increase China's soft power, give a good Chinese narrative, and better communicate China's message to the world."[2] However, China's fast-expanding global presence and influence have caused a certain degree of political, economic and social anxiety in some countries. To a certain extent, China's soft power projection has been constrained by its authoritarian political system.[3] In addition, the 'wolf-warrior' diplomacy—generally referring to aggressive and offensive diplomacy—launched by some Chinese diplomats during the Covid-19 pandemic crisis has fuelled anti-China sentiment.[4]

China's soft power in Cambodia has faced certain constraints due to the certain misconduct of some Chinese nationals. The relatively low quality of some Chinese investment and infrastructure projects has also contributed to China's negative perception.[5] The Chinese investments and presence in Sihanoukville, for instance, significantly damaged the image of China and the Chinese in Cambodia due to increased crime rates, environmental pollution, and social and cultural tensions. Online gambling—it was banned on 1 January 2020—was the root cause of social and economic issues in the province. In the wake of the closing down of the online gambling operations, about 400,000 Chinese nationals reportedly left Cambodia.[6]

Promoting a positive image of China is a process that requires strategically crafted public diplomacy. For China, culture is a critical source of international image projection and nation branding due to its richness in history and culture. Some have even called China a 'civilization state', referring to the critical role of civilization in nation-building.[7] In this connection, China's international appeal is largely associated with Chinese culture and language.[8] Chinese language, in particular, has become more popular among young people across the globe and opened new frontiers of cooperation, partnership and friendship between China and other countries.[9] China has become one of the top ten host destinations for international students.[10] Language diplomacy is one of the key components of China's cultural diplomacy, given that language acquisition processes shape learners' worldviews.[11]

The Chinese government has established various institutions and infrastructure to promote Chinese language learning throughout the world. Such efforts have met with some successes, but the future direction remains to be seen given a certain political push back against Chinese influence.[12] The Confucius Institute, which first opened in 2004 in South Korea, has played a pivotal role in promoting the Chinese language and culture. In some cases, the priorities and activities of Confucius are localized. For instance, the Confucius Institute in South Korea focuses on teaching Chinese, while the Confucius Institute in the United Kingdom prioritizes the promotion of contemporary China to the local people.¹³ In some cases, the Confucius Institutes have been criticized for propagating a Chinese worldview and ideology.¹⁴

While China has made remarkable headway in soft power projection through language diplomacy and the capability to align soft power with desired policy outcomes, there are remaining challenges. China's increasingly assertive and nationalistic foreign policy, together with increased influence and power, have been perceived as a threat by some neighbouring countries. Political legitimacy and language-related public diplomacy are interconnected.¹⁵ In this connection, the following sections discuss the supply-side of the Chinese language in Cambodia.

Confucius Institute

The Confucius Institute was first established in 2009 at the Royal Academy of Cambodia, Council of Ministers, in cooperation with Confucius Institute Headquarters (Hanban) and Jiujiang University. It aims to promote the Chinese language, cultural exchanges, and research and publication. On 22 December 2010, the inauguration ceremony was presided over by the then Chinese Vice-President Xi Jinping and Cambodian Deputy Prime Minister Sok An. At the event, Vice-President Xi said, "the founding of the Confucius Institute at the Royal Academy of Cambodia is a significant accomplishment in the cooperation between China and Cambodia's educational fields as well as a milestone in the history of the Chinese–Cambodian human exchange." He added, the institute will "build a new bridge further to improve understanding and friendship between Chinese and Cambodian peoples". He noted, "Since ancient times, China and Cambodia have learnt from each other, intermingling and making significant contributions to the development and prosperity of oriental culture."¹⁶

The Institute is led by the governing board and co-managed by a Cambodian director and a Chinese director. As of December 2019, there are twenty-two branches across the country. About 14,000 students are registering at the Institutes as of 2020. There are three training programmes under the Institute: a graduate programme in the Chinese language, four levels of a short-term training programme (100 hours for each level), and a preparatory training programme for HSK and HSKK tests (Chinese proficiency tests). The branches are located within the premises of the state and public institutions under the framework of bilateral partnership. The twenty-two branches include the Council of Ministers, General Secretariat of the Senate, Ministry of Foreign Affairs and International Cooperation, Ministry of Culture and Fine Arts, Ministry of National Defence, Ministry of National Assembly–Senate Relations and Inspections, Ministry of Justice, Brigade 70 (elite forces of the Royal Cambodian Armed Forces), Command Headquarters of Special Forces Paratroopers Brigade 911, General Commissariat of National Police, Army Institute, Union Youth Federations of Cambodia in Takeo province, Asia-Europe University, Khemarak University, Heng Samrin Tboung Khmum University, Angkor High School in Siem Reap province, Siem Reap's provincial office, Chea Sim High School Tbeng Meanchey, Aceveda Institute of Business, Canadia Bank, Phnom Penh China Cultural Centre, and Cambodia-China Friendship Radio Station. The Institute aims to establish more branches and build partnerships in all cities and provinces in Cambodia.

The core partner of the Institute is Jiujiang University. The Institute has established an HSK test centre (Chinese proficiency test). From 2009 to 2019, the Institute had sent 500 students under the scholarship programme to study at 213 universities across China. Annually, there are two field visits to China, one for government officials and the other for students. In addition, the Institute has organized many cultural and educational activities to promote mutual understanding and a people-to-people bond between the two countries.[17]

As of December 2020, there were 11 Cambodian staff, 2 local teachers and 69 teachers from China. In October 2020, a graduate programme in "Teaching Chinese to Speakers of Other Languages" was established. However, institutional capacity and coordination and the availability of qualified teachers remain the main challenges that the Institute is facing to expand its partnership, outreach and impacts. The minimum requirement to be qualified as a Chinese language teacher is to acquire an MA in the Chinese language—this explains why there are only a few qualified Cambodians who can teach Chinese. The institute will invest more in training Cambodian teachers of the Chinese language to expand its training services.[18]

Other Chinese Language Training Institutions

The Department of Chinese Language was created in 2010 at the Institute of Foreign Languages at the Royal University of Phnom Penh. The

Department offers a four-year undergraduate programme. The university also provides non-degree Chinese language courses. In November 2020, the Royal Academy of Cambodia established a new graduate programme (four-year programme) in the Chinese language. There are four majors in the programme: Chinese language for commerce, Chinese language for tourism, Chinese language for medicine, and Chinese language pedagogy.

The Phnom Penh China Cultural Centre is another Chinese language training centre. It was inaugurated in 2016 with the presence of Prime Minister Hun Sen and President Xi Jinping. The Chinese Ministry of Culture jointly established it, together with the Yunnan provincial Publicity Department and the Xinzhi Group of Yunnan. The centre contains a full-time Chinese language school, exhibition halls, digital reading rooms, dance rooms, martial arts training rooms and tea experience centres. In addition, regular cultural events are held here.

Some several private schools and universities provide both degree and non-degree Chinese language programmes, such as Tuan Hoa School, Beijing International Academy School (BIA), Zhong Hua international school, Leep Khun school, Chong Zheng Chinese school, Zhong Ying International School, Luan Yu Chinese school, Harvest Education Centre International School, Advanced Stamford International School, Asia–Europe University, Khemarak University, Pannasastra University of Cambodia, and the University of Cambodia. These Chinese language programmes are market-driven as the demand for Chinese proficiency is on the rise among students.

Demand-Side Analysis

The Chinese language is getting more popular among Cambodians and it is making significant headway to becoming a key commercial language. Family factors and personal interest are the key motivations for learning Chinese, and the main objectives of learning Chinese are communication, employment opportunities, business opportunities, cultural interest, and education. It is interesting to know that the family factor has a strong influence over the decision to learn Chinese. A student at the Institute of Foreign Languages Department of Chinese at the Royal University of Phnom Penh (RUPP) said: "I have been learning Chinese since I was 13 years old. At the time, I did not intend to learn Chinese, but because my parents are from Chinese descent, they wanted me to learn Chinese."[19] Another student at the local private school, Tuan Hoa School, said: "My parents want me to connect with Chinese ancestors, traditions and cultures. So they asked me to learn Chinese."[20]

Ethnic Chinese and *Kaun Chao Chen* (children and grandchildren of China or Cambodians of Chinese descent) play a critical role in promoting Chinese culture and language. Over the decades, many Chinese got married to the local Khmer and were absorbed into Khmer culture while introducing Chinese customs into Khmer society. The Khmer culture and Chinese norms and traditions coexist very well. After gaining independence from France in 1953, the Cambodian government started indigenization by implementing an accommodationist policy. However, during the Khmer Rouge regime from 1975 to 1979, ethnic minorities, including ethnic Chinese, were massively executed. The accommodationist policy refers to forming a mechanism or arrangement to promote harmony between distinct cultural identities. Promoting national language and symbols is the key intervention strategy in the indigenization process.[21] In Cambodia, Khmer is the national language, which is the foundation of nationalism and nation-building.

The first wave of ethnic Chinese to Cambodia occurred in the thirteenth century, mainly of Hokkiens. The second wave took place in the seventeenth century, made up predominantly of Cantonese and Hainanese. The third wave took place primarily in the nineteenth and twentieth centuries and was constituted by Teochew and Hakka. Teochew is the largest ethnic community. According to the survey in 1962–63, Teochew accounted for 77 per cent of 425,000 Chinese—about 7.4 per cent of the total Cambodian population.[22] The fourth wave started in the 1990s; it is called the New Chinese. *Kaun Chao Chen* or Sino–Khmers are generally entrepreneurial, and they are raised to occupy a large economic life in Cambodian society. Some are economic elites and influential political figures.

Family factors and personal interests are the two key driving forces for learning Chinese. A lecturer at the Royal University of Phnom Penh said, "I was born in a family where Chinese dialects (Teochew and sometimes Mandarin) are used for daily conversation. Thus, family is the most important driving factor."[23] A government official from the Ministry of Foreign Affairs and International Cooperation said, "Family factor is the main reason for me to learn Chinese. My parents want me to maintain the family traditions."[24]

The Chinese language is the only language associated with Chinese culture and traditions and an increasingly popular language for commerce and employment opportunities. According to the survey findings, the five main purposes of learning Chinese are communication, employment opportunities, cultural interest, education, and doing business.

In addition to the survey findings, the following are the comments from the learners and directors of the training centre.

A School Principal from Toun Fa:

> More people wanted to learn Chinese since our ties became closer with China and there has been more business, factories—so the need is high. Since it was founded in 1914, Toun Fa has catered to Cambodians of Chinese descent, especially the large community of Teochew people from Guangdong province, but these days the student body is diversifying.[25]

Director of the Confucius Institute at the Royal Academy of Cambodia:

> Currently, there is a sharp rise in Chinese investments and businesses in Cambodia, while the relation between Cambodia and China is stronger than ever. Indeed, we need enormous human resources who can speak and write Chinese. No matter what your purpose is for studying the Chinese language, it is always important. If you do not know their language or do not understand their culture, it is very hard to communicate, work or do business with the Chinese.[26]

Student A from the Royal University of Phnom Penh:

> I would like to do business with Chinese entrepreneurs because there are many Chinese businessmen in our country. I also would like to be a foreign affairs official at an institution or a government ministry.[27]

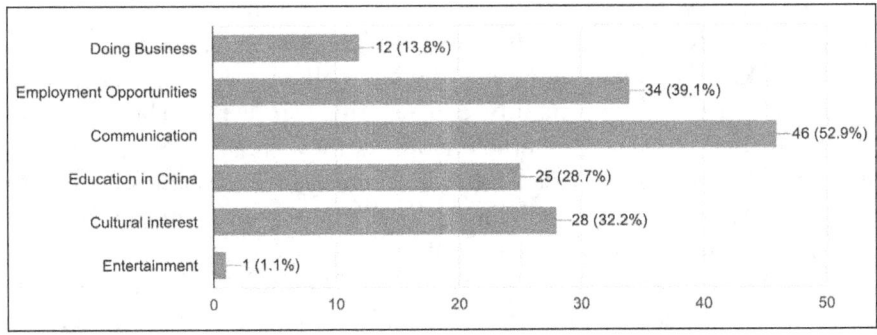

FIGURE 4.1 Purposes of learning Chinese (can choose three answers)

Student B from the Royal University of Phnom Penh:

> Cambodia now has many businesspeople coming here from China. They're investing much money. So it's very important to speak their language.... Cambodian families encourage their children to study Chinese because they want their children to get jobs.... The real money in Cambodia is coming mostly from China.[28]

An owner and manager of a local company:

> My parents inspire me to learn Mandarin, given that it is a business language. To successfully run a family business, we need to have a strong network within the Chinese community, be part of the Chinese associations or groups. They support each other to run a business.[29]

An employee at a private company:

> There are four main purposes of learning Chinese. First, Chinese is a medium for communication with my late grandparent, who originally came from mainland China, siblings and relatives. Second, for entertainment purpose—Chinese movies and music. Other initial aims of learning Chinese are to pursue a career in Chinese companies and to visit China with my parents.[30]

Chinese Learners' Perception

The findings from the survey and interviews are discussed in the following four sub-sections; namely, perception on the New Chinese, Chinese investments, China and the Chinese government, and bilateral relations.

The New Chinese in Cambodia

The New Chinese are those Chinese who arrived in Cambodia after the 1990s. They are mainly petty traders, service entrepreneurs, construction workers, skilled garment workers, and white-collar workers in the banking, logistics, journalism, hospitality and catering services.[31] They embody slightly different cultural characteristics as they are less integrated into the local Khmer society than the Old Chinese, whose cultural identity integrated well with the local Khmer culture due to intermarriage and the fusion of cultural traditions and norms.

The New Chinese promote the ethnic Chinese economic presence, culture and language. Meanwhile, they also widen the gap between the business and political elites and the general population.[32] Social tensions between Chinese immigrants and the local people are other problems caused by the New Chinese. For instance, misunderstanding and social tensions between Cambodian and Chinese construction workers at various construction sites in Sihanoukville are highly present due to language barrier, different working behaviour, cultural mindset, and unfairness relating to wages and benefits.[33]

According to the survey, the Chinese learners perceive that the New Chinese contribute to the local economy (26 per cent), cultural exchanges (14 per cent), and the creation of business opportunities (7 per cent). The New Chinese are seeking business opportunities (9 per cent) and employment opportunities (6 per cent). The New Chinese are less integrated into the local community (14 per cent) and have low awareness of local culture (6 per cent). Some of them cause social tensions or conflicts (10 per cent). Therefore, promoting mutual understanding and cultural integration between the New Chinese and local Cambodians is crucial to improving the local perception of the New Chinese.

Although the New Chinese have been generally perceived as another source of economic growth and business opportunities, social tensions and conflicts remain a problem. The crimes committed by some Chinese,

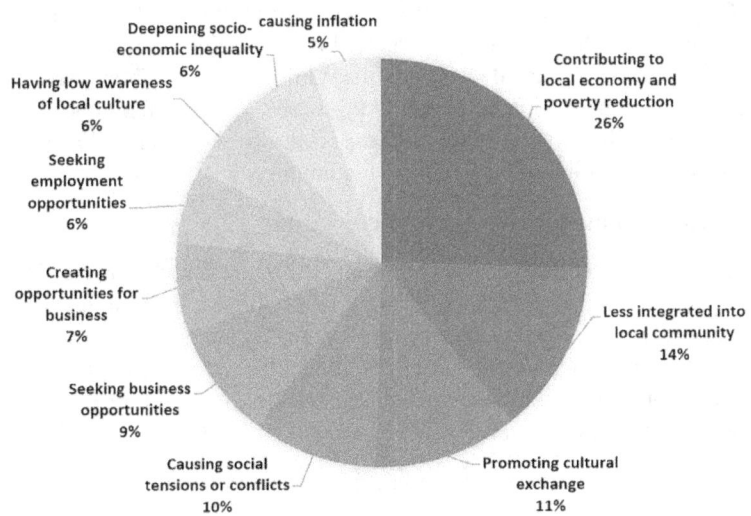

FIGURE 4.2 Chinese Learners' perception of the New Chinese (can choose three answers)

especially in Sihanoukville, add to the negative perception of China. Here are the comments from the Cambodian informants who did not participate in the online survey.

Director of the Confucius Institute:

> The New Chinese people who come here today do not know much about the local culture and traditions, while the Cambodians do not know much about their culture. In such a case, misunderstanding is inevitable. There may be some Chinese people who have improper behaviours, but they do not reflect on the entire population of China.[34]

A Lecturer at the Royal University of Phnom Penh (RUPP):

> I have mixed perceptions, both positive and negative, of the New Chinese in Cambodia. Chinese tourism and investment have greatly contributed to Cambodia's economic growth. The fast-paced illegal Chinese immigration, arrogant behaviour of some New Chinese and improper Chinese businesses have adversely affected China's image.[35]

An official from the Ministry of Foreign Affairs and International Cooperation (MOFAIC):

> Unlike the Old Chinese who came to settle down in Cambodia a long time ago as mainly driven by war and poverty, the new Chinese are more "modern" in thinking and living. The New Chinese who arrived in Cambodia, especially after the 1990s, are chiefly seeking business opportunities. They prefer to live within their circle or community. Some got married to local Cambodians. While some have integrated into Cambodian society, some are not. And there are problems concerning crimes and other illegal activities, especially in Sihanoukville, which harm the overall image of China in the country.[36]

An owner and manager of a private company:

> They help connect business ties between Cambodians and Chinese. They come to do small businesses and work with Chinese companies. Some got married to the local Cambodians. There is an image problem caused by some Chinese who came here to do illegal things such as committing crimes. Some New Chinese do not respect the local culture and drive social and cultural tensions.[37]

An employee from a private company:

> The New Chinese provides business opportunities for the local people, especially those who can speak Mandarin. They also help promote

the business networks between the two countries. Sino-Khmers play an important role to connect and do business with the New Chinese. But there are some concerns with regard to crimes committed by some Chinese nationals, especially in Sihanoukville.[38]

A director of a local NGO:

> The flow of the New Chinese to Cambodia, especially in the past five years, has caused certain social problems. Some of them do not respect Cambodian culture and language. They use incorrect Khmer words in their signboards. They are not sensitive to local culture. Some commit crimes which affect social order and security, especially in Sihanoukville.[39]

Chinese Investments in Cambodia

China is the top source of foreign direct investment to Cambodia. The total investment capital from 2015 to 2019 was about US$11 billion (see Figure 4.3). The main investment sectors are industry and manufacturing (US$7.83 billion), tourism (US$7.04 billion), agriculture and agro-industry (US$2.06 billion), and infrastructure and others (US$7.67 billion). It is predicted that the investment flow from China will increase the year after the bilateral Free Trade Agreement (FTA) signed in October 2020 came into force in 2021.

Cambodian perceptions towards Chinese investment are quite mixed. While the investments have brought opportunities and incomes to the local people, there are some complaints and concerns regarding environmental and social impacts. Some local observers even criticize China for breeding corruption and causing good governance to deteriorate. Chinese contractors prefer to hire Chinese workers rather than locals, although they need to pay more for the Chinese labour costs. In addition, the spill-over effects, particularly in the form of technology and knowledge transfer, are limited.[40]

Quality, accountability, transparency and sustainability are the main issues of Chinese investments. In addition, the lack of social and environmental impact assessments and safeguard measures and economic overdependence on China are some of the concerns and risks.[41] The local people have expressed their resentment towards the Chinese presence in Cambodia due to rising inflation, land conflicts and limited benefits to the local people in terms of employment and business opportunities.[42]

According to the survey, the Chinese learners' perception of Chinese investments is quite positive. They perceive that Chinese investments

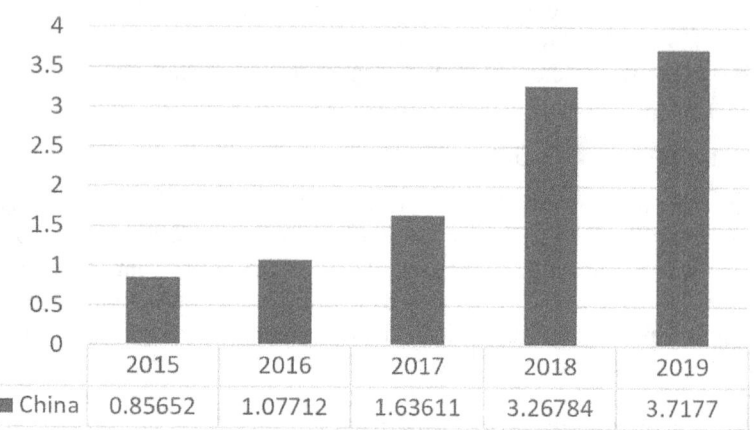

FIGURE 4.3 Chinese investments in Cambodia (Source: Council for Development of Cambodia)

contribute to the local economy (28 per cent), economic diversification (15 per cent), and infrastructure development (11 per cent). The negative impacts caused by Chinese investment projects include environmental degradation (11 per cent), an increase in the crime rate, especially in the gambling industry (11 per cent), an increase in the cost of living and inflation (8 per cent), and the weakening of local governance (7 per cent).

The following are the comments by the local Cambodian stakeholders about the perceived impacts of Chinese investments in Cambodia. The statements highlight the positive as well as the negative dimensions of Chinese investments.

A Lecturer at RUPP:

> I also have mixed perceptions of Chinese investment in Cambodia. Excluding illegal and unhealthy Chinese businesses, China's increasing investment in the country remains significant for decent job creation and robust economic growth. Heavier dependence on China's riches can risk the country's political autonomy. Illegal activities of some Chinese could be one of the adverse consequences.[43]

A government official from MOFAIC:

> The Chinese investments are critical to Cambodia in terms of economic and social development. They help boost infrastructure development,

Cambodian Perceptions of China

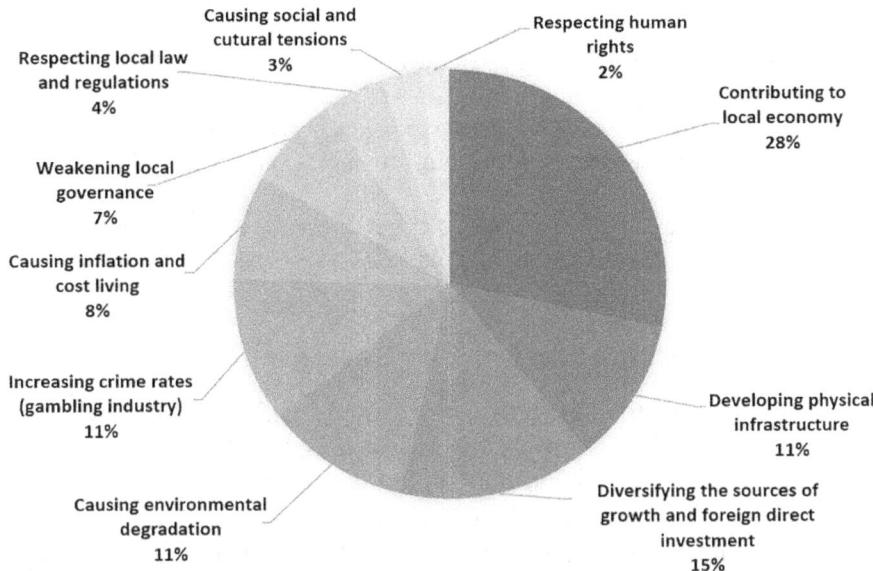

FIGURE 4.4 Chinese learners' perception of Chinese investment (can choose three answers)

provide jobs, and foster the country's economic activity. However, Cambodia needs to enhance institutional building and regulations to maximize the benefits from Chinese investments.[44]

An owner and manager of a private company:

> Chinese investments are good for the local economy and people. They create job opportunities and incomes for the local people. Some local wealthy people have benefitted from selling or renting their real estate. However, some Chinese investment projects are involved in land-grabbing and environmental degradation. There are some concerns over labour rights violations and poor working conditions, especially in the garment industry.[45]

An employee of a private company:

> It contributes to the local economy but also causes certain problems such as environmental issues and corruption. There is a need to improve the quality of Chinese investments by taking care of the local environment and people.[46]

A director of a local NGO:

> The main concerns relating to Chinese investments in Cambodia are environmental degradation, corruption, and the lack of transparency. We don't know much about Chinese investments in the hydropower dams, such as the port facilities in Koh Kong province. Corruption has become a norm of Chinese investment in Cambodia. They need to bribe local politicians and government officials to get things done. In other words, Chinese investments breed corruption.[47]

Perception of China and Chinese Government

Cambodian perceptions towards China and the Chinese government are mixed. Different groups of professions and stakeholders tend to have different views on China and the Chinese government. The government officials and those working in the private sector are largely positive towards China and the Chinese government. The local civil society groups and intellectuals are quite critical of China and the Chinese government. A director of a local NGO said, "China does not have a political value and system that can attract Cambodians. There is no political appeal. The lack of transparency is the key issue in the Chinese government."[48] In addition, a Cambodian researcher argued, "China is a big country with diverse ethnicity and socio-economic class. Therefore, it is necessary to have a strong government that can unite and govern the country. The rise of China presents both opportunities and threats to the region. China's foreign policy has become more assertive or even aggressive, which cause security concerns to some countries."[49]

The Chinese learners are generally positive towards China and the Chinese government. Commenting on the growing number of Chinese learners in Cambodia, a regional analyst argues: "This is about accepting the Chinese leadership in the region. When you study another country's language, you understand, and you accept the leadership of that country."[50] In other words, the Chinese learners tend to be influenced by the Chinese political ideology and worldview through language and values.

According to the survey, the Chinese learners regard China as a success story in poverty reduction, the world's largest economy, fast-developing economy, cultural power, old civilization, and a country with high technological innovation and high-tech industry. The perception can

Cambodian Perceptions of China

be interpreted that economic resources, cultural assets, and technology are the key sources of China's soft power.

The Chinese learners perceive that the Chinese government has strong leadership and governance with an authoritarian regime type. Taking a global leadership role and promoting people-centred development are two other key characteristics of the Chinese government.

A lecturer at RUPP (also a learner of the Chinese language):

> Personally, my perception of China, in general, is neither positive nor negative. If I am asked to choose one, it might be a bit 'positive' for two reasons. The first is grounded in my education and understanding of China's history and civilization. The second is associated with my family's background. Thus far, my family members and I have been accustomed to Chinese culture and other events, including Chinese New Year.
>
> Under President Xi Jinping, Beijing has done a lot to rejuvenate the Chinese nation since 2013. China's BRI, China's engagement in other multilateral institutions and China's contribution to global governance are important for international peace and development.[51]

A government official from MOFAIC (also a learner of the Chinese language):

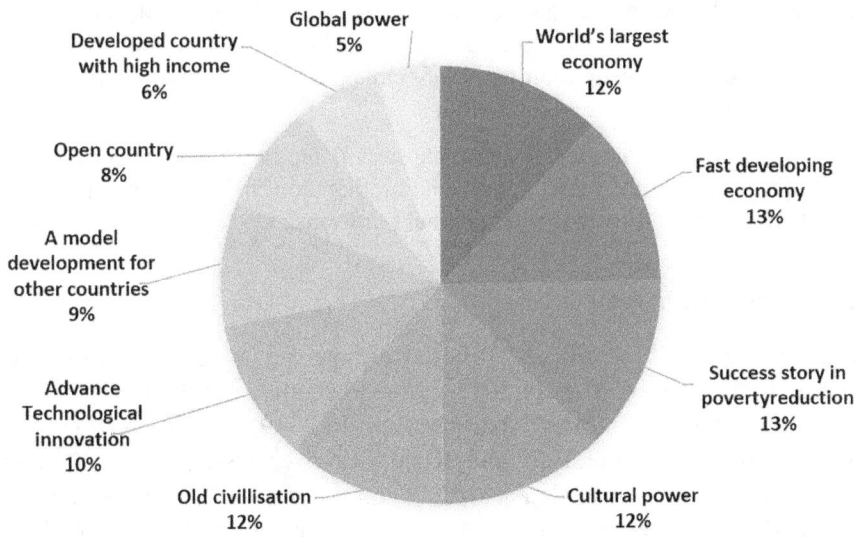

FIGURE 4.5 Chinese learners' perception of China (can choose three answers)

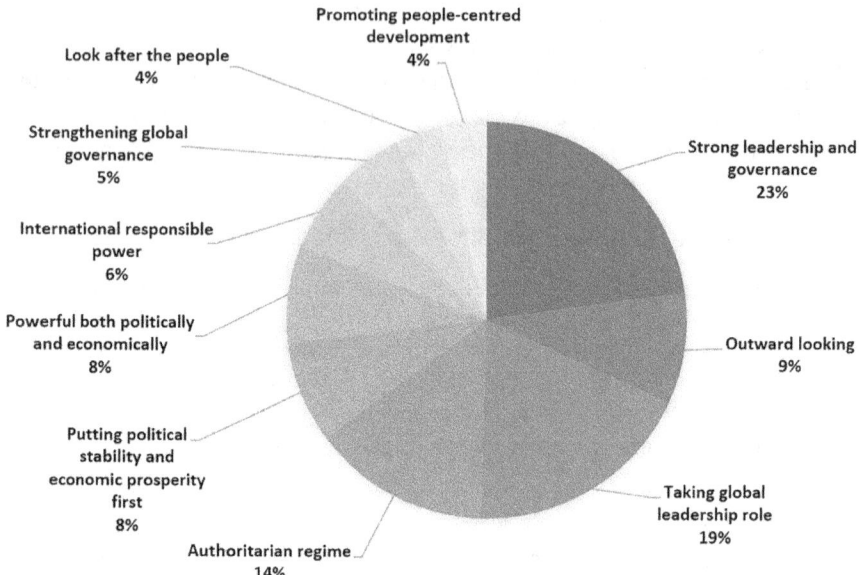

FIGURE 4.6 Chinese learners' perception of the Chinese government (can choose three answers)

China is a big country with an enormous land boundary and people. China has an old and interesting culture and tradition. China has developed a very modern society with high economic growth and a good living standard for the people. In terms of economic power, China is a major power in the region and the world.

The Chinese government has a stable system and far-sighted leadership. China is one of the major donors and brothers to Cambodia, supporting the Kingdom on various international platforms.[52]

Bilateral Relations

The Cambodia-China bilateral relationship has achieved three milestones over the past two decades. In 2010, both sides upgraded their relationship to a 'comprehensive strategic partnership'. In 2019, they signed an action plan to implement the Belt and Road Initiative (BRI). In 2020, they signed the bilateral Free Trade Agreement. It was the first FTA between Cambodia and other countries. Cultural and educational exchanges have been promoted over the years. The weak link in Cambodia-China relations

Cambodian Perceptions of China

is people-to-people ties. Anti-China sentiment reached a new high during 2018–19 due to the influx of Chinese investments in the gambling industry accompanied by increased crime rates, water pollution and sociocultural tensions, particularly in Sihanoukville.[53] There is also a local concern over the loss of Khmer identity and language resulting from ignorance and over the bad behaviour of some Chinese.

Chinese learners play certain roles in promoting mutual understanding and people-to-people ties between the two countries. Out of 87 respondents, 51.7 per cent said that they had contributed to the bilateral relations to varying degrees. Promoting cultural exchanges, educational exchanges, mutual understanding, business relations, and investment are key contributions.

The following comments are from the local Cambodian stakeholders that highlight some of the key activities that they have done to contribute to the bilateral ties.

A Lecturer at RUPP:

> My contributions to enhancing Cambodia's bilateral ties with China are promoting cultural understanding through teaching undergraduate students and communicating with other people, both Chinese and Cambodians, promoting academic research on Sino-Cambodian relations, and being engaged in Track 1.5, Track 2 diplomacy.[54]

An official from MOFAIC:

> I have contributed to the enhancement of Cambodia-China bilateral relations by promoting dialogue, people-to-people ties, and research and publication.[55]

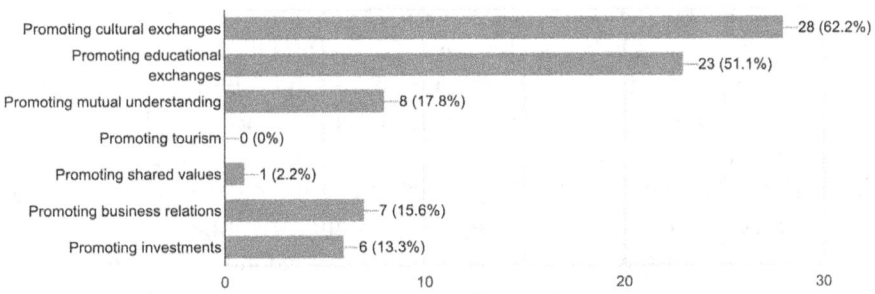

FIGURE 4.7 Chinese learners' perception of their contribution to the bilateral ties

An owner and manager of a private company:

> I have contributed to the bilateral ties by working with the Chinese business community and promoting business ties between Cambodia and China.[56]

An employee from a private company:

> I have contributed to the bilateral relationship through the promotion of bilateral trade and investment cooperation. Many Chinese companies are interested in investing in Cambodia. There are opportunities for Sino-Khmers to partner and work with them.[57]

Conclusion

The Chinese language has become one of Cambodia's most popular foreign languages due to the increased demand and supply of the Chinese language. The Chinese government has invested remarkable resources in promoting the Chinese language and culture, especially under the framework of the Confucius Institute. Due to the influx of Chinese investments and people, increasing Chinese presence presents both opportunities and challenges for the local Cambodians. The Cambodian perception of China is mixed.

This chapter discusses the perception of Chinese learners towards the New Chinese and Chinese investments in Cambodia, China in general, and the Chinese government. It argues that the Chinese learners see China in a more positive light. They have a positive view of the New Chinese and Chinese investments as these provide critical sources of economic growth and diversification opportunities to the Kingdom. They also have quite a positive perception towards China and the Chinese government and contributed in their capacity to the bilateral ties between the two countries.

There are concerns about the lack of mutual understanding, social tensions or conflicts between the New Chinese and the local Cambodians, and the increased crime rate. In relation to the Chinese investments, some negative impacts include environmental degradation, social tensions, increased crime rate (especially due to the investment in the gambling industry), the rising cost of living and inflation, and the weakening of local governance due to the lack of transparency and corruption.

Economic resources, cultural assets, and technological innovation are the key sources of China's public diplomacy and image projection, at least from the perspective of Cambodian learners of the Chinese language.

Therefore, language acquisition does matter in shaping how the learners view China.

Notes

1. *Beijing Review*, "HU Jintao Calls for Enhancing 'Soft Power of Chinese Culture", 15 October 2007, http://www.bjreview.com.cn/17thCPC/txt/2007-10/15/content_80539.htm.
2. Zhang Lihua, "Beijing Focuses on Soft Power", Carnegie-Tsinghua Center for Global Diplomacy, 28 April 2014, https://carnegietsinghua.org/2014/04/28/beijing-focuses-on-soft-power-pub-55458.
3. Eleanor Albert, "China's Big Bet on Soft Power", Council on Foreign Relations, 9 February 2018, https://www.cfr.org/backgrounder/chinas-big-bet-soft-power.
4. Zhu Zhiqun, "Wolf-Warrior Diplomacy: China's New Normal?", *Think China*, 4 May 2020, https://www.thinkchina.sg/wolf-warrior-diplomacy-chinas-new-normal.
5. S. Po, "The Limits of China's Influence in Cambodia: A Soft Power Perspective", *UC Occasional Paper Series* 1, no. 2 (2017): 61–75.
6. *Khmer Times*, "Immigration Dept Says 400,000 Chinese Have Left Because of the Online Gambling Ban", 1 January 2020, https://www.khmertimeskh.com/675447/gdi-attributes-mass-departure-to-online-gambling-ban/.
7. Xia Guang, "China as a 'Civilisation-State': A Historical and Comparative Interpretation", *Procedia-Social and Behavioral Sciences* 140 (2014): 43–47.
8. Jeffrey Gil, "The Promotion of Chinese Language Learning and China's Soft Power", *Asian Social Science* 4, no. 10 (2014): 116–22.
9. Arif Muhammad and Bai Gui, "Role of Chinese Language in Pakistan–China Relations", *International Journal of International Relations, Media and Mass Communication Studies* 1, no. 1 (2015): 17–27.
10. Alexis Hooi, "Country in Top Ranks Hosting Foreign Students", *China Daily*, 13 December 2019, https://global.chinadaily.com.cn/a/201912/13/WS5df2e555a310cf3e3557dd7e.html.
11. Ding Sheng, "Chinese Language and Beijing's Public Diplomacy", *The Asia Dialogue*, 5 June 2014, https://theasiadialogue.com/2015/06/09/chinese-language-and-beijings-public-diplomacy/.
12. Jeffrey Gil, "The Promotion of Chinese Language Learning and China's Soft Power", *Asian Social Science* 4, no. 10 (2008): 116–22.
13. Xin Liu, "China's Cultural Diplomacy: A Great Leap Outward with Chinese Characteristics? Multiple Comparative Case Studies of the Confucius Institutes", *Journal of Contemporary China* 28, no. 118 (2019): 646–66.
14. Oxford Analytica. "China's Language Diplomacy", *Forbes*, 25 July

2006, https://www.forbes.com/2006/07/24/confucius-diplomacy-china-cx_np_0725oxford.html#67a075bf4186.
15. Sheng Ding, "Chinese Language and Beijing's Public Diplomacy", *Asia Dialogue*, 9 June 2015, https://theasiadialogue.com/2015/06/09/chinese-language-and-beijings-public-diplomacy/.
16. Xinhua News, "Chinese Vice President Jinping Xi Unveils the first Confucius Institute in Cambodia", 24 December 2009, http://english.hanban.org/article/2009-12/24/content_146842.htm.
17. Personal interview with the Director of the Confucius Institute in Cambodia, 3 December 2020.
18. Ibid.
19. Him Imrorn, "A Cambodian Student Explains What Prompts Him to Study the Chinese Language", *Cambodianess*, 9 August 2020, https://cambodianess.com/article/a-cambodian-student-explains-what-prompts-him-to-study-chinese-language.
20. Personal interview with a student from Tuan Hoa School, 10 November 2020.
21. Leo Suryadinata, "Ethnic Chinese in Southeast Asia: Overseas Chinese, Chinese Overseas of Southeast Asians?", in *Ethnic Chinese as Southeast Asians*, edited by Leo Suryadinata (New York: Palgrave Macmillan, 1997), pp. 1–25.
22. William Willmott, *The Chinese in Cambodia* (Vancouver: The University of British Columbia, 1967), pp. 16–17.
23. Personal interview with a lecturer at the Royal University of Phnom Penh, 6 November 2020.
24. Personal interview with a government official from the Ministry of Foreign Affairs and International Cooperation, 4 November 2020.
25. James Riddick and Cindy Ko, "In Cambodia's Chinese Language Schools, a Hard Push for Soft Power", *Phnom Penh Post*, 18 December 2017, https://www.phnompenhpost.com/national-post-depth/cambodias-chinese-language-schools-hard-push-soft-power.
26. Rinith Taing, "Chinese Language at the Forefront", *Khmer Times*, 12 July 2019, https://www.khmertimeskh.com/623243/chinese-language-at-forefront/.
27. Him Imrorn, "A Cambodian Student".
28. Irwin Loy, "Learning on the Rise in Cambodia", *The Diplomat*, 22 May 2013, https://thediplomat.com/2013/05/learning-chinese-on-the-rise-in-cambodia/.
29. Personal interview with an owner and manager of a local family business, 8 November 2020.
30. Personal interview with an employee from the local private company, 8 November 2020.
31. Pal Nyiri, *New Chinese Migration and Capital in Cambodia*, Trends in Southeast Asia, no. 3/2014 (Singapore: ISEAS – Yusof Ishak Institute, 2014).
32. Michiel Verver, '*Old*' *and* '*New*' *Chinese Business in Cambodia's Capital*,

Trends in Southeast Asia, no. 17/2019 (Singapore: ISEAS – Yusof Ishak Institute, 2019).
33. Ivan Franceschini. "As Far Apart as Earth and Sky: A Survey of Chinese and Cambodian Construction Workers in Sihanoukville", *Critical Asian Studies* 42, no. 4: pp. 512–29.
34. Rinith Taing, "Chinese Language at the Forefront", *Khmer Times*, 12 July 2019, https://www.khmertimeskh.com/623243/chinese-language-at-forefront/.
35. Personal interview with a lecturer at the Royal University of Phnom Penh, 6 November 2020.
36. Personal interview with a government official from the Ministry of Foreign Affairs and International Cooperation, 4 November 2020.
37. Personal interview with an owner and manager of a local family business, 8 November 2020.
38. Personal interview with an employee from a local private company, 8 November 2020.
39. Personal interview with the Director of a local NGO, 14 November 2020.
40. Vannarith Chheang, *The Political Economy of Chinese Investment in Cambodia*, Trends in Southeast Asia No. 16/2017 (Singapore: ISEAS – Yusof Ishak Institute, 2017).
41. Kin Phea, *Cambodia-China Relations in the New Decade*, Diplomatic Briefing Issue 01/2020, May 2020 (Phnom Penh: KAS and CICP, 2020), pp. 21–25.
42. Luo Jing Jing and Un Kheang, "Cambodia: Hard Landing for China's Soft Power?", *ISEAS Perspective*, no. 2020/111.
43. Personal interview with a lecturer at the Royal University of Phnom Penh, 6 November 2020.
44. Personal interview with a government official from the Ministry of Foreign Affairs and International Cooperation, 4 November 2020.
45. Personal interview with an owner and manager of a local family business, 8 November 2020.
46. Personal interview with an employee from the local private company, 8 November 2020.
47. Personal interview with the Director of a local NGO, 14 November 2020.
48. Personal interview with a Director of a local NGO in Cambodia, 16 November 2020.
49. Personal interview with a Cambodian scholar, 15 November 2020.
50. Irwin Loy, "Learning on the Rise in Cambodia", *The Diplomat*, 22 May 2013, https://thediplomat.com/2013/05/learning-chinese-on-the-rise-in-cambodia/.
51. Personal interview with a lecturer at the Royal University of Phnom Penh, 6 November 2020.
52. Personal interview with a government official from the Ministry of Foreign Affairs and International Cooperation, 4 November 2020.

53. Sovinda Po and Kimkong Heng, "Assessing the Impacts of Chinese Investments in Cambodia: The Case of Preah Sihanoukville Province". Issues and Insights Working Paper vol. 19, WP 4, May 2019, Pacific Forum.
54. Personal interview with a lecturer at the Royal University of Phnom Penh, 6 November 2020.
55. Personal interview with a government official from the Ministry of Foreign Affairs and International Cooperation, 4 November 2020.
56. Personal interview with an owner and manager of a local family business, 8 November 2020.
57. Personal interview with an employee from the local private company, 8 November 2020.

5

China's Soft Power and the Chinese Overseas: Case Study of Xiamen University and the Confucius Institute in Malaysia

Peter T.C. Chang

Locked in a tense geopolitical tussle, China and the United States have expanded their bitter rivalry into the soft power arena. In Malaysia, China's increased presence is felt across the board: from trade investment and manufacturing to e-commerce and the digital economy. One of China's recent initiatives to stand out has been the establishment of Xiamen University in Malaysia (XMUM), marking a milestone in education cooperation between the two countries. This chapter is a study of the XMUM project. It will look at the effect of China's education outreach and examine the potential role of the overseas Chinese in shaping XMUM's imprint on Malaysia and the wider region.

To set the context, the chapter begins with an overview of the soft power competition between China and the United States. Next is a review of the Sino-Malaysia relationship and the Chinese soft power projection in Malaysia. This is followed by a descriptive report on two key Chinese education projects in Malaysia; namely, the Confucius Institute (CI) at the University of Malaysia and the Xiamen University branch campus at Sepang.

The third part of the chapter will then develop three sets of evaluative arguments highlighting the XMUM's importance and potential. The first will draw attention to XMUM's broader significance beyond Malaysia; namely, China's foray into the critical soft power arena—international higher education. The Xiamen move, I argue, signifies Beijing's wider ambition to exert sway in this strategically vital sphere of influence that is still largely dominated by the West.

The chapter then makes the case that XMUM may also be transformed by its relocation to Malaysia. By moving out of the mainland, it could acquire features enabling the university to assume a wider role. One of these agents of change is the overseas Chinese factor. With a campus in Malaysia, Xiamen University is in fact returning to its Southeast Asia roots. Over time, XMUM is likely to re-embrace Malaysia's multiculturalism and recapture the overseas Chinese traditional intermediary role. Transforming itself from a mere conduit of China soft power into a go-between institution, a two-way bridge linking China and Malaysia. A second potential change relates to Malaysia's non-aligned stance on the US-China rivalry. Putrajaya's refusal to take sides could open up geopolitical space for XMUM to assume another unique mediatory role, to conduct impartial scholarship on the ongoing great power rivalry.

Drawing on the XMUM analysis, this chapter ends with some closing observations on the *xin yimin* (新移民). As with their forebears, the new wave of Chinese immigrants will continue to serve as intermediaries, promoting a closer bond between their new and old home. But, unlike the previous generations, these *xin yimin* are much more economically and socially mobile and are likely to evolve into a new cultural force: a distinct transnational, multicultural Chinese soft power.

Overview and Context

China-US Soft Power Rivalry

"The supreme art of war is to subdue the enemy without fighting", wrote the legendary Chinese strategist Sun Tzu 2,500 years ago (Giles 2007). Today, political scientists speak of 'soft power' as means to avert war and to win over others, including one's enemies, without the need to use coercive force. Joseph Nye of Harvard University defines soft power as such:

> A country may obtain the outcomes it wants in world politics because other countries—admiring its values, emulating its example, aspiring to its level of prosperity and openness—want to follow it. In this sense, it is also important to set the agenda and attract others in world politics, and not only to form them to change by threatening military force or economic sanctions. This soft power—getting others to want the outcomes that you want—co-opts people rather than coerces them. (Nye 2004)

Nye categorized soft power into three components: cultural, political values, and foreign policies. And surveys conducted in the past decade have shown the United States as scoring high marks in all three categories: American popular culture and mass media enjoy near-universal appeal. Washington's advocacy of liberal values and human rights are widely respected. And the large diplomatic network of the United States and its leadership in international organizations also won praise around the globe (Nye 2004).

On China's side, Chinese traditional culture and arts, fashion and cuisine have been a source of attraction. In October 2011, at the Seventeenth National Congress of the Central Politburo of the Communist Party of China, General Secretary Hu Jintao focused on the development of 'cultural soft power' as a foreign policy priority.

> The great rejuvenation of the Chinese nation will definitely be accompanied by the thriving of Chinese culture.... We must enhance culture as part of the soft power of our country.... We will further publicize the fine traditions of Chinese culture and strengthen international cultural exchanges to enhance the influence of Chinese cultural worldwide.[1]

Chinese cultural diplomacy, together with active economic engagement and generous foreign aid, has resulted in an uptick in China's standing, especially among developing countries in Africa and Asia. Despite these efforts, polls show that China's authoritarianism continues to be a minus factor in the Chinese soft power indices, scoring low in terms of political values (Glaser and Murphy 2009).

Overall, China continues to lag behind the United States in its soft power appeal. That said, the gap between the two rivals is narrowing, in large part due to the American's own undoing. The Trump administration's abandonment of international multilateralism and negation of US commitments to global issues of climate change have eroded the American standing (French 2020). And this is providing an opening for the Chinese to gain some grounds. Beijing is seizing the moment, embarking on a concerted and concentrated campaign to elevate its international stature. And one country that is receiving considerable attention is Malaysia.

China's Soft Power in Malaysia

The start of the Chinese and Malay civilizational contact is commonly traced back to the fifteenth century when the Ming Dynasty's Admiral Zhenghe, in his epoch-making maritime expedition, made numerous stopovers in the Melaka Sultanate. In the modern era, it was the then Prime Minister Abdul Razak's visit to Beijing in 1974 that formalized the China-Malaysia relationship. This was a historic event, as Malaysia was the first ASEAN country to establish diplomatic ties with a China, which was just emerging from its self-imposed isolation. However active engagement between the two countries only started to gather pace after Deng Xiaoping launched the 1978 open-up reform policy. And Malaysians of Chinese descents were some of the first to visit China, to rekindle lost ties with their ancestral homeland. And some Chinese Malaysians became part of the international pool of overseas Chinese capital channelled to a country that was reeling from decades of economic stagnation (Abdullah 2018).

In the early 1990s, when China regained its economic prowess, the flow of capital started to reverse outwards. And since then, trade and investment between China and Malaysia have grown steadily, reaching a record high in recent years. Then, in 2013, President Xi Jinping launched the ambitious Belt and Road Initiative, drawing countries across the region, including Malaysia, deeper into China's economic orbit (Klemensits 2018).

These Sino-Malaysia developments are taking place amid a wider geopolitical reconfiguration. China's rise is a challenge to the pre-existing regional and world order; namely, the presumptive global leadership of the United States. And the Chinese encroachment is generating tensions across the region. China's disputed nine-dash-line claims over the South China Sea is one example. Small countries like Malaysia are caught in the middle of this big power competition, a geopolitical contestation that has also expanded into the soft power realm (Saha 2020).

China's response to the US soft power dominance has taken on diverse forms across multiple spheres. Aside from the Belt and Road Initiative, the Chinese counter-responses include measures such as keeping an open border policy in order to promote tourism and people-to-people contact, and increased arts and cultural interactions. As the world continues to grapple with a persistent pandemic, public health diplomacy has become key in China's soft power arsenal. Beijing has promised Malaysia 'prioritized' status in China's forthcoming rollout of the vaccination programme (*The Star* 2020; *Malay Mail* 2020). In these wide-ranging deployments of soft power, there is one critical arena where China has long sought to expand its influence in Malaysia, and that is the education sector.

China's Education Outreach

With Confucianism as their cultural anchor, the Chinese have long regarded themselves as the embodiment of a scholastic civilization. Yet it was only in the modern era and during recent decades that China has embarked upon an outbound mission to showcase its intellectual heritage to the world. In Malaysia, two projects have become the flagship of the Chinese knowledge-based soft power display; namely, the Confucius Institute and Xiamen University.

Confucius Institute

Formed in 2004 by Hanban (an agency of the Chinese Ministry of Education) and Beijing Foreign Studies University (BFSU), the Confucius Institute (CI) is an international programme to establish public educational partnerships between China and universities in other countries. The stated aim of these government-run institutions is to introduce Chinese culture through the teaching of the Chinese language, history and tradition and to encourage study in China. By 2017, there were 525 CIs around the world. The majority of these were located on university campuses and are subsidized by China's central government.[2]

In 2009, Hanban set up the first CI in Malaysia on the grounds of the University of Malaya (UM).[3] China's then vice-premier, Li Keqiang, officiated the launch, marking the importance Beijing places on this cultural and educational collaboration and the bilateral relationship between the two countries.[4] As elsewhere, the staple offerings of the CI in UM are language classes and cultural activities. And in the decade since its inception, the CI has expanded its outreach beyond the UM campus, with the setting up of satellite teaching sites in schools and other learning institutions across the country. More recently, Hanban established four additional CIs in Malaysia: at Segi University in Kuala Lumpur, University Pahang Malaysia, University Malaysia Sabah, and University Sarawak at Sibu (Tien and Bing 2021).

Despite these expansions, the impact of CI as a language institution remains limited. One of the main reasons for this is that Malaysia already has a vernacular school system that teaches the Chinese language.[5] The CI's significance lies in its international relations symbolism, to affirm the two countries' diplomatic ties. However, the programme is not without pitfalls. The teaching and learning of the Chinese language remain a sensitive domestic political issue. Excessive promotion of the Chinese language can generate a nationalistic backlash as it can be construed as a challenge to the primacy of the Malay language, thus undermining Malaysia's national identity. That said, on the whole, the CIs in Malaysia have maintained a relatively low profile, attracting little controversy, unlike their counterparts in the West (Siow 2020).

XMUM (Xiamen University in Malaysia)

The other major education outreach by China was the establishment in 2015 of the Xiamen University overseas campus in Sepang. Located on the outskirts of Kuala Lumpur, Xiamen's full-scale campus was built brand new from the ground up. A fully fledged teaching and research university, XMUM is designed to offer undergraduate, postgraduate and doctoral courses.

The idea of opening a comprehensive Chinese university in Malaysia was first conceived in 2011 by Malaysia's former Prime Minister Najib Razak and then Chinese Premier Wen Jiabao as a means to enhance the ties of both countries (*The Star* 2013). By the time the plan finally came into fruition in 2015, XMUM had also become associated with the broader aim of the Belt and Road Initiative as a vehicle to share Chinese technological know-how (*Guardian* 2017).

Indeed, as China's economic footprint continues to grow in the region there have been increasing calls for localization and technological transfer to ensure small countries like Malaysia can acquire the expertise necessary to stay in step with China's rapid advancement. On that account, in Phase I of its development, XMUM priority was directed towards starting classes on the major hard sciences (engineering, computing and environmental science) and professional courses (business, management and accounting), supplemented by minor programmes in social sciences and humanities.[6] Huawei, for instance, has agreed to establish a joint teaching lab at the Sepang campus as a means to transfer Huawei's latest technologies to the XMUM students (*Enterprise It News* 2015).

A key challenge facing China's education endeavour in general and XMUM in particular is to ascertain that these efforts benefit Malaysians of all races. To that end, deliberate efforts have been made to ensure the composition of XMUM's staff and students is representative of Malaysia's diverse demography (*The Star* 2017). In fact, XMUM's stated mission extols an even wider vision: to establish a multicultural, multinational campus with a proportionate ratio of students drawn from China, Malaysia and other ASEAN countries.[7] With the exception of traditional Chinese medicine and the Chinese studies programme, English is the university's medium of instruction.

In 2016, the university opened its doors to the first intake of 180 students. In 2019, XMUM celebrated its inaugural convocation graduating its pioneering class of 120 students.[8] At present, student enrolment stands at around 4,000 and is anticipated to reach a full maximum capacity of 10,000 students within the decade.

XMUM: Significance and Exceptions

CI and XMUM are part of China's 'going global' campaign. Both are expected to impact Malaysia in varying degrees and ways. XMUM in particular will prove consequential in terms of China's technological transfer to Malaysia. If uninterrupted, XMUM has the wherewithal to develop into a highly competitive, regional, if not world-class, engineering-based university. It also has the potential to assume wider roles distinct from its parent university on the mainland. In fact, XMUM marks China's strategic entry into a critical global stage; namely, international higher education.

International Higher Education

International higher education has in recent decades mushroomed into a multibillion-dollar industry. This huge market is dominated by the West; specifically, the English-speaking countries of the United States, United

Kingdom, Canada, Australia and New Zealand. Every year, tens of thousands of students from across the world would travel to these countries to pursue tertiary degrees, paying substantial tuition fees, and generating significant downstream economic outgrowth. International higher education has become an essential and lucrative source of revenue for many of these Anglosphere universities (Ruby 2009).

Aside from the economics, international higher education is also a critical cultural arena. As they head to the West, many of the world's brightest youth are introduced to, become immersed in and, over time, embrace the liberal, democratic values of the West. In fact, American higher education is widely recognized as one of the most effective components in the United States soft power arsenal. Secretary of State Colin Powell, for example, said in 2001: "I can think of no more valuable asset to our country than the future world leaders who have been educated here" (Nye n.d.).

With near-monopoly of the market share, the United States and its allies—namely, the Five-Eyes alliance—had unmatched soft power to shape the outlook of generations of international students, including tens of thousands from China. According to one recent report, one third of the 1.1 million international students in the United States are from China, with even higher proportions in Australia (38 per cent) and the United Kingdom (41 per cent) (Altbach 2019). As a rising global power, it is no surprise that Beijing would seek to carve out its own sphere of influence in this critical soft power arena.

This began in the 1990s, when Chinese campuses started to open their doors to students from abroad, mostly from developing countries of Asia and Africa. Alongside this open-door policy towards the third-world has been an increase in student exchange programmes and research collaboration with universities in the West. More recently, some Chinese universities started to form high-profile twinning partnerships with the likes of New York University and John Hopkins University. Some, such as Nottingham University from the United Kingdom, have set up branch campuses in China. With these engagements and alliances, China aims to gain a foothold in the lucrative business and, more importantly, the influential soft power arena of international higher education. As a result of these concerted efforts, 2018 marked the milestone of a record high of 258,122 inbound international students to China (Gu et al. 2019).

This brings us to the importance of the XMUM. With the campus in Malaysia, China's internationalized campaign is moving to the next level, from opening up to the world to stepping into the world. Just as campuses on the mainland continue to seek to attract international students, China is also embarking on an outbound mode, exporting its scholastic soft power overseas.

To be sure, China is a latecomer. England's Southampton University and Australia's Monash University, for instance, have already established their presence in Malaysia. The XMUM project is nonetheless an important milepost, marking the Chinese entry into the crucial soft power arena of international higher education outside of its home turf.

To some extent, the Confucius Institute was China's first expedition abroad. But XMUM could prove different, with deeper and wider consequences. To begin with, in contrast to CI, XMUM is a standalone, comprehensive university and as such is competing directly for market share and soft power influence with Western competitors like Southampton University and Monash University. And with the Chinese government backing, XMUM has the resources to develop into a regionally, if not globally, competitive university.

Herein lies the wider significance of the XMUM move. It signifies China's ambition to make inroads into the strategically vital sphere of influence that is still largely dominated by the West. XMUM is conceivably the precursor of many other Chinese universities anticipated to make the foray into the global arena of higher education. And as universities in the United States and its allies continue to grapple with falling enrolment due to rising anti-China sentiments, and the Covid-19 pandemic, China is expected to step up the projection of its scholastic soft power abroad.

Clearly, the Chinese are determined to have a stake in shaping the global intellectual landscape. Yet, even as China ventures out to change the world, it could also be transformed by its encounter with the world. In the case of Xiamen University, the relocation to Malaysia may in fact bring about some unexpected changes, and in the process open up new possibilities.

The Overseas Chinese Effect

To begin with, the choice to set up China's first university abroad in Malaysia is not coincidental. The decision was shaped by one historical figure, Tan Kah Kee, a well-known philanthropist in British Malaya and founder of the mother university of XMUM, Amoy University (later renamed Xiamen University) in China.

Born in Xiamen, Fujian Province, in 1874, Tan travelled to Singapore at the age of sixteen and subsequently built a successful business empire that encompasses rice trading and rubber plantations, manufacturing and ocean transport. A prominent leader in the overseas Chinese community, he was responsible for gathering support to aid China during the Sino-Japanese War. Tan also set up education funds and contributed to the establishment of schools and institutions of learning in Southeast Asia, and notably the founding in 1921 of Xiamen University in China's Fujian province (Yong 2013). Thus, with the extension of a branch campus in Malaysia, Xiamen University is returning to its founder's Southeast Asian roots.

This leads us to a key factor shaping the development of XMUM: the overseas Chinese effect. The Xiamen campus in Sepang has the potential to assume the conventional Chinese immigrants' role; that is, to act as an intermediary to foster bonds between their new home, Malaysia, and their ancestral homeland, China. To be sure, XMUM remains a Chinese university, under the administration of China's Ministry of Education. And its mandate is to project Chinese soft power as a means to enhance China's interests in the region. But XMUM can also serve as a bilateral platform for Malaysia to reciprocate and enhance mutual understanding between the two countries.

One example is to develop a Malay Studies programme. As a matter of fact, in 2003 Xiamen University in China decided to inaugurate the Institute of Malaysian Studies. At that time, it was the first research centre of its kind on the Chinese mainland devoted solely to the study of Malaysia, including research on Malaysia's multicultural, multireligious heritage.[9] The Xiamen's campus in Malaysia should build on this legacy and put together an equivalent programme to promote scholastic interaction between the Chinese and Malay civilizations. The XMUM social sciences and humanities faculty in its present Phase 1 structure is centred around the School of Chinese Language and Culture. The future addition of a Malay Studies programme could broaden the humanities scope and help facilitate a two-way cross-cultural civilizational exchange between the Chinese and Malay milieu.

By virtue of its physical presence, over time XMUM is likely to embrace some distinct Malaysian features and characteristics. There is in fact a conscious policy on the part of the university to ensure the campus community reflects Malaysia's multiracial, multireligious demography. The university, for example, is promoting scholarships targeting Bumiputra applications. And just as importantly, English has been adopted as the university's medium of instruction.

Herein lies the first exception of the XMUM project: with a more diverse campus and internationalized ethos, XMUM can set itself apart from its other mainland counterparts and can take on an added role, one that has been traditionally played by the overseas Chinese; namely, as an intermediary linking China to Malaysia, and perhaps even the world. Indeed, the relocation to Malaysia could potentially provide XMUM with another crucial opening: to mitigate the Sino-US rivalry.

The Malaysia Factor

As part of the non-alignment movement, Malaysia has historically taken a non-partisan stance in big power rivalry. And today, as with most countries in ASEAN, Malaysia continues to affirm its impartiality, resisting pressure to take sides in the ongoing US-China standoff. Malaysia's neutrality has far-reaching implications. Among others, it could posit the possibility for XMUM to serve as a platform for independent scholarship on the ongoing geopolitical tussle. This is crucial not least because, as the United States and China become locked into an increasingly tense confrontation, the ability of American and Chinese scholars on either side of the divide to conduct objective analysis has become compromised.

On the US side, the perception of China's rise as an existential threat has fuelled the fear of the foreboding return of McCarthyism. There is in fact heightened scrutiny of Chinese scholars' activities across US campuses, with some China-related research collaborations being suspended and Chinese students' visas revoked. These developments lend to a climate of suspicions that is undermining the US academia's ability to maintain a more detached, even-handed analysis of the challenges posed by China (Pei 2020).

During the reform era, China's universities were accorded wider space for liberal scholarship. But, in contrast to the West, academia in China never had the same leeway for overly self-critical research. And under the present tightening ideological grip of the Xi administration, room for impartial scholarship in Chinese universities is constrained further (*Guardian* 2014).

This is a worrisome development because objective assessments are vital instruments in any conflict resolution. The lack of impartial analysis on the part of Americans and Chinese scholars is impeding efforts to defuse the US-China tensions. Herein lies the other significance of the XMUM move. Malaysia's neutrality can provide the geopolitical setting and an open academic environment to conduct impartial studies on the current geopolitical impasse. On the South China seas dispute, for example, XMUM could host in-depth analysis and oversee open discourse between the various competing stakeholders.

This brings us to the second exception of the XMUM project: if unimpeded, the campus in Malaysia can yet again set itself apart from its mother university on the mainland, this time by taking on the critical role as mediator in the big power rivalry. XMUM could leverage the geopolitical space provided by Malaysia to assume a non-partisan stance and help bridge the US-China divide (Chang 2020).

Overseas Chinese, the *Xin Yimin* (新移民) and Chinese Soft Power

The possibilities that await XMUM can in fact be seen as part of a broader development; namely, the evolving status of the overseas Chinese.

In the 1980s, Chinese Malaysians whose forebears fled a China in turmoil began to reconnect with their ancestral homeland. They played a crucial role in bridging their new home country with a China that was just coming out from a period of self-isolation and prolonged economic stagnation. In the decades since, China has re-emerged as an economic powerhouse, seeking to reclaim its place in the Western-led world order. And some Chinese Malaysians, especially those trained in the West, have found themselves as intermediaries, helping to connect China with the West. These developments sit within the earlier discussed geopolitical landscape, where Putrajaya's non-alignment neutrality allows Malaysia to take on a mediatory role in the Sino-US rivalry.

Similar dynamics are shaping the *xin yimin*'s status, including some associated with the XMUM community. As with the present generation of Chinese Malaysia, the new migrants are likely to assume a bridging role linking China to Malaysia and the West. But the *xin yimin* do have distinct features that allow them to access a bigger stage and assert a broader impact.

For instance, in contrast to earlier waves of Chinese migrations, the *xin yimin* in general are drawn from a better-educated and economically stronger constituent. With greater socio-economic mobility, they are a far more transient migratory population. In fact, most see Malaysia as a stepping stone for a destination that lies beyond the region, and for some towards the West.

In this regard, *xin yimin* represent the next phase in the evolution of the overseas Chinese story. To some extent, they may be seen as the development of a distinct branch of China's soft power. But, to be more precise, it is the unfolding of a new unique form of overseas Chinese soft power, one that remains multicultural but increasingly transnational.

Conclusion

The world order of the twenty-first century is undergoing a paradigmatic geopolitical reconfiguration, and small countries like Malaysia have become the proxy battleground for the big-power rivalry. China has upped the ante in Malaysia with an across-the-board projection of its increasingly wide-ranging soft power arsenal. Among others, these include the establishment of the Confucius Institutes and the Xiamen University Malaysia campus. And it is the latter that has the longer-term strategic importance, with the potential to reshape the nature of Chinese cultural power.

For one, XMUM marks China's ambition to enter one of the few remaining Western bastions; namely, international higher education. But the Xiamen move also shows that, in venturing abroad, China could also be transformed by its encounter with the world. XMUM, for instance, may over time embrace the transnational role of the overseas Chinese of mediating between China, Malaysia and the West. More broadly, the Xiamen project draws attention to the wider dynamics, transforming the overseas Chinese in general and the *xin yimin* in particular into an increasingly cosmopolitan and mobile global actor.

Notes

1. See "Mapping China's Cultural Genome, China's Soft Power Campaign" (Wilson Centre, webpage).
2. See "Kong Zi Institute University Malaya History" (Kong Zi Institute University Malaya, webpage).
3. Malaysia's first CI was actually formed in 2006 with a local private education centre. The partnership faltered, however, due to an unresolvable disagreement. When the CI in UM was proposed, one of the conditions was to remove any

'religious' connotation and to set the institute up chiefly as a language centre (Tien and Bing 2021).
4. See "Kong Zi Institute University Malaya History" (Kong Zi Institute University Malaya, webpage).
5. The CI constituents are predominantly Malay students from local universities, civil servants from various government agencies, and cadets from the Malaysia Defence Ministry academies. The CI at UM has two directors, one each from China and Malaysia, to ensure co-partnership and joint-leadership. The CI teachers are recruited from and teachings materials sourced from China. The Malaysian Director of the Kongzi Institute is reported to have remarked: "The primary responsibility for KZIUM is the teaching of Mandarin language to non-Chinese speaking citizens, particular among the Malaysians" (Tien and Bing 2021, p. 73).
6. See the webpage of Xiamen University Malaysia.
7. The breakdown of the 2016 student body is as follows: 1,720 Malaysian, 950 Chinese, and 30 other international students (Guo Jie 2018).
8. See the webpage of Xiamen University Malaysia.
9. See the webpage of Xiamen University Malaysia. In fact, the Institute of Malaysian Studies at Xiamen University was the inspiration for the then Malaysia Prime Minister Abdullah Badawi to reciprocate with the establishment of the Institute of China Studies at the University of Malaya, where the author of this paper is currently based.

References

Abdullah, Razak. 2018. *China-Malaysia Relations and Foreign Policy.* UK: Routledge.
Altbach, Philip. 2019. "The Coming 'China Crisis' in Global Higher Education". *University World News.* 6 April 2019. https://www.universityworldnews.com/post.php?story=20190403104242366.
Chang, Peter T.C. 2020. "As Academic Ties between US and China Unravel, Malaysia Could Fill The Gap". *South China Morning Post*, 18 October 2020. https://www.scmp.com/week-asia/opinion/article/3105891/academic-ties-between-us-and-china-unravel-malaysia-could-fill.
Enterprise It News. 2015."Huawei Signs MOU with Xiamen University Malaysia Campus". 3 February 2015. http://www.enterpriseitnews.com.my/huawei-signs-mou-with-xiamen-university-malaysia-campus/.
French, Howard. 2020. "When It Comes to Soft Power, China is Already Outpacing the U.S.". *World Politics Review*, 9 September 2020. https://www.worldpoliticsreview.com/articles/29041/when-it-comes-to-soft-power-china-is-already-outpacing-the-u-s.

Giles, Lionel. 2007. *The Art of War by Sun Tzu – Special Edition.* Sweden: Tuttle Special Edition Books.

Glaser, Bonnie S., and Melissa E. Murphy. 2009. "Soft Power with Chinese Characteristics: The Ongoing Debate". *Centre for Strategic and International Studies.* https://csis-website-prod.s3.amazonaws.com/s3fs-public/legacy_files/files/media/csis/pubs/090310_chinesesoftpower__chap2.pdf (accessed 7 January 2021).

Gu, Mini, Rachel Michael, Claire Zheng, and Stefan Trines. 2019. "Education in China". *World Education News & Review,* 17 December 2019, https://wenr.wes.org/2019/12/education-in-china-3.

The Guardian. "Chinese President Signals Tightening of Control over Universities". 30 December 2017. https://www.theguardian.com/world/2014/dec/30/chinese-president-signals-tightening-of-control-over-universities.

———. 2017."'Going Global': China Exports Soft Power with First Large-Scale University In Malaysia". 7 July 2017. https://www.theguardian.com/world/2017/jul/07/going-global-china-exports-soft-power-with-first-large-scale-university-in-malaysia (accessed 7 January 2021).

Guo, Jie. 2018. "Xiamen University Malaysia: A Chinese Branch Campus". *International Higher Education* 95: 9–11.

Klemnesits, Peter. 2018. "Geopolitical Consequences of the 21st Century New Maritime Silk Road for the Southeast Asian Countries". *Contemporary Chinese Political Economy and Strategic Relations: An International Journal* 4, no. 1: 107–38.

"Kong Zi Institute University Malaya History". *Kong Zi Institute University Malaya.* http://www.kongzium.edu.my/about-us/ (accessed 7 January 2021).

Malay Mail. 2020. "China Tests Soft Power in Southeast Asia amid Covid-19 Outbreak". 20 February 2020. https://www.malaymail.com/news/world/2020/02/20/china-foreign-minister-to-meet-asean-peers-at-covid-19-meeting/1839162.

Nye, Joseph. 2004. *Soft Power: The Means to Success in World Politics.* New York: Public Affairs.

———. n.d. "Soft Power and Higher Education". *Forum.* http://forum.mit.edu/articles/soft-power-and-higher-education/ (accessed 7 January 2021).

Pei, Minxin. 2020. "Why Cultural Decoupling from China and Barring Chinese Students Will Hurt the US More*". South China Morning Post,* 20 August 2020. https://www.scmp.com/comment/opinion/article/3097945/why-cultural-decoupling-china-and-barring-chinese-students-will.

Ruby, Alan. 2009. "Global: International Students: A $100 Billion Business?". *University World News,* 27 September 2009. https://www.universityworldnews.com/post.php?story=20090925022811395.

Saha, Premesha. 2020. "US–China Tensions and Its Impact on the South China

Sea Dispute". Observer Research Foundation. https://www.orfonline.org/expert-speak/us-china-tensions-impact-south-china-sea-dispute/(accessed 7 January 2021).

Siow, Maria. 2020. "What Does US Confucius Institute Move Mean for Chinese Soft Power in Asia". *South China Morning Post*, 23 August 2020. https://www.scmp.com/week-asia/politics/article/3098396/what-does-us-confucius-institute-move-mean-chinese-soft-power.

The Star. 2013. "Xiamen University to Set Up 1st Overseas Campus in Malaysia". 21 January 2013. https://www.thestar.com.my/News/Nation/2013/01/21/Xiamen-University-to-set-up-1st-overseas-campus-in-Malaysia/.

———. 2017. "Xiamen Lures Bumi and Indian Students". 31 March 2017. https://www.thestar.com.my/news/nation/2017/03/31/xiamen-lures-bumi-and-indian-students-xmum-offering-scholarships-for-new-intake-in-drive/.

———. 2020. "Malaysia and China Sign Pact over Covid-19 Vaccine". 18 November 2020. https://www.thestar.com.my/news/nation/2020/11/18/malaysia-and-china-sign-pact-over-covid-19-vaccine.

Tien, Ngu Ik, and Ngeow Chow Bing. 2021. "Soft Power, Confucius Institute and China's Cultural Diplomacy In Malaysia". *Kajian Malaysia: Journal of Malaysian Studies* 39, no. 1: 55–76.

Wilson Center. "Mapping China's Cultural Genome, China's Soft Power Campaign". https://www.wilsoncenter.org/mapping-chinas-cultural-genome (accessed 7 January 2021).

Xiamen University Malasia. "Schools and Departments". http://www.xmu.edu.my/14676/list.htm (accessed 7 January 2021).

Yong, Ching-Fatt. 2013. *Tan Kah-Kee: The Making of an Overseas Chinese Legend*, rev. ed. Singapore: World Scientific.

6

China Dream and Singapore Heart: A Comparison between the China Cultural Centre (CCC) and the Singapore Chinese Cultural Centre (SCCC)

Ho Yi Kai

Some people ask the question, "Why does Singapore need two Chinese cultural agencies?" Those who are aware of the chronology may ask, "Why is there a need to establish the Singapore Chinese Cultural Centre (SCCC) when there is already a China Cultural Centre (CCC)?" Associate Professor Eugene K.B. Tan posed a similar question on SCCC's opening day: "Is there one Chinese culture or a variety of Chinese cultures? One might be confused, as there are now two Chinese cultural centres in Singapore in close proximity to each other."[1] This chapter seeks to answer these queries through a comparative study of these two models and attempts to define their roles more clearly in the hope that they can complement each other more effectively and benefit the local cultural scene.

Establishment

The CCC in Singapore, which was established and fully funded by the Chinese government, is one of thirty-five such centres worldwide.[2] It is the thirteenth of the series,[3] and third to be established out of the six currently in Southeast Asia.[4] In 2009, former Chinese President Hu Jintao and Singapore Prime Minister Lee Hsien Loong witnessed the signing of the memorandum of cooperation in setting up the CCC by both parties. The ground-breaking ceremony in the following year was officiated by then Chinese Vice President Xi Jinping and then Singapore Senior Minister Goh Chok Tong. That year also marked the twentieth anniversary of diplomatic ties between Singapore and China. Five years later, in 2015, Chinese President Xi and Singapore Emeritus Senior Minister Goh co-officiated the launch.

Unlike the CCC, the SCCC is unique as it was established by the non-government organization Singapore Federation of Chinese Clan Associations (SFCCA). The idea was mooted by the SFCCA Council and presented by then Chairman Chua Thian Poh to Prime Minister Lee in 2012, who then announced government support. The SCCC was then incorporated by SFCCA the following year, and the ground-breaking ceremony officiated by PM Lee took place another year later, in 2014. In 2016, the cultural exhibition "Blossoms of Vitality, Colours of Life" premiered. In 2017, the Opening Ceremony was officiated by PM Lee, with the government partially funding the centre through the Ministry of Culture, Community and Youth (MCCY).

The centres' chronological development of the idea of the SCCC being mooted three years after the signing of the memorandum for the CCC and the SCCC officially opening two years after the CCC leads to questions such as "Is SCCC a response to the CCC?" and "Did Singapore feel the need for a place to tell its own story as a result of the CCC, thus leading to the establishment of the SCCC?"

According to Mr Perng Peck Seng, Secretary-General of the SCCC and a member of its Board of Directors, the idea was actually mooted in 2011 or 2012 during an SFCCA Council discussion on its forthcoming thirtieth anniversary celebration in 2016 (he could not recall the exact year in our interview). The Council felt that the Chinese Heritage Centre at Nanyang Technological University and the Sun Yat Sen Nanyang Memorial Hall (also known as Wan Qing Yuan) were not what they had in mind to promote Singapore Chinese culture. However, he could not firmly say that CCC bore no influence on the decision-making either. Mr Kwa Chong Guan shared with me that the SCCC would have happened with or without the CCC, following the establishment of the Malay and Indian heritage centres (Chinese, Malay and Indian being the three main ethnic groups in Singapore); it was just catalysed by the CCC. It is explicitly clear that with the establishment of the SCCC, "in effect, symbolising and accentuating the differentiation between 'Chinese culture' and 'Singapore Chinese culture' (or 'Chinese–Singaporean culture')",[5] some may argue that "at face value, it seems to be a push back against the China Cultural Centre".[6] My research shows that while it may not have been initiated as a direct response, the CCC had the two-pronged effect of serving as a catalyst that accelerated the SCCC's establishment and shaped its direction of emphasizing 'Singapore Chineseness'.

Location and Building

The CCC, which stands at 217 Queens Street, is "located in Singapore's Arts and Heritage District and is close to numerous cultural institutions such as Nanyang Academy of Fine Arts, National Library and Singapore Art Museum".[7] Its designer, Dr Liu Thai Ker, who is also one of the founding Executive Board members nominated by the Singapore government, disclosed during our interview that the Chinese government's initial intention was to locate it in Chinatown, but he counter-proposed the current site with the considerations that it was closer to the other local heritage centres (Malay and Indian) for promoting future interaction.

Meanwhile, the SCCC, located at 1 Straits Boulevard in the Central Business District (CBD), is just behind the Singapore Conference Hall, home to the Singapore Chinese Orchestra. This location was probably chosen due to the 'centralized' feel and in anticipation of further development of the area. Otherwise, being in a part of town that is dead quiet at night would seem to be a misjudgement—a sentiment similarly expressed by Mr Kwa.

This CCC in Singapore is "the first such [CCC] to be designed by a local architect",[8] and according to Dr Liu, the Chinese Embassy in Singapore is also the first of such Chinese embassies to be designed by a local architect (it was also designed by him). Can one perhaps perceive this as a gesture of sincerity in collaboration, and also recognition and confidence in the understanding and appreciation by the local Chinese of what the PRC perceives to be 'Chinese culture'? As for SCCC, it is designed by homegrown DP Architects, fully 'made in Singapore', in line with its Singapore-centric direction.

Objective

The primary objective in establishing CCCs, as printed in the front of its Special Editions, is "the stories of China should be well told, voices of China well spread, and characteristics of China well explained (讲好中国故事，传播好中国声音)".
According to the CCC website:

> The establishment of a cultural centre is an important symbol of the further deepening of bilateral relations. It aims to strengthen cultural exchanges and cooperation between the two countries, and enhance mutual understanding and friendship between the two peoples. Since the 1980s, China began to set up cultural centres abroad, and the past decade has seen rapid development.[9]

For Singapore in particular, translating from the Chinese pages, the four objectives are: quality service and cultural activities; public outreach; enhancement of mutual understanding and the development of friendship; and the building of a collaborative relationship that enhances cultural exchange.[10] Quoting then Chinese ambassador to Singapore Chen Xiaodong, the Singapore CCC is to be "a window offering the Singaporean public a glimpse of China and a taste of Chinese culture ... [thereby] making new contributions to strengthening China-Singapore cultural exchanges and enriching 'All-Round Cooperative Partnership Progressing with the Times' between the two countries."[11] Singapore's CCC is one of the earliest in ASEAN, as mentioned above, and according to Dr Liu Thai Ker in our interview, possible reasons might be Singapore being the hub of ASEAN, having ethnic Chinese as its majority population, the Singapore government's transparency, and commercial considerations—China being Singapore's largest trading partner, and Singapore being China's top foreign investor.[12]

There are other views on China's intent, such as "to promote cultural affinity with China to a younger generation of Chinese Singaporeans who feels less identification with China", functioning "as part of a broader effort to create a common identity between Chinese China and Chinese Singapore".[13] This may be an additional intention due to Singapore's uniqueness in that the majority of the population are ethnic Chinese, but I believe the overarching objective should still be in line with the rest, to primarily promote China's soft power through showcasing and collaboration.

The SCCC's mission is to "nurture Singapore Chinese culture and enhance social harmony", and its vision is of "a vibrant Singapore Chinese culture, rooted in a cohesive, multi-racial society".[14] On its website, it states that it "collaborates with arts and cultural groups and community partners to promote and develop local Chinese culture. By creating accessible and engaging content, we strive to nurture greater appreciation of our multi-cultural identity and sense of belonging."[15] In a nutshell, its eyes are on 'Singapore Chineseness' as part of the nation's multiracial and multicultural effort to achieve social harmony.

Uniqueness

According to Dr Liu Thai Ker, the CCC in Singapore is the largest of the series. It is also the only one in the world with its Executive Board members nominated by both China and the partnering country, "a trait that was unique among overseas China Cultural Centres". All members were nominated by their respective governments.[16] The initial four from Singapore out of the eleven in total were Prof Chan Heng Chee (Chairman, National Arts Council), Dr Liu Thai Ker (Founding Chair, Morrow Architects & Planners), Mr Anthony Tan (Deputy CEO, Singapore Press Holdings) and Mr Low Sin Leng (Chairman of the Board, Nanyang Academy of Fine Arts).[17] "The unique mode of the Executive Board and our productive discussions serve as a model of mutual benefit between China and Singapore."[18]

The SCCC is unique in the sense that it should be the only one of its kind in the world, as Mr Perng Peck Seng concurred during our interview. Its Board and Committee members are all locals. This is probably due to Singapore being the only country outside China to have a Chinese-majority population, and "the only country that has adopted explicit cultural pluralism".[19]

Activities

In the three years after its opening in 2016, the CCC organized more than 800 activities, received over 300,000 people, and had more than forty partnering organizations, which were mainly arts related.[20] The main functions of the CCC are to organize cultural activities and classes, provide a platform for intellectual exchange, and also become an information hub on Chinese history, culture and life in the contemporary society.[21]

We see three characteristics in the activities mentioned above:

Importation from China

These activities come directly from China, either as performances or exhibitions, or competitions from China to recruit competitors from Singapore. Major and regular ones include "Happy Chinese New Year", "Cultural Year" and "A Moment We Share", which are also common across the centres worldwide.

Collaboration with Singapore

"[The] China Cultural Centre in the past five years has organized hundreds of activities…, about half of which were programs organized by local Singaporean cultural and art institutions".[22] It is well aware of the Nanyang style and *Xinyao* etc., thus engaging the locals actively and seeking collaborations consciously.[23] It treasures that Singapore Chinese share the same roots and language, and is hence not satisfied in merely displaying but emphasizes collaboration as well.[24] CCC also fulfils physical needs, fully supporting local book launches and exhibitions, such as the Singapore Arts Federation 20th Anniversary Exhibition in 2017, and serving as a performing space. Chinese Opera and Drama Society Founder and President Bian Huibin commented in 2016 that the CCC had brought life and hope to the Chinese Opera scene, providing a premium space for performance, with a good and convenient location, and a 200-seater theatre. Ping Sheh Singapore Chairman James Yeo Huai-seng also commended the premium space and thanked CCC for the venue sponsorship.[25]

Direct Engagement with Singapore Communities

The CCC invited locals to performances and 'walked into schools' (although to my knowledge, there were not many of such activities). It organized competitions and classes to engage Singaporeans as well, and a list of the activity highlights can be found in the Appendix.

As for SCCC, from 2017 to 2019, three years after it opened, it received over 340,000 visitors, more than 35,000 outreach attendance members, and over 410 live-stream audience members.²⁶ The main aspects include a permanent exhibition (SINGAPO 人: Discovering Chinese Singapore Culture), an award (Singapore Chinese Cultural Contribution Award), supporting local arts and cultural groups,²⁷ grants (Chinese Arts and Culture Research Grant, Open Call for Programming Ideas, Publication Grant), and, like the CCC, it serves as an information hub with resources such as the Singapore Chinese Arts & Cultural Group Directory and other publications and resources. Other SCCC events are mainly with and for local Singaporeans. The list of highlights of regular events, competitions, exhibitions, talks and conferences can be found in the Appendix.

Observation and Evaluation

In this segment, we ask the following questions: "Are the activities of these two centres adequate or relevant? Are their objectives thus met?"

The CCC has noticed the uniqueness of Singaporean Chinese, recognizing that "as a highly developed country with a majority Chinese population, [there is] a stark difference in interest, understanding, appreciation and expectation of the Chinese culture compared to other countries",²⁸ and so it is believed to pay more attention to the quality and characteristics of what it brings in. It seems to be bringing in more of the northern culture, complementing Singapore's southern heritage (CCC has only organized one Teochew Opera and one Cantonese Opera, in 2016). It can also be seen as a support, inspiration and morale booster to the 'dying arts'—Chinese opera, through venue sponsorship, performances, talks and workshops to engage the public; facilitating collaboration between China's best and Singapore institutions, such as the China National Peking Opera Company and Ping Sheh Singapore.²⁹ We have heard how grateful local Chinese Opera groups were for the venue sponsorship. The major competition, "Chinese Culture and I", held in 2017, saw mainly youth participants and included both non-Chinese and New Immigrants (*xin yimin*). But is such engagement of youth and non-Chinese significant within the 800 activities? I do not have the figures, but harbour reservations.

Another observation is on the usage of English or the bilingual format. The CCC website and Facebook pages are bilingual, but the

Chinese version of the former is more comprehensive. Its WeChat account is understandably in Chinese, but the majority of the activities seem to use less English as well. In print, the newspaper advertisement for the concert celebrating the thirtieth anniversary of Singapore-China diplomatic relations was published in both the Chinese and English papers;[30] however, for the Anniversary Special Editions, only the first year is bilingual—the second and third years are only in Chinese. This leads to the question: Who is the main target audience? Since the Chinese language is more heavily used, is it the Singaporean Chinese (and not so much the older Peranakans or English-educated who had not learnt Chinese)? Or sojourners and *xin yimin* from China (there are about half a million in Singapore since a decade ago, after all)?[31] In order to realize the China Dream, which places emphasis on wooing "the Chinese overseas to work for the national interest of China", all should be included.[32] So how about the non-Chinese, both local and foreign? The CCC has the potential to be a hub to reach out to foreigners in Singapore and even the region, given Singapore's strategic geographical position and the adoption of English as the working language. Having received visitors from Korea, Thailand, Malaysia, Indonesia, France, Italy, etc. is already a good start for the CCC.

So, are the objectives of the CCC met? Are the stories well told? Are cultural exchanges enhanced and cooperation with Singapore strengthened? With respect to the first question: Are the stories, voices, characteristics of China well told, disseminated and explained? Since more Chinese than English is used, it should be more efficient in telling its stories, although it would be ideal if it could reach out more to local non-Chinese and foreigners. The next question to ask, then, is what stories does it want to tell? It seems to be focussed mainly on the arts. Perhaps it can look into broadening the scope and in general trying to enhance its influence. For instance, *China's Footprints in Southeast Asia* and *The Rise of China and the Chinese Overseas: A Study of Beijing's Changing Policy in Southeast Asia and Beyond* include no mention at all of soft footprint of soft power discussions. Instead, the Confucius Institutes (CIs) took centre stage.[33] Jamestown Foundation *China Brief*, however, only mentioned the CCC and not the CI.[34]

As for whether cultural exchanges are enhanced and cooperation with Singapore strengthened, though half of the activities were in collaboration with Singapore organizations, how was the turnout and engagement?

Judging from the activities and the initial intention of the Chinese government to locate at Chinatown, it seems to indicate they were more inclined towards 'representation' rather than 'outreach', and targeting Chinese audiences, both local and from China (sojourners and *xin yimin*), more than the non-Chinese.

In asking the same questions about the SCCC, are its activities adequate or relevant? And, hence, are the objectives met? Since SCCC is more for locals, it is understandable to have less collaborations with China relative to the CCC. We can see its efforts—through the award, grants and collaborations—to 'nurture Singapore Chinese culture'. But we would then have to ask, "So what is 'Singapore Chinese culture' in comparison to that from China?", and "who is 'Singaporean Chinese'?"

A permanent exhibition is important, as "museums do not only tell us about what happened in the past, or help us study about the past. Good curators of museums can also inspire new ideas and values, fresh ways of looking at people of the past, but also new ways of looking at people today."[35] A promising step has been taken with the SINGAPO 人 exhibition, which asks the fundamental questions: 'What makes a Chinese, Singaporean?', 'What makes us, us?' But it can consider introducing more depth. It currently has six zones: Zone 1 attempts to answer the fundamental questions more directly, featuring very briefly the 'Five Aspects that Shape Chinese Singaporean Culture' (Life in Southeast Asia; Early Migrants from Southern China; Life as a British Colony; Both Nation and a Global City; Diverse Ethnicities, Multiple Cultures).

The "Blossoms of Vitality, Colours of Life" exhibition, held prior to the opening of SCCC in 2016, conceptualized by Mr Toh Lam Huat, would complement it well. It is thus a good reference as a starting point. It comprises three pillars (Chinese Culture, Migrant Culture, National Culture), Life (seven aspects), and the Arts (Visual and Performing). Professor Kevin Tan feels that history would be a good clue as well, and I think the feature of prominent figures would be especially helpful as it is more visual and relatable in the representation of identity and culture— "Singapore's success story is essentially a 'people' story" after all.[36]

So, are the objectives of the SCCC met? With regard to 'nurturing Singapore Chinese culture', SCCC has been a platform for performances and engagement. For instance, it provided 56 and 89 performers for TGIF Music Station in 2018–19 and 2019–20, respectively. But what is 'Singapore Chinese culture'; what is our overarching heritage? Are those activities above enough? Is the SINGAPO 人 exhibition definitive enough? As mentioned above, perhaps at least the permanent exhibition can be enhanced further.

As for the 'enhance social harmony' aspect, we do see some multicultural engagements, such as the "Creativity in Pulses" Special Exhibition, which included work by a Malay artist, the Tian Tian Xiang Shang Exhibition, which reached out to other races and engaged students, the IMPART Collectors' Show, which included key works by notable Singaporean and Indonesian artists, the "Whispers from the Dragon's Teeth Gate", which brought together Chinese and Malay dance, and "Memoirs of Nanyang", which featured a bold fusion of *nanyin* music, Malay cultural music, Mandarin pop tunes and Peranakan culture. However, is the quantity and frequency enough? Other than collaboration, the cross-racial outreach is probably more important in order to influence and enhance harmony, and I do not have the statistics yet. And how about the integration of *xin yimin*? Singapore will have to help them find their Singapore Heart, if they are here to stay, as part of the effort to 'enhance social harmony'.

Engaging the youth is a major focus of the current SCCC CEO Mr Low Tze Wee, echoing PM Lee's vision.[37] We do see more effort pumped into this area, harvesting achievements such as Jun Chong's 'Ke', from their commissioned film *667* (which won the Best Asian Short at the 13th Sapporo International Short Film Festival), and TGIF Music Station, which is a 'young' and vibrant platform for engagement.

Moving Forward

From the evaluation above, the CCC would need to do more for 'cultural exchanges [to be] enhanced and cooperation strengthened'. The CCC should look more into the engagement with local non-Chinese, collaborating more with them and perhaps even with the SCCC. It did collaborate with SCCC, but probably not significantly in scale as such collaboration is not featured and it did not surface during interviews, with only a brief mention in an issue of *Special Edition*.[38] In our interview, the incumbent SCCC CEO Mr Low welcomed the idea.

To clarify, the core 'What is China?' question remains important. And perhaps expanding beyond the arts, which seems to be the main focus of activities at the moment. A permanent exhibition that encapsulates the essence of Chinese culture would also be essential, just as that of the SCCC's. The theme and content should focus on history, since China is after all "a modern economic power with ancient roots", and Xi Jinping's approach to realizing his dream for China is also by "connecting China's global future to the country's long history".[39]

As for the SCCC, it should attempt to identify a clearer direction. Is its intention to display, seek or create Singapore Chinese identity and culture? It can only 'display' if it is sure of what the identity and culture is; can 'seek' only if the identity and culture are sure to be there; and 'create' if we do not even think they are there. As mentioned above, SCCC can consider broadening and deepening the current Singapo 人 exhibition, at least considering incorporating the initial "Blooms of Vitality, Colour of Life" exhibition. The Peranakan Chinese culture is an important reference, but just enough will do to complement the Peranakan Museum. And, as suggested above, beefing up the part on the history of the local Chinese would help, perhaps emphasizing the prominent figures. The "Fifty Prominent Chinese in Singapore" in *A General History of the Chinese in Singapore* (Appendix II) would be a useful guide.[40] Prof Kwok Kian Woon, during our discussion on Singapore identity, suggested also looking into the language and arts. In short, it would be more practical if SCCC were to select an aspect to focus on, as culture is multifaceted after all. Its patron PM Lee gave the direction of 'arts and culture',[41] but it is still too broad. To continue developing existing culture, SCCC can continue to focus more on the southern culture, such as the southern Chinese operas. To 'create' Singapore culture, activities such as the SG: SW20XX I Write the Songs should continue. For more depth, perhaps the international academic conference collaboration with the National University of Singapore can be held regularly.

As per my suggestion to CCC, I would recommend that SCCC engage more with local non-Chinese. This is important, not just as part of an effort to pursue national identity, but also at least to 'strengthen cohesive diversity' to assure the minority races of Singapore that the Chinese can "consciously overcome what one insightful blogger has called the mindset of Chinese Privilege".[42] After all, "Chinese Singaporeans are different from Chinese elsewhere as they're part of [the] multi-racial whole", and this "integration makes Singapore Chinese identity distinct".[43]

Conclusion

Now, returning to answer the questions posed at the beginning: "Why does Singapore need two Chinese cultural agencies?" and "Why is there a need to establish SCCC when there is already a CCC?" The following quote explains the difference between the two centres:

> It appears that the Chinese Cultural Centre (by Singapore) and China Cultural Centre (by China) have a different focus. While the latter is focused on promoting China's soft power in overseas host countries through its arts and culture, the former is more concerned with strengthening the bonds not only among the Chinese community but also between the Chinese and non-Chinese communities in Singapore. In this sense, there is a clear demarcation in the roles and functions of these two cultural institutions. They are therefore likely to complement rather than be in competition with each other.[44]

As concluded by Dr Neo Peng Fu during his presentation in this workshop, the establishment of the CCC in Singapore can be a win-win situation, as per the case of CI. Besides promoting their own cultural influence and soft power, being a similar external institution actually benefits the local cultural centre as it accelerates Singapore's own reflection of local culture and identity. The SCCC's collaborations with other local organizations, such as the second- and third-year collaborations, triggered Ding Yi Music Company to ponder: "How do local Chinese celebrate Chinese New Year? How do local Chinese youth perceive Chinese New Year? And what will be the development of local Chinese Orchestra?"[45]

Moving forward, we have to keep asking: Is the CCC on track to spread China's soft power, telling the China story well, and realizing the China Dream? How about the 'cultural exchanges'? For SCCC, is it on track to find the heart of the local Chinese in the hope to eventually find that of the nation's through multiracial and cultural engagements? I can only ask questions, as it is always a 'work in progress'. What I am sure is that finding the Singapore Chinese Heart is challenging but important. My proposal is to first unite the Chinese, including different dialect groups and two-way assimilation-acceptance of the *xin yimin*, paying particular attention to the latter nowadays as, "new residents from China, Taiwan, and Hong Kong all form their own cliques which also largely exclude the Singaporean Chinese".[46] The next step should eventually integrate, not assimilate, with other ethnic cultures, to formulate the national identity—"We are also a multi-racial, multi-religious, and multi-cultural society. This diversity is a fundamental aspect of our respective identities. Our aim is integration, not assimilation."[47] Taking reference from China and other past empires, there is a need to have "a national identity to protect the country's sovereignty", and "the civilizations stemmed from combinations of cultures that together developed systems of ideas and values that made them even more resilient and powerful".[48]

Lastly, these two centres, though unique, still bear valuable pointers for similar cultural agencies:

1. Having a clear objective and target audience are essential.
2. The introduction of core culture, and the engagement, sensitivity and collaboration with local organizations should bear equal weightage.
3. Co-nomination of board members for the CCC could be considered for the other centres in its series.

Acknowledgments

I am indebted to Professor Leo Suryadinata, convener of this workshop, for this opportunity to share my studies, and to my supervisor at work, Dr Neo Peng Fu, who gave me his full support and valuable academic advice. I also have to thank both the incumbent and former senior management of the two centres in my investigation—Dr Liu Thai Ker, Mr Low Tze Wee, Mr Choo Thiam Siew, Mr Perng Peck Seng and Mr Toh Lam Huat—for their valuable time with my interviews. Last but not least I would like to thank the senior scholars who generously spent their time enlightening me with their insights on local history and culture—namely, Professor Kevin Tan, Mr Kwa Chong Guan and Professor Kwok Kian Woon.

Appendix (Activity Highlights)

China Cultural Centre

Import from China:
- Guangxi: exhibition and evening gala (2016), but involved three local schools, including Nan Hua High School
- Cultural Year: Shandong (2016), Chongqing (2017), Anhui (2018), but invited four local artists to Chongqing in 2017, including a Malay Singaporean (Abu Jalal Sarimon)
- Discovering China Lectures: mainly from China (2016)

- Exhibition of China Fine Works of Culture: mainly from China (2016)
- China programmes in Singapore: "Voice of China", "Water Cube Cup" Chinese Song Competition for Overseas Chinese Teenagers, CCTV's Voice (开讲了) (invited local speakers), Global Chinese Network Host Competition
- CCC First Anniversary Celebration: "Fine Arts Exhibition of Contemporary Chinese Young Artists" (2016)
- A Moment We Share (2017): previous and following year collaborated with Singapore

Collaboration with Singapore:
- Art Exhibition Commemorating China-Singapore 25th Anniversary of Diplomatic Ties: 50 masterpieces, half from each side (2015)
- Chinese New Year Concert by Ding Yi Music Company (2016–18), 2017 including local acapella group, 2018 including local singers
- China-Singapore Calligraphy and Painting Exchange Gathering (2016)
- China-Singapore Children's Arts Festival (2016–18)
- China-Singapore Water Colour Joint Exhibition (2017 in China, Shantou, 2018 in Singapore)
- Experts discussing Children's Arts Education: 1 from China, 2 from Singapore (2016)
- A Moment We Share: with Singapore Youth Chinese Orchestra (SYCO) (2016), following year only from China (2017), then Singapore Ruan Ensemble and Enjoy Music Centre (2018)
- Teochew Opera "Opera Century – Flowers Blossom": co-hosted with Singapore Chinese Opera Institute (2016)
- Second Singapore International Opera Festival: with Chinese Opera and Drama, Singapore (CODS) (2016)
- OBOR Initiative Forum: collaborated with local organization, invited local speakers (2017)

Direct Engagement with Singapore Communities:
- Invited residents in neighbourhood and employees of the builders of the centre to a performance (2016)
- "Walking into School" Programme: China National Theatre into Tao Nan School (2016);

- "China–Singapore Children's Arts Festival" walked into schools as well in 2017
- "Chinese Culture and I" competition (2017)
- Malanhua Performing Arts School for Children: import from China, but for Singapore children. (The enrolment statistics are contradictory. The *CCC Third Anniversary Special Edition* 2018 states on page 15 that there were nearly 10,000 students in three years, but the table on page 81 gives a total of only 465.)

Singapore Chinese Cultural Centre
Other events (mainly with and for locals)

Regular:
- Spring Reception and Chinese New Year events
- Dragon Boat or Duan Wu Festival
- Mid-Autumn events
- National Day Sing-Along
- Cultural Extravaganza
- Zaobao Cultural and Creative Space (series of sharing sessions and workshops)
- TGIF Music Station (twice per month)
- SG: SW20XX I Write the Songs, The Sing•Lang concert

Competitions:
- "My Singapore Story" Micro Film Competition Award Ceremony
- Singapore Family History Writing Competition

Exhibitions:
- "Blossoms of Vitality, Colours of Life" Exhibition (2016)
- "Creativity in Pulses" Special Exhibition (including work by a Malay artist) (2017)
- Tian Tian Xiang Shang Exhibition (2018)
- IMPART Collectors' Show (2018)

Talks and Conferences:
- "Quirky Chinese Phrases" Talk (2017)
- Inaugural International Conference on "Diversity and Singapore Ethnic Chinese Communities" (2019)

Notes

1. Eugene K.B. Tan, "A Tale of Two Chinese Cultural Centres", *Today*, 19 May 2017, pp. 40–41.
2. Zhongguo Wenhua Zhongxin 中国文化中心, http://www.cccweb.org/portal/site/Master/zxjs/index.jsp (accessed 21 November 2020).
3. According to Dr Liu Thai Ker during our interview.
4. The two before Singapore are Thailand (2012) and Laos (2014), and the other three are Cambodia (2016), Vietnam (2017) and Myanmar (2017).
5. Kwok Kian-Woon and Teng Siao See, *Singapore Chronicles: Chinese* (Singapore: IPS and ST Press, 2018), p. 10.
6. Joshua Lee, "China Uses Cultural Centre in S'Pore to Engage in 'Influence Operations': US Report", "Mothership" website, 18 July 2019, https://mothership.sg/2019/07/china-cultural-centre-influence-propaganda/.
7. *CCC First Anniversary Special Edition* (2016), p. 3.
8. Zheng Yongnian, and Lye Liang Fook, *Singapore-China Relations: 50 Years* (Singapore: World Scientific Publishing, 2016), p. 15.
9. China Cultural Centre (Singapore), http://www.cccsingapore.org/en/index.php?s=/home/index/index.html (accessed 21 November 2020).
10. 中国文化中心(新加坡), http://www.cccsingapore.org/index.php?s=/home/index/jieshao.html (accessed 7 December 2020).
11. *CCC First Anniversary Special Edition* (2016), p. 55.
12. "In 2017, Singapore's largest trading partner was China, and Singapore was China's top foreign investor from 2013 to 2017. In 2017 alone, Singapore invested US$4.8 billion (S$6.6 billion) in China." "Asia's Largest Economy and Singapore's Top Trading Partner", *Enterprise Singapore*, https://www.enterprisesg.gov.sg/overseas-markets/asiapacific/china/market-profile (accessed 28 November 2020).
13. Russell Hsiao, "A Preliminary Survey of CCP Influence Operations in Singapore", *China Brief* 19, no. 13 (16 July 2019).
14. Singapore Chinese Cultural Centre, https://singaporeccc.org.sg/about-sccc/ (accessed 21 November 2020).
15. Ibid.
16. *CCC Third Anniversary Special Edition* (2018), p. 16.
17. Ibid., pp. 6–7.
18. Both quotes in this paragraph are from Prof Chan Heng Chee (Singapore member of the CCC Executive Board): *CCC First Anniversary Special Edition* (2016), p. 56.
19. Leo Suryadinata, *The Making of Southeast Asian Nations: State, Ethnicity, Indigenism and Citizenship* (Singapore: World Scientific, 2015), p. 77.
20. *CCC Third Anniversary Special Edition* (2018), p. 13.

21. China Cultural Centre (Singapore), http://www.cccsingapore.org/index.php?s=/home/index/jieshao.html (accessed 7 December 2020).
22. Xiao Jianghua (Director and President of the Executive Board, China Cultural Centre in Singapore), "A Message from China Cultural Centre" in newspaper ad for "Classic Forever Concert: Celebrating 30 Years of China–Singapore Diplomatic Relations", *Straits Times*, 16 October 2020, p. A11.
23. *CCC Third Anniversary Special Edition* (2018), p. 15.
24. Ibid., p. 51.
25. Bian and Yeo comments: *CCC Third Anniversary Special Edition* (2018), pp. 105–06.
26. 2017 statistics: SCCC Annual Report FY2017/2018, p. 17; 2018–19 statistics: SCCC Annual Report 2018/2019, p. 14; 2019–20 statistics: SCCC Annual Report 2019/2020, p. 18.
27. Art Housing Programme (Drum Feng, Nan Hwa Opera, TENG Company), Visual Arts Partnership (signed MOU with eight local groups), Artspace@SCCC, MOU with NUS Department of Chinese Studies.
28. *CCC Third Anniversary Special Edition* (2018), p. 14.
29. Ibid., pp. 108–09.
30. Newspaper advertisements, both on 16 October 2020, in *Lianhe Zaobao*, p. 3, and *Straits Times*, p. A11.
31. According to the statistics shared by Prof Leo Suryadinata during his session in this workshop.
32. On "China Dream" and the term "Chinese overseas" refer to Leo Suryadinata, *The Rise of China and the Chinese Overseas: A Study of Beijing's Changing Policy in Southeast Asia and Beyond* (Singapore: ISEAS – Yusof Ishak Institute, 2017), pp. 17–18 and pp. 5–7, respectively.
33. Maria Serena I. Diokno et al., *China's Footprints in Southeast Asia* (Singapore: NUS Press, 2019). Leo Suryadinata, *The Rise of China and the Chinese Overseas: A Study of Beijing's Changing Policy in Southeast Asia and Beyond* (Singapore: ISEAS – Yusof Ishak Institute, 2017).
34. Russell Hsiao, "A Preliminary Survey of CCP Influence Operations in Singapore", Jamestown Foundation China Brief 19, no. 13 (16 July 2019).
35. Wang Gungwu, *Nanyang: Essays on Heritage* (Singapore: ISEAS – Yusof Ishak Institute, 2018), pp. 74–75.
36. Pang Cheng Lian, ed., *50 Years of the Chinese Community in Singapore* (Singapore: World Scientific, 2016), p. xix.
37. PM's vision to engage the youth: from his speech at SFCCA 30th Anniversary Gala Dinner in 2016.
38. *CCC Third Year Special Edition* (2018), p. 16.
39. Wang Gungwu, *China Reconnects: Joining a Deep-Rooted Past to a New World Order* (Singapore: World Scientific, 2019), pp. 21, 24.

40. Kwa Chong Guan and Kua Bak Lim, eds., *A General History of the Chinese in Singapore* (Singapore: World Scientific, 2019).
41. "I hope the SCCC will strengthen the Singapore Chinese arts and cultural scene. Make it accessible to all races and appeal to all ages, and ensure that Singaporeans remain rooted in our multi-cultural identity for many years to come." From the PM's speech at the official opening, https://www.pmo.gov.sg/Newsroom/pm-lee-hsien-loong-officialopening-singapore-chinese-cultural-centre (accessed 29 November 2020).
42. Ho Kwon Ping, *The Ocean in a Drop: Singapore: The Next Fifty Years* (Singapore: World Scientific, 2016), p. 116.
43. "Integration Makes Singapore Chinese Identity Distinct: PM", *Straits Times*, 4 February 2019, https://www.straitstimes.com/singapore/integration-makes-singapore-chinese-identity-distinct-pm
44. Zheng and Lye, *Singapore–China Relations*, p. 16.
45. *CCC Third Anniversary Special Edition* (2018), pp. 38–39.
46. Ho, *The Ocean in a Drop*, p. 114.
47. PM's speech at the official opening, https://www.pmo.gov.sg/Newsroom/pm-lee-hsien-loong-official-openingsingapore-chinese-cultural-centre (accessed 29 November 2020).
48. Wang, *China Reconnects*, pp. 62, 113.

PART III
New Chinese Migrants and Local Communities

7

"Old" and "New" Chinese Communities in Laos: Internal Diversity and External Influence

Bien Chiang and Jean Chihyin Cheng

Member states of the Association of Southeast Asian Nations (ASEAN) are encountering both opportunities and concerns in the face of an ever-accelerating Chinese economic expansion. For the countries in mainland Southeast Asia, especially along the Mekong, the concerns are all the more acute because of a shared riverine system and, in some cases, shared land border with China (Santasombat 2015, 2017). With the launch of the Greater Mekong Subregion (GMS) Development Programme sponsored by the Asian Development Bank (ADB) and the corresponding China-sponsored Yunnan Gateway Project, it has become apparent that China's national economic strategy in this area is to (1) create maritime accessibility for the 'Greater Southwestern China', (2) extract natural resources from the comparatively underdeveloped neighbouring countries, and (3) enhance the regional market as well as investment opportunities for Chinese enterprises. Where then does Laos stand in this context?

Laos is the only landlocked Southeast Asian country. Except for the proposed Kunming–Bangkok high-speed railway, most of China's economic operations in Laos since the 1990s extend to resource extraction and the exploration of market and investment opportunities. It is worth noting that, among the three countries that share land borders with China—Vietnam, Laos and Myanmar—Laos is the only one to have not witnessed much anti-Chinese protests in recent years.[1] While this is not the place to examine the sources of these protests—to what extent were they civic-led or partially government-induced—the fact remains that, compared to Myanmar and Vietnam, Laos is generally accommodating to the increasing presence of Chinese economic interests in the country. Shared political ideology contributes to this accommodation. Not only does communist comradeship and similar political-administrative mentalities between Laos and China provide a fundamental like-mindedness for the decision makers of the two countries, Laos is also the only nominal socialist country in the region that maintains an amicable relationship with China (Chiang and Cheng 2015, p. 90).[2]

In addition to maintaining a warm relationship with China, a number of geographical and historical factors are also significant in the position of Laos towards Chinese economic expansion. Because it was landlocked, the area consisting of the current Laos was the last to be incorporated into French Indochina in 1893. The French colonial administration brought in a large number of Vietnamese clerks, teachers, technicians and farmers to help them in running this sparsely populated and mostly rural country.[3] Other than road construction and opium monopolization, the French did little in terms of economic development, let alone human resource development. In 2021, according to the World Bank's World Population Review, Laos had a population density of 31 persons per square kilometre, ranking 178 among all the countries in the world. Its GDP per capita in 2015 was US$5,300, which ranks 164 in the world.[4] In short, after experiencing a laissez-faire French colonization (1893–1953) and over two decades of devastating revolutionary warfare, followed by post-revolutionary persecutions from the 1960s to the 1980s, including the destructive US air bombing in the 1970s, Laos remains largely underdeveloped and is a major receiver of foreign aid (Phraxayavong 2009). While the Laotian government generally welcomes foreign investment, the Chinese government and businesses in particular view Laos as a land of plentiful opportunities. In the eyes of numerous Chinese labourers and petty traders who have meagre resources, Laos offers a humble but easy start in life.

"Old" and "New" Chinese in Laos

The Chinese in Laos can be divided into two broad categories: those whose families came before the end of World War II and have Laos citizenship (Old Chinese), and those who came after the 1990s under the Open and Reform policy and who are mostly Chinese nationals (New Chinese).[5] These two communities show conspicuous differences in terms of community formation, language usage, religious practices, leisure life, daily demeanour and embeddedness in Laotian society. From an objective point of view, Chinese economic expansion, including the much-publicized Belt and Road Initiative (BRI), should have created plentiful opportunities for the New Chinese businessmen to recruit Old Chinese as partners, managers, translators and secretarial personnel, and for the businesses of the latter to experience rejuvenation. In other words, it should have brought about the implementation of the so-called 'bamboo network' (Weidenbaum 1996). While it is true that young Laotians with a Chinese language background find more job opportunities with the coming of new Chinese businesses, and the Laotian big conglomerates welcome new prospects for joint ventures, many of the Old Chinese business proprietors, especially SMEs, would shrug off these seemingly promising prospects. Socially and psychologically, the Old and the New Chinese remain separated from each other.

In this section, we will look at how the Old Chinese regard the presence of New Chinese economic operations and immigrants or sojourners from China. We will look further into the internal diversity of the two communities to reflect upon the correct but probably simplified dichotomy. One may say that the New Chinese demonstrate some of the long-standing characteristics of first-generation Old Chinese immigrants. An Old Chinese community leader comments that,

> Many [New] Chinese came here. They are really hardworking and are willing to do any kind of work, from the most difficult task to the middle and top level enterprises. Here in Savannakhet we have only around 800 Old Chinese; the New Chinese [number] several times more. With the prospects of economic growth following the building of [the] high-speed rail, many foreigners consider Laos a piece of [a] gold bar. We local Chinese will suffer from this kind of intense competition.[6]

There is also a prevailing perception that Chinese goods are of inferior quality. In the words of an old lady from a pre-revolution entrepreneurial family:

Those Chinese (from China) do their own businesses; we (Old Chinese) don't deal with them. We do ours and they do theirs. They sell parts and motorbikes from their country. We also don't like to buy their products, easily broken, and their foodstuffs are not of good quality. It is also the case in Thailand, Chinese foodstuffs also not selling well in Thailand. But the local Laotians will buy from them because their goods are cheaper.[7]

A wholesaler who imports foodstuff and general household items from Thailand echoes this opinion. According to him, local consumers—ethnic Chinese and Laotian alike—find the style and taste of Thai merchandise more acceptable than those from China. In addition to evaluating the products of China against the local preference, leaders of the Old Chinese also comment on the social distance between the two communities. According to the vice-chair of one of the Chinese associations:

Only one or two of the New Chinese took part in the affairs of our Chinese Association. Others would not come. They send their children back to China for schooling instead of attending Chinese schools here. In the early days, people who came to Laos, Cambodia and Thailand were all from Fujian and Guangdong, like myself from Teochew (a part of Guangdong). Nowadays they come from Kunming, Hunan and Hubei. Their characters are different from us. There is no disharmony between us, but they live in their area and we ours; they have their associations and we have ours. They can join ours but it is okay if they do not come.[8]

A former chairperson of another Chinese association highlights the lack of rapport between the two communities:

We used to invite some New Chinese business leaders to take part in our temple festivals but very few came. They were reluctant to associate with us and paid attention instead to the activities hosted by their embassy. The Chinese from China are mostly atheistic. When we include them in our festival, they donate very little money. For example, if our lion dance troupe goes to visit their shops or houses during the New Year, one visit will cost one million (Laotian kip), and the owner tips us only two hundred thousand (kip); it is not worthwhile. So gradually we stop inviting them to come. On the other hand, we have better relationships with the local Vietnamese temples. Although with minor differences in ritual details, we are of similar mentality about religion and festivals. So we will go worshipping in their temple and invite their lion-dragon dance troupes to join our celebrations.[9]

This is in accordance with our observation that, on almost all the frontcourt wood or marble tablets recording names and donation amounts for the building or renovation projects of temples and schools in Lao cities, the amounts donated by the Chinese Embassy and New Chinese businesses are often among the most meagre or modest. These New Chinese organizations and groups show little interest in taking part in the activities of the Old Chinese communities. One of our Old Chinese informants described the life of these New Chinese as "starting business seven in the morning and closing eight in the evening, going home, shutting door and watching TV programmes from China".[10] A key observation here is that the New Chinese, unlike the first generation of the Old Chinese who emigrated to foreign lands, enjoy connectivity to the motherland via internet or satellite TV. As such, for the New Chinese, social connectedness and networks take on different forms compared to those of their predecessors from the last century.

It is important to note that the New Chinese are not homogeneous or easily categorized. For example, while the majority of the New Chinese in Laos come from Central and Southwest China, there are also those from South and Southeastern China, the traditional homeland of the Old Chinese. Some of them even come from families with pre-existing extensive family connections in Southeast Asia. Mr H, a man in his sixties, came to Laos in the 1980s from Guangdong. This is how he relates his story:

> My hometown is Meixian, Guangdong. All my relatives are in Singapore, Malaysia and Indonesia. My grandparents lived in Malaysia. They sent my father back to China for education in the mid-twentieth century but then he was banned from coming back to Malaysia. There are many people with overseas connections in Meixian. I am trained in traditional Chinese medicine. I heard that here in Laos there were abundant plants with medicinal effects and that Laos was in need of a Chinese doctor so I came and practised. In the beginning, after saving some money, I bought land with other people's names because that was the only way to buy land. Of course, it was risky because the person who lent you his name might trick you and really take your land away. But I treated that as gambling; once the price for land became higher I sold the land and made a profit. After seven or eight years, the Laotian government urged people to apply for citizenship. I did, which cost me US$100, and became qualified to legally own land. Now the government changes that policy because they fear that more foreigners would become citizens and

buy up all their land. I learn to speak Lao and can use that language quite effectively now. I served one term on the Control Committee of Chinese Association; and I regularly take part in the religious or charity functions, including having lion dance in front of my clinic. Very few New Chinese do that. I came earlier and got along very well with the Laotians. One of my sons is in local Chinese school and two are in colleges in China. I think this is a very good country. In terms of economy it is underdeveloped but people are friendly and the general situation is secured and peaceful because this is a Buddhist country.[11]

Although Mr H arrived in Laos from Guangdong only in the 1980s, he exhibits the traits of the Old Chinese. A native Hakka speaker from an overseas Chinese family, he demonstrated the adventurous spirit of first-generation immigrants, learned the local language, took part in the community affairs and local religious practices and, when the chance came, picked up Laotian citizenship without much hesitation. From Mr H's case, we see that the distinction between the Old and the New Chinese is not a matter of chronology but social categorization and affiliation.[12]

In the same vein, the Old Chinese community is also a diverse one. Aside from the long-standing classification of Haw (Yunnan Chinese) and Chin (Southern Chinese), common among the countries of Mainland Southeast Asia (More 1967; Forbes and Henley 1997), another major distinction comes from those who fled the communist regime and those who stayed. According to anthropologist Grant Evans (2002, pp. 177–78), "The first years of the Lao People's Democratic Republic (LPDR) saw the fleeing of Chinese merchants and most educated Lao.... By 1980, ten per cent of Lao's population left." Florence Rossetti (1997, p. 26) estimates that "the Chinese sector of the population in Laos has dropped from 100,000 people—before the change of regime in 1975—to about 10,000 today". This massive 'secondary diaspora' saw many Old Chinese from Laos taking refuge in Taiwan, France, Canada, the United States and Australia. It was not unusual for members of the same family to be dispersed over many different countries. The next twenty years witnessed the mixed fortunes of the Laotian Old Chinese diaspora. Soon, however, this diaspora began to return.

> After the mid-1990s, with a more liberal economic policy and more business opportunities in Laos there emerged a noticeable trickle of returning former emigrants. There are people returning to Laos either with money to invest or with professional know-how to work. There

is also a sizable cohort of retirees who have come back to Laos with pensions from their decades of employment in the foreign countries, to retire to a rather comfortable life, to recover their lost juvenile memory of their 'hometown', and, not infrequently, to marry (or remarry) a Laotian spouse. (Chiang and Cheng 2015, p. 93)

Mr L, the Vice Chairman of one of the Chinese Associations in Laos, is a returned 'refugee' of the 1980s. At the age of twenty-three he managed to acquire a Chinese passport when the Lao regime changed. With this passport he travelled to Bangkok and acquired a forged Thai passport, which allowed him to travel to Germany without a visa. But it was too risky to fly directly from Thailand because of tighter immigration security. He thus made his way to Kuala Lumpur in Malaysia and boarded a plane from there. After arriving in Germany, he managed to cross the border into France to be reunited with his family who were already there. In his words:

> I returned to Laos for the first time twenty years ago [in the mid-1990s] but had been moving around a lot since. Four or five years ago I started to settle down here in my old hometown and they [Old Chinese community] asked me to be the vice chairman of the [Chinese] Association. They trusted me so I was happy to help. The first few years after I came back, I was in Savannakhet doing gravel business. It was easier to ship construction material from there to Thailand. Earlier timber business was good, but afterwards the forest was depleting and people exported higher priced mahogany furniture to China. After Xi Jinping cracked down on corruption, the mahogany market also reduced in size. Now I am applying for Laotian citizenship but not yet approved so I still hold on to my French passport.[13]

Mr L's story of return is not uncommon. Many former political refugees have chosen to launch a second career in Laos after decades of living abroad. They bring with them capital, professional skills, vision, international connections or, in some cases, humanitarian aid to Laos.[14] There are a number of alma-mater-based or hometown-based organizations that coordinate homecoming and reunion events for these people. During these occasions, long-lost friends, old school mates or even relatives from Laos and overseas would gather together to catch up with each other's lives, go tomb-sweeping and, not infrequently, exchange business information. Laotian high officials would also take these opportunities to lobby these emigrants to invest in Laos. The Deputy Prime Minister of the Lao PDR, Thongloun Sisoulith, encouraged such investments in his welcoming speech at the 2011 Global United Chinese Organizations from Vietnam, Cambodia and Laos Chinese event. In some cases, such reunions revive old grudges over the handling of property that emigrants left in the hands of relatives or friends who had remained in the country.

Grudges notwithstanding, these former emigrants, returning either to visit or to stay, are generally well received by the Old Chinese community. In addition to shared memories of the pre-revolutionary years, they would also find comfort in each other through similar language, attitudes towards religious practices, lifestyle and general disposition. However, the returning emigrants are different from the Old Chinese community who remained in Laos as the former are more cosmopolitan and professionally competitive. Yet, unlike the New Chinese from Central and Northern China, returning emigrants are not treated as outsiders by the Old Chinese. These returning Laotian Chinese are capable of bringing new ideas, new business conduct and vision into Laos society to make a real difference. Therefore, the simple dichotomy between the 'Old' and the 'New' Chinese in Laos, while not entirely refutable, can be simplified. From the above discussions we have demonstrated that it is not a dichotomy based purely on chronological arrival but, more importantly, on social distinctions. While the majority of New Chinese keep to themselves, the New Chinese who come from the traditional *qiao-xiang* (hometowns) of Old Chinese and who already have families in Southeast Asia are better adapted to, as well as adopted by, the local communities, both Chinese and Laotians.

'Education, the Best Investment'

Among Southeast Asian Chinese communities, three traditional institutions serve as major focal points; namely, the temple, cemetery and the school. In the late nineteenth and early twentieth century, these three institutions were often part of dialect or hometown-based associations. With the founding of the Republic of China (ROC) in 1911, these dialect-based schools were encouraged by local Chinese leaders as well as by the ROC government to merge into trans-dialect Chinese schools that used mandarin instead of specific dialects as the medium of education. In the early twentieth century, the French colonial authority in Laos encouraged not only the integration of schools but also the combination of dialect-based associations into a single Chinese association for each major city.¹⁵ Since then, a single Chinese Association became the umbrella organization in each major Laotian city and was entrusted with the administration of cemeteries, temples and schools. As we have seen, the New Chinese, including their enterprises and the Chinese embassy, have shown relatively low interest in participating in the major rituals of the Old Chinese community, such as those of Chinese temples. The operation of Chinese schools, however, was a very different situation.

Chinese schools throughout Southeast Asia were once highly contested grounds between the governments of the ROC and the PRC (People's Republic of China) after the founding of the latter in 1949. In the late nineteenth century, Sun Yat-sen, himself an overseas Chinese from Honolulu, visited the Southeast Asian Chinese organizations seeking support for the revolution with the aim of funding the ROC. The bonds between the Southeast Asian Chinese communities and the ROC government endured even after it was defeated by the communists and retreated to Taiwan. For decades after the founding of the PRC on the Chinese mainland, the Overseas Community Council of the ROC government continued to supply Chinese schools in Southeast Asia with textbooks, teaching equipment and teachers wherever feasible. This was, of course, considered an unwelcome situation by the PRC. However, during the years of 'Exportation of (Communist) Revolution' in the 1950s and 1960s, with the extensive persecution of ethnic Chinese suspected of being communist sympathizers and the prohibition of Chinese media and education in many Southeast Asian countries, the PRC government kept a low profile regarding affairs of the Chinese communities in Southeast Asia. The situation began to change after the 'Reform and Open' policy in the 1980s. Not only did the PRC government become more assertive in working with the overseas Chinese communities, the demand for Chinese language education grew because of a booming China market. Chinese schools in Southeast Asia thus became battlegrounds.

The formal operation of the Chinese National Office for Teaching Chinese as a Foreign Language (NOTCFL, or *hanban*) and its predecessor started in 1987. Since then the office spearheaded efforts to persuade Chinese schools in Southeast Asia to change their textbooks from those of traditional characters to those of simplified characters. NOTCFL also launched programmes to finance the supplying of textbooks and teachers to Southeast Asian Chinese schools that were willing to work with it.

Considered a significant element in the 'United Front' strategy, education, including propagating specific viewpoints of history, was handled systematically under official guidelines. Today, all Chinese schools in Laos are recipients of educational aid from China.

Among the three major Chinese schools, the Lieutou School of Vientiane has more than 2,500 students, with 28 teachers financed by the Chinese government, the Huaqiao School of Pakse has over 600 students and 11 teachers sponsored by China, and the Chungtek School of Savannakhet has 850 students and 18 teachers sponsored by China. All three schools have classes from kindergarten to twelfth grade. All the schools claim to have enrolled more students who have no Chinese ancestry than students who have. Each year, China provides around fifty scholarships for graduates of Chinese schools in Laos to continue their higher education in China, mirroring the generous educational investments of the United States after World War II that saw large numbers of sponsored international students coming to America to study. The strategy itself is praiseworthy as an investment in human resources on behalf of developing countries, except for widespread concerns over the ideological influence China may have on Laotian students.

For this reason, there are occasional disagreements among headmasters or board members of Chinese schools in Laos. One of the headmasters, worried about losing the control of the school's agenda to external agents, commented:

> I am not in favour of the policy that relies too much on external financial support for the running of schools. Some other schools prefer relying heavily on these kinds of external financial aid. But I believe a school should rely basically on the tuition, board member donation and proper management of its assets. Only in this way can we keep the orientation of the school in our own hands. After we achieve this basic financial security, external funds become optional rather than indispensable.[16]

There was also the case where one of the alumni associations of a certain Chinese school got into a fight with the headmaster. The headmaster was deemed to be too much a protégé of the Chinese Embassy by the members of the alumni association. The fight was about the proper uses of funds from alumni donations.

Chinese schools have been one of the major overseas Chinese institutions in Southeast Asia to have attracted the attention of the Chinese government in its efforts to engage the Old Chinese communities. China's economic boom has paved the way for greater financial and material aid to Chinese schools in Laos. The long-term goal of such aid is to spread the values and viewpoints propagated by the Chinese government.

Conclusion

Southeast Asia has witnessed several waves of Chinese immigrants over the centuries. Such waves have resulted in different layers of communities over the region. A well-known example is the distinction between the *peranakan* (assimilated Chinese) and the *toktok* (newly arrived Chinese) in Indonesia. This is also true for Laos, with the distinction between the Old Chinese and the New Chinese. The New Chinese in this context refers to those who came to Laos during or after the 1980s with full official sanction and sometimes assistance from the Chinese government. The differences in life experiences, primary education, business mentality, citizenship and sociality combine to sharpen this distinction. However, as this chapter argues, if we consider the internal diversities of each group, we will find that the real distinction between the two communities is not simply a matter of chronology. New Chinese who originated from the same areas of earlier emigrants and have Southeast Asian Chinese family backgrounds or links can integrate into the Old Chinese community more easily than newcomers from Central, Northern or even Southwestern China. On the other hand, those Old Chinese who fled the country during and after regime change in the 1970s are distinct from those who stayed behind. Possessing higher education, professional skills and a more cosmopolitan worldview, they are nonetheless well received upon returning to Laos by both the government and the Old Chinese community.

Finally, there is a general perception that the first generation of immigrants usually arrive without the backing of national governments and are generally better integrated into the local community, such as was commonly the case for Chinese arriving in insular Southeast Asian countries in the eighteenth or nineteenth centuries. This is in contrast to latecomers who focus more on money-making and paying less attention to the need to integrate. This chapter argues that, while it is true that the New Chinese community has little interest in participating in the social production and reproduction of the Old Chinese community through ritual practices, the Chinese government has taken a keen interest in the syllabus, administration and operations of Chinese schools in Laos. It remains to be seen, however, the extent to which the Chinese government would prevail in its united front strategy over education in Laos, and under what circumstances the Old Laotian Chinese communities would assert their interests over this traditional Chinese institution.

Acknowledgements

The authors want to thank the invaluable help from the Lao Overseas Chinese Association (Republic of China), especially the late Dr Lu Pishing, current Chairperson Mrs Fu Yuluan, and Mr Lin Sziyuan, who made the fieldwork in Laos possible. Parts of the fieldwork funding came from the Thailand Research Fund project, "Variegated Dragon: Territorialization and Civilising Mission in Southeast Asia (2011–2014)", under the directorship of Professor Yos Santasombat, Faculty of Social Sciences, Chiangmai University.

Notes

1. In May 2014, riots against Chinese factories and workers broke out in Southern and Central Vietnam triggered by territorial conflict between the People's Republic of China and Vietnam over the South China Sea. At least one Chinese worker was killed and hundreds injured (Buckley 2014). In Myanmar, protests happened in 2013 and 2016 against the operation of a copper mine located a hundred kilometres west of Mandalay, the construction of the Sino-Myanmar pipeline and the Myitsone dam (Aung Hla Tun 2016; Kyaw Min 2013).
2. This kind of agreeable relationship can also be traced way back in history. Laos, known as Nan-zhang, had always been documented as the more 'loyal' and 'docile' vassal throughout the Qing Dynasty (1616–1911) (Chiang and Cheng 2015, pp. 89–90).
3. According to Meg Regina Rakow (1992, p. 93), "By 1937 ethnic Vietnamese comprised seventy-five per cent of school tutors, and seventy per cent of clerks, secretaries, secret police, and navy personnel."
4. Central Intelligence Agency 2016.
5. The Chinese Association of Vientiane claims that there are around 30,000 'registered members' of the association nationwide. According to the estimation of the Overseas Community Affairs Council, Republic of China (Taiwan), there are around 150,000 Chinese in Laos. Professor Zhuang Guo-tu (2004) of Xiamen University sets the number at 160,000. These two estimates

apparently include both Old and New Chinese. One of our informants, Mr CY, estimate, the number of Old Chinese as between 20,000 and 30,000 for the whole country and between 3,000 and 4,000 in Vientiane, while that of the New Chinese is between 200,000 and 300,000. See Chiang and Cheng (2015, pp. 91–101).
6. Interview with Mrs Ma Li-fang, former chairperson of the Chinese Association of Savannakhet, on 7 January 2016.
7. Interview with Mrs Lin on 4 January 2016.
8. Interview with Mr Lin Sheng-rong, vice chair of Pakse's Chinese Association, on 3 January 2016.
9. Interview with Mrs Ma Li-fang, former chair of the Chinese Association of Savannakhet, on 7 January 2016.
10. Interview with Mr Shao Xi-zhong, former official of Vientiane's Chinese Association, on 23 August 2011.
11. Interview with Mr Hsieh Xin, a pharmacy owner, on 14 January 2016.
12. Mr H is certainly not the only case of an Overseas Chinese returnee whose family moved back to China from Southeast Asia, got stuck inside China for several decades and was finally allowed to emigrate again after the 1980s. Mr C, a temple superintendent, aged more than eighty, went back to China in the 1950s with his mother while his father continued his business in Thailand. He was persecuted during the Cultural Revolution and tried several times to escape to Hong Kong or Myanmar without success. He was allowed to leave the country, finally, in the 1980s. With all the wealth of his father having been inherited by his other siblings who remained in Thailand, he was penniless and offered a job as temple superintendent in Vientiane. The current headmaster of Vientiane's Chinese school is also a "New" Chinese. He is capable of working together with the Old-Chinese-based Chinese Association there partly because he is a Teochew from Guangdong.
13. Interview with Mr Lin Sheng-rong, vice chair of Pakse's Chinese Association, on 3 January 2016.
14. Dr Zhao Shu-zhong, a Vientiane Yunnanese who fled the change of regime, received his medical education in Taiwan. He married a Taiwanese woman and converted to Christianity. In 1997, he went back to Laos on a preaching and medical mission. He has since moved back to Vientiane semi-permanently with his wife and daughter to operate charity medical care projects in remote areas of Laos. He is fluent in the Laotian language because of his primary education in the country, and is therefore well received by Laotian government authorities.
15. In most of the cities in Laos, the Teochew and the Hakka used to have separate associations as well as schools.
16. Interview with a headmaster.

References

Aung Hla Tun. 2016. "Hundreds Protest Restart of China-Backed Copper Mine in Myanmar". Reuters, 6 May 2016. http://www.reuters.com/article/us-myanmar-mine-protests-idUSKCN0XX15A.

Buckley, Chris. 2014. "Anti-Chinese Violence Convulses Vietnam, Pitting Laborers against Laborers". *New York Times*, 15 May 2014. https://www.nytimes.com/2014/05/16/world/asia/anti-chinese-violence-turns-deadly-and-spreads-in-vietnam.html?_r=1.

Central Intelligence Agency. 2016. "The World Factbook". https://www.cia.gov/library/publications/the-world-factbook/docs/faqs.html (accessed 7 January 2017).

Chiang, Bien, and Jean Chihyin Cheng. 2015. "Changing Ethnoscape and Changing Landscape in Lao PDR: Social Impacts of PRC's Participation in the Greater Mekong Subregion Development Project". In *Impact of China's Rise on the Mekong Region*, edited by Yos Santasombat. New York: Palgrave Macmillan.

Evans, Grant. 2002. *A Short History of Laos*. Crows Nest, NSW: Allen and Unwin.

Forbes, Andrew, and David Henley. 1997. *The Haw: Traders of the Golden Triangle*. Chicago: Art Media Resources.

Kyaw Min. 2013. "China-Myanmar Gas Pipeline Becomes Fully Operational". *Myanmar Business Today*, 28 October 2013. http://mmbiztoday.com/articles/china-myanmar-gas-pipeline-becomes-fully-operational.

Phraxayavong Viliam. 2009. *History of Aid to Laos: Motivations and Impacts*. Chiang Mai: Mekong Press.

Rakow, Meg Regina. 1992. *Laos and Laotians*. Center for Southeast Asian Studies with the School of Hawaiian, Asian, and Pacific Studies at the University of Hawaii at Manoa.

Rossetti, Florence. 1997. "The Chinese in Laos: Rebirth of the Laotian Chinese Community as Peace Returns to Indochina". *China Perspectives* no. 13. http://www.cefc.com.hk/article/the-chinese-in-laosrebirth-of-the-laotian-chinese-community-as-peace-returns-to-indochina/ (accessed 3 August 2017).

Santasombat, Yos, ed. 2015. *Impact of China's Rise on the Mekong Region*. New York: Palgrave Macmillan.

———. ed. 2017. *Chinese Capitalism in Southeast Asia: Cultures and Practices*. New York: Palgrave Macmillan.

Zhuang Guo-tu. 2004. "Changing Social Status of Overseas Chinese in Laos since World War II". *Overseas Chinese History Studies*, no. 2: 28–35.

8

Xin Yimin in the Philippines: Challenges and Perspectives

Teresita Ang-See

Xin yimin (新移民), or new Chinese migrants, have continued to be a hot topic for discussion for the last three decades. In fact, it is now often difficult to distinguish which group of Chinese migrants and what period of entry can be considered *xin yimin*. This large-scale migration of the Chinese started in the early 1980s after China's opening up when opportunities to study abroad, travel, do business overseas, and join families became more prevalent. In Southeast Asia, *xin yimin* refers to those who came in during the new millennium or the beginning of the twenty-first century.[1] For the purposes of this chapter, I use the common practice in the Philippines to differentiate the *laoqiao* (老僑), *jiuqiao* (舊僑), *xinqiao* (新僑),[2] and the *xin yimin* who are migrants who came in during the 1990s to date. I will focus on those who came to the Philippines in the new millennium, but particularly highlight new developments, issues and new organizations formed starting 2016, the beginning of President Rodrigo Duterte's presidency.

Historically, there have been Chinese migrants to the Philippines since Spanish colonial rule. However, the contemporary influx of Chinese migrants into the Philippines started in the 1970s, especially after the establishment of Philippines diplomatic relations with China in 1975. It escalated in the 1980s with the market reforms instituted by Deng Xiaoping and the opening up of China to foreign markets. This influx increased even more considerably after President Duterte was elected in 2016.

The influx of new Chinese migrants to the Philippines for the last two decades has been contentious, and President Duterte's pivot to China has brought the problem to the forefront. Philippines-China bilateral ties have reached new heights and brought an increase in investments and infrastructure development and other much welcome economic benefits, but have also triggered an escalation of anti-Chinese sentiments due to many factors, founded and unfounded.

One of the key challenges is the fact that seventy per cent of the newcomers in the work force are hired in POGOs (Philippine offshore gaming operations) or are employed in the online gambling and downstream businesses related to them. While it has brought benefits in terms of increased income for the public and private sector, it has also brought with it problems in criminality, with money laundering being a primary concern on top of other crimes such as kidnapping, extortion, prostitution, human trafficking and others.[3]

Amidst these challenges, Chinese businessmen and investors (among the *xin yimin*) established different organizations as a new norm of social networks, protection and connection with government agencies and authorities. Starting with the establishment of the Philippines China Chamber of Commerce (中國商會), many other business and social organizations sprouted. Hometown or village associations likewise organized new chambers of commerce in response to China's directive to organize such bodies to enable smooth implementation of the One Belt One Road (or BRI) initiative.

This chapter will focus on these new migrants, with their new organizations and the challenges and new dynamics in their relations with the local Tsinoy community and Philippine society.

Composition of the *Xin Yimin* Community

The total Philippine population stands at 104 million and we estimate the Tsinoys (Tsinong Pinoy or Chinese Filipino) to make up 1.2 per cent of the population, or roughly 1.25 million people. There is no accurate figure about the size of the *xinqiao*, but a reasonable estimate put the range at

250,000 to 300,000 Chinese nationals staying in the Philippines with legal or illegal status. This estimate was extrapolated from the following available figures: (1) the enrolment numbers of Chinese language teaching schools where children of the new immigrants are enrolled; (2) the ratio between local-born and the children of the new immigrants; (3) the arrival and departure records of the Bureau of Immigration; and (4) the alien registration records and the Labor Department records of those who apply for work permits.[4] Added to the Chinese Filipino population, there is therefore an estimated 1.5 million Tsinoys and Chinese nationals in the Philippines today (Teresita 2018, p. 11).[4] The new migrants, or *xin yimin*, in the Philippines were more popularly called *xinqiao* (新僑) up to the early 2000s. Only lately was the term *xin yimin* (新移民/中國人) used to refer to the new migrants following the common term used in Southeast Asia. Many of these took advantage of the special investor visas and special retirement visas instituted by the Philippine government to encourage investment.[5]

The division is not as neat as presented, for there is a lot of overlap, especially for those who went back and forth to China in earlier years. There are vast differences among these groups in terms of identities, upbringing and orientation. Each group evolved through time and adapted to, or are shaped by, the Philippines' history and socio-economic environment. Even the children of the so-called *jiuqiao* or *xinqiao* are a new generation quite different from the *laoqiao*.

Breakdown of *Xinqiao* Population[6]

The Bureau of Immigration (BI) reported that more than three million Chinese citizens arrived in the Philippines as tourists, investors, students and professionals from January 2016 to May 2018.[7] More than three quarters, or 2.4 million, of these Chinese hail from the mainland, while the rest are from Hong Kong, Macau and Taiwan. My figures before 2016, published in the *Southeast Asian Affairs 2019*,[8] indicated an estimated 150,000 to 200,000 new Chinese migrants, but in this chapter the number has been adjusted to 250,000 to 300,000, as shown by the figures provided by the Department of Labor and the Bureau of Immigration on the number of applicants for special work permits and alien work permits (shown in the section on workers).[9]

Tourists. Tourism is the sunrise industry in the Philippines, showing an impressive growth for the last decade. The Department of Tourism (DOT) reports that, as of 2018, tourist arrivals broke the millionth mark.

TABLE 8.1
Chinese Arrivals to the Philippines, 2015–19

Year	Volume
2015	491,000
2016	676,000
2017	968,000
2018	1,250,000
2019	1,710,000

Source: DOT, 2019.

Out of the 2.4 million Chinese arrivals to the Philippines, more than half were tourists. While tourists are indeed much welcome in the Philippines as a source of revenue, the problem is that many of these tourists stay on in the Philippines to work or go into the retail business. In particular, after the visa-upon-arrival (VUA) provision was opened to Chinese nationals to ease travel to the Philippines, the number of tourists rapidly increased.[10] Some of these tourists who stayed on found legitimate means to get special working permits, some illegally extended their tourist visas, and some opted for more permanent creative solutions by marrying Filipinas to enable them to stay on and do business.

Investors. A 2019 news report said, "According to the data from Chinese Enterprises Philippine Association, there are some 50 large Chinese companies operating in the Philippines. 'They are directly hiring more than 14,000 Filipinos while the number of Chinese workers stands at less than 1,300,' the association said."[11] This means that for large Chinese enterprises, the ratio of Chinese to Filipino workers is nine per cent. While the report describes the figure as standing "at less than 1,300", a nine per cent ratio of Chinese to Filipino workers is rather high. This figure is corroborated by the preliminary study conducted by Dr Liu Peng, associate professor of the Center for China's Neighbor Diplomacy Studies in Yunnan University, on "The less representative actor, enterprise and its local employee in BRI: the case study of Chinese enterprises in the Philippines."[12] Liu's data showed that among the enterprises he studied, 67 per cent of the employees are at the managerial level rather than the low blue-collar level. His data also showed that the educational levels of the workers show 51 per cent college level and 43 per cent secondary level. However, the data presented in Liu's study cover the big enterprises like banks, aviation and bigger manufacturing concerns rather than the construction, infrastructure and mining enterprises that hire low-level workers. It would be interesting to get the final study with more complete data. Admittedly, big Chinese enterprises hire professional workers whose positions cannot be filled by Filipinos, and hence do not compete with Filipino workers.

Workers. Ninety per cent of the *xin yimin* in the Philippines are workers who received special working permits (SWP) from the Department of Labor and Employment (DOLE) or an alien employment permit (AEP) from the Bureau of Immigration. Of these workers, 71 per cent are in the POGO industry.

As shown in Table 8.2, 71 per cent of the workers who received special work permits are workers hired in POGOs, 11 per cent in the construction business and 5 per cent in manufacturing. In a Senate hearing on the influx of foreign workers, Senator Joel Villanueva, who heads the Labor Committee of the Philippine Senate, said on 21 February 2020 that laxity in regulating POGOs in the country had led to a "loss in government income and opportunities for Filipinos". Villanueva lamented that the POGOs are not withholding taxes from the employees, resulting in a loss of revenues.[13] In an earlier hearing of the same committee, Labor Secretary Silvestre Bello said that aside from Chinese working for POGOs, which requires fluency in Chinese language, other jobs that end up being given to foreigners are those that Filipinos cannot perform.[14] On close questioning during the senate inquiry, DOLE Undersecretary Ciriaco A. Lagunzad III disclosed how the system breaks down and allows the proliferation of

TABLE 8.2
Profile of Chinese Workers in the Philippines

Sector	%
Online gambling	71*
Arts, entertainment and recreation	7
Construction	11
Manufacturing	5
Others	6

Notes: * Around sixty POGOs received permits to operate, mostly in Philippine cities, particularly in the NCR, under the Duterte administration. More than forty-five POGOs operate e-casinos.
Source: Department of Labor and Employment, March 2019; Bureau of Internal Revenue, Philippine Amusement and Gaming Corporation.

illegals. He told senators that first, "A lot of [Chinese nationals] come in as tourists and later on convert their visas to work."[15]

The last two years saw a sharp increase in the number of Chinese nationals applying for special work permits. The figure rose from a five-year average of 1,051 SWP applicants in 2008–12 to a five-year average of 14,895 in 2013–17. The increase was first observed in 2016, the year President Duterte was elected to office. The number of applicants rose to 14,775, which is double the 7,200 in 2015. As of September 2018, the number of applicants for SWP permits has reached 70,121.[16] The DOLE also issues separate AEPs, which are more expensive but are valid for three years. The DOLE reports that it has issued AEPs to 53,111 Chinese nationals for the period of January 2016 to May 2018. The SWP is issued by the Bureau of Immigration to permit a foreigner to work temporarily in the Philippines for up to six months. This period allows the foreigner to secure an AEP from the DOLE.

Taken together, the official figures suggest that there is a total of 123,232 Chinese nationals in the Philippines on AEPs and SWPs. However, the DOLE has warned that there are around 150,000 Chinese nationals who have failed to obtain permits from them, including those who have

TABLE 8.3
Permits Issued to Chinese Nationals

Special Work Permits Issued to Chinese Nationals	
Year	Number of SWP Issued
2008–12 (five-year average)	1,051
2013–17 (five-year average)	14,895
2015	7,200
2016	14,775
2017	70,121
Alien Employment Permits Issued to Chinese Nationals	
Year	Number of AEP Issued
2016	18,920
2017	23,951
2018	33,516
2019	127,269

Sources: Special work permits: BI; Alien employment permits: DOLE, http://ble.dole.gov.ph/downloads/AEP/AEP%20Yearend%202019%20Exec%20Summary_FINAL28July.pdf.

overstayed or violated the terms of their visas. Such Chinese nationals further violate the laws by working without permits or engaging in retail trade, which contravenes the Philippine Retail Trade Nationalization Law.[16] These two figures approach the estimated 250,000 to 300,000 of Chinese nationals staying in the Philippines. The perception that there are just too many Chinese workers around is bolstered by the fact that even the Department of Labor showed that Chinese nationals take up more than 80 per cent of the alien employment permits issued to foreign nationals as of the first and second quarter of 2020.[17]

Media reports and the recent Social Weather Stations (SWS) survey have shown that Filipino workers are worried and that they have complained about the influx of and competition from the Chinese workers here.[18] While the ratio of Chinese to Filipino workers in Chinese enterprises is not high, it is a cause for worry, considering the extent of unemployment in the Philippines, which averages from five to six per cent but has nearly doubled as a result of the Covid-19 pandemic.[19] Filipinos are worried these lower-level workers who have stayed on as resident migrants in the Philippines will compete for jobs with Filipino workers.

New Organizations of Chinese Migrants

The increased presence of new migrants has given rise to new organizations formed particularly in the last decade. Surprisingly, though the number of new migrants in the Philippines are dominated by tourists and workers in online gambling and casino operations, none of the newly formed organizations were directly related to these new enterprises. Travel and business agencies catering mainly to new migrants have grown considerably, especially with the increased number of Chinese citizens travelling to the Philippines.

After diplomatic relations between the Philippines and China were formally established in 1975, pro-China organizations were established. The list includes:

- Filipino–Chinese Amity Club 菲華聯誼總會 (1975)
- Federation of Filipino–Chinese Associations 菲華各界聯合會 (1977)
- Philippines–China Friendship Association 菲中友好協會 (1975), reorganized c.2000
- Association for Philippines–China Understanding 菲中了解協會 (1970s)

- Chinese Alumni Associations in the Philippines 旅菲各校友會聯合會 (1997)
- Feihua Xinlian Gong Hui 菲华新联公会 (1981)

The first two organizations—Amity Club (菲華聯誼總會 1975) and Federation of Filipino Chinese Associations (菲華各界聯合會 1977)—were formed to act as hosts to and entertain visiting dignitaries from China. At that time, the lead organization, Federation of Filipino–Chinese Chambers of Commerce and Industry, Inc. (FFCCCII 菲華商聯總會), was largely predisposed towards Taiwan.

More and more China-affiliated organizations have been established recently. The bigger organizations include:

- Philippine Council for the Peaceful Unification of China 菲律濱中國和平統一促進會 (2002)
- Philippines Soong Ching Ling Foundation 菲律濱宋慶齡基金會 (2004)
- Philippines East China Amity Club 菲律濱中國華東聯誼總會 (2007)
- Promotion of Peaceful Development, Philippine Chapter 中華和平發展促進會菲律濱分會 (2016)
- Philippines–China Friendship Foundations 菲中友好基金聯合會 (2017)
- World Youth Federation, Philippine Chapter 世界青年聯會菲律賓分會 (2018)
- Fujian Province Overseas Association 福建省海外聯誼會 (2018)

New business-related Chinese organizations were likewise formed. Among them:

- Philippine China Chambers of Commerce 菲律濱中國商會 (2007)
- Migrant Chinese Chamber of Commerce and Industry of the Philippines 旅菲華僑工商聯總會 (2007)
- Philippine Chinese Chamber of Commerce and Economics 菲律濱華商經貿聯合會 (2014)
- Junior Chinese Chamber of Commerce 菲華青商會 (2015)

A relatively new development has been that, following a directive from China for overseas organizations to help in its Belt and Road Initiative, hometown and village associations (同鄉會) began organizing chambers of commerce 商會 under their auspices starting in 2015. Even friendship associations like the Amity Club 菲華聯誼總會 recently formed the 菲律賓聯誼總商會 (2018), and the Jinjiang, Xiamen, Shishi village (同鄉會) associations also formed their chambers of commerce 商會. Another new phenomenon arising from the presence of new migrants have been the organizations outside of Fujian (i.e., Anhui, Jiangsu, Guizhou, Hubei, Hunan, etc.).

Interviews with officers and members of some of the organizations reveal that one of the reasons for their proliferation is that it gives the organizers and officers added status and a chance to be recognized and potentially be elected to the bigger traditional organizations. Another member shared: "The new business organizations are made up of a combination of 新僑 and long-time residents (舊僑) here. Most of them have businesses in the localities where the chambers are organized. For example, when they were forming the Xiamen Chamber of Commerce 廈門商會, organizers welcome people who have studied in Xiamen, owned properties and have business there. I also believe they want to boost their status by joining 同鄉會 both here and in their hometowns."[20]

More importantly, the presence of new migrants outside Fujian has given rise to groups like 菲律濱湖北同鄉總會 (2018), 菲律賓湖南同鄉會 (2018), 菲律濱山東聯誼會 (2011) and chambers of commerce that include Hong Kong, Zhejiang, Anhui, Hunan, Hubei and other chambers of commerce. Another manifestation of the new migrants' presence is shown in the 'cultural groups' formed lately, such as the 菲律賓酒文化研究會 (2018) Wine or Spirits Culture (meaning the art of drinking), the Cheongsam Cultural Association 菲律賓旗袍文化協會 (2017), organized mainly by spouses of the new business leaders, 菲律濱中醫藥總商會 (2018), 菲律濱中國美術協會 (2006), Traditional Medicine Association 菲律濱福建青年聯合會 (2017), and Fujian Youth Association.

These new organizations play a positive role in mobilizing the resources of the new migrants in many relief and charity projects. Most were active during the Covid-19 pandemic in giving aid, distributing masks and PPEs, and pooling resources in the Chinese Filipino Disaster Relief Fund. They are also active in helping the Chinese embassy in the Philippines in disseminating information and directives.

What is quite surprising, however, is that while there is a predominant presence of workers among the new Chinese migrants, there are no organizations formed by them or established on their behalf for the purpose of protecting or promoting workers' welfare. In the Philippines, there are hundreds of NGOs or institutions that watch out for migrants' rights or promote the welfare of overseas Filipino workers (OFWs), like the Center for Migrant Advocacy, the Scalabrini Migration Center, Kabalikat ng Migranteng Pilipino, Philippine Migrants Rights Watch and many others.[21] This is unfortunate, as will be seen when we look, in the last section, at problems OCWs encounter or problems that arise from their presence, which NGOs could have helped mitigate. Except perhaps for NGOs under the ambit of the All-China Federation of Trade Unions, which look into migrant workers' welfare, there seems to be no dedicated government agency for OCWs, unlike the POEA or OWWA that we have in the Philippines.[22]

Positive Impact of New Migrants

The local-born generation of Tsinoys or Chinese Filipinos are well integrated and assimilated and many have lost their Chinese language fluency and facility. Most Chinese organizations, Chinese language newspapers and schools, and selected Chinese business enterprises depend on new migrants to continue to survive and are unable to function without them. Many business enterprises hire Chinese professionals to the top managerial positions. They render a positive contribution by training and teaching new skills and methods to Filipinos. The new immigrants likewise revitalize the Tsinoy community and help in maintaining or restoring the sinicization of Chinese institutions in the community, especially those that require Chinese language facility.

To illustrate the urgent need for new migrants, a huge problem confronting Chinese language schools at present is the continuing decline in the number of Chinese students; "華生流失" is the term given to this phenomenon. At present, the estimate of children of new migrants enrolled in these Chinese schools is 36,000 nationwide. A quarter of these students are from mainland China; the other 75 per cent are local born (children of new migrants who came in the 1990s). Without this infusion of new migrants, even more Chinese language schools would have closed. From a high of 135 Chinese language schools, the remaining number is just about a hundred, and many of these are barely struggling to survive. The new migrants' children are much needed additional students that make the difference between doom or survival for these schools.

The new migrants' income contribution to the Philippine economy and the gaming industry is perceived to be the biggest contributor to revenues.

The reluctance to shut down POGOs is an offshoot of the perceived amount of revenues that they bring into the Philippine economy.²³ PAGCOR estimates that the sector contributes revenues amounting to between PhP8 billion and PhP10 billion in licensing fees and royalties, as well as windfalls from rentals and living expenses of the hundreds of thousands of workers hired by the POGOs.²⁴ In the three years since the Duterte administration, when the influx of POGO operations increased, demand for office and living spaces also increased. David Leechiu, CEO of Leechiu Property Consultants, a leading real estate services firm, estimated that between PhP400 and PhP500 billion in salaries were contributed to the Philippine economy. There was no clarification, however, as to how much of the salaries were paid to Chinese workers who did not pay taxes to the Philippines and who may have remitted a large part of their income back home to China. For sure, the workers spend a part of their income in the Philippines for their personal expenses.²⁵ In addition, licensing and royalty incomes from POGOs increased steadily from PhP6 billion in 2017 to PhP14 billion in 2019.

In personal interviews with business agencies handling the affairs of workers employed by Chinese BPOS IT (Business Processing Outsource Services Information Technology) and POGOs, some managers shared that in most circumstances the POGO operators and financiers provide housing and facilities for their workers. The standard practice is that several rooms in an apartment or condominium or an entire repurposed building or hotel would be rented, and the workers are housed there in two shifts and bussed to their working places. The conditions of some of the housing facilities are appalling, with thirty to forty workers squeezed into one unit to cut the cost of rent and utilities and groceries. Private interviews with some of the workers revealed that the company usually takes care of transportation, lodging and utilities but they take care of personal expenses like food, hygiene supplies and entertainment, at an average of PhP100,000 annually. Hence, for a low estimate of 150,000 workers, this translates to a conservative PhP15 billion in revenues infused into the economy.

Issues and Challenges Posed by New Migrants

The improvement in Philippines–China relations and the easing of contentious issues and disagreements since President Duterte took office yielded positive results in recent years in terms of increased investments, infrastructure development, financial aid and other forms of assistance.

However, they also brought new challenges and problems. The huge increase in the number of new Chinese immigrants in the offshore gambling business and its negative social impact have been one of the greatest challenges. Crimes involving POGO workers and the very public misbehaviour of the new migrants have hogged the news headlines for the past two years.

Contribution to the Philippine economy. While admittedly, the importance of the Philippine casino and gaming industry to the economy is growing, following a gross gaming revenue of PhP216.5 billion (US$4.3 billion) in 2018 from PhP 176.73 billion in the previous year, there are doubts as to the overall impact it has for Philippine economic growth in general, contradicting claims of the POGO and real estate enterprises. A risk assessment conducted by the Anti-Money Laundering Council (AMLAC) in 2019, "Understanding the Internet-Based Casino Sector in the Philippines: A Risk Assessment", reported clearly: "Despite its recognition as among the significant contributors and drivers to the economic growth, the entire casino industry accounts for about less than 1.4 per cent of the economy. Taking the gross revenues from 2017 to 2018, the Internet based casino sector accounts for only about 2.5 per cent of the gross revenues of the entire casino sector. Thus, the internet-based casino sector represents only about 0.03 per cent of the economy."[26] Senate inquiries and other studies concur that POGOs have little contribution to the Philippine economy and in fact the revenues brought in do not compensate for what the government spends for the crimes and social unrest created by the presence of the workers. While the earnings and profits raked in by the POGOs and casino operators are substantial, no one knows how much of these really go to the Philippine economy, and there are understandable worries that most of the income is repatriated to China and other countries in an elaborate money laundering scheme. Senator Franklin Drilon castigated the PAGCOR for continuing to support POGO operations. "The social problems that POGO has brought to our country is not worth the relocation fees that you earn for Pagcor", he said.[27]

Involvement in crimes. Crimes related to casino or online gambling are on the rise. They no longer just result in torture and extortions but also in kidnapping, suicides, outright homicide and murders as well as prostitution and human trafficking. The incidents are rising because rarely do the victims cooperate with authorities to pursue the case and punish the perpetrators. In many cases, crime pays and pays lucratively. In a Senate hearing in October 2020, the Philippine National Police reported ten police operations versus POGO sex dens, which mostly cater exclusively to Chinese workers. Some 199 women who got involved in prostitution have been rescued. There have also been seventy-three casino-related kidnapping cases in the last three years that targeted Chinese nationals.[28] In 2019 alone, local authorities closed down around 200 internet-based casinos and service providers that illegally serviced online gaming operations. In the same year, the local government ceased the operations of one of the largest service providers for an internet-based casino. This service provider was also the subject of investigation for alleged links with an individual and entity involved in the Bangladesh Bank heist (an elaborate cyber hack that stole US$81 million from the bank and transferred the funds to the Philippines). The AMLC likewise mentioned the increasing level of threat from money laundering and other fraudulent activities involving domestic internet-based casino operators and service providers. From 2017–19, the recorded casino-kidnapping-related incidents totalled sixty-three cases.

Immigration problems and rampant corruption. The abuses in the application and granting of SWPs as well as the abuses in the visa-upon-arrival privilege from the BI were subject to congressional hearings by both the Philippine Senate and House of Representatives. Reports describe transactions to allow those who enter through tourist visas to extend their stay and even to obtain working visas. Upon payment of a hefty bribe, Chinese are fraudulently given an SWP through connivance with Chinese travel agencies as facilitators in the transaction. Even for as low as 10,000 pesos (US$200), Chinese nationals were allowed entry through the visa-upon-arrival provision. No questions were asked, and some of those arrested were in fact convicted criminals or fugitives from China. Immigration officials caught in this bribery scheme had been dismissed.[29] But one of the latest hearings conducted by Sen. Risa Hontiveros, who heads the Senate Women and Children Committees, uncovered an even more elaborate scheme of human trafficking through the connivance of corrupt immigration officials. Hontiveros,[30] the Department of Justice and the National Bureau of Investigation have conducted an investigation into these allegations and, as of September 2020, the NBI has filed cases against twenty individuals—19 BI officials and an owner of a Chinese travel agency—who are allegedly involved in the operation, popularly tagged as the "*pastillas* scheme", involving BI officials and Chinese nationals, especially financiers of gambling and prostitution dens.[31] A total of 324 Chinese nationals have been arrested by authorities with the Philippines Bureau of Immigration (BI) on allegations they were engaged in cybercrimes, including operating unauthorized online gaming. Unscrupulous Chinese agents advertise in Chinese social media platform like WeChat for any form of services wanted by Chinese businessmen, investors, POGO workers and, especially, criminals who need such services as drivers' licences, bank certifications, credit cards, legal immigration papers, and even the services of prostitutes.[32]

China against POGOs. Contrary to the allegations of anti-China opinion makers, the Chinese government is vehemently against POGOs and has been assiduously working to ban its citizens from becoming involved in the same. China has repeatedly protested against these gambling operations that cause a financial drain from China's domestic economy. The Chinese Embassy in the Philippines clearly expressed its objection to online gambling in its statement on 8 August 2019: "All gambling aside from the state-run lottery is illegal in China. Hence, gambling syndicates in online gaming networks unlawfully target the Chinese, many of whom, like the overseas Filipino workers, were illegally recruited with false promises." A statement in response to this was issued to the PAGCOR at the congressional hearings about the POGOs: "According to the Chinese laws and regulations, any form of gambling by Chinese citizens is illegal. The casinos and offshore gaming operators (POGOs) and other forms of gambling entities in the Philippine target Chinese citizens as their primary customers. In many cases, the employers of Philippine casinos, POGOs and other gambling entities do not apply necessary legal work permits for their Chinese employees. Some Chinese citizens are even lured into and cheated to work illegally with only tourist visas."[33]

The Chinese Embassy statement further elaborated how China itself has been severely and adversely affected by the Philippine casinos and POGOs and other forms of gambling entities targeting Chinese customers: First, huge amounts of Chinese funds have flowed out of China and into the Philippines illegally, involving crime such as cross-border money laundering through underground banking, which undermines China's financial supervision and financial security. A conservative estimate puts gambling-related funds flowing illegally out of China and into the Philippines at hundreds of millions of Chinese yuan (renminbi) every year, going into the local real estate markets and other sectors in the Philippines. Second, illegal gambling has resulted in an increase in crime and social problems in China. Gambling crimes and telecom fraud are closely connected, which have caused huge losses to the victims and their families. Third, many of the Chinese workers in Philippine casinos or POGOs and other forms of gambling entities are subject to 'modern slavery' due to severe limitations of their personal freedom. Their passports are taken away or confiscated by the Philippine employers. Some of them have been subject to extortion, physical abuse and torture, severe injuries or even murder.[34] In fact, many media reports describe the workers' slave-like conditions, long hours without rest, and their suffering physical and mental abuse (including threats to harm their families back home).

To demonstrate that China is serious about cracking down on cross-border telecommunication fraud, the Ministry of Public Security of China, on 27 January 2020, just before the Covid-19 pandemic erupted, issued a notice to its overseas nationals stating that it had obtained a list of Chinese nationals suspected of committing long-term telecommunication fraud in different countries. It required these POGO workers abroad to return to China by 8 February otherwise, "all those involved in overseas telecommunications fraud and gambling will have their passports cancelled". Since then, China has revoked thousands of its citizens' passports[35] on grounds that they violated laws by traveling to work in the Philippines' online gaming industry. In interviews with a few who received notices that their passports would be cancelled, they revealed that the Chinese Embassy at least acknowledges that they have been victims of illegal recruitment and they were given travel documents to enable them to go home. This revocation of passports has spawned new problems, especially with migrants who were determined to stay on through any means. Acquisition of Philippine passports through unscrupulous means and fake documents was one such measure. On 17 September 2020, a couple was arrested in Quezon Province, south of Manila, after paying ₱800,000 for a 'genuine' Philippine passport obtained fraudulently from the Department of Foreign Affairs. Confiscated from them was the money used for the payoff, Philippine birth certificates and other documents for residency. With them was a Chinese who facilitated the transaction. He had been in the Philippines for some time and could speak Filipino.[36]

The above section on the negative impacts of new Chinese migrants in the Philippines is not meant to make a blanket accusation against their presence. I wish to emphasize that many of the positive impacts of the presence of new migrants may be negated because of the POGO-related crimes they spawn. Many social commentaries have repeatedly underscored that the supposed profits and benefits accrued from the presence of POGOs and illegal Chinese immigrants do not compensate for the adverse social disorder it triggers.

Public opinion.[37] The problems and concerns raised about the increased presence of new Chinese migrants (including illegal Chinese workers), and the problems and conflicts arising from the South China Sea disputes and China's building of massive infrastructure in disputed areas, are a potentially combustible combination. Trust ratings of China have continued to go downhill and the Covid-19 pandemic further exacerbated the Filipinos' trust rating of China despite many positive moves from China, the Chinese and the Tsinoy community to help the Philippines cope with the Covid-19 pandemic.

This opinion is further worsened by many incidents of misbehaviour of some Chinese tourists and new migrants in public confrontations arising from refusal to wear masks in a restaurant, spitting on the floor, letting a child defecate in a public place, verbally and physically abusing persons of authority (policemen and traffic enforcers), continued smoking in public in the midst of the pandemic, and many other unacceptable behaviours.

Conclusion

The worsening image of new migrants prodded the Federation of Filipino–Chinese Chambers of Commerce to take out a public advertisement in the Chinese newspapers warning the Chinese to be more circumspect in their actions to prevent an escalation of racism. This is especially true during the pandemic and the economic crisis and the consequent widespread poverty it has spawned. The racial divide happens not just between the new migrants and the Filipinos but also among the new migrants and the Tsinoys who resent the fact that the new migrants' misbehaviour damages the centuries-old good relations between the Filipinos and Chinese Filipinos.

New migrants are here in the Philippines to stay as attested by their children's enrolment in local schools and the many new organizations formed by new migrants. These organizations should help in addressing the problems that arise from their presence here. Just like in the early years, when the Tsinoy organizations directly and indirectly imposed social sanctions against their erring members, the new organizations must exercise their influence, too, to police their own ranks. They hopefully can play an active role in helping to improve the image of the new migrants not just in mainstream society but also in the Tsinoy community. The divisiveness in the ranks between the old and new migrants is not healthy, but the schism is understandable in the face of the incidents of misbehaviour of the new migrants. Though they are isolated incidents, media, especially social media, tend to play up and exaggerate them, thus further exacerbating the tensions generated.

While government-to-government relations between China and the Philippines have improved considerably under President Duterte's term, people-to-people relations have deteriorated and measures must be taken to rectify the situation before the racial conflict worsens. The Philippines has much to learn and to benefit from China, but the latter's diplomacy and exercise of soft power must include cautioning its own citizens to be law-abiding and be sensitive to the social norms of their host country.

Notes

1. Leo Suryadinata, "New Chinese Migrants in Indonesia: An Emerging Community that Faces New Challenges", *ISEAS Perspective*, no. 2020/61, 11 June 2020.
2. I first introduced these terms, popularly used in the Philippines, in my paper, "Influx of New Chinese Immigrants to the Philippines: Problems and Challenges", in *Beyond Chinatown: New Chinese Migration and the Global Expansion of China*, edited by Mette Thunø (Denmark: NIAS Press, 2007), pp. 137–64. See also Teresita Ang See and Carmelea Ang See, "The Rise of China, New Immigrants and Changing Policies on Chinese Overseas: Impact on the Philippines", in *Southeast Asian Affairs 2019*, edited by Daljit Singh and Malcolm Cook (Singapore: ISEAS – Yusof Ishak Institute, 2019), pp. 275–94; and "Influx of New Chinese Immigrants to the Philippines: Problems and Challenges", in *The Chinese in the Philippines: Problems and Perspectives*, vol. 4, edited by Teresita Ang See (Manila: Kaisa Para Sa Kaunlaran, Inc., 2013), pp. 200–35.
3. Ang See and Ang See, "The Rise of China", introduced some of the problems. See also Hannah Torregoza, "Senate Panel to Conduct Probe on POGO-Related Sex-Trafficking, Prostitution", *Manila Bulletin Online*, 23 February 2020, https://mb.com.ph/2020/02/23/senate-panel-to-conduct-probe-on-pogo-related-sex-trafficking-prostitution/; Lorna Patajo-Kapunan, "Sexual Trafficking, POGOs and the Coronavirus", *BusinessMirror Online*, Legally

Speaking, 10 February 2020, https://businessmirror.com.ph/2020/02/10/sexualtrafficking-pogos-and-the-coronavirus/; Aika Rey, "PNP Says Rise in Chinese Kidnappings Linked to POGO Worker Influx", *Rappler*, 5 March 2020, https://www.rappler.com/nation/pnp-says-risechinese-kidnappings-linked-pogo-worker-influx.

4. "Integration, Indigenization, Hybridization and Localization of the Ethnic Chinese Minority in the Philippines", in *The Chinese in the Philippines: Problems and Perspectives*, vol. 5, edited by Teresita Ang See (Manila: Kaisa Para Sa Kaunlaran Inc., 2018), pp. 1–30; also in Leo Suryadinata, *Migration, Indigenization and Interaction: Chinese Overseas and Globalization* (Singapore: Chinese Heritage Centre, 2011), pp. 231–52.
5. Ibid. Also in Leo Suryadinata, "New Chinese Migrants in Indonesia: An Emerging Community that Faces New Challenges", *ISEAS Perspective*, no. 2020/61, 11 June 2020.
6. Figures in this section were combined from two sources: Ang See and Ang See, "The Rise of China" and Rommel Banlaoi's upcoming paper presented in various conferences and webinars on "Current Chinese Migration in the Philippines under Duterte Administration: Law Enforcement Concerns and Security Challenges in Philippines–China Relations before and during the Covid-19 Pandemic". Updated figures came from the Department of Labor and the China State Enterprises Association of the Philippines 2019, AMLAC Report 2019 and other data from concerned government agencies.
7. From official response of the Bureau of Immigration, dated 24 September 2018, signed by Immigration Commissioner Jaime H. Morente to this author's letter request.
8. Ang See and Ang See, "The Rise of China".
9. Ibid.
10. Xinhua, "Gov't Figure Shows More Chinese Tourists Visit Philippines in First Half of This Year". *People's Daily online*, 20 August 2018, http://en.people.cn/n3/2017/0820/c90000-9257703.html.
11. "Chinese Companies Create Lots of Jobs in the Philippines: Trade Secretary", Xinhua, 30 March 2019, http://en.people.cn/n3/2019/0330/c90000-9562217.html.
12. The data was presented by Dr Liu Peng at a webinar on "Assessing Belt and Road Initiatives in the Philippines", jointly convened by the Philippine Association for Chinese Studies and the Institute of Southeast Asian Studies of Jinan University, on 22 August 2020, in commemoration of the forty-fifth year of the establishment of Philippines–China diplomatic relations. Liu's study is part of a research project on BRI and Chinese enterprises in Southeast Asia under the auspices of the Overseas Chinese Enterprise and Employee Survey OCEES 海外中國企業與員工調查.

13. Aika Rey, "Gov't Income and Jobs for Filipinos 'Lost' to Chinese Workers – Villanueva", *Rappler*, 21 February 2019, https://www.rappler.com/nation/chinese-workers-influx-government-incomejobs-filipinos-lost.
14. Dharel Placido, "Chinese Workers Grabbing Jobs Meant for Filipinos? Labor Chief Reacts", ABS–CBN News, last updated 28 December 2018, https://news.abs-cbn.com/news/12/27/18/chineseworkers-grabbing-jobs-for-filipinos-labor-chief-reacts.
15. Raissa Robles, "Chinese Workers 'Flood' the Philippines, Yet Duterte's Officials 'Don't Know' How Many There Are", *South China Morning Post*, 22 December 2018, https://www.scmp.com/week-asia/economics/article/2178749/chinese-workers-flood-philippines-yet-dutertesofficials-dont.
16. Ang See and Ang See, "The Rise of China".
17. "Alien Employment Regulation 2019 Year-end Report", Department of Labor and Employment, 10 August 2020, http://ble.dole.gov.ph/downloads/AEP/AEP%20Yearend%202019%20Exec%20Summary_FINAL28July.pdf.
18. CNN Philippines Staff, "SWS: 70% of Filipinos 'Worried' about Rise in Number of Chinese Workers in PH", CNN, 5 December 2019, https://cnnphilippines.com/news/2019/12/5/sws-chinese-workersin-ph.html?fbclid.
19. "Employment Situation in July 2020", Philippine Statistics Authority, Ref. No. 2020-246, 3 September 2020, https://psa.gov.ph/content/employment-situation-july-2020; "Philippines Unemployment Rate", *Trading Economics*, https://tradingeconomics.com/philippines/unemployment-rate (accessed 23 October 2020).
20. Personal interview with various heads of organizations.
21. The report of the Center for Migrant Advocacy – Philippines, submitted to the United Nations' Migrant Workers Convention in 2009, lists forty-four organizations that help promote migrants' welfare. See the complete report at https://www2.ohchr.org/english/bodies/cmw/docs/ngos/PMG_Philippines10.pdf.
22. See report of Chloe Frossart, "NGOs Defending Migrant Workers' Rights: Semi-union Organisations Contribute to the Regime's Dynamic Stability", translated by N. Jayaram, https://journals.openedition.org/chinaperspectives/5549.
23. Pia Ranada, "Duterte won't ban POGOs: 'We Need It'", *Rappler*, 4 September 2019, https://www.rappler.com/nation/duterte-will-not-ban-pogos.
24. Ralf Rivas, "POGO Revenues Online Gambling Contributes P551 Billion to Philippine Economy Yearly", *Rappler*, 17 September 2019, https://www.rappler.com/business/online-gamblingcontribution-philippine-economy-yearly.
25. Bernie Cahiles-Magkilat, "POGO Overtakes IT-BPM Office Space Takeup", Leechiu Property Consultants, 16 September 2019, https://leechiu.com/news_events/pogo-overtakes-it-bpm-officespace-takeup/; also in *Manila*

Bulletin, Business, 16 September 2019, https://mb.com.ph/2019/09/16/pogo-overtakes-it-bpm-office-space-takeup/.

26. Anti-Money Laundering Council, "Understanding the Internet-Based Casino Sector in the Philippines: A Risk Assessment", Republic of the Philippines Anti-Money Laundering Council, March 2020, http://www.amlc.gov.ph/images/PDFs/AMLC%20RISK%20ASSESSMENT%20ON%20INTERNETBASED%20CASINO%20SECTOR%20IN%20THE%20PHILIPPINES.doc.pdf (accessed 23 October 2020).
27. Aika Rey, "Drilon to Pagcor: 'Stupid Mindset' to Allow POGOs for Money", *Rappler*, Nation, 5 March 2020, https://www.rappler.com/nation/drilon-pagcor-stupid-mindset-allow-pogos-formoney.
28. Reynaldo G. Navales, "Senator Says Pogos Have Little Contributions to Philippine Economy", *SunStar Pampanga*, 2 July 2020, https://www.sunstar.com.ph/article/1862205/Pampanga/LocalNews/Senator-says-Pogos-have-little-contributions-to-Philippine-economy; Melissa Luz Lopez, "7-B Revenues Not Enough to Justify POGO Crimes in PH, Senators Say", *CNN Philippines*, 5 March 2020, https://cnnphilippines.com/news/2020/3/5/POGO-revenues-vs-crimes.html.
29. Ferdinand Patinio, "18 BI Personnel in 'Pastillas' Scam Sacked", Philippine News Agency, 20 February 2020, https://www.pna.gov.ph/articles/1094425.
30. "Hontiveros Uncovers Menu of Sex Services, Trafficked Women for Chinese POGO Workers", Senate of the Philippines, 28 January 2020, http://legacy.senate.gov.ph/press_release/2020/0128_hontiveros1.asp; "Senate Panel to Conduct Probe on POGO-Related Sex-Trafficking, Prostitution", *Manila Bulletin Online*, 23 February 2020, https://mb.com.ph/2020/02/23/senate-panel-to-conduct-probe-on-pogo-related-sex-trafficking-prostitution/.
31. Hannah Torregoza, "Hontiveros to NBI: Charge Masterminds of BI 'Pastillas' Scam", *Manila Bulletin Online*, 22 September 2020, https://mb.com.ph/2020/09/22/hontiveros-to-nbi-charge-masterminds-of-bi-pastillas-scam/.
32. Dennis Datu, "Mag-asawang Chinese nagbayad umano ng P800,000 para makakuha ng PH passport", ABS–CBN News, 17 September 2020, https://news.abs-cbn.com/news/09/17/20/mag-asawang-chinese-nagbayad-umano-ngp800000-para-makakuha-ng-ph-passport.
33. "Remarks by Chinese Embassy Spokesperson on Issues of Chinese Citizens Concerning Gambling in the Philippines", Embassy of the Peoples Republic of China in the Republic of the Philippines, 8 August 2019, http://ph.china-embassy.org/eng/sgfyrbt/t1687164.htm.
34. Ibid.
35. "Embassy Spokesperson Answers Reporters' Questions on the Cancellation of Passports of Chinese Employees of Philippine Internet Gaming Company", Embassy of the Peoples Republic of China in the Republic of the Philippines,

24 February 2020, http://ph.china-embassy.org/chn/sgdt/t1748597.htm; "Tai Han Was Kidnapped by a Gaming Company to Survive without Eating or Drinking for Two Days", *Shangbao*, 29 September 2020, http://www.shangbao.com.ph/fgyw/2020/09-29/96104.shtml; Christine O. Avendaño, "PH Envoy Says China Sanctions 'Likely' on Pogo Workers", *Inquirer.net*, 23 February 2020, https://newsinfo.inquirer.net/1232244/phenvoy-says-china-sanctions-likely-on-pogo-workers#ixzz6j8g8t6sF.
36. Dennis Datu, "Mag-asawang Chinese".
37. CNN Philippines Staff, "Poll Shows Filipinos Trust US, Australia over China", CNN Philippines, 19 July 2020, https://cnnphilippines.com/news/2020/7/19/sws-survey-trust-us-australia-china.html?fbclid=lwAR2http://www.sws.org.ph/swsmain/generalArtclSrchPage/?page=1&srchprm=CHINA&arttyp=&stdtrng=&endtrng=&swityp=.

9

New Transnational Chinese Migrants in an Evolving Malaysia

Danny Wong Tze Ken

In 1974, during the height of the Cold War, the Malaysian Prime Minister, Tun Abdul Razak, visited Beijing, long considered a suspect country as a result of the two countries' opposing ideological inclination, and thus belonging to different camps in the contestation for influence of the opposing blocs of countries. Little could Razak imagine that the bilateral relationship between the two countries would grow to a stage of closeness and interdependency that manifested over the past decade. During the past decade, China has grown to be Malaysia's largest trading partner, and one of the principal contributors of direct foreign investment. These developments had inevitably started a new development in the bilateral relationship; namely, the influx of Chinese nationals to Malaysia. This development is interesting considering the historical background of the relations—from that of massive immigration of Chinese into the territories that formed present-day Malaysia.[1] Chinese migration then came to a standstill with the taking over of China by the Chinese Communist Party as Malaya—and later, Malaysia—was fighting an armed insurgency led by the Malayan Communist Party, which was supported by the Chinese.

This resumption of Chinese nationals moving to Malaysia has created some ripples, not least among the authorities but also among the public at large.

The rise of the People's Republic of China that was precipitated by the introduction of the Open Door and Reformation policies since 1978 saw China transform itself from a backward, ideologically dominated country to a modern and economically powerful nation. This transformation process has also undergone changes from a gradual and experimental stage in the 1980s and 1990s to full-blown economic development that saw the country rising to be the fastest growing economy in the world. This transformation also brought massive changes to Chinese business enterprises from the state-owned enterprises that were not performing in line with the changing times to be the multinational corporate bodies that helped to spearhead stronger economic performance for China. In 2010, the country overtook Japan as the second-largest economy in the world. The introduction of the Belt and Road Initiative (BRI) in 2013 further strengthened the development of the Chinese economy and provided impetus for stronger economic performance.

The spectacular economic achievements attained by China, especially in the past two decades, have resulted in an increase in the number of arrivals of Chinese nationals into Malaysia. They have been broadly divided into four groups, including, first, the employees of Chinese enterprises and multinational corporations in Malaysia. Chinese students who came to Malaysia for their tertiary education made up the second group. The third group of Chinese are those who have decided to take up residence in Malaysia due to the attractive 'Malaysia as Second Home' project. The last group of Chinese nationals who have arrived in large number in Malaysia are the Hui, or Chinese Muslims, whose presence in Malaysia is considered to be special.

This chapter will look into the circumstances that led to the surge in Chinese nationals arriving in Malaysia over the last twenty years and how it had impacted the country both in terms of socio-economic development and perhaps even in the political sphere. The chapter argues that the influx of Chinese nationals has been a double-edged sword. On the one hand, they brought about many positive developments to economic development in the tin industry, but on the other hand, this translated into fear of the country being swamped by the Chinese. This fear also translated into influences on the results of the last general elections in 2018. The chapter argues that, while there may be similar experiences, as in the case of other Southeast

Asian countries, including Thailand and Singapore, the Malaysian case could offer some slightly different perspectives that could help in further understanding the transnational Chinese diaspora experience in Southeast Asia. The chapter will also look at how Malaysia handles or copes with this group of new Chinese nationals.

The Chinese in Malaysia

The territories that make up Malaysia consist of the Malay Peninsula, which has eleven states and a federal territory, and the Eastern Malaysian states of Sabah and Sarawak, situated on the island of Borneo. These states, or their earlier entities, were already in contact with China in the distant past. Earlier visitors from the first millennium CE left behind no evidence, but Chinese presence became common after the Song Dynasty in China. Contacts between the two peoples intensified during the Age of the Ming voyages, where Chinese traders and seamen frequented the land as part of their voyages. Many also decided to stay and intermarried with local women, and this gave rise to the emergence of a hybrid community of Baba and Nyonya and other Sino-Native communities.[2]

Today, the ethnic Chinese in Malaysia number seven million and constitutes 23 per cent of the total population, making it a sizeable minority whose position cannot be ignored. Chinese emigration basically ended in the early 1950s, with some exceptions, including those who emigrated from Hong Kong or Indonesian Borneo (Kalimantan). Those who arrived, integrated and became part of the Malaysian citizenry. Even though the community was an immigrant one, its members since the country's independence have become Malaysian citizens and contributed towards the nation-building process of the country. The situation in Malaysia is not unlike other parts of Southeast Asia where the Chinese immigrants settled into the national lives of the respective nation, and they have been treated with varying degrees of acceptance and tolerance by the indigenous communities.[3]

The Malaysian experience is well-documented and well-researched.[4] The bulk of the Chinese population trace their origins to the massive migration of Chinese to the rest of the world since the mid-nineteenth century. These Chinese left China for various reasons. Many went out in search of greener pastures trying to escape the harsh life in China. In Malaysia, many of the Chinese joined the tin- or gold-mining industries, while others worked for the many plantation estates that sprang up for various crops, including pepper and gambier, coffee, tobacco and, later, rubber.

The Chinese in Malaysia also organized themselves in different associations and societies. Most of them identified themselves based on their place of origin, with counties or prefectures serving this basis. This form of identification, coupled with the manner the British set the population census category, which they called *dialect*, gave the Chinese in Malaysia their form of identification. Thus, they were organized largely based on these two related aspects of identification. The Chinese also organized themselves based on dialect or places of origin. Apart from the dialect associations, the Chinese businessmen organized their own chambers of commerce and trade organizations. The chambers remained influential throughout their existence and, in many ways, represented the Chinese community. This was especially true during the colonial era, when there were no Chinese political parties. The coming of independence saw the leadership role of the chambers somewhat diminished, giving way to leaders who came via the political parties.

In politics, the Chinese initially had their allegiance to China, taking part in the revolution against the Manchu Qing Dynasty. During the republican period, the Chinese government that was based in Nanjing introduced a national election, which also included Chinese who were residing overseas, to cast their votes or to stand for elections to the National Assembly. For these, elections were held and representatives were chosen. This practice was discontinued after the Nanjing Government fell to the communist-led government of the People's Republic of China in 1949. The action, in many ways, directed the Chinese allegiance to China. This was to change in the 1950s following the outbreak of the Emergency, when the ethnic-Chinese-dominated Malayan Communist Party launched an armed insurrection against British rule. Contacts with communist China were severed and immigration from China came to a standstill. As the Malayan Communist Party was supported by the Chinese Communist Party in China, no bilateral relations were established, even after Malaya became independent, and this continued even after the establishment of Malaysia. During this lull in bilateral relations, some trading activities went on between Malaysia and China, mainly through Hong Kong. And throughout this time, Taiwan was widely accepted in Malaysia as the other China.

The Chinese in Malaysia took active part in the political lives of the country, starting with the attempts to form political alliances in the 1950s, and later, during the negotiation for independence from British colonial rule.

Thus, in the post-independence years, Chinese were well-represented in the political arena, including appointments to strategic ministerial positions such as finance minister and chief minister of at least two states. The coalition government of, first, the Alliance Party (made up of the Malay-dominated UMNO, Chinese MCA and MIC of the Indian community) was later expanded into the Barisan National (National Front) coalition in the aftermath of the May 1969 racial riot and the post-1974 national elections. Chinese political participation, however, while not suffering much in terms of numbers, was increasingly seen as diminishing in influence and stature, especially within the government coalition. The two Chinese-dominated parties of MCA and Gerakan were seen as mainly playing bridesmaids to the Malay-dominated UMNO. The introduction of the New Economic Policy (1971) in the aftermath of the May 1969 racial riot was seen as further eroding the Chinese political and economic position in the country.[5]

Malaysia and the People's Republic of China established diplomatic relations following the visit of the Malaysian Prime Minister, Tun Abdul Razak, to China in May 1974. This paved the way for the thawing of bilateral relations, which had thus far been conditioned largely by the Cold War. This led to the establishment of diplomatic representations in 1978 and an increase in bilateral trade. Trading activity picked up after Malaysian Prime Minister Mahathir Mohammad's visit to China in 1985. The improvement in bilateral relations was also encouraged by the end of the armed insurrection by the Malaysian Communist Party in 1989. This opened up more bilateral ties, including people-to-people visits. But, despite all these developments, bilateral relations were still slow. It took some structural changes in China to effect greater ties between the two countries. Chinese companies began to enter the country, initially focusing on the trading of commodities and goods. Later, Chinese companies began to seek out partners for joint-venture projects, hence initiating an influx of Chinese nationals into the country.

Rise of China and New Chinese Nationals in Malaysia

The initial presence of these new Chinese nationals in Malaysia came via two sources. The first were the employees of the early state-owned enterprises (SOEs) operating in Malaysia. They began to find their way into Malaysia in the early 2000s. Many were keen to peddle their wares in Malaysia, while others were focusing on establishing joint-venture activities. This was the initial period of Chinese firms making forays into Malaysia. Trading activities became the primary focus, thus the numbers of Chinese nationals were mainly transient and would not stay on for long. There is no clear indication of their numbers, but it was certain that they were few and far between. Most of those who stayed for a longer duration in the country belonged to those Chinese SOEs that started branches in the country. Many of them were interested in joint-ventures with Malaysian firms. Some went into light industry of manufacturing. It must be noted that during this time of operation, most of the Chinese firms had worked with local ethnic Chinese firms in the belief that these local ethnic Chinese firms would provide them with local knowledge—often to serve as intermediaries between the Chinese companies and government-linked companies or government agencies. This was a role played by the ethnic Chinese community in Malaysia for the initial period of the existence of Chinese firms and, hence, Chinese nationals in the country. This role would change later with more Chinese companies coming into the country, especially after the introduction of the BRI in 2013.

Another group of Chinese nationals who have made their ways to Malaysia were the students who came to Malaysia for their tertiary education. Since the introduction of the modernization and reform programme in 1978, Chinese students have been going abroad in large numbers. The move coincided with the opening of the International Islamic University of Malaysia, which was Malaysia's first international university. Many of the Muslim students from China found their way to Malaysia to join the university. At this time, the number of students was still very small, but it was a good beginning.

The arrivals of these new Chinese to the region and to Malaysia could be broadly divided into two phases: before and after the introduction of the BRI in 2013.[6] Prior to 2013, the new Chinese migrants were mainly represented by employees of state-owned enterprises who came out to prospective countries in search of partnerships and joint-venture projects. There were also students at the tertiary level coming out to acquire much-needed qualifications and skills. Many of these early Chinese officials chose to work with the ethnic Chinese community in the country in order to penetrate the local market, including in negotiating with the government. The number of this group of migrants was small and they were quite transient in nature. This situation began to change with the introduction of the BRI in 2013.

The BRI was introduced by President Xi Jinping in 2013 as a way of enhancing mutual development through stronger connectivity with the hope of achieving a common destiny. It involved the establishment of strong connectivity in joint-development projects between Chinese enterprises with local partners from partner countries. Following the launch of the BRI, more Chinese companies have come to Malaysia to set up branches focusing on communication and infrastructure. Trade volume between Malaysia and China also increased year by year. According to data provided by the Chinese Embassy in Malaysia, by 2019 China had been Malaysia's largest trading partner for eleven consecutive years. Trade volume between Malaysia and China accounted for 17.2 per cent of Malaysia's total trade volume—an increase of 0.2 per cent compared to 2018.

For many years, China's foreign direct investment (FDI) in Malaysia was trailing other countries. Following the introduction of the BRI, there began a proliferation of Chinese companies into Malaysia. This resulted in Chinese investment in the country rising steadily. In 2010, Chinese investment in Malaysia began to rise from RM920 million (or 0.9 per cent) of Malaysia's FDI flows in 2010 to RM6.2 billion or 9.0 per cent in 2017. The amount has continued to rise since then. What is interesting is the sharp rise of this investment from a mere 2.0 to 2.2 per cent in 2012–14 to suddenly rise to 3.0 per cent in 2015, to 6.0 per cent in 2016 and then to 9.0 per cent in 2017.[7]

In 2019, Malaysia came in fourth in ASEAN with the largest Chinese FDI, with a total of $7.92 billion. By comparison, Chinese investments in Singapore and Indonesia totalled at $52.64 billion and $15.13 billion respectively. The lack of FDI from China also means that there were less people-to-people connections as well as arrivals of Chinese nationals in the country.[8]

It is evident that the sharp rise in China's FDI is evident as a result of the introduction of the BRI in 2013. With its introduction, it changed the pattern and nature of investments significantly. Investments were no longer confined to state-owned enterprises and were no longer contended with joint-venture projects. The new firms were into mega-size infrastructure development projects, especially pertaining to communication (land, sea, air and telecommunications), energy-related development projects, and finance and banking, as well as accommodation and support services. Hence, mega projects such as the Kuantan–Qingzhou Industrial Parks, East Coast Rail Link, Second Penang Bridge, and the Mass Rapid Transit System in Klang Valley were initiated. And to facilitate the flow of funds and services, major banks from China were invited to open branches in the country. These including Bank of China, Industrial and Commercial Bank of China (ICBC), and Asian Infrastructure Investment Bank (AIIB).

Table 9.1 details the main infrastructure construction projects of Chinese companies in Malaysia as of 2019.

It is clear that since the introduction of the BRI, the number of new Chinese nationals who entered Malaysia has risen rapidly. The new arrivals are different from those who came here earlier.

The New Chinese Nationals in Malaysia

The increase of Chinese companies operating in Malaysia since the introduction of the BRI have brought about an increase in the number of Chinese nationals into the country. However, unlike the pre-2013 years, where the numbers were small and were confined mainly to employees of state-owned enterprises, the circumstances around the new Chinese nationals are different from those of their predecessors. First, there was a sharp increase in the numbers of new arrivals. Second, the new arrivals were no longer confined to the major cities like Kuala Lumpur and Penang. Instead, they are found all over Malaysia, as the new investments are found in almost every state in the country. Third, there are also private enterprises that are not linked to the state; individual businessmen who arrived in the country in search of opportunities. Many were happy to expand their operations in Malaysia. Finally, these new arrivals tend to stay longer. Many also made the decision to arrive with their families and chose to invest privately in the country by sending their children to schools in Malaysia and to purchase private properties as a means of investment.

In this sense, the image conjured by the new migrants is different from those who came in the pre-2013 period. The new Chinese nationals are more confident, posses capital and are more informed. They are also more composed and efficient, as many are the products of top schools in China, and some also came back with overseas education. Having learned from the experience of those who came in the pre-2013 era, they were able to bypass the old migrants (local ethnic Chinese) as conduits or intermediaries in their dealings with the Malaysian state, as well as the government-linked companies. Another new dimension in the new arrivals who came after 2013 is the exponential increase of Chinese students coming to study in Malaysia.

TABLE 9.1
Major Projects by Chinese Companies in Malaysia (as of 2019)

No.	Project Name	Contractor
1	Kuala Lumpur Signature Tower	China State Construction Engineering (Malaysia) Sdn Bhd
2	The Second Cross-Sea Bridge in Penang	CHEC Construction (M) Sdn Bhd
3	Encore Malacca Theater	China Construction Yangtze River (M) Sdn Bhd
4	The CRRC ASEAN Manufacturing Center	CRRC rolling stock center (M) Sdn Bhd
5	Xinyi Group Malaysia Industrial Park	Xinyi Energy Smart (M) Sdn Bhd
6	Kuala Lumpur PANTAI 2 sewage treatment plant	Beijing Enterprises Water Group (M) Sdn Bhd
7	Klang Valley's Second Mass Rapid Transit	China Communication Construction Company (M) Sdn Bhd
8	The Ampang Light Rail Line Extension Project	CHEC Construction (M) Sdn Bhd
9	The Kuala Ketil solar photovoltaic power station in Kedah	CGN Edra Power Group
10	The Bakun Hydropower Station in Sarawak	Sinohydro Corporation (M) Sdn Bhd
11	The Malaysian East Coast Rail Link Project	China Communication Construction Company (M) Sdn Bhd
12	The railway upgrade project initiated by the Sabah State Government in 2005	China Railway Engineering Corporation (M) Sdn Bhd
13	Petroleum National Berhad (Petronas) Automated Storage and Retrieval System (ASRS) Projet	Sinopec Engineering (Group) Co. Ltd, Sinopec Shanghai Engineering Co. Ltd, Sinopec Engineering Group Malaysia Sdn Bhd
14	The 3.5 million tons Steel project at Malaysia–China Kuantan Industrial park	MCC Overseas (M) Sdn Bhd
15	The Pulai River Bridge Project	CHEC Construction (M) Sdn Bhd
16	Xiamen University Malaysia	Sinohydro Corporation Limited
17	SANY IBS (Industrialized Building System) factory in Kijal	SANY International Developing (M) Sdn Bhd
18	The Gemas–Johor Baru electrified double-track project	CRCC Malaysia Berhad

Source: China Enterprises Association in Malaysia, 2019: China–Malaysia 45th Anniversary of The Establishment of Diplomatic Relations Photo Album, pp. 21–30.

The introduction of the BRI in 2013 marks a turning point in the transnational experience of new Chinese nationals in Malaysia (as well as other parts of Southeast Asia). It is estimated that there are now between 120,000 and 150,000 Chinese nationals residing in Malaysia. They are broadly divided into the following four categories: students, workers, those who participated in the "Malaysia as My Second Home Scheme", and the Muslim Chinese.

a) Students

In 2006, the Malaysian Government introduced a plan to turn Malaysia into a major education hub in Southeast Asia. This was partly to reduce the outflow of revenue abroad by the opening of more universities and institutions of higher learning. It was also intended to generate revenue by attracting international students to study in Malaysia. It began to attract a large number of international students to take up places at the various institutions of higher learning in the country. From a negligible number when it started in the mid-2000s, the number has risen in 2016 to more than 130,000. Of these, students from China numbered 10,899, making up about 10 per cent of the total international student population. By 2017, the percentage of Chinese students in Malaysia went up to around 15,000, accounting for 14.85 per cent of total international students in Malaysia.[9]

The Chinese students are enrolled in both public and private universities. There were two main reasons behind the impetus for Chinese students choosing Malaysia as a destination for tertiary education. The first is the push factor in China, where tough competition for places in Chinese universities has encouraged many to seek their higher education abroad. Second, Malaysian universities are well-run and accessible. This encouraged many Chinese students to consider acquiring their degrees in Malaysia. The cost of tertiary education in Malaysia is also considered affordable, and so is the cost of living. The high quality of Malaysian universities, especially the fairly good position of the public universities in world university rankings, prompted many to consider coming to Malaysia for their education.

In 2014, the Xiamen University Malaysian branch campus was opened. This has greatly increased the number of Chinese students studying in Malaysia. The campus now boasts a total of 5,800 enrolments, with about

TABLE 9.2
Total Number of International Students by Nationality, 2017

No.	Country	Total
1	Bangladesh	30,525
2	China	14,854
3	Nigeria	13,529
4	Indonesia	9,762
5	Yemen	6,748
6	Pakistan	6,033
7	Libya	3,317
8	Iraq	3,257
9	Sudan	3,104
10	Iran	3,068
11	Others	40,163
	Total	133,860

Source: Ministry of Education, 2017.

two-thirds of the students being Chinese nationals.[10] The remainder of the students came mainly from Malaysia and other countries. There are also branches of other reputable universities operating in Malaysia, making the country attractive to Chinese and international students. These branches include Monash University, Wollongong University, Swinburne University, Nottingham University, and Reading University.

A China–Malaysia Students and Alumni Association was started in 2014, initiated first by a group of students who were doing their postgraduate studies in the University of Malaya. The association had by 2015 gained recognition from the Embassy of the Peoples' Republic of China in Kuala Lumpur as one of its outreach and contact channels. Thus, branches of the association were established in different institutions of higher learning and have served as the liaison points for social events and also as a minor mutual assistance channel.[11] The association also organized activities to promote Malaysia as a destination for higher education for Chinese students.

The influx of Chinese students to Malaysia is no longer limited to those who came to study at the tertiary level. Instead, given the increase in the number of Chinese workers and their families in the country, there is also an increasing number of high schools and primary schools.

b) Chinese Workers in Malaysia

The number of Chinese workers in Malaysia grew in correspondence to the rise in the number of Chinese companies that operate in the country. Earlier arrivals were mainly employees of state-owned enterprises. Their numbers were small and many were groping their way through the complex business conditions of Malaysia, especially in dealing effectively with Malaysian government-linked companies (GLC). But their numbers soon increased sharply after the introduction of the BRI in 2013. With the increase in Chinese investments through the initiation of new mega-sized projects, the number of Chinese workers in Malaysia has also increased.

It must be stressed that the composition of Chinese workers in Malaysia differed sharply from other countries. Most of those countries despatched their workers to serve as unskilled labour, whereas Chinese workers, after an initial stage of finding their way, were able to focus on having more workers in the white-collar sector who were mainly professionals.

When Chinese companies started to operate in Malaysia, they began to bring in Chinese workers. This was especially true in the construction sector. Previously, the construction sector in Malaysia had relied on other

TABLE 9.3
Number of Foreign Workers in Malaysia, 2017

No.	Country	Total
1	Indonesia	728,870
2	Nepal	405,898
3	Bangladesh	221,089
4	Myanmar	127,705
5	India	114,455
6	Pakistan	59,281
7	Philippines	56,153
8	Vietnam	29,039
9	China	15,399
10	Thailand	12,603
11	Sri Lanka	5,964
12	Cambodia	5,103
13	Laos	39

Source: Ministry of Home Affairs, Malaysia, 2018.

foreign workers and a negligible number of locals as unskilled workers. Chinese companies however, preferred their own workers and their own utility services, including cooks from China, and having the ingredients for their food/diet being supplied from China—by Chinese companies. This method of operation had strong implications for the local operators. In the first instance, the Chinese companies preferred to use their own labour force, have minimized the many hitches faced by local companies who were dependent on foreign workers. The Chinese companies became more efficient and could complete their tasks in shorter times.

With such efficiencies, Chinese companies are now posing a threat to local companies competing for these job in the market. Second, by relying entirely on their own labour force, complemented by its own eco-system (food, utilities, etc.), there is no spill-over effect on the local suppliers. This became a sore point in working relations between Chinese firms and local markets, especially in the case of labour. In fact, this issue emerged as a factor in accusations against the former Malaysian government, who, in their all-out effort to attract Chinese investments, have given way to Chinese companies to operate relying solely on Chinese workers. This became an issue during the 14th general elections. It was used by the opposition party to discredit the then Malaysian government for being overly dependent on Chinese investments.

Chinese Companies in Malaysia are involved in the following industries: tourism, media, IT, trading, hostel management, mining, construction, telecommunications, education, hardware, retail, real estate, logistics, exhibitions, manufacturing, healthcare, therapy, oil and gas, medical, energy, accountancy and tax, law, machinery, printing and publishing, culture and events, safety equipment, services, AI and robotics, sound and lighting, technology, food and beverages, commodities inspection, the financial sector, rubber, textile, and electronic commerce.[12]

As many of the Chinese companies operating in Malaysia had initially started as joint-ventures, it was understood that the Chinese partners would work with their local partners and that there would be jobs available for the locals. As more and more Chinese multinational companies began operations in Malaysia, the number of Chinese nationals acting in senior and executive levels also increased. This gave rise to the same question as to whether these companies would expand their employment targets to bring in more local Malaysians to work in their establishments.

c) Participants of the Malaysia My Second Home Programme (MM2H)

As a way to attract investments and to promote tourism, the Malaysian Government introduced the International Residency Scheme/Migration Programmes in 1987, from which the Malaysia My Second Home (MM2H) Programme had developed. The idea was to attract wealthy senior foreign nationals to live in Malaysia. The programme was rebranded and revamped in 2002 to open up to anyone regardless of age. In 2006 it was placed under the purview of the Ministry of Tourism, where a one-stop centre was established to administer the programme.

The programme allowed the participants to have ten years of residency in the country through the investment of a certain amount and to invest in a property. For Chinese nationals, the condition was for the potential resident to invest RMB1 million, out of which RMB650,000 would be spent on investing in a property and with RMB100,000 for living expenses.[13] Many Chinese took the opportunity to invest in a property and were granted the opportunity to stay, but on a short-term basis, as there was no intention on the part of the Malaysian government to grant citizenship to those who joined the programme, though permanent resident status is allowed. This was in line with sentiments over ethnic sensitivity. From 2002 to 2017, the programme approved a total of 35,821 applications, and out of that, 9,902 of them are Chinese nationals. This made the Chinese the largest group in the programme.[14] This was a great increase from the initial 154 Chinese participants in 2010. It reflected a change of economic conditions in China, where massive transformation has allowed many to be able to afford having a second home abroad. This coincided with the Malaysian government's seriousness in making the programme work. Indeed, for a long time Malaysia was a favourite destination in Southeast Asia for retirees from abroad to settle.

The initial stage of the programme attracted many Chinese retirees, as had originally been envisaged. Later, the programme began to attract younger Chinese nationals who were still active in their vocations and businesses but were keen to have a long-term presence in Malaysia. According to one Ms Jing Baobao, she chose Penang as the base of her family's MM2H after a short visit to the state. The idea was to allow her daughter, a junior high school student, to have a less stressful learning environment and to gain access to top schools in the world without having to go through the highly pressurized and extremely stressful Gaokao (University Entrance Examination). The family had originally planned on heading for Melbourne in Australia, but they decided to stay in Penang after the visit.[15] In this sense, Ms Jing has become what is now commonly known as Peidu Mama (Mother Who Accompanies Children for Education). Jing Baobao is not alone. Another Peidu Mama, Ms BW, also brought her daughter to settle in Penang under the MM2H Programme. Her daughter was still in pre-school when they made the decision. The idea was quite similar to that of Jing Baobao, to provide a conducive environment for her daughter to grow up. Ms BW's husband remained in Shanghai, working for a major corporation, but he would visit the family in Penang whenever possible. Ms BW was trying to make the best out of her role as a Peidu Mama by engaging in a small bookstore business, catering for her fellow Peidu Mamas.[16]

Another Chinese national who was attracted by the programme is Paul Yang Qian, who has been in Malaysia since 2009. Both his children were born in Malaysia. He joined the MM2H Programme and is now staying in the high-end Kuala Lumpur suburb of Mont Kiara. He travels between his hometown in Wuhan and Malaysia, spending several months at both places each year. His wife stays in Malaysia with the children. According to Yang, before he made his move, his father had moved to Malaysia. Yang found life in Malaysia agreeable and comfortable: "It is easy to join the culture here, and not feel like a total outsider. The different races get on well, and it's quite near China. The education is good, and the country maintains its traditional face while also experiencing development." He also considers the weather another reason for him to live in Malaysia: "Back home the seasons (weather) are very dramatic with extremely hot summers and very cold winters. Malaysians are very friendly. I feel this is a good place for my next generation."[17]

Part of the success of this programme among the Chinese nationals is the complimentary role played by Chinese investments in Malaysia, both in terms of the workers brought in by the various Chinese companies who were lured by the beauty and affordable lifestyle of Malaysia, and thus decided to partake in the scheme. The other major complimentary factor has been the direct Chinese investment projects, such as the $100 billion Forest City project, which is a mixed development project by Country Garden Holdings, which built a massive city out of nowhere in Johor, with the purpose of attracting Chinese nationals to invest in the country. The

TABLE 9.4
Total Number of Residents under the MM2H by Country, 2017

Country	Total
China	9,902 (27.6%)
Japan	4,372
Bangladesh	3,746
United Kingdom	2,499
South Korea	1,514
Iran	1,351
Singapore	1,346
Taiwan	1,175
South Korea	1,271
Pakistan	1,992
India	1,937
112 other countries	7,891 (22.0%)

Source: http://www.mm2h.gov.my.

project, the largest overseas project by a Chinese property developer in the world, has 42 per cent of its equity held by Malaysians, including the Sultan of Johor.[18] The project was heavily promoted in the national mass media in China, and was enormously popular. It promotes the Forest City as the ideal destination to invest for retirees, especially after working so hard throughout their working lives.

For Chinese nationals, several reasons were given as determining factors in their choice of Malaysia as their destination for a second home. The first is good quality of life: less competitive environment compared to China; friendly people; affordable living expenses and tuition fees; cultural and language proximity—able to communicate in Chinese and Chinese dialects. For Chinese Muslims, religion and the halal environment are the main reason. In terms of location, Malaysia is nearer to China than Western countries that have a similar quality of life and education. And, finally, for some workers who were assigned to work in Malaysia for a period of time, it is hard for them to cope with changes back in China when they return. Many decided to move their family to settle down in Malaysia while continuing to work in China-invested companies in Malaysia, or started their own businesses.[19]

It must be emphasized that despite the attractiveness of MM2H and its popularity among the Chinese, they also understood that what was granted by the programme was a short-term residency of ten years, and of course renewable subject to conditions. There is no promise of granting permanent residency nor any prospect for citizenship, as might be possible elsewhere. The project did not result in an immigration experience due to the sensitivity of race politics and concerns with racial imbalance. Malaysia is not an immigrant-receiving country for Chinese emigrating abroad, rather it represents more of short-term stay, depending on the type of occupation—whether they be students or workers/employees of Chinese firms—and perhaps should be more accurately known as sojourners.

Recent events, however, especially after the imposition of restrictive measures by the Chinese government in 2017 restricting Chinese nationals from buying property or spending more than $50,000 a year outside of China, have dampened the prospects of further Chinese investments in property developments like the Forest City. Many Chinese nationals who are owners of units in the property decided to sell off their units, and many at terrible losses. The new Malaysian government under Mahathir Mohammad, who was highly critical of the project and hit out at it during the 2018 general elections, and who had barred foreigners from buying into the Forest City, created uncertainties. All these issues were to have severe implication on the participation of Chinese nationals in the MM2H programme.

Despite all these uncertainties, including the temporary suspension of the programme in October 2020, the MM2H programme is still an important programme to attract Chinese nationals to settle in the country. The resumption of the programme, with new features and criteria, will probably attract further participation from Chinese nationals, but its success will depend heavily on how attractive the new criteria are and the easing of capital controls in China for external spending. The new criteria published in September 2021 are definitely more restrictive and challenging for qualification.[20]

d) The Hui in Malaysia

The notion of Chinese nationals in Malaysia took on a new dimension with the arrivals of Chinese Muslims from China in significantly noticeable numbers since the 1980s. Their numbers began to rise in the late 1990s and early 2000. By 2015, their presence was widely accepted as part of the Chinese Transnational experience, though the circumstances of their arrivals could differ significantly from other Chinese Transnational diasporas. One important dimension is the religion factor, which was basically absent from the experience of their Han Chinese counterparts. More recently, Ngeow and Ma[21] provided some very interesting perspectives on the Hui in Malaysia and the background to their emigration to Malaysia and how pockets of communities of the Hui also emerged. They were well-received by the Malays as they share the same religion. However, it is unclear if they would be welcome to stay on permanently in the country.

It is clear that the Hui group (and Uighur, Ningxia and Dongxia, etc.) take advantage of Malaysia's Islam fraternity by coming to Malaysia first as students and later as businessmen or workers. The International Islamic University of Malaya (IIUM), supported by the Organisation of Islamic Cooperation (OIC), became a favourite institution of higher learning for Hui students, though they are also found in other universities, both public and private.

There has been a growing number of religiously motivated and economically driven Hui migrants since 2000. They come to Malaysia to learn about Islam, to act as an imam (religious leader) to the Chinese Muslims or simply to live in a Muslim-majority environment, as well as to seek job opportunities or expand their business networks. The first arrivals took place during the 1980s when a small group of Hui students were sent to study in the many Islamic religious institutions of learning. Later, after the establishment of the International Islamic University (IIUM), many of the Hui students were enrolled in this university.

The recent mushrooming of Hui-established restaurants, Chinese halal markets and travel agencies, as well as the visibility of Hui imams, are clear evidence of their presence, as well as their ability to adapt to the Malaysian environment. Some Hui students confessed that living as a Muslim in China was easier as apart from observing the prohibition against consuming pork there were few other rules and regulations that manifest in the Muslim way of life. This is different in Malaysia, where adherence to Islam is a way of life, thus providing impetus for a stricter observation of the religion.[22]

There are no official figures of Hui migrants in Malaysia. It is estimated that there are about 2,000 Hui students studying in Malaysia and about 100 Hui families living there, most of whom would have first come as students and later engaged in business activities. Many Hui students in Malaysia were worried they might be stigmatized by their ethnicity.[23]

It is worth noting that although the Chinese Muslim and non-Muslim communities in Malaysia are also from China, their lifestyles, social networks and business networks are very different and they have little interaction with each other. There is more interaction and a closer relationship between Chinese Muslims and Malays, which are obviously inseparable by their shared religious identity.

More recently, part of the Chinese Muslim community, including some Uighur, began to use Malaysia as a transit point to eventually move to Turkey—a common route also allegedly taken by Uighur Muslim separatists. This development has become a point of contention between the Uighur on the one side and the Malaysian and Chinese governments on the other. In 2017, the then Deputy Prime Minister of Malaysia, Zahid Hamidi, announced that the Malaysian government had since 2012 repatriated fifty-nine alleged Uighur militants or separatists to China.[24] The revelation caused an uproar among the Uighur and human rights NGOs (non-government organizations) as it was likely that those who were repatriated would inevitably be arrested and sent to prison. The move at that point, however, would definitely win the friendship of China, which was investing heavily in Malaysia.

The Malaysian government had a change of plan in October 2018 when eleven Uighurs who had escaped from Thai prisons landed in Malaysia. Instead of repatriating them to China, the newly elected Malaysian government, led by Prime Minister Mahathir Mohamad, decided to send them to Turkey, the ultimate destination desired by the Uighur escapees. The decision was said to be defying the Chinese at a time when relations were at a low point since the Mahathir-led coalition had swept to power in the May 2018 general election.[25] Even though the Mahathir government fell in 2020, the policy of not repatriating the Uighur to China seemed to have remained in force as late as November 2020.[26]

Concluding Remarks

This chapter addresses a new phenomenon known as the arrivals of Chinese nationals in Malaysia and Southeast Asia. This new transnational experience by the Chinese began as part of the Open Door and Modernization Policy introduced in 1978. The initial pre-BRI period did not see an immediate increase in the number of Chinese nationals coming to Malaysia. This changed with the introduction of the BRI in 2013, and the number of new Chinese nationals arriving in the country, either as businessmen, workers, students or people who decided to take up residency in Malaysia, have increased at an unprecedented rate. This brought about a possible new experience, which this chapter has tried to address.

The experience of the new Chinese nationals in Malaysia is definitely different from the traditional ideas of diasporas and migration. If, in the past, the experience would involve acculturation, assimilation or multiculturalism, these terms are quite inadequate for understanding the new phenomenon such as "circulatory mobility, migrants' constant contacts with the sending country societies, de-territorialized imagination of ethnic community, cultural reproduction and hybridity reinforced by constant cross-border flows of symbols and value".[27] From the outset, the current transnational Chinese diaspora experience may seem to be a later wave of Chinese emigrating to the region including Malaysia. However, a closer examination presented a scenario quite unlike the experience of the earlier Chinese who emigrated to Malaysia and other parts of Southeast Asia. One glaring difference is that in Malaysia, the new Chinese nationals were not given the option of remaining in the country permanently as citizens.

Notes

1. The Federation of Malaysia that was established on 16 September 1963 was originally made up of eleven states on the Malay Peninsula, Singapore, Sabah (formerly known as North Borneo) and Sarawak. Earlier, the Federation of Malaya consisting of the eleven states on the Peninsula was proclaimed on 31 August 1957.
2. See Felix Chia, *The Babas* (Singapore: Landmark Books, 2015); and Danny Wong Tze Ken, "A Hybrid Community in East Malaysia: The Sino-Kadazans of Sabah and their Search for Identity", *Archipel* 84 (2012): 107–27.
3. See Wang Gungwu, *The Chinese Overseas: From Earthbound Chinese to the Quest for Autonomy* (Cambridge, Massachusetts: Harvard University Press, 2000), pp. 88–92.
4. Victor Purcell, *The Chinese in Malaya* (London: Oxford University Press, 1958); Lee Kam Hing and Tan Chee Beng, eds. *The Chinese in Malaysia* (Kuala Lumpur: Oxford University Press, 2000). See also Lee Hock Guan and Leo Suryadinata, eds., *Malaysian Chinese: Recent Development and Prospects* (Singapore: Institute of Southeast Asian Studies, 2012).
5. Gordon Means, *Malaysian Politics* (Kuala Lumpur: Oxford University Press, 1970); and Gordon Means, *Malaysian Politics: The Second Generation* (Kuala Lumpur: Oxford University Press, 1991).
6. For a study of the BRI, see Wang Yiwei, *The Belt and Road Initiative: What Will China Offer the World in Its Rise* (Beijing: New World Press, 2016).

7. Bank Negara Malaysia as cited in "China's Investment in Malaysia: Perceptions, Issues and Prescriptions", a report by Social Economic Research Centre (SERC), Associated Chinese Chamber of Commerce and Industry Malaysia, 2017, p. 13.
8. Official website of Ministry of Commerce of the People's Republic of China. http://images.mofcom.gov.cn/hzs/202010/20201029172027652.pdf (accessed 7 March 2022).
9. Ministry of Higher Education Malaysia.
10. "Xianmen University Malaysia Campus", Edufair, https://edufair.fsi.com.my/xmumalaysia (November 2021).
11. Interview with Zhang Runxian, President of the China–Malaysia Students and Alumni Association, PhD Student at University of Malaya, and businessman, 31 January 2019.
12. China Enterprises Association in Malaysia and China Entrepreneurs Association in Malaysia.
13. For the latest requirements, see Ministry of Tourism, Malaysia webpage, http://www.mm2h.gov.my.
14. See Ministry of Tourism, Malaysia webpage, http://www.mm2h.gov.my (accessed 7 March 2022).
15. Interview with Jing Baobao, verbal and correspondence.
16. Interview with Ms BW.
17. "The 3rd Wave of Chinese Migrants: Rich and Happy", *Free Malaysia Today*, 27 March 2017.
18. *Berita Harian*, 24 November 2017.
19. *New Straits Times*, 13 July 2017.
20. New Rules for MM2H Programme. https://www.mm2h.com/new-rules-2021/ (accessed November 2021).
21. Ngeow Chow Bing and Ma Hailong, "More Islamic, No Less Chinese: Explorations into the Overseas Chinese Muslim Identities in Malaysia", *Ethnic and Racial Studies* 39 (2016): 12, 2108–28.
22. Interview with Ma Ying, PhD Student at University of Malaya, 30 January 2019.
23. Interview with Zhang Runxuan, 31 January 2019.
24. *Berita Harian*, 13 January 2017.
25. *New Straits Times* 11 October 2018.
26. *Malay Mail*, 15 November 2020.
27. Ngeow and Ma, "More Islamic, No Less Chinese".

10

Xin Yimin in Indonesia: A Growing Community That Faces New Challenges

Leo Suryadinata

The issue of New Chinese Migrants (*xin yimin*, 新移民) has been prolifically discussed globally since Deng Xiaoping introduced market-based economic reforms and greater engagement by China with the global community. Some scholars argue that this migration mainly went to Western developed countries rather than to Southeast Asia, with the exception of Singapore.[1] Understandably, English language scholarly work on *xin yimin* has tended to focus on this phenomenon in developed countries,[2] and less attention on the topic has been paid to Southeast Asia, at least until recently.

According to the International Organization for Migration of the United Nations (UN), 'migrant' is "[a]n umbrella term, not defined under international law, reflecting the common lay understanding of a person who moves away from his or her place of usual residence, whether within a country or across an international border, temporarily or permanently, and for a variety of reasons".[3]

Xin yimin, or new Chinese migrants, are further defined as migrants from mainland China (and to a much lesser extent from Taiwan) who stay in another country for more than one year, some with the intention to stay longer or permanently.[4]

According to a rough estimate, there were 10.3 million *xin yimin* across the world in 2008, of which about 8 million came from mainland China.[5] Of those from China, only twenty per cent went to Southeast Asia.[6] It is difficult to get accurate figures on this since almost no country in Southeast Asia has released any relevant figures. According to Indonesia's Labour Minister, Hanif Dhakiri, there were 24,800 Chinese workers in Indonesia in 2017,[7] the majority of whom were classified as skilled workers. However, many argue that the real number may be double that.

This chapter will focus on the *xin yimin* in Indonesia, an undertaking that forms part of my larger project on Chinese migration in Southeast Asia. There have been copious descriptions of the diverse nature of Chinese migration into the region, but statistics have been less forthcoming, both as a result of the sensitive nature of the subject and the uneven data collection of country-level surveys. However, from scattered information that is available, it is still possible for us to gain a rough picture of the *xin yimin* in Southeast Asia and to understand their activities (see Table 10.1). To a limited extent, their impact on the local socio-economic and political scene can also be assessed.

TABLE 10.1
Chinese New Migrants in Southeast Asia
(thousands)

Country	Up to 2007 (Zhuang Guotu)	Other Estimates
Singapore	200–250	300
The Philippines	150–200	50–70
Thailand	200–300	200
Malaysia	100–150	50
Indonesia	100–120	50
Vietnam	50–100	50–60
Laos	10 or more	20
Cambodia	10 or more	20
Myanmar	100?	50–60

Source: Leo Suryadinata, "Chinese Migration in the Globalizing World: A Brief Comparison between Developed and Developing Countries", *CHC Bulletin*, nos. 13 and 14, November 2009, p. 4.

Situating the *Xin Yimin* in Indonesia

Indonesia has many restrictions on new migration. For instance, the ratio of foreign workers to local workers is 1 to 10. Only workers whose skills are not available in Indonesia can get a permit, and they have to leave the country as soon as their project is completed. The permit is usually for only six months. This is due to strong ethno-nationalism and protectionist policies in support of the economic well-being of 'indigenous Indonesians'. Many 'indigenous Indonesians' still live below the poverty line, and they hold strong suspicions and prejudices towards foreigners, especially the Chinese. Worse, opposition politicians often use identity politics to promote their interests, making Chinese new migrants targets for attacks.

In fact, ethnic prejudices prevail not only against new migrants but also towards Chinese Indonesians who have been there for generations. The Basuki Tjahaja Purnama (alias Ahok) affair is a case in point.[8] Even the former Commander-in-Chief of the Indonesian military, General Gatot Nurmantyo, promoted anti-Chinese sentiments while he was aiming for a high political position as his retirement job.[9]

Regardless of the strict policy towards the Chinese migrants, *xin yimin* are found in many places in Indonesia. There have been tensions between these Chinese workers and the local population.

In 2015, for instance, a cement factory in Lebak, Banten province, was said to have hired 799 Chinese migrant workers mainly to do non-skilled work, and the local people, claiming that these workers had caused damage to the environment, demanded that their work permits be withdrawn.[10] Joint project companies in Bali and Kalimantan were said to have hired many more Chinese migrant workers than permitted. The issue persisted for several months and was eventually debated in Parliament.[11] The government investigated the matter and found that the numbers were within quota. More recently, during the Covid-19 pandemic, the presence of 49 Chinese workers in the Konawe district, Southeast Sulawesi province, led the local population to demonstrate and to urge the local government to expel these new arrivals.[12] Soon after this episode, another 500 new Chinese workers were scheduled to enter Konawe. The plan was leaked before their arrival, resulting in strong opposition from the local government. The entry of these workers was temporarily halted.[13]

It is worth noting that illegal *xin yimin* are also present in major cities such as Jakarta, Surabaya, Medan, Bandung, Semarang and Yogyakarta.

These are usually overstayed visitors in Indonesia. Some of them are petty traders selling Chinese porcelains and other products in malls and markets; some work in restaurants, factories and other outfits; and some are sex workers working under local syndicates.[14] Due to their large numbers in major Indonesian cities, sex workers from China are now known as Cungkuok, a local Indonesian slang of "Zhongguo"—meaning China.[15] Despite the large number of illegal *xin yimin*, very few have been deported.[16]

China Chamber of Commerce in Indonesia and *Xin Yimin* Businessmen

Although Deng Xiaoping's open-door policy started in the 1980s, new migrants came to Southeast Asia, especially to Indonesia, much later. It appears that it started only during the Hu Jintao presidency, around 2005. With the launching of the Belt and Road Initiative (BRI) by Xi Jinping in 2013, the number of Chinese new migrants to Indonesia increased dramatically in tandem with the great numbers of state-linked and private Chinese companies arriving in the country. According to an estimate of the local *xin yimin* observer, there are over 1,000 Chinese companies in Indonesia, of which 260 are members of the China Chamber of Commerce in Indonesia (CCCI).[17]

The CCCI only accepts mainland Chinese business companies as members. Almost all large state-linked companies in Indonesia are members of the CCCI. So are private-owned companies, which are mainly small and medium enterprises (SMEs). The large companies have often collaborated with some local companies, while the SMEs are often independently run and have few interactions with local Chinese-Indonesian businessmen. Chinese-Indonesian business firms are not members of the CCCI, and they have formed their own Chinese chambers of commerce, such as Yinni Zhonghua Zong Shanghui (印尼中华总商会) and Huashang Zonghui (华商总会), which only accept Chinese Indonesian companies as members.

The CCCI originated in the Chinese Business Association in Indonesia (Zhongzi Qiye [Yindunixiya] Xiehui 中资企业 [印度尼西亚] 协会), first established in May 2005. It changed its name in September 2010 to China Chamber of Commerce in Indonesia (CCCI, 印度尼西亚中国商会).[18] In other words, the CCCI has fifteen years of history. This also shows that *xin yimin* businessmen have been active in Indonesia for at least that long.

The former chairman of the chamber, Zhang Min (张敏), who was in Indonesia between 2010 and 2016 and managed the China Bank in Jakarta, stated that China is very good in many businesses such as construction, building power plants, the smelting industry, and the electronics business. Experts in these sectors are needed in Indonesia, while Indonesia's rich natural resources are in demand by China.[19]

The current composition of the Council of the CCCI is clearly controlled by China's major state-linked enterprises: its general chairman is Zhang Chaoyang (张朝阳, who is the director of the China Bank Jakarta branch); the honorary chairman is Zhang Jinxing (张金星, from the Industrial and Commercial Bank of China, ICBC); the council chairman is Zhang Wei (张伟, from the China Railways Corporation); the daily deputy chairman is Liu Cheng (刘城, from Global Machinery Company in Indonesia); and the secretary is Xue Baohua (薛宝华, from the China Pacific Insurance). There are also twelve deputy chairmen who are from various of China's industries operating in Indonesia.[20]

A former general chairman of the CCCI, Gong Bencai (宫本才, from China's State Oil Company), revealed in a seminar in Jakarta in November 2018 that 50 per cent of the activities of the Chinese companies took place on Java and the rest on the Outer Islands (beyond Java Island). With regard to their investments, 17 per cent were in the construction industry, 15 per cent in the mining industry and 13 per cent in the electronics industry. He further revealed that China's companies also moved into infrastructure, logistics, power plants and the food industry in order to fulfil Indonesia's needs.[21]

Not only have trade volumes between China and Indonesia continued to increase, but the inflow of direct investment has also been significant. China is now the largest trading partner of Indonesia, while, as a source of direct investments to Indonesia, China jumped from number 10 in 2008 to number 3 in 2016.[22] Nevertheless, the amount is still very small when compared with the FDI from Japan and the United States. Luhut Pandjaitan, now the Coordinating Minister for Maritime and Investment Affairs, appealed to China in late 2018 to invest more in Indonesia, claiming that the investment environment was more conducive.[23]

Indeed, China is very interested in doing business in Indonesia. Outside of Java, another centre is the Riau Archipelago Province (Kepulauan Riau, or Kepri). In September 2015, China's Businessmen Association in Riau (Asosiasi Pengusaha Tiongkok di Kepri, APTK) was officially established.

Its Chinese name is Yinni Liaonei Qundao Zhongzi Qiye Shanghui (印尼廖内群岛中资企业商会), which translates to the Chamber of Commerce of China's Enterprises in the Riau Archipelago of Indonesia. The office is located on Batam.[24] It has twenty members, including PT Bank ICBC Indonesia, PT Damai Indo Pertama Sukses, PT Cindo International Marine Trading, PT TJK Power and PT China Communications Construction Industry Indonesia.[25] The chairman of APTK is Shen Xiaoqi (沈晓祺), who is the CEO of ICBC in Indonesia. He announced that the APTK would immediately join the CCCI and become its Riau Islands branch, and he looked forward to the guidance of the Chinese embassy and consulate-general so that the association would be on the right track.[26]

In 2017, China's investment in Kepri was still small. Both the investments of the People's Republic of China (PRC) and Hong Kong combined came to only US$232 million, placing it as the fourth-largest investor in Kepri. Separately, Hong Kong was number 5, while the PRC was number 12.[27] However, by 2019, investments by the PRC had reached US$1.3 billion and it had emerged as the second-largest investor in Kepri, behind Singapore (US$2.7 billion), but ahead of Hong Kong (US$600 million), Japan (US$600 million), and the United States (US$500 million).[28] China's state-linked and private businesses in Indonesia do recruit local Chinese Indonesians, though not in great numbers. These firms require staff who speak and understand Mandarin, in which most young Chinese Indonesians are not fluent. Therefore, they need to rely heavily on *xin yimin* students who graduated from Indonesian universities.

Xin Yimin Students

A significant number of Chinese have been studying in Indonesia in recent decades. In 2001, a Chinese Indonesian banker, Li Wenguang (李文光), of the Panin Group, established President University (Universitas Presiden) in a suburb of Jakarta.[29] It offered a hundred scholarships annually to mainland Chinese students to enrol in that university.[30] Also, since 2010, the China Hongkong and Bay Areas Enterprise in Indonesia (中国港湾印尼有限公司) has offered fifteen to twenty annual scholarships to the university.[31] According to a study on Chinese businesses in Indonesia, more than a thousand of these graduates have served as the backbone for China's businesses and companies in Indonesia.[32] These graduates are well versed in both Mandarin and Indonesian.

There are also many Indonesians, both indigenous and of Chinese descent, who have studied in China. In 2015–18, as many as 57,031 Indonesian students went to mainland China's universities for their education.[33] Although no data is available on what they have been doing since their return to Indonesia, one may assume that some would have joined Chinese firms.

Chinese Indonesians who grew up during the New Order period are generally not well versed in Chinese dialects of any kind. The still sizeable older generation, on the other hand, went to Chinese-medium schools and are often literate in Chinese, and are readers of Chinese language newspapers. According to one estimate, Indonesia has about 30,000 Chinese language newspaper readers, supporting at least seven or eight such newspapers, five of which are based in Jakarta.[34]

Since the younger generation of Chinese Indonesians in general no longer have an active command of Mandarin, these newspapers often hire mainland Chinese studying in Indonesian universities as reporters, writers or editorial staff.[35] Some continue to work after graduation, contributing to the survival of the Chinese press in post-Suharto Indonesia.

Conclusion: An Uneasy Relationship between *Xin Yimin* and Chinese Indonesians

Most *xin yimin* have a limited command of the Indonesian language. Some interaction between them and older Chinese Indonesians who still speak Chinese does occur. This cannot be said about interactions between them and the younger generation of Chinese Indonesians who are Indonesian- or Western-educated. According to observers, the ties between *xin yimin* and Chinese Indonesians are not close, and the groups are divided by different life experiences and by the language barrier.[36]

Even ties between *xin yimin* businessmen and Chinese-speaking Chinese Indonesians have not been cordial. Many *xin yimin* businessmen are seen to be arrogant and dismissive of the local Chinese, while Chinese Indonesian *towkays* often distrust *xin yimin* businessmen.[37]

But from my observations, major *xin yimin* corporations do collaborate with local Chinese-speaking businessmen. The local contacts help the *xin yimin* to develop their businesses in Indonesia. This is especially the case in the Outer Islands, where many Chinese Indonesians are still able to speak Mandarin.

The *xin yimin* continue to enter Indonesia. While Indonesia welcomes Chinese investments, a surplus-capital China also needs resources from Indonesia. Most new Chinese migrants are quite young and are often better educated than the old migrants. They are also more adventurous, and chances are they will be more successful than their forefathers.

It is worth noting that the presence of the Chinese workers had invoked protests and demonstrations among the indigenous population, but the presence of Chinese businessmen did not elicit the same reaction. During the 2019 presidential elections, Prabowo Subianto attacked mainland Chinese investments and Chinese workers, but this did not result in noticeable anti-China sentiments or anti-Chinese riots. This was probably because, apart from the success of Joko Widodo's security policy, these Chinese businessmen were not seen in public and did not have direct contact with the indigenous population. Prabowo himself later joined the Joko Widodo administration and became more sympathetic to Chinese investments. Nevertheless, tensions between new Chinese migrants and the indigenous population remain.

With the arrival of *xin yimin*, a new type of Huaqiao (overseas Chinese) community is in the making. Indonesia may experience a Totok-and-Peranakan situation again. These new Chinese migrants (Totok) may come into conflict with the Chinese Indonesians (Peranakan) who consider new migrants as competitors and a threat. There may also be tension—and conflict—between *xin yimin* and the indigenous population, who see them as foreign exploiters. In addition, Beijing's Overseas Chinese policy may also affect the situation of the *xin yimin* in Indonesia should Sino-Indonesian relations turn sour.

Notes

1. For instance, Zhuang Guotu, (庄国土), 中国新移民与东南亚文化 "China's new Migrants and the Culture of Southeast Asia", *CHC Bulletin* (华裔馆通讯) 9 (May 2007): 9. I also agree with his observation.
2. The study of the *xin yimin* began to emerge in the second decade of the twenty-first century. Examples of such studies include Leo Suryadinata, ed., *Migration, Indigenization and Interaction: Chinese Overseas and Globalization* (New Jersey and Singapore: World Scientific, 2011); Leo Suryadinata and Lee Guan Kin, eds., *Chinese Migration in Comparative Perspective: Adaptation and Development* (Singapore: Chinese Heritage Center, 2009); Liao Jianyu (廖建裕), Liang Bingfu (梁秉赋) eds. 《华人移民与全球化: 迁移、本土

化与交流》[Chinese Migrants and Globalization: Migration, Localization and Interactions] (Singapore: 华裔馆 [Chinese Heritage Centre], 2011).
3. International Organization for Migration, https://www.iom.int/who-is-a-migrant (accessed 2 April 2020).
4. It should be noted that our academic usage of the term "migrants" (*yimin* 移民) to refer to new Chinese workers is often misunderstood, particularly in the Indonesian context. Migrants in Indonesia are often understood as foreign nationals who plan to settle down in other countries. However, Indonesia does not regard foreign workers as "migrant workers" per se because they entered Indonesia not as migrants but as foreign manpower (Tenaga Kerja Asing, TKA) without entitlement to settle down in Indonesia. In theory, they need to leave Indonesia when the project is completed. Even businessmen are not considered as migrants either. These are reasons why the Indonesian government claims that it does not have new Chinese migrants.
5. Wang Wangbo and Zhuang Guotu, *2009 nian haiwai huaqiao huaren gaishu (2009 年海外华侨华人概述)* [The general description of Chinese overseas in 2009] (Beijing: World Knowledge Publishing, 2010), p. 3.
6. Zhuang Guotu (庄国土), "Zhongguo xin yimin yu dongnanya wenhua (中国新移民与东南亚文化)", *CHC Bulletin (华裔馆通讯)* 9 (May 2007): 10.
7. Andri Donnal Putera, "Ini Data TKA di Indonesia dan Perbandingan dengan TKI di Luar Negeri", *Kompas*, 23 April 2018, https://ekonomi.kompas.com/read/2018/04/23/154732226/ini-data-tka-di-indonesia-dan-perbandingan-dengan-tki-di-luar-negeri. The figure given was based on the end of 2017 figures.
8. Ahok, a Chinese Indonesian Christian, was defeated during the gubernatorial election in 2017 by his opponents, who used identity politics. For a brief analysis, see Liao Jianyu (廖建裕), *Yajiada shouzhang xuanju hou de Yinni zhengju (雅加达首长选举后的印尼政局)* [The political situation in Indonesia after the Jakarta gubernatorial election], *Lianhe Zaobao* (联合早报), 25 April 2017.
9. Leo Suryadinata, "General Gatot and the Re-emergence of Pribumi-ism in Indonesia", *ISEAS Perspective*, no. 2017/49, 7 July 2017.
10. Bisnis.com, 26 June 2015, https://ekonomi.bisnis.com/read/20150626/12/447727/waduh-para-pekerja-asal-china-di-lebak-suka-bab-sembarang.
11. See Leo Suryadinata, "Anti-China Campaign in Jokowi's Indonesia", *Straits Times*, 10 January 2017, https://www.straitstimes.com/opinion/anti-china-campaign-in-jokowis-indonesia.
12. Kiki Andi Pati, "Bupati Konawe Minta Gubernur Sultra Stop TKA dari China", *Kompas.com*, 19 March 2020, https://regional.kompas.com/read/2020/03/19/12500601/bupati-konawe-minta-gubernur-sultra-stop-tka-dari-china?page=all.

13. Ade Miranti Karunia, "Kemenaker Sebut Kedatangan 500 TKA China ke RI Tak Dalam Waktu Dekat", *Kompas.com*, 30 April 2020, https://money.kompas.com/read/2020/04/30/183900326/kemenaker-sebut-kedatangan-500-tkachina-ke-ri-tak-dalam-waktu-dekat?page=all#page3.
14. For a series of reports on illegal Chinese migrants, see Iwan Santosa, "Banjir Imigran Gelap China", in *Peranakan Tionghoa di Nusantara: Catatan Perjalanan dari Barat ke Timur* (Jakarta: Kompas Media Nusantara, 2012), pp. 201–31.
15. Ibid., p. 202.
16. Ibid., pp. 218–19.
17. https://new.qq.com/omn/20190626/20190626A04VKO.html (accessed 15 April 2020).
18. http://www.chinachamber.co/inside/1/12.html (accessed 1 February 2020).
19. http://toutiao.manqian.cn/wz_17C2fjYS9lv.html (accessed 19 March 2020).
20. Ibid.
21. Teguh Firmansyah, "Kadin Cina: Ada 1.000 Perusahaan Cina di Indonesia", *Republika*, 27 November 2018, https://republika.co.id/berita/piui22377/kadin-cina-ada-1000-perusahaan-cina-di-indonesia.
22. Siwage Dharma Negara and Leo Suryadinata, *Indonesia and China's Belt and Road Initiatives: Perspectives, Issues and Prospects*, Trends in Southeast Asia, no. 11/2018, (Singapore: ISEAS – Yusof Ishak Institute, 2018), pp. 5–6.
23. Teguh Firmansyah, "Luhut Ajak Investor Cina Perbesar Investasi di Indonesia", *Republika*, 27 November 2018, https://republika.co.id/berita/piu4n4377/luhut-ajak-investor-cina-perbesar-investasi-di-indonesia.
24. Yusuf Riadi, "Asosiasi Pengusaha Tiongkok Kepri Dukung Kemajuan Investasi di Kepri", *Tribun Batam*, 9 September 2015, https://batam.tribunnews.com/2015/09/09/asosiasi-pengusaha-tiongkok-kepri-dukung-kemajuan-investasi-di-kepri.
25. Delta Kepri, "Asosiasi Pengusaha Tiongkok – Kepri Resmi Dikukuhkan", 10 September 2015, https://deltakepri.co.id/asosiasi-pengusaha-tiongkok-kepri-resmi-dikukuhkan/.
26. http://www.guojiribao.com/shtml/gjrb/20150910/234633.shtml (accessed 23 April 2020).
27. Charlotte Setijadi, "Chinese Investment and Presence in the Riau Islands", *ISEAS Perspective*, no. 2018/4, 10 May 2018, p. 5.
28. https://www.cnbcindonesia.com/news/20200420140140-4-153122/singapura-china-masih-juara-investasi-terbanyak-di-ri (accessed 14 May 2020). I would like to thank Dr Siwage Dharma Negara for drawing my attention to this sudden jump.
29. 李文光 (印尼泛印集团董事长、印尼总统大学创办人) 的介绍-520问题网 (520wenti.com). However, other sources noted that the founder was

the chairman of the Jababeka Group, S.D. Darmono. His Chinese name is Xu Longchuan 许龙川. See 教育园 – Jababeka. See also Setyono Djuandi Darmono Profile, Indonesia Tatler (accessed 16 September 2021).
30. http://www.chinachamber.co/detail/1189.html (accessed 1 February 2020).
31. This university offers courses on engineering, computer science and business. The medium of instruction is English and Indonesian. In 2019 there were 5,000 students, of which 500 were foreign students, mainly from China, Vietnam, South Korea and Australia. See http://www.chinachamber.co/detail/1189.html (accessed 1 February 2020).
32. http://www.chinachamber.co/detail/1189.html (accessed 1 February 2020).
33. Ibid.
34. Interview with one of the Chinese newspaper directors, Jakarta, 22 August 2015.
35. Correspondence with a Chinese newspaper reporter in Jakarta, 20 April 2020.
36. 印尼老杜, "浅谈印尼老侨和新侨的关系 [Talking about the relationship between old Chinese and new Chinese in Indonesia]", 26 September 2019, https://new.qq.com/omn/20190626/20190626A04VKO.html.
37. Ibid.

11

Indonesian Elites' Perceptions of New Chinese Migrants during the Jokowi Presidency

Johanes Herlijanto

In the last two decades, the relationship between Indonesia and China has undergone a significant change. While in the past, particularly in the first two decades of the period of New Order Indonesia, the two countries had a tumultuous relationship,[1] today their relations have been significantly enhanced. Such a good relationship began to develop in the year 2000, after President Abdurrahman Wahid entered his presidential term. President Wahid even made China the first country that he officially visited as the president. Since then, cultural exchanges between China and Indonesia have intensified, while their economic relations have increased unprecedentedly. Indonesia's subsequent presidents have continued President Wahid's friendly attitude towards China. In 2005, President Susilo Bambang Yudhoyono (popularly known as SBY) signed a strategic partnership agreement with President Hu Jintao, an agreement that was followed by an influx of Chinese investments into Indonesia. Less than a decade later, during President Xi Jinping's visit to Jakarta in 2013, Indonesia and

China signed another agreement that made both countries comprehensive strategic partners.

The above phenomenon has opened the way for much more frequent encounters between the Chinese and Indonesian people. Such encounters have not only occurred due to the increased visits by Indonesians to mainland China, but also as a result of the coming of Chinese people to this Southeast Asian country. In the last few years, people from mainland China have become among the largest groups of foreign visitors to Indonesia.[2] While the majority of these people come for tourism, and hence only stay for a short period, a number of them arrive in the country for other purposes, including work, study and business. This latter group constitutes a group of 'new Chinese migrants' (*xin yimin*) in Indonesia.

These new Chinese migrants have a number of differences from the so called '*lao yimin*' (old migrants), particularly in terms of levels of education, proficiency in the local language, values, and adaptability to the local situation.[3] While the descendants of the Chinese old migrants have transformed into a major ethnic group—popularly known as the ethnic Chinese in Indonesia (Chinese Indonesians)—and have also had a high degree of interactions with other ethnic groups in the country, these new Chinese migrants are relatively alien to the majority of the Indonesian people, who are usually called the 'pribumi' (indigenous) Indonesians.[4] Furthermore, as their presence in a significant number in Indonesia is a new phenomenon, studies that focus on these new migrants have not been sufficiently conducted.[5] It is against this background that this chapter wishes to focus its discussion on the Chinese new migrants in Indonesia. In particular, emphasis will be given to the way in which these new migrants are perceived by the 'pribumi' Indonesians, more specifically by the 'pribumi' Indonesian elites.

The data used for this chapter was mainly collected between January and June 2016 in Jakarta amongst members of various elite groups in Indonesia, when the author conducted research on the Indonesian 'pribumi' elites' perceptions of China and the ethnic Chinese in Indonesia.[6] The term 'elite' in this study is broadly defined so that it includes government elites, which in this research consists of the individuals who hold mid-ranking and high-ranking positions in the government,[7] and the non-government elites comprising former senior officials, retired high-ranking military officers, senior politicians, senior scholars and researchers, religious leaders, non-government organization (NGO) activists, and high-profile professionals.

Some other interviews, conversations and text-based communications with members of these elites were also conducted between 2016 and 2019.

Xin Yimin in Indonesia: Types and Characteristics

The *xin yimin* phenomenon—a phenomenon that Zhuang Guotu and Wang Wangbo categorize as the fourth wave of Chinese migration—can actually be traced back to the 1980s.[8] Unlike the other three waves of Chinese migration, which took place between the mid-seventeenth and the mid-twentieth centuries, the new wave of migrants that began in the 1980s did not make Southeast Asia their destination.[9] Instead, as Zhuang and Wang point out, these new migrants tended to go to more affluent countries. Nevertheless, the improved political relations and the intimate economic interactions between China and Southeast Asian countries, combined with China's growing investments in the region, have driven the mainland Chinese to migrate to Southeast Asia as well, particularly since the early 1990s.[10]

The impact of the Chinese new migrants on the local communities in Southeast Asia is by no means negligible. In Cambodia, where the capital influx from China has arrived since 1999, the coming of these people has altered the way Cambodians understand what it means to be Chinese, an understanding that previously was shaped by Sino–Khmer cultural elites.[11] In Thailand, notably in the major Thai border town Chiang Saen, the border-crossing Chinese who started to enter Thailand in the 1990s have transformed the town into a competitive marketplace in which the locals have found themselves progressively displaced.[12]

Indonesia has received a large number of Chinese new migrants in the last two decades, though when compared to the Indonesian population, the size of these migrants is relatively small. A media report in May 2020 estimates that the number of the Chinese workers in 2020 was 35,781. However, because many Chinese migrants come to Indonesia on a tourist or a sixty-day business visa,[13] the actual number of these migrants may be higher than the official number. Ping Lin, an associate professor at National Chung Cheng University, Taiwan, estimates that even in the mid-2000s the number of Chinese new migrants in Indonesia had already reached 50,000.[14]

The presence of Chinese temporary migrants in Indonesia can be traced back to the early 1990s, after the resumption of diplomatic ties between

Indonesia and China. Amongst the first groups of the new migrants who entered Indonesia in 1990 were a number of Chinese students who came to study Bahasa Indonesia in the University of Indonesia, Depok, and the Chinese technicians who participated in the construction of a steam power plant belonging to PT Indah Kiat Pulp & Paper.[15] But the large influx of the Chinese new migrants only started to take place much later—in the early years of the new century. A small group of these new migrants came as a part of the volunteer programme launched by the Office of Chinese Language Council International (Hanban). Hanban began the volunteer programme to Indonesia in 2004 by sending twenty Chinese teachers to teach Mandarin in schools and universities in the country. Concurrently, professional Mandarin instructors have also come to the country to work at private education providers, many of which have offered Mandarin as one of the subjects taught in their institution.

Meanwhile, Chinese workers, technicians and managers have also come to Indonesia to work for the Chinese companies participating in various projects in Indonesia. For example, the construction project of the Surabaya–Madura Bridge (also know as the Suramadu Bridge), an inter-island bridge that connects Surabaya city in East Java to the Madura Island, was carried out by a consortium consisting of Chinese contractors and their local partners. These Chinese companies brought with them around 300 Chinese workers and 46 engineers to participate in the project.[16] The presence of such Chinese investors and companies in Indonesia has significantly increased since 2013. The Bandung–Jakarta high-speed railway project, the industrial park in Konawe, Southeast Sulawesi, and the industrial park in Morowali are examples of the projects financed and carried out by the Chinese.

Some Chinese nationals have also come to Indonesia to study in Indonesian universities. Qianqian Luli, a researcher at Fujian Normal University, estimates that there were around 300 Chinese students in Indonesia by the end of 2010.[17] This number rose to 500 students by the end of 2016, and nearly 700 students by the end of 2017.[18] Many of these students have studied in President University (Universitas Presiden), a private university located in Cikarang, West Java, which since its establishment in 2001 has offered a number of scholarships to mainland Chinese students.[19]

In addition to the Chinese professionals, workers, teachers and students, some *xin yimin* have also come to work in the service sectors in Indonesia, such as those who work in Chinese restaurants.[20] Other examples include Chinese women who work in the entertainment industry in Indonesia's metropolitan cities, such as Jakarta, Surabaya and Medan.[21] There are also Chinese women who migrate to Indonesia after marrying Indonesian (usually Chinese Indonesian) men. While the latter case is interesting, their number is too low and therefore may have only an insignificant impact on Indonesian society.

Perceptions of Chinese New Migrants in the Yudhoyono Era

The increased influx of the *xin yimin* in Indonesia has begun to attract people's attention since the second half of the 2000s, although it has not been widely discussed amongst the Indonesian public. In the era of President Yudhoyono (2004–14), an appreciation of these Chinese migrants, particularly of their work ethic, was observable amongst middle-class Indonesians. This appreciation can be seen in the popular discourse on China circulating during that period that positively portrayed *xin yimin* as hardworking individuals.[22] The discourse circulated in the form of written materials published between 2000 and 2010 as well as statements made by important figures of the country. For example, Yudhoyono's vice president, Mr Boediono, was reportedly impressed by the work ethic in the Chinese society during his three-day visit to Nanning and Beijing in October 2010.[23]

Other than in popular discourse, the admiration of the Chinese work ethic amongst some Indonesian people may also be observed being expressed in their frequent encounters with Chinese migrants. For instance, some Indonesian technicians and workers on the Suramadu Bridge project who had an opportunity to meet, observe and collaborate with the Chinese migrant workers were among those who had a positive view of their work ethics. A coordinator of the technical consultants in the project praised the Chinese engineers and workers for their work ethics, which in his view included their discipline, courage and hardworking attitude.[24] The consultant also commented positively on the ways in which the Chinese managers were able to find a more innovative way to complete the task within the expected time. Similar praise was also given by an Indonesian worker who worked for the Indonesian contractors participating in the project. The worker even thought that Indonesian workers should learn from their Chinese counterparts' work ethic.[25] Meanwhile, a Chinese Indonesian community leader in Surabaya mentioned how the people in the city were amazed with the work ethic performed by the Chinese workers who participated in the construction of the Suramadu bridge. According to the leader, a top university in the city even invited the managers of the Chinese companies involved in the project to share their insights on how to build such a good working culture.[26]

Elite Perception of New Chinese Migrants during the Joko (Jokowi) Widodo Presidency

The perception of the new Chinese migrants has undergone a substantial change since 2015, less than one year after Joko "Jokowi" Widodo entered his presidential office. The negative tones toward these migrants became increasingly apparent alongside rising concerns regarding China of the Indonesian public. The concerns emerged widely in the Indonesian media and are particularly related to the increased number of China's infrastructure and mining projects in Indonesia.

One of the issues pertaining to the Chinese new migrants that became popular in 2015 was the alleged massive migration of individuals from China to Indonesia. The concern spread in the aftermath of the speech delivered by the then vice premier of China, Madam Liu Yandong, during her visit to Jakarta. Madam Liu Yandong stated that, in order to enhance relations with Indonesia, China would encourage Chinese youth to go to Indonesia for their studies. In return, China would welcome Indonesian students to study in China.[27] The statement sparked concerns regarding the possibility of mass migration of Chinese citizens from China to Indonesia. In 2016, a news article which reported that China had allegedly planned to send ten million Chinese migrants to Indonesia became widespread, albeit only in non-mainstream Indonesian media.[28] The information about China's aforementioned plan, however, was unverifiable and was very likely false. Mainstream Indonesian news agencies such as Kompas, Koran Tempo. co and Sindonews.com did not mention this massive arrival of Chinese people in their reports on the vice premier's visit.[29]

Another issue that ignited public debate, also since 2015, was the increased influx of Chinese workers for Chinese companies in Indonesia. While the number of these workers is relatively low, the debates over the arrival of the workers persisted between 2015 and 2019. The presence of the large number of blue-collar Chinese workers employed by Chinese companies has been exposed by mainstream media, such as *The Jakarta Post*, which in 2017 published a series of reports about the development of an industrial park in Morowali, Central Sulawesi, which was managed by a Chinese joint venture.[30] Another rumour that about ten million Chinese workers were inundating Indonesia emerged in 2018, forcing the government to take some actions to deal with the rumour.[31] Suspicions that Chinese military personnel, disguised as migrant workers, might infiltrate Indonesia also emerged following the arrest of a number of Chinese workers dressed in military-like attire at a military base that belongs to the Indonesian Air Force in East Jakarta.[32] The issue regarding the arrival of Chinese migrant workers has come under scrutiny again during the pandemic in 2020.[33]

Many of the issues that have appeared in the Indonesian public discourse are reflective of the perception of the Indonesian elites towards Chinese new migrants. Concerns regarding Chinese workers may be found amongst both the government and non-government elites. The majority of the government elites regard the issue as manageable, though in need of serious attention. In contrast, the non-government elites, particularly those who oppose Jokowi's administration, tend to be more critical in general. Their views often comprise suspicions, at least at a certain level, that China has a hidden agenda behind the coming of these migrants.

Perception amongst the Non-government Elites

The perceptions of new Chinese migrants amongst members of the non-government elites are mostly negative and are based on several viewpoints. First of these is the belief that the arrival of the low-skilled Chinese workers may have a negative impact on local people. Such an argument is observable even amongst members of the elites who support President Jokowi. For instance, a top Indonesian lawyer who supports President Jokowi criticized the practice of importing blue-collar workers from China to do unskilled jobs and suggested that the Indonesian government should ensure that these jobs be done by Indonesian workers.[34] In another interview, a pro-Jokowi NGO activist questioned the abolition of the regulation that requires that learning Bahasa Indonesia (Indonesian language) be mandatory for foreigners applying for a work permit.[35]

Criticism based on the above argument also come from labour union activists. A leader of an Indonesian labour union compared the employment practices by Chinese companies against those by European, Korean and Japanese companies in Indonesia. In her view, the latter only employed skilled professionals from their countries and made a contribution by transferring knowledge to their Indonesian counterparts. In contrast, Chinese companies import blue-collar Chinese workers who do not facilitate such knowledge diffusion, and may instead even result in the rise of unemployment amongst the local people.[36] The union leader also expressed concerns regarding the tension that might arise between Chinese new migrants and the local people who felt that the former's existence potentially reduced their employability. The labour union leader also expressed concerns about the horizontal conflict that might emerge due to the cultural differences and communication problems that resulted from the Chinese workers' inability to communicate in Bahasa Indonesia.[37]

Another belief that becomes the basis of the negative perception of the new migrants is the view that the arrival of the Chinese new migrants may pose a threat to Indonesian national security. Suspicions that these migrants are either undercover intelligence agents or military personnel infiltrating Indonesia can be found amongst the non-government elites. For example, the labour union leader mentioned earlier reported that quite a few labour union activists were worried that the Chinese migrant workers were actually Chinese spies. Meanwhile, a prominent political scientist posed the following rhetorical question at an interview: "How could you be sure that they (the Chinese migrant workers) are not military personnel? We have so many unemployed labourers, why do they have to use labourers from China?"[38]

White-collar Chinese new migrants are also seen with suspicion by some 'pribumi' elites. A well-connected senior researcher who heads an independent research centre is one such example. In the researcher's view, Indonesians need to direct their suspicion towards the top or at least mid-level Chinese managers instead of towards the blue-collar workers, who do not pose a serious threat to the country's security. The researcher stated that "these top and middle level managers come as a part of a mission. Those [Chinese] diaspora, [are dispatched] to identify the 'target area'."[39] The researcher regards the presence of top and mid-level Chinese managers as an intelligence issue.[40] As such, he also sees the influx of Chinese investments in Indonesia not only as an economic issue, but also an intelligence one.

A third viewpoint, which is related to the second one, associates the influx of the Chinese new migrants to the 'migration strategy' that China is allegedly adopting. The elites that believe in such an argument argue that China may be implementing such a 'migration strategy' to deal with their population-related problems. A retired high-ranking officer of the

Indonesian Army opined that China began to develop an expansionist character because it needed a place to relocate its people.[41] The retired general believes that China's investments in infrastructure projects in Indonesia is one of the ways to carry out the aforementioned migration strategy. In his view, the Jakarta–Bandung high-speed railway project is a clear example of this:

> It is a long-term project. The concession agreement grants China the right to manage the operation of the railway for fifty years. In that period, they [the Chinese migrants working in the project] will have children and grow into a sizable community. China must have designed it. For me, it is a demographic movement strategy.[42]

A similar view was presented by a former speaker of the Indonesian House of Representatives (Dewan Perwakilan Rakyat, or DPR). Instead of through infrastructure projects, however, he felt that mainland Chinese citizens might relocate to Indonesia through buying property.[43] He explained that such a practice was feasible because of the government regulation that permitted foreign nationals who lived in Indonesia to own a property.[44]

A fourth argument, which is very rare but observable among the above groups of elites, concerns the involvement of Chinese nationals in smuggling drugs to Indonesia. The fact that a number of drug dealers from China have been arrested by the Indonesian police in the last few years has sparked concerns amongst the non-government elites.[45] Conspiracy theories that China might have used these Chinese drug dealers to corrupt the younger generation of Indonesians is sometimes heard in discussions among the non-government elites.[46] However, this concern is less popular compared to the other issues discussed earlier.

Despite the presence of the above negative perception, positive views of Chinese new migrants can still be found among the non-government elites, usually in the form of appreciation of their work ethic. The presence of this appreciation shows that the admiration of the Chinese new migrants which emerged during the Yudhoyono period persists, albeit only to a certain extent.

Views of the Government Elites

Government elites are aware of the presence of negative views of Chinese new migrants amongst non-government elites and society in general. Most of them agree that the issues pertaining to Chinese new migrants are a source of concern, but their views on the ways in which Indonesia should respond to the issues are varied. Professor Dewi Fortuna Anwar, a senior political scientist affiliated with the Indonesian Institute of Science (LIPI), understands that cases pertaining to Chinese migrant workers have sparked public concerns in Indonesia. In an article published in 2019, she wrote about how, "in the run-up to the 2017 Jakarta gubernatorial election, a hoax proliferated on social media about the influx of up to ten million Chinese nationals illegally entering Indonesia, allegedly to vote for the ethnic Chinese incumbent governor, Basuki Tjahaja Purnama (Ahok)."[47] Meanwhile, the arrest of the Bandung–Jakarta High-Speed Railway project's workers for illegally digging in the military base in 2016 has raised public suspicion towards the identity of these Chinese migrant workers. In her view:

> This case has two dimensions. First of all, many people are caught by surprise with the fact that the contractors have again brought the workers from China to participate in the Bandung–Jakarta High Speed Project. But more than that, they also questioned what these workers did, 'how dare they dig there without permission?' This sparks speculative concerns among the Indonesians, 'are they members of the intelligence agency?', 'is there any security issue related to the case?'[48]

She suggests that the government carefully handles such issues. According to her, "if such an issue is not handled with care, it can trigger a backlash".[49]

Professor Anwar's view is echoed by a senior diplomat who also regards the increased influx of the Chinese blue-collar workers as a problem, though he believes that the issue should be seen mainly as a violation of the immigration rules, which may be committed by many foreign visitors, and not only by the Chinese. The diplomat believes that one of the ways for Indonesia to solve the problem is by enforcing the law more strictly.[50] Similarly, a senior military officer mentioned in an interview that the Indonesian government should regulate the influx of migrant workers, such as by permitting only skilled workers or higher-level staff and managers to enter Indonesia for work.[51]

Historical Legacy, Internal Politics and the Perception of China

The last section of this chapter has discussed in detail the ways in which the Indonesian 'pribumi' elites view the Chinese new migrants that have arrived in Indonesia in recent years. Most of the elites, particularly the non-government elites, focus their attention on Chinese new migrants who have come to work at Chinese companies, tending to view these people negatively. What does the phenomenon described in the last section indicate? What are the factors that lead to such negative perceptions? This section will be devoted to discussing these questions.

The fact that suspicion plays an arguably significant role in the perception harboured by the non-government elites—particularly those who are critical of President Jokowi—reveals the negative perception existing amongst these elites is that China is an expansionist country that potentially poses a threat to Indonesia. Such a perception existed already in the 1960s,[52] but became ingrained in Indonesian society during the New Order period.[53] The study conducted by Daniel Novotny shows how such a negative view existed amongst the Indonesian elites during the Yudhoyono period despite the pragmatic attitude that these elites had towards China.[54] Meanwhile, surveys and research in recent years have shown that both a certain group of the elites and the Indonesian public in general harbour a certain degree of a negative perception of China.[55] But if the appreciation of China and of the Chinese people also began to appear among the Indonesian public during Yudhoyono's presidency,[56] why then has the perception of China and of the Chinese new migrants in the Jokowi era become predominantly negative?

As Professor Dewi Fortuna Anwar has noted, economic factors play an important role for the re-emergence of the negative perception of China, which in turn influences the ways in which Indonesians view the Chinese new migrants.[57] Other factors, such as China's assertive behaviour in the South China Sea, and particularly in the waters near Natuna Islands, may contribute to such negative perception as well. But the recent developments in Indonesian politics have also played a significant role in the return of the anti-China and anti-Chinese sentiments among certain groups of the non-government Indonesian elites.

The interviews on which the stories narrated in this chapter are based were mainly conducted in early 2016, just over a year after a Chinese Indonesian politician, Basuki Tjahaja Purnama (popularly known as Ahok), was inaugurated as the governor of Jakarta in November 2014, and less than a year before the 2017 gubernatorial election in which Mr Purnama participated. Mr Purnama's appointment as the governor of Jakarta, while supported by a large number of political elites and activists, caused resentment among certain groups of the 'pribumi' elites. These groups of elites were worried that the Chinese Indonesians, who in their view have dominated the Indonesian economy, would now dominate Indonesian politics as well. The concern increased as Mr Purnama planned to participate in the 2017 gubernatorial election. The suspicion that the governor colluded with Chinese Indonesian business tycoons by letting the latter build properties in the reclaimed islands in the bay of Jakarta, to be marketed to the mainland Chinese, was observable amongst some members of the non-government elites. Such a suspicion shows how the perception that ethnic Chinese individuals will always retain their connection with the 'ancestor land' prevails in the minds of the aforementioned group of elites. This also illustrates how the perceptions of China, Chinese new migrants and Chinese Indonesians may be interconnected, though only amongst some groups of Indonesian elites.

But the negative views of Chinese new migrants, as well as of the Chinese state, may have also been directed against Jokowi and his government, which has had an increasingly close relationship with China. Later in 2019, Professor Anwar reported that "Jokowi has become the target of a massive black campaign on social media that accuses him of being a handmaiden of both China's and local Tionghoa's interests."[58] For Professor Anwar and some other Indonesian scholars who express concerns with the recent political situation, the above practice is considered worrisome because "in the increasingly charged political climate the rise in anti-Chinese sentiment could again be manipulated for political purposes".[59]

Concluding Remarks

To summarize, this chapter portrayed how Chinese new migrants have been perceived by the 'pribumi' elites in Indonesia. While Chinese new migrants may be found in different sectors in this country, attention from the 'pribumi' elites were mainly given to blue-collar migrant workers in infrastructure and mining projects. Many non-government 'pribumi' elites expressed a negative view of the Chinese new migrants. They were worried that the arrival of the blue-collar Chinese workers, who in their view constitute a large part of the Chinese new migrants, would disadvantage the Indonesian workers that live in the region where a Chinese project exists. Some elites viewed the coming of these new migrants as a security issue. They were suspicious that China might collect intelligence through these migrants. Meanwhile, a concern that the influx of these new migrants is part of China's strategy to deal with its population problem was also apparent among certain groups of the non-government elites. Finally, a concern regarding the Chinese nationals' involvement in smuggling illegal drugs to Indonesia was also present, albeit rather rare, amongst members of the 'pribumi' elites. Meanwhile, government elites acknowledged the presence of the above concerns but focused more on how the government should respond carefully to the issue.

The above negative views of the Chinese migrants have emerged as a result of a number of factors. As discussed in the last section, the historical portrayal of China as an expansionist country that might pose a threat to Indonesia is still present amongst some groups of the Indonesian elites. Meanwhile, resentment towards various impacts of the rise of China, concerns about China's assertive behaviour, particularly in the waters near the Natuna Islands, and concerns regarding possible Chinese Indonesian political domination in addition to their perceived domination of the Indonesian economy have also become important factors that have contributed to the growing negative views of the Chinese migrants and of China. The last factor is interesting because it shows how the perception of the new Chinese migrants is linked to the perception of Chinese Indonesians. Finally, Indonesian internal politics, including the political atmosphere at the national level, has also affected the ways in which negative views of China spread amongst the Indonesian elites, particularly amongst the non-government elites who are critical of Jokowi's administration.

Notes

1. See Rizal Sukma, *Indonesia and China: The Politics of Troubled Relationship* (London: Routledge, 1999).
2. For example, between January and June 2017, Chinese were the largest group of visitors who entered Jakarta. See Badan Pusat Statistik Kota Jakarta Barat, "Wisatawan Asal Tiongkok (China) Tetap Merupakan Wisatawan yang Terbanyak Masuk ke Jakarta" [Tourists from China still make up the majority of those entering Jakarta], 14 February 2018, https://jakbarkota.bps.go.id/pressrelease/2018/02/14/84/wisatawan-asal-tiongkok-china-tetap-merupakan-wisatawan-yang-terbanyak-masuk-ke-jakarta.html.
3. Leo Suryadinata, "Chinese Migration and Adaptation in Southeast Asia: The Last Half Century", in *International Migration in Southeast Asia*, edited by Aris Ananta and Evi Nurvidya Arifin (Singapore: Institute of Southeast Asian Studies, 2004), pp. 71–93.

4. Despite its contested meaning, the chapter uses the term 'pribumi' in order to be consistent with the majority of the interviewees who used it to refer to the indigenous peoples of the archipelago.
5. The recent publications on this issue include, among others, Leo Suryadinata, "New Chinese Migrants in Indonesia: An Emerging Community that Faces New Challenges", *ISEAS Perspective*, no. 2020/61, 11 June 2020; Leo Suryadinata, "Tensions in Indonesia over Chinese Foreign Workers during COVID-19 Pandemic", *ISEAS Perspective* no. 2020/73, 6 July 2020; Qianqian Luli, "Chinese Students in Indonesia and the Belt and Road Initiative", *Translocal Chinese: East Asian Perspectives* 14 (2020): 95–114; Ping Lin, "Discovering the Xinyimin in Jakarta: New Chinese Migrants from the PRC", *Translocal Chinese: East Asian Perspectives* 14 (2020): 66–94.
6. The project was commissioned by the Indonesian Studies Programme, ISEAS – Yusof Ishak Institute, Singapore.
7. The active government officials interviewed during the research consist of three first-echelon officials, one second-echelon official (director), four third-echelon officials (deputy directors) and four senior military officers.
8. Zhuang Guotu and Wang Wangbo, "Migration and Trade: The Role of Overseas Chinese in Economic Relations between China and Southeast Asia", *International Journal of China Studies* 1 (2010): 174–93.
9. Ibid.
10. Ibid.
11. Pál Nyiri, "Investors, Managers, Brokers, and Culture Workers: How Migrants from China Are Changing the Meaning of Chineseness in Cambodia", in *Chinese Encounters in Southeast Asia: How People, Money, and Ideas from China Are Changing a Region*, edited by Pál Nyiri and Danielle Tan (Seattle: University of Washington Press, 2017), pp. 25–41.
12. Aranya Siriphon, "Border Guanxi: Xin Yimin and Transborder Trade in Northern Thailand", in *Chinese Encounters in Southeast Asia*, pp. 79–96.
13. Interview with an immigration officer, Jakarta, November 2015; Lin, "Discovering the Xin Yimin in Jakarta", p. 80.
14. Lin, "Discovering the Xin Yimin in Jakarta", pp. 79–80.
15. "Pelajaran Mahal dari Serang" [Tough lesson from Serang], *Tempo*, 5 September 1992, https://majalah.tempo.co/read/nasional/8919/pelajaran-mahal-dari-serang (accessed 26 January 2021).
16. Interview with a technical consultant coordinator participating in the Suramadu Bridge Project, Surabaya, 6 March 2009.
17. Luli, "Chinese Students in Indonesia", p. 104.
18. Ibid., p. 105.
19. Suryadinata, "New Chinese Migrants in Indonesia", p. 6.
20. Among these are the Hui Muslims who come to Indonesia to open their restaurants. See Hew Waiweng, "Translocal Pious Entrepreneurialism: Hui

Business and Religious Activities in Malaysia and Indonesia", in *Chinese Encounters in Southeast Asia*, pp. 58–76.
21. Ko-Lin Chin and James O Finckenauer, *Selling Sex Overseas, Chinese Women and the Realities of Prostitution and Global Sex Trafficking* (New York: New York University Press, 2012), pp. 102–4.
22. See Johanes Herlijanto, "Search for Knowledge as Far as China! Indonesian Response to the Rise of China", in *Chinese Encounters in Southeast Asia*, pp. 200–203.
23. "Boediono Kagumi Etos Kerja Bangsa China" [Boediono admires Chinese work ethic], *Kompas.com*, 21 October 2010, https://internasional.kompas.com/read/2010/10/21/07153047/Boediono.Kagumi.Etos.Kerja.Bangsa.China.
24. Interview with a technical consultant coordinator, Surabaya, 6 March 2009.
25. Interview with an Indonesian worker who participated in the Surabaya Madura Bridge construction project, Surabaya, 15 May 2009.
26. Interview with a Chinese Indonesian leader, Surabaya, 8 September 2009.
27. Xinhua, "China Vows to Promote People-To-People Exchange with Indonesia", State Council of the People's Republic of China, 28 May 2015, http://english.gov.cn/news/top_news/2015/05/28/content_281475116219904.htm.
28. For example, http://www.mediapribumi.com/2016/07/pm-china-kirim-10-juta-warga-negara.html (accessed 21 August 2016); "Jokowi akan datangkan 10 Juta Orang Cina ke Indonesia" [Jokowi will bring 10 million Chinese people into Indonesia], Warta Priangan, http://www.wartapriangan.com/jokowi-akan-datangkan-10-juta-orang-cina-ke-indonesia/5131/ (accessed 21 August 2016).
29. "Kepada Wakil PM, Jokowi Minta Tiongkok Tak Sekadar Janji Investasi di Indonesia" [To vice prime minister, Jokowi requests that China not only offer empty promises on investing in Indonesia], *Kompas.com*, 27 May 2015, http://nasional.kompas.com/read/2015/05/27/19373091/Kepada.Wakil.PM.Jokowi.Minta.Tiongkok.Tak.Sekedar.Janji.Investasi.di.Indonesia; "Jokowi: Cina Segera Percepat Proyek Investasi" [Jokowi: China to expedite investment project], *Tempo.co*, 27 May 2015, https://m.tempo.co/read/news/2015/05/27/090669989/jokowi-cina-segera-percepat-proyek-investasi; Marieska Harya Virdhani, "China Ajak UI Kerja Sama Pendidikan" [China invites University of Indonesia to educational collaboration], *Sindonews.com*, 27 May 2015, http://nasional.sindonews.com/read/1006009/144/china-ajak-ui-kerja-sama-pendidikan-1432722279.
30. Dewi Fortuna Anwar, "Indonesia–China Relations: Coming Full Circle?", in *Southeast Asian Affairs 2019*, edited by Daljit Singh and Malcolm Cook (Singapore: ISEAS – Yusof Ishak Institute 2019), pp. 156–57.
31. As an example, in August 2018 President Jokowi stated that the information regarding the arrival of ten million Chinese workers to Indonesia was a hoax. See Fabian Januarius Kuwado, "Bantah Isu Serbuan 10 Juta TKA

China, Jokowi Sebut Hanya 23,000 Orang" [Debunking the rumour of a swarm of 10 million Chinese migrant workers, Jokowi mentioned there were only 23,000], *Kompas.com*, 8 August 2018, https://nasional.kompas.com/read/2018/08/08/10590981/bantah-isu-serbuan-10-juta-tka-china-jokowi-sebut-hanya-23000-orang?page=all.
32. Intan Pratiwi and Andi Nur Aminah, "*Ngebor* di Wilayah Lanud Halim, 5 Pekerja Cina Ditahan" [Digging in Halim airport, 5 Chinese workers arrested], *Republika.co.id*, 27 April 2016, http://nasional.republika.co.id/berita/nasional/jabodetabek-nasional/16/04/27/o6a1tc384-ngebor-di-wilayah-lanud-halim-5-pekerja-cina-ditahan.
33. For example, see Rachmawati, "Saat 500 TKA Asal China Akan Didatangkan di Tengah Pandemi Corona, Klaim untuk Hindari PHK Pekerja Lokal" [When 500 foreign workers from China are slated to be brought in during Corona pandemic, demands arose to avoid retrenchment of local workers], *Kompas.com*, 3 May 2020, https://regional.kompas.com/read/2020/05/03/06400071/saat-500-tka-asal-china-akan-didatangkan-di-tengah-pandemi-corona-klaim?page=all.
34. Interview with a top Indonesian lawyer, Jakarta, 14 May 2017.
35. Interview with a pro-Jokowi NGO activist, Jakarta, 5 March 2016.
36. Interview with a labour union leader, Jakarta, 9 May 2016.
37. Ibid.
38. Interview with a prominent political scientist, Jakarta, 29 February 2016.
39. Interview with the director of an independent research centre, Jakarta, 16 January 2016.
40. Ibid.
41. Personal communication with a retired high-ranking army officer, 12 February 2019.
42. Ibid.
43. Interview with a senior politician, Jakarta, 26 May 2016.
44. The regulation was signed by President Jokowi on 22 December 2015. See Humas, "Terbitkan PP, Pemerintah Resmi Izinkan Orang Asing Miliki Rumah Tempat Tinggal di Indonesia" [Issuing regulations, government officially allows foreigners to own residential house in Indonesia], Sekretariat Kabinet Republik Indonesia, 12 January 2016, https://setkab.go.id/terbitkan-pp-pemerintah-resmi-izinkan-orang-asing-miliki-rumah-tempat-tinggal-di-indonesia/.
45. For instance, Ervan David, "Jaringan Narkotika China Selundupkan Sabu dalam Paket Mainan Anak" [Chinese drug network smuggled methamphetamine in children's toy parcel], *iNewsJabar.id*, 17 December 2019, https://jabar.inews.id/berita/jaringan-narkotika-tiongkok-selundupkan-sabu-dalam-paket-mainan-anak; Agung Pambudhy, "Polri Bongkar Jaringan

Narkoba Asal China" [Indonesian police uncovers drug network from China], Detik News, 24 January 2017, https://news.detik.com/foto-news/d-3404362/polri-bongkar-jaringan-narkoba-asal-china; and Ratna Puspita, "Polri: Tim Halilintar Kembangkan Kasus Narkoba Asal China" [Indonesian Police: Halilintar team further investigates drug case from China], *Republika.co.id*, 25 June 2020, https://republika.co.id/berita/qch5hb428/polri-tim-halilintar-kembangkan-kasus-narkoba-asal-china.

46. For example, the issue was raised in a discussion forum attended by retired high-ranking military officers and former government officials, conducted in Jakarta, 21 March 2018.
47. Anwar, "Indonesia–China Relations", p. 156.
48. Interview with Professor Dewi Fortuna Anwar, Jakarta, 24 May 2016.
49. Ibid.
50. Interview with a senior diplomat, Jakarta, 3 June 2016.
51. Interview with a senior military officer, Jakarta, 7 March 2016.
52. Carl Taylor, "Indonesian Views of China", *Asian Survey* 3, no. 3: 165–72.
53. See Sukma "Indonesia–China Relations".
54. Daniel Novotny, *Torn Between America and China: Elite Perceptions and Indonesian Foreign Policy* (Singapore: Institute of Southeast Asian Studies, 2010).
55. See Anwar, "Indonesia–China Relations", p. 157; Diego Fossati, Hui Yew-Foong, and Siwage Dharma Negara, *The Indonesian National Survey Project: Economy, Society, and Politics*, Trends in Southeast Asia, no. 10/2017 (Singapore: ISEAS – Yusof Ishak Institute, 2017), pp. 41–46; Johanes Herlijanto, "How the Indonesian Elite Regards Relations with China", *ISEAS Perspective*, no. 2017/8, 4 December 2017.
56. Herlijanto, "Search for Knowledge as Far as China!"
57. Anwar, "Indonesia–China Relations", p. 157.
58. Ibid., p. 158.
59. Ibid. My conversation with a retired senior professor who was previously affiliated with the University of Indonesia also revealed a similar concern.

PART IV

New Chinese Migrants and Local Economies

12

Vietnam–China Economic Ties and New Chinese Migrants in Vietnam

Nguyen Van Chinh

Much effort has been made to account for the new waves of Chinese migration. And globalization, transnationalism and the changing economic and political context have often been used as potential explanations. For example, Kuhn (2008) suggests that Chinese overseas emigration has important connections to domestic migration trends, and that new Chinese migration has been shaped by historic events. Similarly, Rallu (2002, p. 6) believes that the recent trend in the flow of Chinese migrants is rooted in domestic pressures—including high unemployment, rural underemployment and the rapid increase of the "floating population" within Chinese society. In addition, the close nexus between the rise of China's economic role and Chinese new migration has also received attention in both academic and policy circles.

This chapter, based on fieldwork conducted in Vietnam, explores the flow of Chinese migration in relation to China's regional economic integration. In the past, waves of Chinese migration abroad were mainly the result of social conflicts and poverty. Nowadays, the interconnectivity between migration and other economic flows such as trade, investment and economic aid, as well as development policies, are among the main actors (Xenogiani 2006, p. 39). Recent studies by Zhuang and Wang (2010), Chong (2013) and Nyiri (2013) also support this research lead.

In this chapter, new Chinese migrants are categorized into two subgroups for analysis, though it should be noted that these categorisations may not always be clear-cut. The first group is contracted labourers who are brought to Vietnam by Chinese contractors and companies; the second group is independent migrants who assume all risks in making their way to Vietnam and engage in business in various economic sectors.

The Ethnic Chinese in Vietnam

The term 'ethnic Chinese' is referred to as *người Hoa* in Vietnam, which is derived from the Chinese word *Huaren*. While this term generally refers to Chinese migrants who live overseas and their descendants, it may not convey whether or not they are Chinese nationals. In the context of Vietnam, 'ethnic Chinese' means the descendants of Chinese, including the *Hán* and other sub groups that originated from China such as *Hakka*, *Xạ Phang* and *Ngái* who settled in the country before it gained national independence in 1945. The *Người Hoa* is distinguished from the *Hoa Kiều* (Huaqiao) or "Overseas Chinese". The latter is commonly used to refer to Chinese sojourners who temporarily reside in the country while maintaining their Chinese citizenship (Wang Gungwu 1992; Hirschman 1988). The term *Hoa Kiều* has since had a politically sensitive meaning due to the assimilation policy of the South Vietnam Government in the years 1955–56 and particularly during the crisis of relations between Vietnam and China (1978–79).[1] The *Người Hoa* is now used as an official ethnonym in Vietnam, though this term is rather flexible and can include several sub-groups.

According to Vietnam's General Statistical Office, the population of Chinese in Vietnam in 1999 was 862,071 but declined to 823,071 in 2009 (GSO 2010). About 85 per cent of ethnic Chinese are residing in the southern parts of the country, especially in Ho Chi Minh City, where over 500,000 of these citizens live.

The ethnic Chinese in Vietnam today are the descendants of migrants who arrived earlier in history, between the sixteenth and mid-twentieth centuries. Migration continued during the French colonial period but then nearly ceased after the People's Republic of China (PRC) was founded in 1949 (Martinez 2007).

During the period from 1889 to 1906, nearly 1.2 million Chinese migrated to South Vietnam (*Cochinchina*), but approximately 850,000 Chinese also returned to their homeland concurrently. The general trend in the period between 1910 and 1950 was that the number of Chinese migrants in Vietnam increased from about 100,000 in 1910 to 1.2 million by the 1950s. By 1952, there were about 1.5 million ethnic Chinese living in Vietnam, accounting for six per cent of the national population. The wave of Chinese migration to Vietnam was strongest between 1935 and 1950, the period when Chinese society had political and economic upheaval due to the war and internal strife (Luong Nhi Ky 1963). Until the 1970s, the Chinese population in Vietnam was about 1.55 million, compared to 360,000 Chinese people in Cambodia and more than 100,000 in Laos. Tran Giao Thuy (2014) shows the proportion of Chinese groups in Vietnam by their dialects, of which a majority are Cantonese (41 per cent) and Teochew (37 per cent), with the remaining Hakka, Hokkien and Hainanese. Other groups from Guangxi and Yunnan were present but not in significant numbers.

Southern Vietnam was selected as a preferred destination probably because most Chinese immigrants were those who ran away from the chaos and internal strife in China, and therefore wanted to get as far away from the mainland as possible (Engelbert 2007). However, there were also minority groups who could not cross the border by sea but only by road. They entered Vietnam through border gates in the northeastern border region of Vietnam in different waves. Most of them are Ngái and Hakka who left southern China for the Sino-Vietnamese borderlands and landed in Hải Ninh, that is the present-day Quảng Ninh Province. A portion continued to move deeper to the northern border provinces. They were victims of the Taiping Rebellion, a bloody civil war in southern China during the Qing Dynasty from 1850 to 1864. When Vietnam was divided as a result of the Geneva Accords in 1954, there were over 50,000 Chinese immigrants who had left the North for the South (Nguyễn Văn Chính 2021; Trần Hồng Liên 2008). In the big northern cities, the Chinese were running small businesses. Most Chinese workers were involved in heavy labour. They lived in relatively closed communities and often practised ethnic endogamy instead of marrying locals. The Chinese population in Hanoi in 1913 was only about 2,000 people and this increased to 13,000 in 1978. In 1913, in Hải Phòng, there were only 8,500 Chinese people, and by 1979 there were more than 30,000 (Han 2009).

Prior to the reunification of Vietnam in 1975, the Overseas Chinese Associations played an essential role as a place of networking for the Chinese immigrants. In places with large Chinese communities, association halls were built to facilitate their meetings and activities. During the French colonial period, these associations were also used to control the Chinese immigrants. According to Engelbert (2007), the colonial state restored the Chinese traditional association system in 1863 after a series of unsuccessful experiments on direct administration of Chinese emigrants. Known as *congregations*, the system was set up on the basis of the immigrants' origins and language dialect groups. Pursuant to this system, Chinese immigrants were required to register at the Overseas Chinese Associations at the province where they had settled. For example, Sài Gòn-Chợ Lớn had five major associations: Guangtung Association, Fujian Association, Teochew Association, He (Hakka) Association, and Hainan Association. Enforced by the *French Service de l'Immigration for* Chinese immigrants in Indochina until the end of the French colonial system in 1954, the leaders of the associations were responsible for the policing of their new members—which included record keeping and monitoring of their activities—under the system. Any fines incurred by their members as a result of illegal actions, such as tax evasion or escape from law enforcement, had to be paid by the association on their behalf. Emigrants who did not register with the associations, if found, were forced to return to their homeland or expelled to other countries.

Despite the significant roles played by the Overseas Chinese Associations in the management of Chinese immigrants and tax collection, they were not financially supported by the colonial government. Their operational costs were derived from membership fees as well as income raised from various activities conducted by them. Apart from governance, these associations were also active in maintaining and promoting culture, customs, rituals and education within their own communities. While they generally did not intervene in their members' economic affairs, they were willing to assist their members who were in various forms of need.

During the American War of 1954–75, Overseas Chinese Associations in South Vietnam were managed by the *Groupements administratifs chinois régionaux* (Chinese Regional Administration Grouping) which had earlier replaced the *congregations* system (Luong Nhi Ky 1963). They were allowed to set up their own organizations under the Chinese Chamber of Commerce for the purpose of coordinating and organizing trade and industry programmes for the Chinese communities. Although the ethnic Chinese achieved great economic success, very few of them participated in or held high positions in the political arena of South Vietnam. Keeping Chinese citizenship as *Huaqiao* was perhaps a way for the Chinese immigrants to protect their business and to demonstrate loyalty to their motherland.

The ethnic Chinese played a significant role in Southern Vietnam's economy until the economic reforms after 1975. Up to the beginning of the 1970s, the largest investments in Southern Vietnam were owned by the overseas Chinese. Nearly half of the enterprises in the south were owned by them, and they controlled most of the processing industries, rice mills, exports and imports (Trần Khánh 1993, pp. 41, 43, 56). Unlike the Chinese communities living in the South, the Chinese in the North were much smaller in number and relatively weaker in the economy (Trần Khánh 1993).

Vietnam–China Economic Relations after Normalization in 1991

The relationship between Vietnam and China is not one simply based on diplomacy, but one that is geopolitically determined. This prominent feature is believed to have influenced the relations between the two countries in the past and in the present, and it will continue to be a key factor in the future. It is interesting to note that while the two countries are characterized by a common political regime ruled by a one-party state since the mid-twentieth century, each of them has pursued a different diplomatic strategy aimed to serve their national interests and maintain the power of the communist party. The diplomatic relationship between Vietnam and China during the past several decades is also a reflection of the long historical relationship between these two neighbouring countries in which China persistently attempts to pull Vietnam into its political orbit and Vietnam struggles to step out of China's shadow.

Trade with China

Trade between Vietnam and China has increased exponentially, from as little as US$30 million in the 1990s to more than US$41 billion by 2012 (VECITA 2012; *Thương Mại Việt-Trung Bulletin* 2012; *VnExpress* 2013).

At the same time, Vietnam's trade deficit with China grew from US$188 in 2001 to US$16.3 billion in 2012. The trade deficit ratio was 14.8 per cent in 2001, and by 2011 it had increased to over 220 per cent (Nguyễn Duy Nghĩa 2010).

Trade relations between the two countries have transformed Vietnam into a ready market for Chinese imported goods. There are several reasons for this. First, accepting Chinese imports is essential to good trading relations with China. While the Chinese market will not be affected if China stops exports to Vietnam—the latter comprises only one per cent of China's total foreign trade—the reverse is true for Vietnam as its trade with China comprises 28 per cent of its total foreign trade (Lê Đăng Doanh 2014). Second, as the two countries produce similar products for export, Vietnamese-made products will find it harder to compete with China-made goods because of price. Finally, domestic industries have not been able to meet the increasing demands in local consumption in Vietnam. Therefore, some industries source for goods from China in light of the geographical proximity between the two countries. Moreover, the cost savings gained from importing lower quality but cheaper Chinese equipment and technology help to mitigate the financial constraints of small and medium factories in Vietnam.

China is also a major provider of concessional loans and it has won major construction projects in the Vietnamese engineering, procurement and construction sector (EPC). There is no clear data on economic cooperation with China vis-à-vis EPC contracts because information on foreign economic aid is regarded as strictly confidential by both governments, leaving the exact value of Chinese aid to Vietnam unknown. A study by Le Hong Hiep (2013) reported that Chinese engineering companies, by the end of 2009, were involved in projects worth US$15.4 billion, making Vietnam their largest EPC market in Southeast Asia.

The increase in number and value of EPC contracts won by Chinese contractors is one of the most important factors driving the increasing flow of Chinese contract labour migration into Vietnam. To realize these EPC projects, Chinese contractors not only bring in Chinese technicians and managers, but also equipment, technology, materials and manual workers. Chinese state-owned companies, such as Shanghai Electric Group Co Ltd. (SEC), Wuhan Kadi Power Chemicals Co Ltd. China, China Donfang Electric Co (DEC), China Huanqiu Group, China Aluminium Intl. Engineering Company, Wuhan Engineering Co (WEC), and ZTE

Corporation Shanghai, are major partners contributing to this trend in Vietnam's EPC sector.

Reports issued by the Ministry of Industries and Commerce of Vietnam revealed that many EPC contracts won by Chinese contractors are upstream projects in sectors allied to national defence and security such as those in energy and mining. As much as 90 per cent of Vietnam's thermal power plants have been built by Chinese contractors (Nhật Minh 2012; Phạm Huyền 2010). Vietnam's dependence on Chinese contractors in these sectors has generated serious concerns. Among them are the poor quality of projects from Chinese companies, the perennial trade deficit with China, and conflict of interest over Vietnam's national security, especially in relation to energy security. In light of Vietnam's dependence on China on several fronts, it is understandable why the Vietnamese government has reacted slowly and passively to the types of illegal migrants from China into the country.

China's Foreign Direct Investment (FDI)

China officially became a foreign direct investment provider to developing countries from 2000 when the Chinese Communist Party launched its "going-out strategy", which encouraged and supported investment activities overseas aimed at making use of both domestic and foreign resources and markets. It was during this period that foreign investment of China increased from US$2.5 billion in 2002 to US$56.5 billion in 2009.

China's FDI inflows into Vietnam, however, have changed dramatically since 2015, especially since the US government imposed a 25 per cent import tax on goods imported from China, forcing Chinese businesses to look for opportunities abroad to cope with the US measures. Vietnam is one of the neighbouring countries sought by Chinese enterprises to expand their trade scale and increase direct investment projects. The table below shows the growth of Chinese FDI in Vietnam.

The statistics in Table 12.1 show that China's total cumulative investment as of December 2020 is 18.5 billion dollars, with 3,123 projects, placing China in the seventh position among foreign investors in Vietnam. However, the rapid growth of China's foreign direct investments also raises doubts about its consequences. The ongoing discussion about foreign investment of China often revolve around three main issues: (i) Chinese investments might cause trade deficit and imbalance, thus posing a threat

TABLE 12.1
Chinese FDI Inflows into Vietnam, 2015–20 (million US$)

Year	Total capital (million dollars)	Project number
2015	10,174	1,296
2016	10,521	1,555
2017	12,084	1,812
2018	13,348	2,149
2019	16,246	2,807
2020	18,128	3,807

Source: Ministry of Planning and Investment (2020), Investment flow from China to Vietnam, http://investvietnam.gov.vn/vi/tin-tuc.nd/tinh-hinh-dong-von-dau-tu-tu-trung-quoc-vao-viet-nam.html November 2020.

to host countries; (ii) Strategically, China might try to use its commercial dominance to pave the way for its industries to climb up the value chain, and; (iii) Chinese investments tend to concentrate on the mining of natural resources, which may lead to serious environmental problems.

Thanks to increased FDI inflows and loan supply, for many years China has continuously been the largest supplier of goods to Vietnam, but, also, Vietnam is a country with a large trade deficit with China. In 2020, two-way trade between Vietnam and China totalled US$133 billion, of which Vietnam had exported products worth US$48.9 billion to China, while the country had spent US$84.1 billion on imports from China, a trade deficit of US$35.2 billion. The main drivers for the trade growth were still processing and manufacturing goods and building materials.

Although the number of Chinese investment projects in Vietnam grew rapidly, they were generally not stable and the average size of projects were relatively small. From the 1990s to 2001, China's FDI projects were only small and medium scale, and there was even a project investment that covered just US$100,000. Since 2001, the average project capital has increased from US$1 million to US$10 million, and until 2007 the number of projects has been on the increase, with large capital investment ranging from US$10 million to US$100 million. The total investment capital of Chinese enterprises has increased since 2015, but it poses new challenges. For example, in 2015 China invested in twenty-nine projects with a total investment of US$150.87 million in plywood production. However, the unusual increase in Chinese plywood investment in Vietnam and the increase in plywood exports from Vietnam has led to doubts about the transparency of trade. As a result, in June 2020 the United States officially issued a decision to investigate Vietnam's plywood products (VietnamNet 7 July 2020).

China's FDI projects in Vietnam have expanded to seventeen different sectors, in which manufacturing and processing occupied the majority (76 per cent), followed by construction (5.3 per cent) and agriculture and forestry (3.8 per cent). However, there are minimal investment projects using advanced technology with large capital investment. China's FDI projects mainly exploit cheap labour and resources that are available locally. In the mining and communication and energy sectors, Chinese investors do not use FDI but opt for preferential buyer's credit and concessional loans provided by the Chinese government as a method to monopolize the construction contracts and buy the product.

While Chinese FDI projects in Vietnam are on the increase, Chinese companies do not seem to focus much on FDI projects but instead prefer projects that provide funding to Vietnamese investors in order to receive bids for major EPC construction projects. Generally speaking, EPC projects by Chinese contractors in Vietnam involve the Chinese government in the name of concessional loans. In order to implement this form of economic cooperation, the Chinese contractors often seek the support of their government by instituting the constraint that the firms that conduct these projects must be Chinese. Such projects are not considered FDI but a form of cooperation or economic aid. In fact, such subsidies are one of the main forms of support from the Chinese government for their enterprises, which aim to facilitate economic activities overseas to obtain the raw materials that China lacks. The subsidies also aim to stimulate the export of goods by equipment or technology that China has a comparative advantage in and in labour service exports, and to make use of internationally advanced technology, management and human resources.

During the past decade, Chinese companies have been the most important contractors for all major construction works in Vietnam. The total value of major construction projects won by Chinese contractors continues to increase, and this development is directly related to the flow of contract labour migration from China to Vietnam. A significant proportion of the construction projects implemented by Chinese companies are in the form of EPC. It is apparent that EPC contracts with Chinese partners are one of the key elements contributing to the increasing labour migration from China to Vietnam and the trade gap between Vietnam and China, which was discussed earlier in this chapter.

Chinese capital into Vietnam increased, partly due to the US–China trade war, which caused a trend to shift production out of China. Vietnamese civilians are also worried FDI inflows from China may turn Vietnam into a 'basecamp' for Chinese enterprises that import goods into Vietnam and then export them to the United States and European countries, causing Vietnam to violate international regulations. Furthermore, the wave of investment from China also creates pressure on domestic enterprises. By 2020, the impact of the Covid-19 pandemic has slowed this trend. Affected production and business activities, the travel of investors, new investment decisions and expansion of the scale of foreign investment projects tended to decrease, which caused not only Chinese capital flows entering Vietnam but also from other countries to decrease (Kiều Linh 2020).

China's Economic Aid

Since the normalization of diplomatic relations between the two countries in 1991, China has begun to resume its economic aid to Vietnam, which was stopped in 1975. China's aid to Vietnam from the 1990s onwards did not, however, emphasize the principle of 'politics first', as it did before, but instead used aid as a tool to achieve two major goals: political interest and economic gains.

In 1992, China signed a package of US$20 million aid to Vietnam, opening a new era of relations between the two countries. Presently, China continues to provide aid to Vietnam, and it has increased in both scope and amounts, representing the symbolic meaning of economic-political ties between the two nations and two communist parties.

China's aid to Vietnam from 1992 to the present has typically been in the form of concessional loans and preferential export buyer's credit. Concessional loans are mostly focused on the new investment projects such as copper and bauxite mining, thermal power plants and infrastructure contracted by Chinese companies and which therefore prioritizes Chinese companies in construction contracts. As regulated by EXIM Bank (2012), all projects using China's concessional loans must use Chinese technology, machines and equipment, and the Chinese government reserves the right to appoint Chinese contractors to implement the projects it aids instead of inviting competitive-based tenders. In addition, the human resource training projects that use China's government aid must be conducted in China and by Chinese partners. Undoubtedly, these conditions have enabled Chinese contractors to win EPC projects and have contributed to the dominance of Chinese engineering companies in Vietnam. With such support, Chinese companies are able to offer lower prices. It is apparent that China's concessional loans have become an increasingly important source of funding for Vietnam's investment projects and mainly function as a channel to promote China's foreign trade and investments aimed at prioritizing economic gains.

New Chinese Migrants in Vietnam

Contracted Labourers

The increasing presence of Chinese migrant workers in Vietnam and Southeast Asia indicates that China's economic cooperation and integration with the region has been growing where they are considered a 'resource to generate foreign exchange' (Skeldon 1996; Walsh 2009).

According to Vietnam's General Statistical Office (2011), the influx of migrants from China to Vietnam has been increasing. By 1995, statistics indicated that about 62,000 Chinese migrated into Vietnam for various purposes. The figure of Chinese migrants then rose to 723,000 in 2002, and 905,000 in 2010.[2] We do not know how many amongst these migrants came to find jobs, do business or work as contracted labourers. The number of Chinese entering Vietnam has continuously increased in recent years. From 2015 to 2018, the number of Chinese entering Vietnam accounted for more than thirty per cent of the total number of 15 million foreigners coming to Vietnam in the same period. According to the National Assembly's Foreign Affairs Committee (Thanh Niên 2019), 13 million foreigners entered Vietnam for tourism purposes; more than 1 million came to Vietnam to work. It is noteworthy that while the number of Chinese people working in Vietnam was the largest, only 6,121 people were licensed.

Together with the increase of human influx from China, available data reveals that the number of Chinese labourers working at Vietnamese construction sites has also been on the rise. There are no official statistics but unpublished reports by the Ministry of Labour, Invalids and Social Affairs (MOLISA, 2010) and a monitoring report by the National Assembly do provide some clues to confirm this trend, as indicated in Table 12.2.

Although the data provided by MOLISA, as indicated in Table 12.2, is not adequate, it shows that within the last decade Chinese workers in

TABLE 12.2
Chinese Working as Contracted Labourers in Vietnam (by year/person)

Year	Number of workers (person)
2005	21,217
2006	34,117
2007	43,766
2008	52,633
2009	55,482
2010	75,000
2014	34.161
2018	25,100
2020	33,770

Sources: Data for 2005–10 and 2020 provided by MOLISA. The figures presented in this table are obtained from unpublished reports by the Ministry of Labour, Invalids and Social Affairs (MOLISA) and Information Office, Social Affairs Committee of the National Assembly (SAC). They do not necessarily reflect the real volume of Chinese labours working in Vietnam because a majority of Chinese manual labours do not register with local authorities. Data for 2014 and 2018 were extracted from "Monitoring report of the National Assembly's Social Affairs Committee" provided by the National Assembly's Information Office, 26 October 2018.

Vietnam have increased more than three times. Since there are no reliable statistics on Chinese workers at the national level, we had to conduct fieldwork at several construction sites to obtain some facts on Chinese immigrants working in Vietnam. Details are indicated in Table 12.3.

Chinese manual workers are mainly found to work for major construction projects where Chinese enterprises were contracted by Vietnamese investors. In our conversations with various Chinese contractors, it was reported that most of their workers were employed to work on a short-term contract, from three months to one year or longer, depending on the specific project. A number of Chinese workers who participated in our survey were found, however, to have stayed in Vietnam for longer, from two or more years, particularly for cases in Hai Phong, where it was reported that they had stayed for longer than ten years and worked at various projects in Vietnam. These workers did not return home after completing the contract but moved to work at other construction sites for the same or different Chinese employers. At every work site with Chinese labourers, we found Chinese workers who got married to local women and resided in their wife's home or cheap lodgings nearby their worksites.

TABLE 12.3
Chinese Workforce at Different Worksites

Worksites	Quantity (persons)	Legally registered	Year
Hải Phòng Thermo-power Plants (Hải Phong City)	4,000	300 (7%)	2010
Quảng Ninh Thermo-power Plants (Quảng Nam)	4,200	1,195 (28%)	2011
Ninh Bình Industries Complex (Ninh Bình Prov.)	2,400	714 (29%)	2011
Bauxite Mining Nhân Cơ (Daknong Province)	1,091	215 (19%)	2011
Bauxite Mining Tan Rai (Lam Dong Province)	1,400	255 (18%)	2011
Nong Son Coal & Electricity (Quang Nam Prov.)	500	100 (20%)	2012
Cà Mau Complex of Gas, Electricity & Nitrogen	1,700	654 (38%)	2012
Nghi Sơn Cement Factory (Thanh Hóa Province)	326	93 (28%)	2013
Sông Bung Hydro Power Plant (Quảng Nam)	296	50 (17%)	2013
Formosa Steel Corporation (Hà Tĩnh Province)	4,300	800 (18%)	2011
Formosa Steel Corporation (Hà Tĩnh Province)	10,339	1,913 (19%)	2018
Đắk N'Drung wind power project (Đắk Nông Prov.)	101	100 (99%)	2020
Pou Chen Vietnam Enterprise (Đồng Nai Prov.)	1,400	465 (33%)	2020
Krông Búk Wind Power Project (Đắk Lắc Prov.)	87	85 (97%)	2021

Sources: Fieldwork investigation.

Similar to many construction sites in Asia and Africa that are implemented by Chinese contractors, the majority of Chinese labourers found working in Vietnam are manual or unskilled labour and involved in 'heavy' jobs. Because most of them stay illegally, not licensed by the local government (illegal entry, illegal stay and illegal work), they do not cross the border back to home in China after completing the contract but search for new jobs in the local area, moving from their original worksite to other sites to avoid detection and fines by local authorities. Chinese employers see this as a good opportunity, as it can save some transaction costs to recruit new workers from China. As we discovered, Chalieco Company (Chinalco Corporation) was contracted to build an aluminium processing factory in Tân Rai Bauxite Mining of Lâm Đồng. They brought in 700 workers when the project began in 2008. The number of Chinese workers was then doubled to 1,400 persons in 2009 but later reduced to 922 in late 2011. Most of the labourers working in Tân Rai finished their contracts in 2011, and they were recruited and moved to Nhân Cơ aluminium factory (Đắk Nông Province). This adjustment apparently ensures availability of labour force for the Chinese contractors but causes local authorities more difficulties in management because of their mobility.

At the Quảng Ninh Thermo-Power Plant (Quảng Ninh Province) and Bauxite Nhân Cơ (Đắk Nong Province), we found that during some periods Chinese workers can constitute 80 to 90 per cent of the total workforce. As indicated in the report by MOLISA (2010), local authorities also acknowledge that Chinese workers are an important labour force in all construction projects implemented by Chinese contractors. However, the concern is that the majority of Chinese workers are not registered with the local authorities nor have a work permit as regulated by labour and immigration laws of Vietnam.[3]

The involvement of Chinese workers in some major construction projects in Vietnam is shown in Table 12.3. In our interviews with the local authorities of Thủy Nguyên District, where roughly 4,000 Chinese labourers were working at the construction site, the Chairman of the District said:

> The information on Chinese workers we gave to you was synthesized from reports by contractors and investors. We do not know exactly how many they are in reality, so we have to trust them. Our public security force has been checking the worksites, but to be honest, it is not easy to figure out because the workers may stay here in our district for a few months and then move to other worksites afterwards, depending on the

management of their contractors. We cannot follow them everywhere. Recently, one Chinese worker was found dead in My Son commune. The local authority informed the Chinese contractors about the case but they responded that they didn't have any workers missing. We finally had to organize the funeral for the death after completing the legal procedures because we cannot treat the death in such a bad way.

As we discovered, there are at least three key reasons to explain why the local authorities could not manage the Chinese workers in the location they are responsible for:

1. The demand for manual labour at construction sites is high but most of the tasks do not require high skills so Chinese contractors are able to mobilize a good number of cheap workers from the floating population roaming in China's cities within a short time and bring them to Vietnam for work. If their cases are found, they will be returned home or moved to other worksites without asking for compensation.
2. The procedure of applying for work permits is time-consuming and complicated. However, despite low wages, many Chinese workers are willing to travel to Vietnam for temporary jobs in order to make some quick money, and thus choose to skip such legalities. Contractors widely acknowledge that such low-wage workers are usually not granted a work permit, but they choose to ignore local laws to meet the demand for the progress of the project.
3. Chinese contractors usually take advantage of Vietnam's loose regulations to bring in cheap workers. The popular remedies they often employ are: (i) Moving workers regularly among worksites they have contracted; (ii) Only applying work permits for technical staff, specialists and engineers; and (iii) Using fake documents certifying the standard of occupation for manual workers. When there are inspections, the worker will be moved to other worksites.

If we compare the wages of Chinese workers with those of workers in the mainland, we can see that wages for migrant workers in Vietnam are comparatively low and are not as attractive for Chinese workers.[4] Our conversations with Chinese workers reveal, however, that when they get a job in Vietnam, they are able to accumulate savings when returning home. Moreover, they often evade paying personal income tax by working without permission.[5]

Although their job is tough, Chinese workers rarely complain about their working conditions. Vietnamese workers who worked with Chinese workers commended their hardworking, disciplined and robust character. Although rumours about physical punishments by Chinese overseers against their workers exist, we did not hear of such complaints in our conversations with workers at construction sites.[6] Chan and Wang (2004), basing their empirical research on comparing Taiwanese investors' practices in managing factories in Vietnam and China, remarked that even though wages in Vietnam are not as high as expected, Chinese workers' rights are respected. They were not abused, as was the case at many worksites and factories in mainland China. Chan and Wang argued that this was one of the main reasons why Chinese workers from the mainland preferred working in factories run by Taiwanese firms in Vietnam. Their explanation was that "in China, Taiwanese managers can use a 'militaristic' management method, where physical punishments were very common, including even hitting, like in the military", but "in Vietnam we feel they need to use 'soft' management methods", because "their protection of labour rights is too stringent" in Vietnam. Chan and Wang quoted an interview with a Chinese worker in Hai Phong, who said: "In Haiphong ... we frequently have to work overtime, even to midnight. But I feel that we are lucky here compared with our work in China, where I worked much longer." (Chan and Wang 2004, p. 637). However, it is noted that the working conditions in factories run by Taiwanese are well organized, with the monitoring of labour unions and other massive organizations, which is completely different from worksites under the management by Chinese contractors where labour unions are almost non-existent.

Chinese construction workers share some common characteristics in their daily lives. Generally, their work and daily activities are arranged by sub-contractors. For instance, in Hải Phòng Thermal Power Plant, there were six sub-contractors from Guang-xi, Hubei and Shantung. These sub-contractors are responsible for different assignments as per contracts with the main contractors and employment of workers to implement their assigned jobs. At this construction site, temporary dormitories for workers were built on-site to ensure accommodation for thousands of workers. Visiting one of the dormitories built by Nhất An Company (Guang-xi) at this construction site, we found that each unit had 130 bedrooms. Each room was equipped with 4 to 8 bunk beds, which was enough for 8 to 16 workers. As a principle of work organization, workers are divided into small groups and placed under the direct management of the unit head. These small units have their own office and a collective kitchen for workers. The sub-contractors also provide workers with a karaoke bar and some canteens for their other necessities. In this way, the arrangement of these workers' lives is quite similar to that of a military unit.

Apart from a few Chinese women recruited to do light jobs, cleaning and cooking, most of the workers in worksites are male. After their long working hours, they engage in various types of entertainment close to their worksites, including massages, herbal baths, gambling and sex. In the evening, they join groups searching for entertainment outside of the construction sites, get drunk and make noise. It is to meet the demand from Chinese workers that there is the provision of such 'relaxing' services to maximize the service zones around construction sites. These places are called new "Chinese villages".[7] All instructions for guesthouses, hotels, restaurants and more are written in both Chinese and Vietnamese. These places also attract a large number of sex workers, causing a ruckus and thereby disturbances for local residents every night.[8]

From the view of Vietnamese investors and labour managers, the increasing presence of Chinese workers in Vietnamese construction sites is a new development that policymakers have not been able to respond to immediately in the right manner. The labour law that permits foreign workers to stay in Vietnam for less than three months without permission is a policy gap that must be addressed. Furthermore, the government's bureaucratic system does not seem to work very well. The required procedures under Decree 34/2008/NĐ-CP and Decree 46/2011.NĐ-CP for work permits are much too complicated, time-consuming and unfeasible. In addition to this, the quality of local workers is said to be low as they lack discipline and career ambitions.[9]

From the side of Chinese contractors and managers, they seem to share the common concerns that Vietnamese workers are unable to stand the heavy workload and lack discipline. They often quit without notice and ignore the guidance given by Chinese technicians. The largest issue for Vietnamese workers is the language barrier. They are not able to understand instructions by Chinese engineers, while hiring interpreters is expensive. The utilization of Chinese workers thus provides contractors with many advantages as they often work under the pressure of tight timelines. The account by Dave Zhang, a Chinese employee at Pou Chen Vietnam

Enterprise in Đồng Nai province, helps us to understand why Taiwanese contractors need Chinese workers:

> We were sent to resolve any 'bottlenecks' in the production lines that were slowing down the rest of the plant because during the launch of every new production line Vietnamese workers would strike and get into disputes. As far as I know, there were over a thousand Chinese employees managing various aspects of the production lines in the company's Vietnamese factories.

The account below is also helpful:

> In fact, what our Chinese employees have done in Vietnam for more than a decade can be said to be very simple but very difficult. That is to teach Vietnamese workers our experience of working on a production line, improve the productivity of the Vietnamese workers, and help the factories become localized. (He 2020)

Even deputy manager Ha tinh of the Formosa Steel Corporation (owned by a Taiwanese) admitted that his company eventually recruited Chinese workers because Vietnamese workers applying for the positions needed to know a foreign language (i.e., Chinese) and be experienced in the field, and only Chinese workers were able to do the job (interview with Vương Tường, June 2018).

The Traders

Today, although the Chinese new migration to Vietnam and Southeast Asia is diverse and much more different than in the past, there are two groups of migrants that seem to continue the traditional flow of out-migration from China. They are the hawkers and healers. According to our interviews, most of the new migrants working as small traders and healers in Vietnam seem to concur that their priority is not to seek permanent resettlement in Vietnam, but rather to find opportunities to earn good money. These migrants do not try to integrate into local society. Instead, they usually move abroad without their family and maintain their Chinese citizenship. They maintain close connections with the mainland during their out-migration with the expectation of returning home.

Chinese immigrants working in construction sites and as petty traders make up a large proportion of the immigrants, although it is difficult to differentiate between the two in the human flow of the border crossings each day. At the trade centres located in Móng Cái, Tân Thanh and Lào Cai borderlands, we can observe the flow of cheap goods from China penetrating into Vietnam transported by local porters, both Chinese and Vietnamese. No Vietnamese agencies have been able to collect specific data on the volume and value of goods brought in by Chinese traders. Upon return, Chinese businessmen buy almost all agricultural products available, comprising fruit, coffee, rice, sweet potatos, cassavas, seafood, rubber, and herbs for medicine, among others. They also collect small amounts of iron ore, coal and various kinds of minerals acquired by family and private groups and transport them to China for large profits. At the border markets, we can see individuals selling and buying minerals.

Observation of the trade of lychees in Lục Ngạn District (Bắc Giang Province) may help us understand the roles and behavioural patterns of petty Chinese traders. The district authorities reported that during the lychee season of 2011, there were 121 petty Chinese traders buying lychees in this district. These traders came during the lychee season, from the beginning of June, and stayed until the end of the month. When the lychee season ended, they transitioned into selling other agricultural products. The Chinese traders normally use their long-term relationship with locals, especially with the local ethnic Chinese communities in the district, to run an agency for collecting and selecting lychees with the highest quality and transporting the products to the borders at the two main border gates of Lào Cai and Lạng Sơn. However, there are also petty traders illegally entering the country, scrambling to buy and sell, disrupting the lychee market. In coping with the situation of illegal entry, since 2015 Bac Giang authorities have coordinated with the Chinese Embassy in Hanoi to register 190 Chinese traders who come to Vietnam to buy lychees. Electronic exchanges also work with traders who do not come in person, which have helped increase lychee exports to China. Information by Bắc Giang Province indicated that approximately 70,000 tons of lychees (equivalent to more than 52 per cent of the lychee production of Lục Ngạn District in 2011) were exported to China by Chinese petty merchants through border trade. This figure increased to 130,000 tons in 2021.

Chinese merchants collect and transport the products from Vietnam to the border in order to deliver these products to their Chinese partners. Many petty traders started working as hired labourers and later switched to doing business when they had acquired enough capital. Some even purchase property through their local partners' name. For them, building a good relationship with local partners is essential. The choice of marrying local women for some Chinese male traders can be seen as a turning point in their sojourning lives because from this point they are able to think of a permanent settlement and expand their business. The cases of Chinese immigrants who worked on aquaculture in Vũng Tầu (Khánh Hòa) and Vũng Rô (Phú Yên) below could be useful for obtaining an overview of the work and life of Chinese petty traders in Vietnam.

> In Vũng Tầu, we met a group of six Chinese immigrants from Fujian. They arrived here in 2007. Their main business is to buy white bass fish and lobsters and sell them back to China. Since they had good networking relations with traders in mainland China, their business went smoothly. Two years later, one of them, Mr Lin, got married to a local Vietnamese Chinese woman. They separated from the group and set up a company named Song Phong. The company was registered under the name of his wife, a Vietnamese citizen, who is able to legalize their fish and lobster farming and trading business. Following his friend's footsteps, Mr Zheng also got married to a local woman, who was born and raised in China Town, Ho Chi Minh City. They established Hải Hoành Company and engaged in the same business of fish and lobster farming in Đầm Môn, which is ten kilometres from the shore. The company is also registered in the name of his Vietnamese wife. Their fish cages increased from three at the beginning in 2009 to three hundred fish and lobster cages in 2011, and their farming area also expanded to ten hectares. They employed local labourers to work on fish and lobster hatching. Their stories give a clear idea of the 'cooperation' between new and old Chinese migrants in doing business, where marriage to a local woman is often chosen as a strategy. I don't know if cooperation is the right word...

...to penetrate into local society and take advantage of ready business network created by local ethnic Chinese.

The Healers

The Vietnamese have a strong belief in Chinese herbs and traditional methods of treatment. For the poor, medicines from natural materials such as traditional herbs are safe, accessible and cheap. Since the border re-opened in the 1990s, Chinese traditional healers have found their way back to Vietnam and it is here that they see a great potential market for their business.

Data provided by the Ministry of Health indicate that from 2005 up to present, they have licensed a total of 168 Chinese clinics for operation in Vietnam (44 licenses in 2008, 47 licenses in 2009, and 67 licenses in 2010). Of such clinics, 76 were registered as legal Vietnamese entities and operate in the form of joint-ventures, while the other 92 clinics were invested in directly by Chinese doctors of traditional medicine (Ministry of Health 2010). The licence for these clinics normally lasts between three to five years and is renewable. Chinese clinics are found in 17 provinces and cities, but most of them are concentrated in Hanoi (52 clinics), Ho Chi Minh City (32 clinics), Cần Thơ (19 clinics) and Đà Nẵng (13 clinics). According to information given in their registration documents, each clinic employed between 4 and 6 staff, including nurses, doctors and health workers. However, these clinics were found to recruit employees without labour permits (Người Lao động 2012).

Up until 2000, Hanoi had 144 registered traditional medical clinics, while there were 1,647 such clinics in Ho Chi Minh City. In our interviews with officers of Hanoi's Health Department, it was revealed that the figure of registered Chinese traditional clinics is far from the reality because the operation of such clinics is usually done under the name of legal Vietnamese entities and/or under the form of joint-venture clinics. In such clinics, Chinese traditional medical practitioners and medical doctors are invited to work temporarily based on verbal agreements. They normally stay for several days or up to a few months. The mobility of Chinese traditional healers and medical doctors is high, but local authorities are not able to control and monitor their movements.

Apart from spending large sums for advertising, Chinese traditional healers rarely invest in improving the conditions of their clinics. They often rent a small office space just large enough for one or two tables, several simple medical tools and room for staff. We found that some Chinese clinic toilets were even utilized as drug stores due to a room shortage. Such simple and space-constrained clinics for both health examination and selling drugs were also found in many commercial centres and open markets in the North.

Most Chinese healing practitioners were found to have been working in Vietnam for several years or more. They were unable, however, to speak Vietnamese—their examinations and treatment instructions were usually sent through interpreters. Nevertheless, we did not meet professional interpreters at any of the medical clinics we visited. More often, we found students of Chinese language training colleges or medical staff who could speak some Chinese acting as interpreters.

Clients of those Chinese clinics mostly come from poor rural areas. They know about these clinics mainly via advertisements on television or word of mouth. The patients also noted that they found the same drug prescribed for different ailments and therefore questioned its effectiveness. One student of Chinese language, who was hired to work as an interpreter in a clinic, said in one of our interviews that she could not understand all the medical terms. She sometimes had to use 'body language' to convey patients' problems and expectations.

The boom of Chinese clinics and its suspect practices forced local health authorities to inspect many Chinese clinics. In 2009 and 2011, health authorities in Hanoi and Ho Chi Minh City conducted inspections on twenty Chinese medical facilities and found that all of them violated the law (Người Lao Động 2012). Their violations were demonstrated by (1) the physician's use of a false licence; (2) selling drugs that are out of date or of unknown origin, charging too much for medical examinations and treatment services, and deceiving or treating patients unethically; (3) false advertising.

A matter of concern is that Chinese migrants undertaking self-employment often choose to emigrate illegally. They enter Vietnam mainly to work in the informal and underground economies such as gambling, internet fraud and loan sharking. They enter via trails along the border with the help of brokers or use passports with visas on entry but do not extend them when their visas expire. Most of the people who entered the country illegally were aged between 20 and 45 years old. Marrying a local Chinese or Vietnamese who knows Chinese is a common solution to reach out to the local community and build social capital for their business. However, they also often gather in large groups for illegal activities. For example, in 2019 the Hải Phòng police busted a high-tech gambling ring in the city and took more than 380 Chinese into custody. Investigations found that the ring has been operating for six months, facilitating gambling bets worth more than 3 billion yuan, equivalent to US$435.7 million (*VnExpress* 2019). In 2020 and 2021, Vietnamese police detected 199 cases of illegal entry from China, with 1,343 people entering illegally. Once in Vietnam, they spread out to the provinces and live in residential areas with the help of local brokers, making it very difficult for the authorities to detect (Lao Động 2021).

Conclusion

The massive migration from China to Vietnam in recent years is not a unique phenomenon but part of a broader trend of Chinese out-migration to foreign countries in search of better fortunes after China's economic reforms in 1979. These contemporary Chinese migrants seem to share some common features.

First, most Chinese who contracted labourers and migrants to Vietnam are not highly educated or from well-off families, unlike those who migrate to developed countries. Contract workers and traders, who run their own businesses and are expected to shoulder all risks, are prominent within the human flow from China. Because of limited resources, Chinese migrants often rely on their own networks based on their ethnicity, kinship relations or business ties with local people, particularly with the ethnic Chinese in Vietnam. In recent years, illegal migration brokers are becoming increasingly popular in border areas. Additionally, marriages between Chinese male migrants and Vietnamese local women are on the rise as they can be seen as a 'warranty' for Chinese migrants to create new social networks and facilitate their integration into Vietnamese society.[10] New Chinese villages and Chinatowns have also emerged in many places where new Chinese migrants have gathered.

Second, the usual route for Chinese migrants to enter Vietnam is via tourist visas that are valid for between one and three months. However, instead of arriving for tourism, they come to seek jobs and business opportunities. Chinese migrants often remain in Vietnam longer than the validity of their visas without applying for work permits or licences. This pattern results in their illegal status, which causes difficulties in adjusting to their new life and hinders their integration into local society. Nevertheless, there are no official statistics from Vietnam providing reliable data on the volume of Chinese migrants to Vietnam thus far. The open policy and friendly relations between the two countries, along with the rapidly improved infrastructure system, have created more advantages for migrants.

Third, Vietnam's policies and regulations on migration are inadequate to respond to situations in which Chinese contractors employ a large number of manual workers for their contracted projects in Vietnam. At the same time, further problems for local authorities in migration management arise when workers whose contracts have expired do not return to China but instead run businesses illegally. Several policy amendments to deal with Chinese migrant workers do not seem to work well. One policy is to get foreign contractors to provide employment plans in their bidding documents; another is to require foreign contractors to apply for work permits in an attempt to prevent the migration of manual workers (as per Decree 46/2011/NĐ-CP). In actuality, Vietnam has created robust laws with regards to contemporary foreign labour, but they face a dilemma in dealing with Chinese illegal migrants because of Vietnam's special relationship with China. And the reality is that Vietnam needs more capital for development projects from the Chinese government. Furthermore, 'economic cooperation' between the two countries is often defined as an internal collaboration among the socialist-oriented economies led by communist parties. Dealing harshly with Chinese migrants is deemed to be harmful to the bilateral relations of the two neighbouring communist countries. This explains why local Vietnamese authorities cannot fully apply laws in the cases of illegal migration.

Finally, the boom of Chinese new migration around the world is not only an individual's decision but also one largely influenced by China's policies of exporting labourers, foreign investment and economic aid, in line with the Chinese Communist Party's strategy of 'going-out' in the early twenty-first century. This strategy has recently received great support from the state through the Belt and Road Initiative. The use of economic strength and high volumes of trade as a policy instrument to create dependence of other countries on China is also a matter of concern (Xu 2010; Cui 1991). Nevertheless, studies on the impacts of external economic policy in general and out-migration as an important part of this state's strategies still receive little attention.

Notes

1. Regarding the policy of assimilation of Hoa Kiều (overseas Chinese) in the South, the Government of the Republic of Vietnam promulgated the Law on Vietnamese nationality in 1955, followed by a series of edicts (Edict No. 48 signed on 21 August 1956; Edict No. 52 signed on 29 August 1956; Edict No. 53 signed on 6 September 1956), forcing Hoa Kiều who were born in Vietnam to naturalize and declare Vietnamese nationality. In case they do not accept citizenship, they can apply for repatriation. See Trinh Mai Linh (2010, pp. 13–138).
2. The data of Chinese labour used in this paragraph were processed from various sources provided by the GSO (Ministry of Planning and Investment

- MPI), Immigration Department (Ministry of Public Security – MPS) and the Department of Labour and Employment (Ministry of Labour, Invalids and Social Affairs – MOLISA). Since the data were preserved at the archives but not officially published, they were mainly used within the functioning bodies of ministries as sources of internal references. I am aware clearly that these sources of data are partial and may not be sufficient to provide a comprehensive understanding of the current situation.
3. According to the current Vietnam Labour Laws and Immigration Laws, foreign labourers who are recruited to work in Vietnam for a period less than three months do not need to apply for work permission, but they have to register with the local authorities where they reside at least seven days before commencing work by submitting required documents such as the certificate(s) of profession and personal profile (Decree No. 34 /2008/NĐ-CP on Recruitment and Management of Foreign Labour in Vietnam). The Decree No. 46/2011/NĐ-CP, issued on 17 June 2011, indicates clearly that only foreign workers with well-trained skills and experience are permitted to work, but their recruitment must be put in the contract documents of their project contractors. As we discovered, such regulations are all ignored by Chinese contractors and Vietnamese investors.
4. According to World Salary (2005), *Average Salary in China – Job and Sector Comparison*, the average salary of construction workers in China was US$533/month in 2005, equal to US$22.2/day for 9 working hours or 2.5 US$/hour (http://www.worldsalaries.org/china.shtml), *Tiên Phong Newspaper* (20 February 2012), cited in the *New York Times*, showing that the medium salary of one Chinese producing worker is US$3.1/hour, compared to US$22.3/hour paid to an American worker with the same job.
5. As per the Law of Personal Income Tax (PIT), which was ratified by the Vietnamese National Assembly on 21 November 2007, those who have a total income of 9 million VND and above per month are subject to pay PIT.
6. According to *Daily Mail Reporter* (1 May 2011), an investigation of the 500,000 workers by the Centre for Research (Sacom) revealed that excessive overtime was rife despite a legal limit of thirty-six hours a month, while badly performing workers were humiliated in front of colleagues.
7. In mid-2011, BECAMEX Bình Dương Corporation embarked on building a 'Great ChinaTown' valued at more than US$320 million on an area of twenty-six square hectares in Thủ Dầu Một City, Bình Dương Province. This project aims to build a modern Chinese-style town to serve Chinese communities who live and work in Bình Dương. It is reported that there are more than 700,000 Asian immigrant workers working in Bình Dương Province, of which 70 per cent are ethnic Chinese (http://www.becamexijc.com/Default.aspx?mod=guide&atv=guide&id=42&idtype=31).

8. There have been many conflicts between Chinese and local workers. One example was at Nghi Sơn construction site (Thanh Hóa Province) and reported in the media. More than a hundred Chinese workers wrecked a local restaurant on 22 June 2009 because of a misunderstanding while buying cigarettes. Two local people were beaten and suffered severe injuries (VietnamNet 2009).
9. In response to our interview question to an officer of Hải Phòng Thermal Power Plant on the issue of using Chinese manual workers, he said that "it is the Chinese contractors who are responsible for the recruitment of workers. The Vietnamese investors' obligation is just to monitor the project progress and quality; they are unable to interfere in the utilization of labours and wages."
10. The Institute of Social Development Studies ISDS 2011, "Migration of Vietnamese Women to East Asia for Marriage" (2011), reports that about thirty thousand Vietnamese women married Chinese men, and the majority of these marriages have no legal documents.

References

Chan, Anita, and Hong-zen Wang. 2004. "The Impact of the State on Workers'Conditions, Comparing Taiwanese Factories in China and Vietnam". *Pacific Affairs* 77, no. 4: 629–46.

Chong, Terence. 2013. "Chinese Capital and Immigration into CLMV: Trend and Impact". *ISEAS Perspective*, no. 2013/53, 29 August 2013.

Cui, Huo Shen. 1991. *Cuộc đấu tranh giành giật biên giới mềm* [The struggle to fight for soft border]. Hanoi: Marx-Lenin Publisher. (Translated from the Chinese version: Cui Huo Shen. 1990. *Zhengduo "Ruanbianjiang" de xin jiaozhu*. Sichuan: Education Publishing House.)

Đặng, Vũ Chinh. 2009. "Chiến tranh biên giới Việt–Trung 1979" [Vietnam–China border war 1979]. http://sites.google.com/site/chinhdangvu/vietnam/history-of-vietnam/sino-vietnamese-war/chien-tranh-bien-gioi-viet-trung-1979 (accessed 23 May 2013).

Đào, Trinh Nhất. 1924. *Thế lực Khách trú và vấn đề di dân vào Nam Kỳ* [The Chinese immigrants and the question of their migration into Nam Ky]. Hanoi.

Engelbert, Thomas. 2007. "'Go West' in Cochinchina, Chinese and Vietnamese Illicit Activities in the Transbassac (c.1860–1920s)". *Chinese Southern Diaspora Studies* 1: 56–82.

EXIM Bank. 2012. "Chinese Government Concessional Loan and Preferential Export Buyer's Credit". http://english.eximbank.gov.cn/businesarticle/activities/loan/200905/9398_1.html (accessed 30 December 2012).

General Statistics Office (GSO). 2010. *The 2009 Census*. Hanoi: Thong Ke.

Han, Xiaorong. 2009. "Spoiled Guests or Dedicated Patriots? The Chinese in North Vietnam, 1954–1978". *International Journal of Asian Studies* 6, no. 1: 1–36.

He, Huifeng. 2020. "Coronavirus: Chinese Workers in Vietnam Cry Foul after Being Fired by Taiwanese Firm Making Shoes for Nike, Adidas". *China Economy*, 9 May 2020.

Hirschman, Charles. 1988. "Chinese Identities in Southeast Asia: Alternative Perspectives". In *Changing Identities of the Southeast Asian Chinese since World War II*, edited by Jennifer Cushman and Wang Gungwu, pp. 1–21, 23–31. Hong Kong: Hong Kong University Press.

Kiều, Linh. 2020. "Vốn FDI Trung Quốc vào Việt Nam quay đầu giảm mạnh" [China's FDI into Vietnam has dropped sharply]. *VnEconomy*, 30 December 2020. https://vneconomy.vn/von-fdi-trung-quoc-vao-viet-nam-quay-dau-giam-manh.htm.

Kuhn, Philip A. 2008. *Chinese among Others: Emigration in Modern Times*. Singapore: NUS Press.

Lam, Tom. 2000. "The Exodus of Hoa Refugees from Vietnam and their Settlement in Guangxi: China's Refugee Settlement Strategies". *Journal of Refugee Studies* 13, no. 4: 374–90.

Lê, Đăng Doanh. 2014. "Điều chỉnh chính sách kinh tế trước tình hình mới" [Economic adjustment to face the new situation]. *Sai Gon Times*, 23 May 2014.

Le, Hong Hiep. 2013. "The Dominance of Chinese Engineering Contractors in Vietnam". *ISEAS Perspective*, no. 2013/4, 17 January 2013.

Luong, Nhi Ky. 1963. "The Chinese in Vietnam: A Study of Vietnamese-Chinese Relations with Special Attention to the Period 1862–1961". PhD dissertation, University of Michigan.

Martinez, J.T. 2007. "Chinese Rice Trade and Shipping from the North Vietnamese Port of HaiPhong". *Chinese Southern Diaspora Studies* 1: 82–96.

Ministry of Health. 2010. "Foreign Doctors of Traditional Medicine in Vietnam 2008–2010". Internal report by the Department of Traditional Medicine archives, Hanoi.

Ministry of Labour, Invalids and Social Affairs MOLISA. 2010. Vấn đề lao động nước ngoài trong thời kỳ hội nhập quốc tế [The question of foreign labour in Vietnam during the international integration: A research proposal]. MOLISA archives.

Ministry of Planning and Investment. 2020. "Tình hình dòng vốn đầu tư Trung Quốc vào Việt Nam" [Investment flow from China to Vietnam]. http://investvietnam.gov.vn/vi/tin-tuc.nd/tinh-hinh-dong-von-dau-tu-tu-trung-quoc-vao-viet-nam.html (accessed November 2020).

Người, Lao Động. 2012. "Hoạt động của phòng khám Trung Quốc: Bộ Y tế chỉ cấp giấy phép?" [Chinese clinic activities: The Ministry of Health's responsibility is just to grant the licence]. http://nld.com.vn/20120625115023637p0c1002/bo-y-te-chi-cap-giay-phep.htm (accessed 26 June 2012).

Nguyễn, Duy Nghĩa. 2010. "Suy ngẫm về quan hệ thương mại Việt-Trung"

[Thinking of the Vietnam–China Trade Relation]. http://vnexpress.net/gl/ban-doc-viet/kinh-doanh/2010/03/3ba1a188/ (accessed 25 March 2010).

Nguyễn, Văn Chính. 2021. "Ethnic Chinese in the Sino–Vietnamese Borderlands: Debates over Loyalty and Identity". *Journal of Vietnamese Studies* 16, no. 4: 1–35. https://doi.org/10.1525/vs.2021.16.4.1.

Nhật, Minh. 2012. "Việt Nam ngày một thua thiệt khi buôn bán với Trung Quốc [Vietnam suffers increasing disadvantages in trade with China]. *VnExpress*, 28 November 2012.

Nyiri, Pál. 2014. *New Chinese Migration and Capital in Cambodia*. Trends in Southeast Asia, no. 3/2014. Singapore: ISEAS – Yusof Ishak Institute.

Phạm Huyền. 2010. "Choáng ngợp với nhập siêu từ Trung Quốc" [Being shocked with trade deficit from China]. http://vef.vn/2010-12-27.choang-ngop-voi-nhap-sieu-tu-trung-quoc (accessed 27 December 2010).

Pháp Luật. 2021. "Người Trung Quốc nhập cảnh trái phép vào Việt Nam để làm gì?" [What do Chinese people illegally enter Vietnam for?]. 5 May 2021. https://plo.vn/ban-doc/nguoi-trung-quoc-nhap-canh-trai-phep-vao-viet-nam-de-lam-gi-929002.html.

Rallu, Jean Louis. 2002. "International Migration in South-East Asia: The Role of China". Paper presented at the IUSP Conference on Southeast Asia Population in a Changing Asian Context held at Chulalongkorn University, Bangkok, Thailand, 10–13 June 2002.

Skeldon, Ronald. 1996. "Migration from China". *Journal of International Affairs* 49, no. 2: 434–56.

Song Moi. (2012). "Nhập siêu từ Trung Quốc lên tới 16,7 tỷ USD" [Trade deficit with China reached to US$16.7 billion]. http://songmoi.vn.kinh-te-thi-truong/nam-2012-nhap-sieu-tu-trung-quoc-len-toi-167-ty-usd (accessed 28 December 2012).

Thanh Niên. 2019. "Người Trung Quốc chiếm hơn 30% số người nước ngoài nhập cảnh vào Việt Nam" [Chinese citizens account for more than 30% of foreigners entering Vietnam]. In *Thanh Niên*, 10 November 2019.

Trần Giao Thủy. 2014. "Người Hoa tại Việt Nam và tương quan Hoa-Việt" [The Chinese in Vietnam and Chinese – Vietnamese correlation]. http://dcvonline.net/2014/04/30/nguoi-hoa-tai-viet-nam-va-tuong-quan-hoa-viet-iii/ (accessed 28 April 2014).

Trần Hồng Liên. 2008. "Các nhóm cộng đồng người Hoa ở tỉnh Đồng Nai, Việt Nam. Hội thảo quốc tế Việt Nam học lần 3" [Chinese communities in Dong Nai Province, The 3rd International Conference on Vietnamese Studies]. Hanoi, 4–7 December 2008.

Trần Khánh. 1993. *The Ethnic Chinese and Economic Development in Vietnam*. Singapore: Institute of Southeast Asian Studies.

Trịnh Mai Linh. 2010. "Understanding the Policy Towards Overseas Chinese of

the Saigon Government through the Edicts on Nationality and Economic Issues (1955–1956)". *Journal of Science* 23: 134–38.
VietnamNet. 2020. "Trung Quốc ồ ạt đổ vốn vào Việt Nam, Mỹ lập tức điều tra" [China massively poured capital into Vietnam, the US immediately investigated]. 7 July 2020. https://vietnamnet.vn/vn/kinh-doanh/dau-tu/von-trung-quoc-do-vao-go-dan-654678.html.
VnExpress. 2013. "Thương mại Việt Trung dự kiến đạt 50 tỷ đô la" [Vietnam–China bilateral trade reaches 50 billion dollar]. http://kinhdoanh.vnexpress.net/tin-tuc/doanh-nghiep/thuong-mai-viet-trung-du-kien-dat-50-ty-dola-2925357.html (accessed 18 December 2013).
———. 2019. "380 Chinese Arrested in Gambling Bust in Northern Vietnam". 28 July 2019. https://e.vnexpress.net/news/news/380-chinese-arrested-in-gambling-bust-in-northern-vietnam-3959129.html.
Walsh, John. 2009. "The Rising Importance of Chinese Labour in the Greater Mekong Sub-Region". http://www.jbic.go.jp/en/about/topics/2009/0421-01/2-12%20The%20Rising_Walsh.pdf.
Wang, Gungwu. 1992. *Community and Nation: China, Southeast Asia and Australia*. St. Leonards, Australia: Allen & Unwin.
Xerogiani, Theodore. 2006. "Migration Policy and Its Interactions with Aid, Trade and Foreign Direct Investment Policies: A Background Paper". OECD Working Paper no. 249, June 2006.
Xu Yunhong. 2010. "How China Deals with the U.S. Strategy to Contain China". *Seeking Truth*, English version by China Scope. http://www.sinocism.com/archives/2007 (accessed 23 March 2011).
Zhuang, Guoto, and Wang Wangbo. 2012. "Migration and Trade: The Role of Overseas Chinese in Economic Relations between China and Southeast Asia". *International Journal of China Studies* 1, no. 1: 174–93.

13

Chinese Engagement in Laos: Past, Present and Uncertain Future

Danielle Tan

On 7 April 2010, the Lao government signed an agreement with China that sets out the financing and the construction of a high-speed railway line (420 km) linking the capital Vientiane to southwestern China. The construction was initially set to commence on 25 April 2011 to celebrate the fiftieth anniversary of diplomatic relations between China and Laos. However, the project was postponed after the corruption scandal that led to the removal of China's Minister of Railways in February 2011. Afterwards, the Chinese construction companies pulled out of the venture fearing the rail link would not generate enough profit. After several years of numerous setbacks and rumours of cancellation, the construction of the controversial China–Laos railway was officially launched on 25 December 2016, but labour issues and compensation for people displaced still linger (Radio Free Asia 2017). The railway is valued at US$6 billion, and is expected to be completed within five years. China holds a 70 per cent stake in the rail project, while Laos holds the remaining 30 per cent.

Should this megaproject materialize, China would be fully connected to Southeast Asia, from Beijing to Singapore. The rail project is part of the Belt and Road Initiative, which aims to develop infrastructure networks across the ancient Silk Road trading routes. It would join the multiples lines of communication that have been built by China over the past few years. The navigation on the Mekong River and the North–South Economic Corridor (NSEC)[1] seemed unrealistic just a decade ago, given the very difficult terrain of this region. These Herculean works are rather emblematic as the Chinese are on track to achieve the *mise en valeur*[2] of Laos that the French only dreamed of during their colonial rule but failed to implement (Stuart-Fox 1995).

French interest in Indochina was mainly to gain access to the Chinese market to the detriment of the British. That was why building railways and a water road along the Mekong River was crucial to the colonial government. A century later, the same scenario is being replayed, but this time the Chinese have become the dominant players, and they are considering the Greater Mekong Subregion (GMS) as the centrepiece of their "charm offensive" (Kurlantzick 2007, p. 10) in Southeast Asia. Once again, the role of Laos will be to serve as a transit corridor and as a reservoir of natural resources.

Are we then witnessing the emergence of a "neo-colonialism with Chinese characteristics" (Shichor 2008, pp. 73–85), or is there, conversely, a genuine growth opportunity presented to Laos due to the extraordinary human and financial capacity of China? This question is relevant not only with respect to Laos but also with respect to many African countries that have similarly allowed China access to their raw materials in exchange for huge investment amounts (Alden et al. 2008). Western observers tend to depict China as a "spoiler" in Africa whose "insatiable" and "voracious" appetite for mineral resources is nothing more than a neo-colonial grab for raw materials that perpetuates African countries' underdevelopment (Marton and Matura 2011, p. 115). China's development model exported to the world is therefore seen by many analysts as a threat to the sovereignty of weak states (Halper 2010).

I will address this issue by analysing the role played by the new Chinese networks in the economic liberalization of Laos,[3] arguing that China's growing presence is far from eroding the power of the Lao communist regime. Instead, Chinese engagement allows the Lao state to cope with the challenges of globalization *and* to maintain its power at the same time. However, the cost of the *Great Transformation* (Polyani 1944) in Laos is exclusively borne by the weak—that is to say, the minorities, the farmers and the poor living far from the centres of power, Vientiane and the regional capitals. First, I will highlight Chinese engagement in Laos throughout history by emphasizing their recurrent patterns of intermediation. Then, I will describe how Chinese networks have become key partners of the Lao state's development policies. However, rising uncertainties over the neighbouring communist ally's economic potential may push China to revise its development strategy in Laos.

The Chinese and Their Recurring Role as Middlemen

Laos is often depicted as a landlocked country, penalized by its subsistence-oriented economy. Such images fail, however, to account for a longer historical portrait, with evidence of ancient caravan trade integrating the Lao Kingdom of Lan Xang into a regional trade-oriented economy ever since its founding in 1354.

Chinese Caravans Connecting the Lowlands with the Uplands and with the World Economy

While the contribution of Chinese maritime networks to the formation of Southeast Asian coastal states is well established (Reid 1993; Lombard 1990), the role of continental Chinese Muslim traders in the political consolidation of the Tai kingdoms (Lan Xang, Lan Na, Kengtung, Sipsongpanna)[4] is far less well known (Forbes 1988; Hill 1998).

At the end of the fifteenth century, the Lao Kingdom of Lan Xang blossomed due to a favourable economic environment generated by the Chinese caravan trade. Known under different names—*Hui* in Chinese (*huizu* 回族), *Haw* or *Chin Haw* in Thai and Lao, *Panthay* in Burmese—the Chinese Muslim caravan traders served as intermediaries between the highlanders and the lowland societies. They stimulated the economy within each kingdom along the trade routes through paying local taxes, and by supplying and collecting goods from the highlanders. Most importantly, they offered these landlocked kingdoms an outlet for their luxury goods—aromatic and medicinal plants, resins, benzoin, rare timber, ivory and the like—to the international market. In the long run, however, the revenue of the caravan trade alone turned out to be insufficient for Lan Xang to compete with the rising power of Ayudhya, whose economy was based both on maritime trade and agriculture. The Siamese and Vietnamese armies accentuated tensions and divisions within the realm by supporting the rivalry between the princes of Luang Prabang and Vientiane. The south seceded in turn and set itself up as the kingdom of Champassak in 1713. Split into three rival kingdoms, Lan Xang had ceased to exist.

The Overseas Chinese: "Indispensable Enemies" of French Colonial Rule

It was predominantly the disruption of caravan traffic from the mid-nineteenth century caused by the Panthay (1856–73) and the Taiping (1850–64) Rebellions in China that precipitated the decline of Luang Prabang—then under the control of Siam—and also explains its search for protection by the French.

Laos had the particularity—along with Thailand and Myanmar—of harbouring two types of Chinese communities (Halpern 1961; Rossetti 1997). In the north, the early overland Haw migration was characterized by caravan drivers, dealers, traffickers and a few shopkeepers who were forced to settle permanently after the revolts in Yunnan. They were long thought of as hill tribes or as Muslims, but the term Haw became ambiguous because it subsequently incorporated the large number of Yunnan's Han and non-Muslim Chinese immigrants who fled into the Golden Triangle after the defeat of the Kuomintang (KMT) in 1949. Regardless, these overland Chinese rejected this name. In Laos, the Han Yunnanese who had settled for five or six generations in the north—mainly concentrated in the province of Phongsaly—consider themselves both ethnic Chinese and Lao.

In contrast, larger waves of overseas Chinese (called *huaqiao* 华侨) from Guangdong, Fujian and Hainan settled in the main cities of central and southern Laos (Vientiane, Thakhek, Savannakhet and Pakse) during the colonial period. Although they had arrived as coolies to develop the European empires, the overseas Chinese in Laos and throughout Southeast Asia rapidly came to dominate the main economic sectors thanks to their networking abilities. They organized themselves in what the French called *congrégations*[5] (*huiguan* 会馆 or *bang* 帮) according to their dialect and/or provinces of origin (Purcell 1965; Pan 1999). The structures of colonial economies relied on the vast networks of Chinese middlemen to extract agricultural production and distribute basic consumer goods. These middlemen bought, sold, imported and exported everything available in the colonies. In Indochina, they functioned as *compradors* for the French trading houses. More importantly, they controlled a vast banking, commercial and money-lending network—particularly opaque and branched—covering Cochinchina (today's southern Vietnam), Cambodia and Laos. French traders resigned themselves to working with them, considering them "indispensable enemies" (Brocheux and Hémery 2001, p. 194).

Those who ended up in Laos had actually failed to prosper in Thailand, Vietnam or Cambodia (Halpern 1961). The fact that Laos is landlocked is not the only factor that explained the small size of the Chinese communities in the country.[6] The French also encouraged Vietnamese migration to Laos on whom they placed high hopes. Indeed, according to racial criteria established by the French colonial policy, the Vietnamese produced better officials than the Lao due to their Mandarin tradition, and were considered more docile and less expensive workers than the Chinese (Robequain 1948, p. 86).

A Strategic Alliance between the Ethnic Chinese and the Lao Elite

Although the *Huaqiao* were few in number, they managed to control the Lao economy through a marriage-based integration process. The more affluent businessmen traded their economic capital for symbolic capital—that is to say, for the prestige (*kiet*) inherent in the traditional system of patronage monopolized by powerful Lao families (*phu gnay*). Similar to the outcomes in Thailand and Cambodia, these inter-ethnic marriages did not successfully assimilate the Chinese into Lao culture, but rather led to the emergence of a "creolized" community (Skinner 1996, pp. 63–65).

The Vietnam War proved to be a Golden Age for the Chinese in Laos due to American presence indirectly reviving Chinese migration. Fearing that the fall of Laos to the communist Pathet Lao forces might have a domino effect in Southeast Asia, the United States provided abundant assistance contributing to an economic boom and an increase in trade, especially with Thailand. A significant number of Chinese from Thailand settled on the banks of the Mekong River. In 1956–57, it was the turn of the Chinese from Hong Kong and Saigon to take advantage of the mismanagement in the US aid programme (Halpern 1961, p. 2).

The Lao elite benefited substantially from the corruption related to the assistance provided by the United States to keep the Royal Government of Laos (RGL) in power. The corrupt elite mainly comprised members of the royal family who made alliances with the military and with Chinese businessmen. The exercise of power was a means of accumulating wealth, for in exchange for concession rights or monopolies granted to Chinese businessmen the Lao elite received a share of the profits. At that time, the opening of casinos by the Chinese had already become a 'semi-legal' lucrative business: profits were reinvested in the regular economy—for example in the development of the national airline company, Lao Airlines (Evans 2002, pp. 158–59).

In addition, the Secret War conducted by the Central Intelligence Agency (CIA) had catapulted Laos into the echelons of the world's leading opium producers. In the context of its anti-communist efforts, the CIA played a significant role in the opium trade to finance mercenary armies in Laos and Thailand. Chinese merchants (predominantly Yunnanese) continued to serve as intermediaries between the highlanders and the Corsican syndicates who controlled the opium trade since the departure of the French, until its takeover in 1965 by General Ouane Rattikone, on behalf of the RGL, and with the help of Air America, one of the CIA's airline companies (McCoy 1991, pp. 226–34). Unlike Myanmar and Thailand, there were no major drug lords in Laos, whose profits remained modest in comparison with the two other key protagonists of the Golden Triangle, the Shan state-based Haw leaders (among them, Khun Sa, the most notorious drug lord), and the Kuomintang soldiers, secretly supported by the CIA, who had settled in northern Thailand after their defeat by the Chinese Communists in 1949.

The 1960s saw the arrival of a massive number of troops from the Chinese People's Liberation Army (PLA), tasked to build a vast network of roads in Laos's north, then occupied by the Pathet Lao. However, cooling Sino–Lao diplomatic relations towards the end of the 1970s[7] resulted in the withdrawal of 5,000 Chinese military workers (Walker 1999, p. 59) and in the dissolution of Chinese community life in Luang Prabang, Oudomxay and Xiengkhuang.

Chinese Presence in Laos since the 1990s

The political changes of 1975 that culminated in the Pathet Lao takeover led to a mass exodus of most of the Chinese community, which dropped from 100,000 people[8] to approximately 10,000 in the early 1990s (Rossetti

1997). Being targeted by the new communist regime less for their ethnic origin than for their social position and economic influence, the Chinese communities in Laos—like those in Vietnam and Cambodia—sought refuge mainly in the West, particularly in the United States, France and Australia (Condominas and Pottier 1982).

The end of the Cold War in the early 1990s led to a new regional order that endorsed a revival of China's influence in Southeast Asia (Evans et al. 2000). Determined to regain its "rightful place" in a region it considered its traditional sphere of influence (Stuart-Fox 2003), the Chinese government devised a strategic "charm offensive" (Kurlantzick 2007), nurturing close economic partnerships (i.e., aid, investment, creation of a free trade pact between ASEAN and China) and promoting the idea of China's peaceful, non-threatening emergence. Moreover, China's attitude towards its diaspora has changed radically. The Chinese government has recognized the tremendous potential of its diasporic human capital within the country's soft power strategy to restore the great power status that China held for centuries before subjugation by Western superior military powers in the nineteenth century.

The visit of Premier Li Peng to Vientiane in 1990 marked a turning point in China–Laos relations. Suddenly, being Chinese was no longer problematic. Chinese schools and shops gradually began to reopen, even though the Laotian Chinese community had been reduced to a shadow of its former self. Thus, the reawakening of a Chinese community in Laos did not come from the *huaqiao*, unlike in Cambodia where they managed to regain their traditional economic role (Tan 2006). Rather, in Laos, this arose from a new cycle of immigrants (*xin yimin* 新移民), who started pouring into northern Laos in the late 1990s on an unprecedented scale. The vast majority of these Chinese newcomers have settled in the north of the country and in Vientiane.

The first Chinese newcomers arrived in the mid-1990s as workers or technicians on road construction projects and as part of the industrial cooperation between Yunnan and the northern provinces of Laos (Luang Namtha and Oudomxay). At the end of their contracts, some stayed on and started their own businesses. They were quickly joined by a growing number of petty traders from neighbouring Yunnan and from more distant provinces such as Hunan, Sichuan and Zhejiang. They typically engage in miscellaneous trading activities in import–export, transport, hardware and household supplies, motorcycle repair, cell phone shops, restaurants, hotels or beauty salons, and they occupy increasing space in local markets. For most of these new migrants, Laos is not their first point of destination. The overwhelming majority of traders I met at the markets in northern Laos were from Hunan, with many of them first migrating to Yunnan, where they had engaged in commercial activities (see also Hansen 1999). Because of the fierce competition in China, they resigned themselves to exploring other migration options. They moved to northern Laos after having been told that a new road would soon link Kunming to Bangkok and bring economic development to a country still replete with opportunities. Before leaving China, some migrants told me that they had never heard of Laos or were unable to locate the country on a map.

Indeed, the completion of the North–South Economic Corridor (NSEC) has accelerated the migration of Chinese petty traders searching for a better life and new economic opportunities. Their long-term settlement has profoundly transformed the socio-economic landscape of northern Laos in both urban and rural areas. As soon as Chinese bus companies started to connect Yunnan Province (mainly Mohan, Mengla, Jinghong and Kunming) with the main cities of northern Laos[9] and Vientiane, Chinese traders began to settle there, supplying cheap Chinese goods to the urban and rural populations. In particular, they have transformed Lao urban centres: Chinese markets, shops, restaurants and guesthouses have become the most visible markers of this new urbanization (Tan 2014a).

Upon establishing a foothold in Laos, these new pioneers make contact with their home communities in order to recruit labour and business partners. While Chinese migrants in the 1990s were mostly males (Rossetti 1997, p. 33), I observed during my fieldwork that the pattern of migration has increasingly become feminized. Most of the newcomers I met run their businesses with their families, so they can go back to China regularly without having to stop their activities. The families often seize the opportunity to raise more than one child in the Lao PDR. When they have children of school age, they prefer to leave them with the grandparents to receive a Chinese education. I encountered many single or married women who ran their own businesses, leaving their families behind in China. Living mostly alongside their Chinese peers, the newcomers have achieved limited integration in Lao society. Regardless of their length of stay in Laos or future plans to remain there, they view their stay as temporary and strictly for the purpose of economic advancement. Given that this circular and chain migration is still recent, the newcomers have not yet organized themselves into associations, unlike the overseas Chinese during the colonial period. Instead, hotels/guesthouses and restaurants have become crucial nodes within regional business networks. Setting up wherever buses stop over, they play multiple roles, acting as information centres, gambling houses (where *mah-jong* is played), bus ticket offices, small warehouses, intermediaries between traders and private buses, meeting rooms for Chinese companies and so on. They are frequently engaged in other activities such as running a shop in another city even as far away as Vientiane, a transportation business, clinics or rubber production. Due to capital constraints, they tend to have only smallholdings, with many now serving as subcontractors and supervisors for large Chinese companies (Shi 2008; Diana 2009).

According to official Chinese data, there are some 30,000 Chinese currently residing in Laos, though their number may actually be ten times higher (*The Nation* 2007). As reported by a Greater Mekong Subregion (GMS) Migration Policy Briefing, 80,000 Chinese are estimated to be working on Chinese-led projects (ADB 2010). Estimating the Chinese population in northern Laos is difficult due to divergences in official Lao data at the national and provincial levels.[10] Lao provincial officials also acknowledge the difficulties the current administrative system has in precisely assessing Chinese numbers because of their mobility practices.[11] Strict control of cross-border migration in northern Laos is simply not possible due to the porous natural borders formed by the mountains and the Mekong River, and because of the difficult access to some areas during the rainy season. Moreover, the newcomers often run their businesses under a Lao name or settle illegally, with a very small number legalizing their stay though marriage to Lao citizens.

Chinese migration is not limited to the NSEC areas, but has also reached some of the more remote provinces of Laos such as Phongsaly. This is not surprising since Phongsaly has traditionally hosted a sizeable community of Chinese Haw. As they share close historical and linguistic features with Yunnanese Chinese—for example, they can speak both Lao and the Yunnanese dialect—they have managed to take advantage of the dynamism of Chinese traders, as evidenced by the new markets in Oudomxay, Muang Sing and Luang Namtha built by Haw entrepreneurs. The rapid influx of Chinese investment in northern Laos would not have been possible without the crucial go-between role played by the Haw and, to a lesser extent, by other ethnic minority groups belonging to the Chinese cultural sphere, such as the Hmong or the Akha. Since most Chinese traders cannot speak Lao, they hire Haw personnel as translators, middlemen or business partners to overcome the language barrier and deal with Lao clients and officials.

Dispersion and inter-polarity are typical migration patterns of the Chinese diaspora (Ma Muang 2000), a rule to which the recent Chinese networks in Laos make no exception. The success of the small entrepreneurs hinges at least as much on their economic capital as on their social capital (*guanxi*). The poorest among the newcomers usually open a small stall in the village or sell their goods as street vendors. As soon as things go well in one place, the most enterprising among them open a shop in another village and let their relatives take over the old business. Due to the rising competition between the newcomers themselves, some of them head for new destinations in other northern provinces of the country (Xieng Khuang, Sayabouly), and increasingly move southwards as well. The richest settle directly in Vientiane. There, however, the competition is fiercer, as the *xin yimin* (new Chinese migrant groups) have to compete with the established *huaqiao*. The majority of the *xin yimin* have settled around the *Talat Leng* (the 'Evening Market') where they have created a new Chinatown promptly designated 'Little Kunming' by the inhabitants of Vientiane. Since the opening in August 2008 of the new Chinese shopping mall (*San Jiang*) en route to the airport, the new Chinatown has been expanding in that direction. The diversity of the new Chinese community is larger in Vientiane than in the north and we find entrepreneurs there who are from all over China, the majority coming from Zhejiang, Guangdong and Shanghai, alongside the key Yunnanese and Hunanese players who dominate the Chinese trade in Vientiane.

Apart from these new migration flows, China's foreign direct investment (FDI) has been the main driver of change in northern Laos (see also Tan 2012, 2014a, 2014b). The main Chinese investors are state-owned enterprises and large private companies. While the former invest heavily in developing agriculture, industry, hydropower plants and mines (Rutherford et al. 2008; Tan 2014b), the latter have chosen the tourism sector, and particularly the lucrative sector of casinos. These megaprojects have increased the pace of development and radically reshaped the uplands of northern Laos into large-scale rubber plantations and huge gambling enclaves which benefit from a regime of extra-territoriality, ironically recalling the concessions imposed on China in the mid-nineteenth century by the colonial powers (Nyíri 2009, 2012). I will come back to this point later.

In the 1990s, FDI in Laos was dominated by Thailand. Chinese investment in Laos started to increase dramatically in the mid-2000s after the implementation of China's "Going Out" policy (*zou chu qu* 走出去) encouraging its domestic enterprises to invest overseas. China ranked as Laos's top foreign investor for the first time in 2007, surpassing Thailand and Vietnam. As of February 2016, approved Chinese investment (1989–2015) in Laos had reached US$5.48 billion, making China the largest investor in the country. The value of Thai investment has reached US$4.49 billion, while Vietnamese investment is now worth US$3.57 billion, according to the Lao Ministry of Planning and Investment.[12] Thailand lost its first position, while Laos's traditional ally, Vietnam, has followed suit and increased its investment over the past decade (for more details, see Tan 2014b). Large Chinese companies have also extended their explorations southward. In the near future, the trajectory of Chinese migrants is expected to follow this emerging geography of Chinese investment.

If Chinese networks often appear as new regimes of power and accumulation competing with or undermining state authority (Stuart-Fox 2009)—some even speak of a "shadow state" threatening national sovereignty and territorial integrity (Walsh 2009)—in my view, they are far from eroding the power of the Lao communist regime. It is necessary to go beyond the caricatured images regularly on display in the media (Lintner 2008; Crispin 2010; *The Economist* 2011; Gluckman 2011)—in which Laos is variously depicted as a weak state, a victim of globalization and of China in particular—and to consider a less-passive posture. Hence, I will demonstrate the way in which Chinese networks have become the key partners of Laos's strategy of modernization and economic liberalization.

"Turning Land into Capital"

It is not a question of denying the empowerment of Chinese actors or claiming that relationships are symbiotic and harmonious. Rather, it is a matter of recognizing that behind conflict and competition are found techniques of governing—in particular, in establishing indirect rule—which are more elaborate than one may perceive at first glance. With increasing internationalization of the economy, the Government of Laos has tried to inhabit the role of a "catalytic state" (Weiss 1997, p. 17), using external forces—through a series of alliances with other states and foreign private actors—to maximize its control over its territory and to strengthen its national economy by encouraging foreign investment. Laos's reliance on its external environment, especially China, is a deliberate strategy to put regional powers in competition with one another in order to avoid being drawn into the orbit of just one of them (China, Vietnam or Thailand), and to enhance its bargaining power with investors.

Since the late 1990s and early 2000s, the Lao leadership has opted for a "turning land into capital" strategy (Dwyer 2007), based on leasing its land and exploiting its natural resources as the main engine of national development. To them, hydropower along with mining, tourism, timber and agro-processing industries have become high-priority sectors for investment given their potential to stimulate economic growth and generate greater revenues. In that context, Chinese migration and capital were seen as an unexpected opportunity to modernize the country. They would grant the contemporary Lao nation-state the necessary financial, technological and human means—which it never previously possessed in either its colonial or independent guises (Stuart-Fox 1995)—to access the wide array of under-exploited natural resources (agriculture, forest, mining, hydroelectricity, etc.) dormant within its peripheral territories in the country's uplands regions. In addition, they would assist the Lao state in renewing its technologies of power as well as its discourse of modernity to legitimize its *mission civilisatrice* in these so-called backward peripheries by bringing development and prosperity.

The Long-Awaited Development of the Northern Uplands

Chinese immigrants and capital were particularly welcomed in northern Laos to transform the uplands into a new space of productivity and competitiveness integrated into the market economy. Given the low population resources available there, and also because of the customary reluctance of lowlanders (*Lao Loum*) to establish themselves in these difficult mountainous areas, the Lao state has resorted to using the Chinese newcomers to develop new pioneer farming areas and to "monetize" (Scott 2009, p. 4) the northern borderlands. To some extent, the current situation in northern Laos is very similar to the way Southeast Asian colonial and post-colonial governments were dependent on extensive networks of Chinese middlemen and pioneers to exploit local economies and facilitate the enclosure of their peripheries and hinterlands (Trocki 2009). As in the past, Chinese networks once again serve as essential mediators between the state and the global economy.

Through a policy of promoting foreign investment, trade liberalization and privatization based on land concessions and contract farming, the Lao State has fostered the transition from semi-subsistence farming to a market-oriented agriculture. Tax cuts were awarded to foreign investors who settled in priority areas (mountain areas and special economic zones) and invested in specific activities (such as in rubber plantations).

These measures began to bear fruit in the early 2000s. The influx of Chinese investment allowed a take-off of agricultural exports (corn, sugar cane, rubber, cassava, watermelon and non-timber forest products) in the border provinces with China (Tan 2012, 2014a, 2014b). Bearing lower costs than registered Lao companies due to informal and illegal practices,[13] Chinese traders have been able to offer an all-inclusive service (providing fertilizers and seeds, collecting and transporting agricultural products, dealing with customs, etc.) and better prices to Lao farmers. However, the latter are often suspicious about their final payment since they have frequently been cheated, seldom receiving money in time or not at all.

According to a high-ranking official in the Ministry of Agriculture and Forestry,[14] the vision is that Chinese companies will start developing northern Laos, and other investors will follow:

> Before the Chinese, nobody wanted to invest in the North. Since they have started to develop the area, everybody wants to go there now!... The idea of the Lao is, given we are very much underdeveloped, rather than following the conventional way, we need to bring the resources from outside; that will help our society to have access to the transfer of knowledge for example,... to improve the economy and to give good opportunities for the Lao young labour force. So, we see things in a more positive way; we need to open ourselves but in a way that it is manageable.

The Lao rulers have thus relied on Chinese technical expertise as well as financial and human resources to help them civilize their 'backward' margins. Since 2003, the government of Yunnan Province has been actively involved in the design of a new master plan for the development of northern Laos, sending its experts to Vientiane and training Lao officials in Kunming.[15] The Northern Master Plan highlighted the issue that "the mentalities of most people are still at the starting stage of agricultural economic development, which is unsuitable for development of market economy and economic globalization" (Northern Laos Industrial Economic Development and Cooperation Planning Preparation Group 2008, 15). As Baird (2011, p. 11) has shown,

> one of the main motivations of the government of Laos in granting large-scale land concessions is to remove peasants, and particularly indigenous peoples, from their conditions of production because they are seen as making unproductive use of resources and as being resistant to fully integrating into the market economy.

Therefore, the policy of the government of Laos to "turn land into capital" is crucially intertwined with "turning people into labour" (ibid., p. 12).

One of the priorities of the Northern Master Plan is the eradication of opium and its replacement with rubber plantations. This cooperation has proved a bonanza for the government of Laos. On the one hand, it generates an alternative cash crop for northern highlanders now aspiring to emulate their successful relatives in China. On the other hand, the partnership between the Lao state and private Chinese companies allows power-holders—mainly military and some national and/or provincial officials—to benefit through becoming joint venture counterparts with the private companies. Without injecting any capital, they are also able to take advantage of roads built by the same companies, using them to continue logging tropical forests. In the long run, this Sino–Laotian cooperation offers an alternative to UN anti-opium aid programmes tied to expectations of democratic openings (Cohen 2009).

In 2003–4, the northern provinces began receiving an influx of Chinese investment from Yunnan. Chinese rubber companies seized the opportunity to acquire cheap land as a low-risk investment. They started to formally register companies in response to favourable incentives under China's Opium Replacement Policy, implemented in the Golden Triangle (Transnational Institute 2010) and designed to ease labour restrictions, provide financial inducements and access to a special fund of 250 million yuan assisting businesspeople through grants and loans (Shi 2008, p. 27). This strategy reflects China's broader 'Going Out' (*zou chu qu*) policy aimed at encouraging Chinese investment abroad. Though companies are typically headquartered in Mengla, Jinghong or Kunming, investment comes from as far away as coastal China. These companies have strong governmental ties and usually subcontract with existing local

Chinese communities (mostly Sichuan and Hunan migrants engaged in miscellaneous trade and who have been converting their business to rubber enterprises in recent years) and employ Lao Akha or Lue personnel as translators and supervisors. Subsidies and exemptions granted under the Opium Replacement Special Fund apply only to companies that sign a formal contract with the Lao authorities (at the local and national level) and operate plantations of more than 10,000 *mu* (666 ha) (GMS Study Center 2008). This explains why the Lao central government has granted large land concessions to firms with close ties to the Chinese government. For example, China–Lao Ruifeng Rubber, a group originally specializing in the leisure industry, obtained a concession of 300,000 hectares in the province of Luang Namtha (equivalent to the size of Sing and Long districts) in a joint venture with the Lao Army, while Yunnan Rubber Company plans to cover 167,000 hectares. The decision to grant a concession to that company was taken during the visit to Laos of Vice Premier Wu Yi in March 2004 (Shi 2008, p. 25). In collusion with Lao military higher-ups and officials at both national and local levels, Chinese companies have forced upland farmers to change their farming practices or abandon their land in the name of development.

Nonetheless, a myriad of smallholders—Chinese entrepreneurs from neighbouring towns in Xishuangbanna as well as Lao villagers benefiting from the experience of their trans-border networks—are also actively involved in the 'rubber boom' (Shi 2008). When the borders reopened in the 1990s, small waves of Lao Akha and Hmong refugees from the American War were repatriated from the border villages of Xishuangbanna to Mom cluster in Sing district and Ban Hat Ngyao in Namtha district (Luang Namtha Province). Under the influence of their relatives (*pi-nong*) in China who have experienced better standards of living by planting rubber, and because they used to work in the state farms in Xishuangbanna, they were the first rubber-planters in the mid-1990s. Though this community is limited in size, it provided examples and an essential source of knowledge for other villages. Some have successfully developed business relations with their relatives based in Yunnan. Recent studies show, however, that this profitable configuration has not become widespread throughout northern Laos (Wasana 2012; Sturgeon 2013; Dwyer 2014). Although the northern provinces favour the '2+3' model of contract farming[16] (seen as the best way to promote rural development), the arrangement often slips into a '1+4' system. Since the poorest farmers cannot afford the prolonged uncompensated labour input (at least seven years), they only contribute land, in exchange for thirty per cent of future plantation profits and current wages if they work for the company. Ultimately, the '1+4' system is closer to the concession model. Whereas the local urban elite has been able to invest in rubber plantations and thus reap the benefits from Chinese investment, the upland farmers have been converted into a cheap and sedentarized labour force necessary for the development of large-scale plantations and industrial projects.

The Special Economic Zones as "Sites of Exception"

While many see the special economic zones (SEZs)[17] in northern Laos as Chinese colonies or extraterritorial entities that threaten Lao national sovereignty and territorial integrity, I prefer to consider them 'sites of exception' in the sense suggested by Aihwa Ong (2006)—that is, specific areas where the state develops exceptional forms of power at the frontier between the formal and informal economies, legal and illegal practices, and where it experiments with other forms of sovereignty that she calls "graduated sovereignty". These specific technologies of governing involve differential state treatment of segments of the population and territory in relation to market calculations, as well as some aspects of state power and authority being taken up by foreign corporations located in the SEZs, to make them "more 'bankable' than other developing regions" (Ong 2006, p. 78). From this perspective, the ongoing process of privatization in the northern SEZs should not be read as a withdrawal of the Lao state in economic affairs and an incapacity to regulate or control Chinese private actors. Rather, it illustrates an "extension of indirect rule methods" (Hibou 2004) whereby much of Lao sovereignty is vested in private corporations in order for the state to have access to modernity and development. If the current crop of Chinese migrants has very nearly regained the status of tax farmers held under colonial rule, I argue that emergent SEZs constitute full-blown tax farms.

In northern Laos, two SEZs are located in the borderlands (Golden Boten City in Luang Namtha province and the Golden Triangle SEZ in Bokeo Province). They have become important "resource frontiers" (Tsing 2005, pp. 28–30) for the Lao state because they embody "spaces of capitalist transition" (Barney 2009, p. 146). Less competitive than its neighbours in terms of industrial productivity, the government of Laos has chosen to implement casino complexes in the northern borderland SEZs, seeking to tap into the growing and dynamic Southeast Asian gambling market. The idea is to attract foreign tourists—specifically Chinese and Thai, since gambling is strictly forbidden in their countries—and to stimulate a development dynamic by providing tax advantages. Given the area's past reputation as an arena synonymous with illicit drug movements, the government of Laos has envisioned the conversion of these drug enclaves into "regional paragons of economic modernity" (Nyíri 2012, p. 562). However, the outcomes appear to be less grandiose than envisaged.

In April 2003, high-ranking Lao officials granted Hong Kong Fuk Hing Travel Entertainment Group Ltd. a thirty-year concession, renewable twice. The 1,640-hectare concession worth US$103 million was meant to become a "Paradise for Freedom and Development", as promoted by the investment brochures. In fact, in late 2006, instead of luxury resorts, a public-housing-like casino sprang up in the middle of the rainforest, surrounded by shops and warehouses, mostly unoccupied. A few thousand Chinese traders, dealers and sex workers settled in this casino city; only a handful were Lao. The currency used was Chinese yuan, all the products consumed locally were imported from China, everything was written in Chinese, and even the time zone was set according to China. Pornographic items, banned in Laos, could be found in Boten, as well as cabaret shows performed by *kathoey* (male-to-female transgender persons) from Thailand. Most casino clients were professional Chinese gamblers. They were equipped with headsets for receiving instructions from their bosses based in China, who could follow the game on the Internet.

Yet, when I came back in July 2012, the casino lay abandoned and looked like a 'ghost city'. Indeed, Golden Boten City's gambling activities had seriously begun to upset Chinese authorities after several Chinese television stations reported in January 2011 on how hundreds of gamblers were lured, tortured and sometimes murdered if their families did not pay their debts. In December 2010, officials from Hubei Province conducted negotiations to rescue some 'hostages'. In March 2011, China shut down the border and cut off electricity. Eventually, under pressure from Beijing, the government of Laos decided to close the casino in April 2011. Nevertheless, the Lao government still pins high hopes on the project. In April 2012, high-ranking Lao officials surprisingly decided to give the chairman of Hong Kong Fuk Hing Travel Entertainment Group Ltd., Wong Man Suen (also known as Huang Minxuan), another chance (Olsen 2013). Partnering with Yunnan Hai Chang Industrial Group Stock Co., these Chinese investors will increase their investment capital to US$500 million to change the focus of Golden Boten City from gambling to commerce and eco-tourism. The objective now is to transform the special zone into a regional trading hub and to link it to the future high-speed train that will pass through Boten to connect Kunming to Vientiane, and then Singapore.

In the meantime, a new casino has been developing in Tonpheung, Bokeo Province. The project was signed in 2007, and the Golden Triangle SEZ was inaugurated on 9 September 2009. Owning twenty per cent of the project, the government of Laos hopes to attract a million tourists along with more than 300 companies. The Hong Kong–registered Kings Romans Group[18] was granted a ninety-nine-year concession for an area covering some 10,000 hectares, 3,000 of which have been designated as a duty-free zone. The rest has been earmarked for eco-tourism. A concession fee of US$850,000 was allegedly paid to the government for the first year of the lease, with investors rumoured to hail from Hong Kong, Macau and Yunnan Province. The group has to date declined to divulge the names or details of their backers. The first phase of the project cost US$86.6 million,[19] with the conglomerate planning to invest US$2.25 billion by 2020 to build an industrial park and eco-tourism facilities, and to create a truly modern city.

At present, in the heart of the Golden Triangle, a colossal golden crown has ruptured the surrounding carpet of forest. It sits atop the Kings Romans Casino. It would appear that the Lao government has learned several lessons from the shambolic experience of Golden Boten City. As a shareholder in the new project, the Lao government will be better able to maintain control over operations and will directly recover profits should the venture prove successful.[20] Security has also been improved. Private security guards are everywhere. Both the investment group and the Lao state are determined that the new complex should not suffer the fate of Golden Boten City. An average of some 1,000 people visit the casino every day (Hilgers 2012). The majority of croupiers are Chinese, and most gamblers pay in Chinese yuan or Thai baht. The local mobile phone network is provided by a Chinese company. The new city is expected to accommodate more than 200,000 residents, potentially becoming the second-largest urban development in the country after Vientiane. Working conditions are such that, as in Boten, it is likely that only a small number of Lao will work in the Golden Triangle SEZ. Of the more than 4,500 people employed in the zone, only 500 are

Lao nationals. The rest originate from China, Thailand and Myanmar. The majority of them are not registered with the Department of Labour and Social Affairs in Bokeo Province.[21] Many Lao I met in my fieldwork said things like, "Over there, it's not Laos anymore. That's China."

Kings Romans has an ambitious blueprint for the SEZ. It wants to expand the area so that it resembles Las Vegas. The managers have already commenced a few vegetable farms, which currently service the casino and which may in time produce crops for export. The 'gambling enclave' now includes an international border checkpoint and river port, hotels, and a Chinatown market with as many as seventy restaurants and shops selling a variety of retail goods, including illegal wildlife products (EIA 2015). The company claims that there is no drinking or prostitution in the casino, although a row of dubious-looking nearby massage parlours and bars, complete with giant signs displaying ladies in lascivious positions, suggests that these vices are not, however, completely unrepresented. Moreover, hotel rooms provide phone numbers with which clients may order sexual services.

According to Shan journalists and Thai businessmen (Lintner and Black 2009; the author's interviews in Chiang Mai and Chiang Rai, June 2012), Lin Mingxian (林明贤) is the main investor in Golden Boten City and is also one of the investors in Tonpheung. There is as yet no evidence to confirm the rumoured connection. Better known as U Sai Lin, Lin Mingxian is one of the Golden Triangle's most notorious drug lords. He continues to command a militia of between 2,000 and 3,000 foot soldiers known as the National Democratic Alliance Army (NDAA) in Shan State Special Region No. 4. Born in Yunnan, Lin Mingxian was once a member of the Red Guards and, during the Cultural Revolution, was sent to fight alongside the Burmese Communist Party. When most of the Guards were recalled to China in the late 1970s, Lin Mingxian decided to stay.

Lin allegedly thrived on smuggling timber into China and opium into Thailand, before declaring his zone 'opium-free' in 1997 in exchange for financial support from China's opium-substitution policy. At the same time, he began investing in the construction of gambling houses in the Sino-Myanmar border town of Mongla, using drug money as investment capital. He reportedly moved his investment interests to Boten after the closure of his Mongla casinos by Chinese authorities who, for their part, sought to stop the haemorrhaging of capital diverted from China by corrupt officials. While newspapers in the region have begun to describe Kings

Romans as a gigantic machine for laundering drug money (Fawthrop 2011; Al Jazeera 2012), Zhao Wei (赵伟), the chairman of the group rejected these accusations, stating that his company invested in the Golden Triangle to create an economic alternative to the narcotics trade and they are currently improving people's lives (*China Talk* 2011; Hilgers 2012).

The two megaprojects outlined above, in Golden Boten City and the Golden Triangle SEZ, illustrate something of the overlap between legal activities (development of tourism, SEZs) and illegal practices (gambling, prostitution, laundering of drug money, wildlife trafficking, etc.) on which the Lao state has based its poverty alleviation policy. In fact, for the Lao leadership, they offer an ideal framework to cover all sorts of illicit and illegal activities that are at the same time highly profitable. It is also a means to launder illicit money into legal channels in the context of converting the opium-oriented political economy of the region into a series of casinos, under the banner of the GMS Program.[22] As a transit country and a small player in the drugs trade, Laos wants to take a share of that reconversion to boost development in its peripheral frontier territories. In that context, its borderlands can become laboratories for implementing these casinos as a new model of development. Though a 'vice economy' drives these zones, and the Chinese state has cracked down on them at least once, we should not assume, as Nyíri (2012, p. 557) puts it, "that zone managers and the officials they talk to in Laos and China do not view the zones as at least potential enclaves of progress".

Conclusion

This brief insight into the crucial role of Chinese networks in the transformation of Laos's political economy during different periods of its history highlights their recurrent patterns of intermediation. Although the number of Chinese migrants in Laos has soared over the past few decades, their proportion still remains low in comparison with Thailand, Cambodia, Vietnam and Myanmar, which have also experienced a new wave of Chinese migration. These countries share with China larger volumes of trade, and their more substantial ethnic Chinese communities have facilitated the return of the diaspora and attracted a greater number of new immigrants (Tan 2012).

Nevertheless, the numerous imminent megaprojects in Laos are likely to accelerate Chinese migration. The construction of the railway line will entail 50,000 workers and hundreds of thousands of hectares of rubber plantations will soon require a similar number. Because of a lack of skilled labour, importing foreign workers, especially from China, will be inevitable, not only in the north but throughout the country.

Rather than viewing the growing Chinese presence as a threat to Lao sovereignty or a form of neo-colonialism, an allegation often raised in the media and amongst Western commentators, I have instead tried to demonstrate in this chapter how these networks are reshaping the state, allowing it to adapt and to morph in accordance to the exigencies of globalization, and reinforce state power at the nation's margins. By initiating a neoliberal transition, Chinese investors effectively provide Lao leaders with privileged access to private capital and public goods, thus facilitating the conversion of the revolutionary ruling elite into managers of a privatized state. This primitive accumulation process is occurring at the expense of both rural communities and the environment.

However, uncertain benefits may push China to revise its long-term development strategy in Laos. Since June 2014, EximBank—the official export credit agency of the Chinese government—has suspended loans for nine road and bridge projects in Laos that were linked to Chinese firms. The bank said it would only support projects in the mining and hydropower sectors "that give maximum economic results" (RFA July 2014). This shift could be seen as an indication of Beijing's concern over Laos's ability to repay loans for such projects in the absence of immediate guarantees. The ADB and the World Bank also warned that the China–Laos railway project would entail an onerous debt burden that the country could not afford. In addition, the Lao government signed in April 2013 a US$5 billion funding agreement with Giant Consolidated Limited (GCL)—an obscure company based in Malaysia but incorporated in the British Virgin Islands and funded by Rich Banco Berhad, an offshore bank—to build and operate the high-speed railway linking southern Laos to Vietnam and Thailand.

In the past, despite natural resource potential, the country's isolation and difficult terrain meant that Laos largely remained economically unviable to the French. They rapidly gave up the ambition to develop a proper railway network in Laos. It seems that China is willing to take that risk today and bet on developing Laos's economic potential, despite the twisted saga behind the high-speed train. So far, the railway project in Laos has also been put on hold because of Thailand's political turmoil. But then, in December

2014, Thailand's military junta approved a US$23 billion deal for two high-speed rail links with Kunming (via Vientiane) to be built by 2021. This plan is in fact part of China's broader ambition to revive the centuries-old 'Silk Road', both in the continental and maritime domains, to boost connectivity across Asia. In November 2014, China invested US$40 billion in the Silk Road Fund to build roads, railways, ports, airports and other transport links in poorer parts of Asia. President Xi Jinping also unveiled the US$50 billion China-backed Asian Infrastructure Investment Bank, seen as a challenge to the World Bank and the Asian Development Bank (*The Economist* 2014). Yet, it is difficult to say what the future holds for Laos in China's new 'Silk Road'. China's 'high-speed railway diplomacy' and its fashionable 'win-win' rhetoric may not be as successful as Chinese diplomats would like to believe. The delay in the railway project may also reflect concerns among the Lao elite about China 'taking over Laos', thus putting pressure to negotiate a fairer deal. Nevertheless, China can make a more powerful argument in the current negotiation game. Ultimately, the question is not necessarily about whether a railway will be or should be built in Laos, but rather about the cost to rural Lao communities.

Notes

1. In short, the NSEC is basically a highway that links Kunming to Bangkok crossing through the northern provinces of Laos. It was inaugurated on 31 March 2008 during the third GMS Summit held in Vientiane.
2. This term refers to the colonization policy implemented by the French colonial government in Indochina. Indochina was designated as a *colonie d'exploitation* (colony of economic interests) by the French government. The objective for Laos was to provide access for trade with China, or a strategic location from which to extend French influence west to Siam.
3. More specifically, the analysis will focus on the three northern Lao provinces connected to the North–South Economic Corridor (Luang Namtha, Bokeo and Oudomxay), in which I conducted fieldwork between 2007 and 2012.
4. Lan Xang, the 'Kingdom of a Million Elephants' is the precursor of the country of Laos; Lan Na, the 'Kingdom of a Million Rice Fields' is located in present-day northern Thailand; Kengtung is part of the Shan State in Myanmar, and Sipsongpanna, the 'Kingdom of 12,000 Rice Fields' became the Xishuangbanna Dai Autonomous Prefecture in Yunnan Province.
5. The French colonial regime had entrusted these *congrégations* with the responsibility for the registration of Chinese newcomers in Indochina. This

system of indirect rule over Chinese communities also provided mutual aid assistance, organized social and cultural activities, mediated internal disputes, and assisted the government in implementing laws and collecting taxes.

6. By the end of the colonial period in 1947, the overseas Chinese numbered 2.5 million in Thailand, 1.9 million in Dutch India, 300,000 in Myanmar, and 850,000 in French Indochina. Barely 32,500 Chinese were registered, however, in Laos in 1955 (Purcell 1965, p. 2; Halpern 1961, Table 3).
7. Due to the Sino-Vietnamese war (17 February to 16 March 1979) triggered by the invasion of Cambodia in December 1978 by Vietnamese troops.
8. This figure is given by the Association of Overseas Chinese in Vientiane. Most official sources recorded 40,000 people.
9. According to my field observations between 2007 and 2012, the major destinations were the provincial capitals; in order of importance, Oudomxay, Luang Prabang, Luang Namtha, Phongsaly, and Houeisay. The improvement of transportation has also enabled further inroads in secondary cities, such as Muang Sing, Muang Long, Xieng Kok, Vieng Phou Kha, Pak Beng, or Muang Khoa.
10. For a more detailed analysis of these figures, see Tan (2011).
11. A border pass, provided at the international and local checkpoints, allows all Chinese citizens to travel within four northern provinces (Oudomxay, Luang Namtha, Bokeo and Phongsaly) for a period of ten days, extendable for another ten days.
12. See the official website of the Lao Ministry of Planning and Investment: http://www.investlaos.gov.la/index.php/resources/statistics (accessed 5 January 2017). It may be important to point out that all the projects on paper do not necessarily materialize or, if they do, they do not always match the size of the investments.
13. Many traders are not registered companies. They use Lao registered companies to clear documents and pay 'tea money' (i.e., bribes) to customs officers to shorten administrative procedures, to benefit from tax cuts or to smuggle goods. This explains why many of the imported and exported products pass through official channels but on an informal basis, and preferably at local border checkpoints (interviews and field observations at local border checkpoints in Boten, Panthong, Xieng Kok and Meochai, May–October 2008 and June 2009).
14. Interview, Vientiane, June 2009.
15. Personal communication with officials from the National Economic Research Institute (NERI), a think tank under the supervision of the Ministry of Planning and Investment, Vientiane, June 2009.
16. Under this system, the company provides capital, technology and a market for the final product, and farmers provide land and labour. Profits are split, generally with 70 per cent going to the farmer and 30 per cent to the investor.

17. Special economic zones are designated enclaves within national territory operating under a set of administrative and regulatory structures distinct from those throughout the rest of a country. Private enterprises investing in SEZs receive special treatment in things such as services, duties and tariffs, and investment regulations. The social, environmental and labour standards imposed on investments are more lenient than those in national regulations and laws.
18. Kings Romans Group is also known as Dok Ngiew Kham Company or Jin Mumian (金木棉)—meaning 'golden kapok', named after the kapok trees that carpet the area with flame-red flowers.
19. The data was collected from the Department of Planning and Investment of Bokeo Province in 2009.
20. Kings Romans Casino paid US$6,300,000 in taxes to the Lao government for the period 2009 to 2014 (see EIA 2015, p. 21).
21. Interview with the director of the department, Houeysay, 11 June 2009.
22. The creation of an SEZ is one of the major components of the GMS Program towards the realization of economic corridors. Since 2001, the ADB has been involved in forty-one SEZs-related projects in the GMS with an estimated cost of US$1 billion (see ADB's GMS Development Matrix, last updated October 2006, http://www.adb.org/GMS/Projects/devmatrix.asp, accessed 15 April 2013). In Laos, the National Committee for Special and Specific Economic Zones (NCSEZ) received US$700,000 of technical assistance for developing SEZs.

References

ADB. 2010. *GMS Migration Policy Briefing, Forecasting Migration Flows: The Relationships among Economic Development, Demographic Change and Migration in the Greater Mekong Subregion*. Manila: ADB.

Al Jazeera English. "Chinese Casino in 'Golden Triangle' Lead to Questions of Drug Ties". 2 December 2011. http://www.youtube.com/watch?feature=player_embedded&v=P3OPZUjZa5c#.

Alden, Chris, Daniel Large, and Ricardo Soares de Oliveira, eds. 2008. *China Returns to Africa. A Rising Power and a Continent Embrace*. London: Hurst.

Baird, Ian G. 2011. "Turning Land into Capital, Turning People into Labour: Primitive Accumulation and the Arrival of Large-Scale Economic Land Concessions in the Lao People's Democratic Republic". *News Proposals: Journal of Marxism and Interdisciplinary Inquiry* 5, no. 1: 10–26.

Barney, Keith. 2009. "Laos and the Making of a 'Relational' Resource Frontier". *Geographical Journal* 175, no. 2: 146–59.

Brocheux, Pierre, and Daniel Hémery. 2001. *La colonisation ambiguë*. Paris: La Découverte.

China Talk [中国访谈]. "赵伟: 奋斗在金三角经济特区." [Zhao Wei: Struggle in the Golden Triangle Special Economic Zone]. 4 May 2011. http://fangtan.china.com.cn/2011-05/04/content_22492727.htm.

Cohen, Paul T. 2009. "The Post-Opium Scenario and Rubber in Northern Laos: Alternative Western and Chinese Models of Development". *International Journal of Drug Policy* 20, no. 5: 424–30.

Condominas, Georges, and Richard Pottier, eds. 1982. *Les Réfugiés originaires de l'Asie du Sud-Est*. Paris: La Documentation française.

Crispin, Shawn W. 2010. "The Limits of Chinese Expansionism". *Asia Times*, 23 December 2010.

Diana, Antonella. 2009. *Roses & Rifles: Experiments of Governing on the China–Laos Frontier*. PhD dissertation, Australian National University.

Dwyer, Mike. 2007. *Turning Land into Capital. A Review of Recent Research on Land Concessions for Investments in Lao PDR*, Part 1 & 2. Vientiane: Working Group on Land Issues.

———. 2014. "Micro-geopolitics: Capitalising security in Laos's Golden Quadrangle". *Geopolitics* 19: 377–405.

The Economist. 2011. "Busted Flush. How a Sino-Lao Special Economic Zone Hit the Skids". 26 May 2011.

———. 2014. "The New Silk Road. Stretching the Threads". 29 November 2014.

EIA. *Sin City. Illegal Wildlife Trade in Laos' Golden Triangle Special Economic Zone*. London: Environmental Investigation Agency. http://eia-international.org/wp-content/uploads/EIA-Sin-City-FINAL-med-res.pdf (accessed 21 March 2015).

Evans, Grant. 2002. *A Short History of Laos: The Land in Between*. Bangkok: Silkworm Books.

Evans, Grant, Christopher Hutton, and Kuah Khun Eng, eds. 2000. *Where China Meets Southeast Asia. Social and Cultural Changes in the Border Regions*. Bangkok: White Lotus.

Fawthrop, Tom. 2011. "High Stakes as Laos Turns to Casinos". *South China Morning Post*, 23 January 2011.

Forbes, Andrew. 1998. "The Role of Hui Muslims in the Traditional Caravan Trade between Yunnan and Thailand". In *Marchands et Hommes d'affaires asiatiques, XIIIème-XXème siècles*, edited by Denys Lombard, and Jean Aubin, pp. 289–94. Paris: EHESS.

Gluckman, Ron. 2011. "Bungle in the Jungle". *Forbes Asia Magazine*, 8 August 2011.

GMS Studies Center. 2009. *A Study on China-Laos Economic Relations*. Final Report. Kunming: Yunnan University.

Halper, Stefan. 2010. *The Beijing Consensus: How China's Authoritarian Model Will Dominate the Twenty-First Century*. New York: Basic Books.

Halpern, Joel M. 1961. *The Role of the Chinese in Lao Society*. Santa Monica: The Rand Corporation.
Hansen, Mette Halskov. 1999. "The Call for Mao or Money? Han Chinese Settlers on China's South-Western Border". *The China Quarterly* 158: 394–413.
Hibou, Béatrice, ed. 2004. *Privatising the State*. London: Hurst.
Hilgers Lauren. 2012. "Laos Vegas: A Chinese Entrepreneur Crosses the Border to Build His Gambling Empire". *Good*, 14 March 2012.
Hill, Ann Maxwell. 1998. *Merchants and Migrants: Ethnicity and Trade among the Yunnanese Chinese in Southeast Asia*. New Haven, CT: Yale Southeast Asia Studies.
Kurlantzick, Joshua. 2007. *Charm Offensive: How China's Soft Power Is Transforming the World*. Yale: Yale University Press.
Lintner, Bertil. 2008. "China Ascendent – Part 1: Checkbook Diplomacy Raises China's Standing with Laos and Cambodia". *YaleGlobal Online*, 25 April 2008.
Lintner, Bertil, and Michael Black. 2009. *Merchants of Madness. The Methamphetamine Explosion in the Golden Triangle*. Bangkok: Silkworm Books.
Lombard, Denys. 1990. *Le carrefour javanais. Essai d'histoire globale*. Paris: EHESS.
Ma Mung, Emmanuel. 2000. *La diaspora chinoise: Géographie d'une migration*. Paris, Ophrys.
Marton, Peter, and Tamas Matura. 2011. "The 'Voracious Dragon', the 'Scramble' and the 'Honey Pot': Conceptions of Conflict over Africa's Natural Resources". *Journal of Contemporary African Studies* 29, no. 2: 155–67.
McCoy, Alfred W., Cathleen B. Read, and Leonard P. Adams II. 1972 [1991]. *The Politics of Heroin in Southeast Asia*. New York: Harper & Row.
The Nation. "Chinese Investors Invade Laos". 8 October 2007.
Northern Laos Industrial Economic Development and Cooperation Planning Preparation Group, 2008–2020. 2008. *Planning for Industrial Economic Development and Cooperation in Northern Part of Lao People's Democratic Republic*.
Nyíri, Pál. 2009. "Extraterritoriality. Foreign Concessions: The Past and Future of Form of Shared Sovereignty". *EspaceTemps.net*, 23 November 2009.
———. 2012. "Enclaves of Improvement: Sovereignty and Developmentalism in the Special Zones of the China-Lao Borderlands". *Comparative Studies in Society and History* 54, no. 3: 533–62.
Olsen, Robert. 2013. "Hong Kong Invites Fraud to Solve Nonexistent Problem". *Forbes*, 27 March 2013.
Ong, Aihwa. 2006. *Neoliberalism as Exception: Mutation in Citizenship and Sovereignty*. Durham: Duke University Press.

Pan, Lynn, ed. 1999. *The Encyclopedia of the Chinese Overseas*. Cambridge, MA: Harvard University Press.
Polanyi, Karl. 1994 [2001]. *The Great Transformation: The Political and Economic Origins of Our Time*. Boston: Beacon Press.
Purcell, Victor. 1965. *The Chinese in Southeast Asia*. London: Oxford University Press.
Radio Free Asia (RFA). 2014. "China's EximBank Suspends Loans for Roads, Bridges in Laos". 22 July 2014.
———. 2017. "Clearing for Lao–China Railway Begins, but Questions about the Project Still Remain". 4 January 2017.
———. "China to Press ahead with Financing of Lao Railway Project". 19 August 2014.
Reid, Anthony. 1993. *Southeast Asia in the Age of Commerce, 1450–1680. vol. II. Expansion and Crisis*. New Haven: Yale University Press.
Robequain, Charles. 1948. *L'Indochine française*. Paris: A. Colin.
Rossetti, Florence. 1997. "The Chinese in Laos. Rebirth of the Laotian Chinese Community as Peace Returns to Indochina". *Chinese Perspectives* 13: 26–39.
Rutherford, Jeff, Kate Lazarus, and Shawn Kelley. 2008. *Rethinking Investments in Natural Resources: China's Emerging Role in the Mekong*. Cambodia, Denmark, Canada: Heinrich Böll Stiftung, WWF, International Institute for Sustainable Development.
Scott, James C. 2009. *The Art of Not Being Governed. An Anarchist History of Upland Southeast Asia*. Yale: Yale University Press.
Shi, Weiyi. 2008. *Rubber Boom in Luang Namtha. A Transnational Perspective*. Vientiane: GTZ.
Shichor, Yitzhak. 2008. "Sudan: Neo-colonialism with Chinese Characteristics". In *China in Africa*, edited by Arthur Waldron, pp. 73–85. Washington: Jamestown Foundation.
Skinner, William. 1996. "Creolized Chinese Societies in Southeast Asia". In *Sojourners and Settlers, Histories of the Southeast Asia and the Chinese*, edited by Anthony Reid, pp. 50–93. Honolulu: University of Hawai'i Press.
Stuart-Fox, Martin. 1995. "The French in Laos, 1887–1945". *Modern Asian Studies* 29, no. 1: 111–39.
———. 2003. *A Short History of China and Southeast Asia: Tribute, Trade and Influence*. St. Leonard, NSW: Allen & Unwin.
———. 2009. "The Chinese Connection". In *Southeast Asian Affairs 2009*, edited by Daljit Singh, pp. 141–69. Singapore: Institute of Southeast Asian Studies.
Sturgeon, Janet. 2013. "Cross-Border Rubber Cultivation between China and Laos: Regionalization by Akha and Tai Rubber Farmers". *Singapore Journal of Tropical Geography* 34, no. 1: 70–85.

Tan, Danielle. 2006. *La Diaspora Chinoise du Cambodge. Histoire d'une identité recomposée.* Master's dissertation, Sciences Po, Paris.

———. 2011. *Du communisme au néolibéralisme: le rôle des réseaux chinois dans la transformation de l'État au Laos.* PhD dissertation, Sciences Po, Paris.

———. 2012. "'Small Is Beautiful': Lessons from Laos for the Study of Chinese Overseas". *Journal of Current Chinese Affairs* 41, no. 2: 61–94.

———. 2014a. "Chinese Networks, Economic and Territorial Redefinitions in Northern Lao PDR". In *Transnational Dynamics in Southeast Asia: The Greater Mekong Subregion and Malacca Straits Economic Corridors*, edited by Nathalie Fau, Sirivanh Khonthapane, and Christian Taillard, pp. 421–52. Singapore: Institute of Southeast Asian Studies.

———. 2014b. "China in Laos: Is There Cause for Worry?" *ISEAS Perspective*, no. 2014/13, 16 May 2014.

Transnational Institute. 2010. "Alternative Development or Business as Usual? China's Opium Substitution Policy in Burma and Laos". *Drug Policy Briefing* 33.

Trocki, Carl. 2009. "Chinese Revenue Farms and Borders in Southeast Asia". *Modern Asian Studies* 43, no. 1: 335–62.

Tsing Lowenhaupt, Anna. 2009. *Friction: An Ethnography of Global Connection.* Princeton: Princeton University Press.

Walker, Andrew. 1999. *The Legend of the Golden Boat. Regulation, Trade and Traders in the Borderlands of Laos, Thailand, China and Burma.* Richmond: Curzon Press.

Walsh, John. 2009. "The Rising Importance of Chinese Labour in the Greater Mekong Sub-Region". *Asia-Pacific Journal* 12.

Weiss, Linda. 1999. *The Myth of the Powerless State.* Ithaca: Cornell University Press.

Wasana La-Orngplew. 2012. *Living under the Rubber Boom: Market Integration and Agrarian Transformations in the Lao uplands.* PhD dissertation, Durham University.

Xinhua. 2014. "China Becomes Largest Investor in Laos". 30 January 2014.

14

Casino Capitalism, Chinese Special Economic Zone and the Making of a Neoliberal Border in Northern Laos

Pinkaew Laungaramsri

> We hope that this will be a [future] collaboration [between three countries]. When the special economic zone in Thailand connects with the zone here and when the political situation in Myanmar has improved so that the country can develop with their own style and natural resources, we will build a bridge on the Mekong river. It will be a 人 shape bridge, with Laos on the top, Thailand on the left, and Myanmar on the right. It will be a tourist bridge that shows to the world that we have done good deeds here, and that Golden Triangle has already changed.
>
> Laos used to suffer tremendously from various causes. But with the effort by Kings Romans, this place has become peaceful and clean.
>
> (Zhao Wei, Owner of Kings Romans Company)[1]

On 7 January 2014, a bulldozer was sent by a Chinese firm—the Kings Romans Company, which runs the Golden Triangle Special Economic Zone—to clear land to construct an international airport in Ton Phueng district. An area of 236 hectares of rice fields had already been taken by the company from forty-one families, but the villagers refused to accept the offered compensation as it was well below market value. Though the original land dispute was not yet settled, Kings Romans demanded an additional 6 hectares of land to complete its construction. Refusing to comply with the perceived unfair deal, a group of farmers who had cultivated the area for several generations protested in front of the bulldozer, prompting the company to seek intervention from the Lao police. Policemen armed with AK-47 assault rifles were sent to enforce the order by Kings Romans, resulting in a stand-off between villagers and government officials. This was a rare protest by citizens against a developmental project in post-Socialist Laos.[2]

The case of Ton Phueng is just one among many throughout the Lao PDR of local communities similarly affected by the government's Special Economic Zones (SEZs), defined as the creation of large-scale zones of fenced-in industrial estates to attract foreign direct investments. Since the 2000s, Laos has followed its Chinese neighbour in creating SEZs to serve as a new economic engine where special economic policies and flexible governmental measures conducive for business can be implemented. Presently, there are a total of thirteen SEZs in Laos, four of which are operated by Chinese firms. An area of 13,626 hectares has already been granted to SEZ development, while the government is planning to grant as many as forty SEZs in the next ten years. Revenues generated from the development of special economic zones in Laos are mainly from shareholdings, value-added taxes and land concession fees. As of 2015, the total amount of invested capital was US$1 billion. However, the total revenue from the thirteen zones only reached US$11 million.[3]

SEZs in Laos represent an ongoing effort by the Lao government, since the land concession policy during the 1990s, to 'turn land into capital'. However, an SEZ differs markedly from land concessions in several aspects. First, it was designed to overcome the shortcomings of previous land management strategies, such as a confusing approval process that often resulted in overlapping agencies and institutions at provincial and national levels (Kenney-Lazar 2010).[4] With the SEZ, there is a centralized system under the Lao National Committee for Special Economic Zone (chaired by the Deputy Prime Minister) and managed by relevant government units.[5] The newly established management model known as 'One-Stop Service' is believed to help hasten the approval process and provide more incentives to foreign investors.

Second, unlike land concessions that allow investors to turn natural resources such as land or minerals into commodities, the SEZ is a large land sale scheme where the state acts as a business incubator and land broker to help the private sector accumulate capital at a low cost. SEZs in Laos thus signify a significant shift in the state's role over land dispossession. In accelerating the process of land expropriation, the Lao state has shifted from its traditional role as a key economic planner for national development to that of land broker under a neoliberal regime of dispossession.[6]

Third, as a land broker, the state also transfers the rights for development and resource management to foreign investors, thus giving foreign investors equal rights and power to govern the zone and people within the zone without external interference. 'Shared sovereignty', 'flexible citizenship' and temporal suspension of the rule of law have since been used as key marketing strategies to incentivize investors with further benefits. The benefits of SEZs thus include tax breaks, enhanced legal enforcement of property rights, bureaucratic non-interference and autonomy of governance to create environments that are more conducive to foreign investors and increase regional competitiveness.

China has been the most significant player in Laos's economic development. In 2014, China became the largest foreign investor in Laos, with a total investment of US$5.1 billion, edging out Thailand and Vietnam.[7] The asymmetrical economic relationship between Laos and China has turned the former into an extension of the latter's development scheme in which abundant natural resources have been extracted and exported in the name of regional connectivity.

Contrary to China's SEZ models, such as Shenzhen, where both central and local governments play significant roles in the planning process,[8] the Lao SEZs have witnessed the retreat of the Lao state from the entire process of zone development. Instead, the Lao state has granted full planning and regulatory authority to zone developers. As a result, most zones, especially those operated by Chinese investors, have become single-firm zones that are poorly designed and have failed to create further business development within the zone. The Lao state's withdrawal also means SEZ operators enjoy autonomy in designing their own regulatory policies and determining the type of production and export performance. Most SEZs have their own judicial systems and are free to employ as many domestic workers as they wish. Instead of generating quality economic growth, several zones end up establishing shadow economies where underground activities such as gambling, drugs, sex and wildlife trade take place. At the same time, the absence of the state also means that people's livelihoods and property are subjected to expropriation by SEZ operators, thus sparking tensions between local communities and government officials.

This chapter uses the case of the Golden Triangle Special Economic Zone (GT SEZ) to demonstrate the politics of development in post-Socialist Laos. It analyses the collaboration between the Lao state and Chinese developers to transform the agricultural borderland of Ton Phueng into a new Chinese Urban using casino capitalism and other shadow economies as the key economic engine. The chapter argues that foreign intervention, as carried out by transnational casino capitalists and authorized by the Lao state, represents a peculiar mode of government driven by an authoritarian form of neoliberalism. To facilitate economic development, the Lao state has lent its sovereignty to foreign business counterparts. SEZs are, therefore, not simply "demarcated geographic areas contained within a country's national boundaries where the rules of business are different from those that prevail in the national territory" (Farole 2011, p. 23). Instead, they are place-making projects where the "state of exception" (Agamben 2003) operates as a mechanism to normalize the coercive transformation of local resources and economy, and to depoliticize the process of dispossession and displacement. Conversely, Chinese enterprises have claimed that they have created employment opportunities, enhanced economic competitiveness and advanced labour skills to raise the living standards of border communities. However, this chapter will show that such rhetoric legitimizes the appropriation of local resources with unfair compensation while allowing developers to shun their responsibility to local groups.

Golden Triangle Special Economic Zone, Chinese Empire and the Politics of Place-Making

> When I first got there, I saw that Lao people still wore sandals and were very poor. The environment was very bad, making this place very backward. I was interested in this place and asked the guide to take me to the village head. I asked him, "with such beautiful resources you have, would you be interested in doing tourism?" He said no one has invested here.

> The second reason I invested in this place is the image of the Golden Triangle. People found it mysterious and scary. But I did not find it that way. I really liked it here. People here are conservative. Their thinking is at least fifty years behind China. And that interested me. Lao people are kind, honest, and pitiful. That was the reason I wanted to help them. I felt like a parent wanting to take care of his children. My hope is that I will be able to help them. (Zhao Wei)[9]

> For more than ten years, the government has developed Ton Pheung district in Bokeo province to become a special development zone in order to eliminate its negative reputation as a "drug zone". (The National Committee for Special and Specific Economic Zone Secretariat Office [NCSEZ])[10]

In *The Will to Improve: Governmentality, Development, and the Practice of Politics* (2007), Tania Li demonstrates how attempts to improve the conditions of the population, landscape and productivity in Indonesia have had a long and troubled history. From the colonial period to the present, such attempts have ignored structural deficiencies and, instead, focused on technical issues to drive reform. A problem with this approach is that the 'will' to improve is not a singular intention but a diverse one drawn from diverse *dispositifs*—the various institutional and administrative mechanisms and knowledge structures that sustain the exercise of power within the social body (Foucault 1979). The irony of such an improvement programme, as Li notes, is that the gulf between what it attempts to do and its accomplishment is far too wide.

If the establishment of the Golden Triangle SEZ is one example of 'the will to improve' orchestrated by the state and Chinese actors at the border, then certain historical facts have been selectively remade to override the local realities and experiences. In justifying the rationale for 'improvement', the discourses of drug, crime, and poverty have been constructed and accentuated to characterize northern Laos as a 'wild frontier'. But Ton Pheung was not a drug-producing area, at least not from local memory. Located in a wide bend of the Mekong River, the area was part of the ancient Souvanna Khomkham civilization, dating from the fifth century. Interestingly, while the area is referred to by Chinese developers and the Lao SEZ authority as the 'Golden Triangle'—a term coined by the US Vice-Secretary of State Marshall Green during a press conference on 12 July 1971; a term not necessarily shared by other Lao state agencies responsible for heritage preservation, or international organizations such as UNESCO, and local people who see this area as part of the ancient archaeological area that stretches from Bokeo province's Ton Phueng in Laos to Chiang Rai's Chiang Saen on the Thai side.[11] Historically, this transboundary connection of Chiang Saen and Suvannakhomkham shared 500–600 years of ancient history across the Mekong River. Houayxay town, located in the Golden Triangle SEZ, used to be a trading centre between China's Yunnan Province and the Chiang Rai province of Thailand, while cross-border trade has long been going on along Laos's northern border despite its intermittent closure. Unfortunately, this local history of economic connectivity and cross-border trade is often played down in contemporary analysis.[12] Instead, the discourse of deficiency and, in this case, economic isolation and backwardness is the *sine qua non* for the need for improvement as it benefits the interests of various stakeholders.

The Golden Triangle SEZ was established in 2007 with the promise to develop the Ton Phueng district, in Bokeo province, into one of the top entertainment complexes in the world. It is the third SEZ to be located on the Laos–Thailand border, following Savan–seno SEZ in 2003 and Boten–dankham SEZ in 2007.[13] According to the NCEZ, the plan to develop the 'remote' and 'drug trade zone' area of Ton Phueng goes back at least a decade to when the Lao government assigned the Northern Development Agriculture, Import-Export Trade and Services' State Enterprise in collaboration with the PP Group Co., Ltd (Thailand) to develop the zone.[14] However, this collaboration never came to fruition.[15] It took the Lao government ten years to find a committed investor to help improve this area. Initially registered in Myanmar under the name Burma-Macaolandou Co., Ltd., the Dok Ngiou Kham Group (known in Chinese as 金木棉 or golden kapok, a Hong Kong-registered company with an English name, Kings Romans Co., Ltd.) was granted a seventy-five-year contract (extendable to ninety-nine years) in a 3000-hectare area in exchange for a total investment of US$2 billion. The first phase saw 827 hectares covering farmlands and village settlements used to establish a basic infrastructure of roads and buildings with an initially agreed investment value of US$87 million. According to the agreement, between 2011 and 2020, the company will need to upgrade its development project to a full SEZ to include other necessary facilities such as an international airport that will link Laos regionally and internationally.

According to NCSEZ, the GT SEZ now has a full-option entertainment complex that includes a gigantic, golden crown casino building and a three-star hotel. It also has restaurants, fresh markets, six dormitories, a brick factory, rock grinders, Done Sao Cultural Hall, electricity and water supply systems, a concrete road of forty-six kilometres, and housing for Ban Kwan villagers. Interestingly, although gambling in the GT SEZs has been the prime cause of social problems in the area, very little has been made of these problems. In the Development Strategies of SEZ documents, terms such as 'casino' and 'gambling' are avoided, while the consequences of gambling addiction are mentioned only in passing. As the official document noted, "the development of full option entertainment creates some social problems that cause unsafely [sic] in Golden Triangle Special Economic Zone".[16]

Gambling (赌博) is also not an activity that Zhao Wei, the developer and Kings Romans owner, wants to be associated with. As a casino tycoon, Zhao Wei has gained business experience in China's Macau and Mong La, a Burmese border town opposite Dalou in China's Yunnan province. Zhao's casino in Mong La was, however, short-lived. Notorious for being a hub for gambling, prostitution, transsexual cabaret shows and money laundering, regular casino customers at his casino in Mong La were not only Chinese tourists but also government officials, with the latter reported for gambling with state funds.[17] It was not long before pressure from the Chinese government prohibited officials and citizens from crossing the border to Mong La, bringing an end to the once lucrative business, which resulted in Zhao Wei moving his business elsewhere. At the northern Lao border, the casino industry is reborn as an entertainment and development project designed to improve the quality of life of the rural Lao population. In several interviews with Chinese media, the GT SEZ is often portrayed by Zhao as a beautiful place with red gorgeous Kapok flowers blossoming in February; an image set in contrast with the 'ignorant' local Lao people and their lack of knowledge to preserve the fertile natural resources. As Zhao stated,

> We want to build eco-tourism here. Green environment with no pollution so that in the future we can have something green to eat. We have already invested in the construction of reservoir and agricultural development. We will build a place that is different from big city tourism that people have been accustomed to.
>
> The reason why we focus on agriculture is because people here know how to farm but did not care if their slash and burn method would destroy forests.

They will have to learn how to farm. They like farming, we then teach them scientific method of farming. [We already] invited specialists from Agricultural Institute in China and collaborated with Chinese Projects to teach [Lao] farmers a good practice of farming.[18]

In this way, the casino is not simply part of the gambling industry but a development scheme. It is a development scheme that identifies local deficiencies, devises corrective measures and turns problems into technical inquiries. The building of the casino thus becomes a positive development in the lives of Lao citizens, while pertinent questions over deprivation and uneven resource allocation are depoliticized and concealed by the rubric of development discourse (Ferguson 1994). As Zhao puts it: "Doing business is like making merit. Business and society: they grow together."[19]

Zhao Wei, however, claims that his casino business is different.[20] It is a 'good' and 'responsible' casino that complies strictly with laws that prohibit money laundering, and was, as Zhao contends, established in order to replace a worse industry—the drug trade. In his words, "to stop the spread of drug business and replace it with casino, I think it's much worth it."[21] Furthermore, dispossession is often claimed to be a necessary transformative process where the traditional peasantry gives way to a skilful working class in a new industry. Unfortunately, this transformation did not happen as envisioned. While the GT SEZ has indeed become a reservoir of job and economic opportunities for many people, the majority of waged labour is taken up by cross-border migrant Burmese, and not the evicted Lao peasants. Chinese immigrants also gained benefits from the SEZ. The result of this is class differentiation developed along ethnic lines, with the Lao sitting at the bottom of this differentiation. A decade of development, however, has not eradicated the area's reputation for being a 'drug border'. On the contrary, the international media has portrayed it as a zone free from state rules within which all kinds of illicit trade flourish. From drugs to sex and wildlife trade, authorized illicit economic activities have come to characterize the new 'wild' zone of the GT SEZ led by Chinese tycoons.

Resettlement, Dispossession and Suspended Citizens

For over a decade, internal resettlement in Laos has been a controversial issue among social scientists and development practitioners. Central to the issue is the need to interpret the concept of 'resettlement' from the perspective of affected people. In her article, "The Implications of Aspirations: Reconsidering Resettlement in Laos" (High 2008),[22] anthropologist Holy High uses two ethnographic case studies to argue against the binary understanding of resettlement that is often couched in the discourse of coercion against voluntary movement. High proposes looking at resettlement as an "experimental consensus" in which people, despite their bitter and unjust circumstances, critically engage with state policies on resettlement with an aspiration for modernity and new livelihoods. High's proposal was dismissed by Baird and others in their response to her article, "International Resettlement in Laos: Reading Too Much into Aspirations: More Explorations of the Space between Coerced and Voluntary Resettlement in Laos" (Baird et al. 2009).[23] They caution that in situations where coercion is normalized and top-down resettlement is an integral part of development policy, an interpretation of resettlement requires a politically sensitive and reflexive understanding. More importantly, the implication of High's position—aspiration for modernity as the motive of people's willingness to engage in a state-initiated resettlement—should be carefully reconsidered, for it can be the basis to justify the already predominant state's centrally planned resettlement policy against highland people in Laos.

However, what seems to be missing from the debate is a focus on the larger political economic forces that drive resettlement and its impact on people. Since the turn of the twenty-first century, with the Lao government's 'turning land into capital' economic strategy, resettlement has become part of a larger process of accumulation of local resources by the state and transformed into capital by transnational corporations. Here, at stake is not the movement of people per se, but the process of stripping people of their property and transferring ownership rights to the private sector while turning the evicted farmers into labour. Many dispossession schemes that include resettlement are carried out not in the highland area where poor ethnic minorities reside, but among the wealthy lowland communities who have lived in their villages for a long time. While the rationale to eradicate shifting cultivation has continued to be used to justify many state resettlement projects, many targeted villages are not shifting cultivators. In many cases, they are lowland farmers whose diversified livelihoods have long been sustained by rich paddy fields, orchards and livestock. Resistance and negotiation against resettlement schemes in these areas have therefore grown louder while land disputes, especially in land concession areas, have escalated.

Resettlement to make way for the GT SEZ took place in 2007 when villagers in Ban Kwan, the first of nine targeted villages, were informed of the relocation plan.[24] However, the process was not transparent. On 24 January 2007, 320 villagers of Ban Kwan met with Ton Phueng district officials and were first told of the GT SEZ project and the need to relocate all the villages along the Mekong River to build tourist shops and the Don Dok Ngiew tourist site. Kwan and Sibounhueong villages were to make way for a fitness centre, a hotel, food and drink venues, and other entertainment facilities. Government officials told villagers that they would only have to move a few hundred metres away from their original village and that they could still gather fruits and vegetables from their orchards as well as use water from the river. The temple would also be retained for the village's religious needs. Based on this information from authorities, the Ban Kwan villagers approved the proposal believing that the resettlement was not severe. In reality, the new resettlement site was located far from the old village, making it impossible to utilize the river for its water and other agricultural resources. On 1 June 2007, villagers submitted a petition entitled, "A Request to Kindly Exempt the Village and Paddy Fields of Kwan Village from the Development of Tourism Complex Project" to the Prime Minister's Office. Two village representatives were sent to Vientiane to deliver the petition. However, it was rejected because the project had already been approved by the government.

Interestingly, although the main reason for resettlement given by the SEZ developer and government officials was to eradicate shifting cultivation and poverty in the area, Ban Kwan and Si Boun Hueong were relatively wealthy lowland communities with the majority of residents owning paddy fields, corn fields, tree plantations, gardens and cattle.[25] In effect, the resettlement turned these farmers into landless labourers and deprived them of their traditional means of production.

Public resentment is directed more towards the Lao government than the SEZ developers. An interview with a woman who used to own a grocery store at Ban Kwan village and whose farmland was taken for the construction of the casino hotel affirms this. She responded in tears,

> I am more angry with our government. It is them who have agreed to hand in our properties to the investor. The investor did their job as an

investor. But the government who should have protected their citizens, have instead betrayed us, reaped benefit from the people's suffering.[26]

On average, a household received between 60,000 and 80,000 baht (US$2,000–2,500) as compensation for their house. A family with a house, granary, gardens, paddy fields, cattle and grazing land would receive compensation of between 800,000 and 1,000,000 baht (US$26,000–34,000). Not surprisingly, most Ban Kwan villagers feel that a new form of poverty now awaited them as the small amount of cash would not be sufficient to establish a new livelihood.

The promise of employment in GT SEZ industries was generally unfulfilled. Locals who were unable to learn the Chinese language or endure hard work, as well as the elderly, were often denied employment by the developer. As a result, less than a third of the villagers found employment with the developer.[27] The majority of the people who were employed by the developer were Burmese migrants, followed by the Chinese and then the Lao people. But in terms of job benefits, Chinese workers enjoyed higher positions compared to the Burmese and Lao. Some young Lao people who were hired at the casino planned to work there only for a short period of time in order to save some money. This included Kiang Khai, a twenty-six-year-old who was married to a Lao woman who had decided to work at the casino as she needed cash for her house construction.

> I have worked in the casino for three years now. I'm the only person in the family who works there. The casino work is okay. But it is insecure. I might work there for another year or two and then quit. The smoking there is terrible. Chinese people smoke a lot. I'm really fed up with it. It is also hard work. Working on a night shift, I have to be cautious all the time. If I make a mistake, my boss will severely reprimand me. Most Lao who work there are card dealers. The Burmese do the cleaning jobs. The Chinese and Burmese get higher payment than the Lao. Some people explained that it's because they are not local. In the old village we used to earn more than 200,000 baht per year. We only had to pay for clothing and meat. The other necessities could be gathered from the forest. Approximately, the monthly expenses would cost us around 2,000 baht. But living here [in the new village] the cost of living is much higher. (Nang Kiang Khai, interviewed 9 November 2012)

On 28 January 2012, an official opening ceremony was held at the new village, renamed Samliem Kham (Golden Triangle). Ban Kwan villagers were offered modern concrete houses classified into six sizes. However, problems appeared within a few months of moving in. The walls and tiles started to crack, while flood water seeped inside the house during heavy rain. The villagers had to spend the compensation they received from the developer on repairing their houses.

Dispossession in the case of the GT SEZ has been uneven among farmers in Ban Kwan, with some benefitting more than others. The landlords or the elite class tended to gain more from the drastic change brought by the casino developer as they owned the largest plots of rice fields and held positions such as village heads, which could advance their economic status. These households aligned themselves with the Chinese developer and thus received the highest rates of compensation. The former village head, for example, bought a plot of paddy field with his compensation and rented it out to poorer families. He was also offered a salaried job at the casino as a reward for his role in the resettlement process even though he had no official role in the casino and did not speak other languages than Lao. His daughter also worked at the casino as a card dealer. He planned to invest his money in a casino-related business such as a guesthouse for gamblers.

Nevertheless, not everyone could find employment in the casino. In 2012, only twenty-five people were offered jobs as card dealers, all of whom were between 15 and 25 years old, and females were favoured over males. Although incomes from casino jobs were enough to cover the high cost of living at the new village,[28] most of these young employees found working conditions at the casino difficult. Workers were required to be flexible in their working hours and had to be open to working night shifts. For example, a female Lao who worked as a card dealer reported that her working hours changed every fifteen days and there was no pattern to her hours, which ranged from 6.30 p.m. to 3.30 a.m., 3.30 a.m. to 10.00 a.m., or 10.30 a.m. to 7 p.m. The only holiday she was entitled to was Chinese New Year.[29] As a result, many of these young workers would eventually leave for other jobs outside the SEZ.

Little is known about the ground reality beyond the image of a successful GT SEZ as propagated by the Lao state and the developer, Kings Romans Company. Although dispossession is often justified as necessary for industrialization, not everyone has access to the casino-related new economy, while those who are engaged in casino work do so under difficult conditions, thus underlining the economic and developmental uncertainty under the GT SEZ.

Border SEZ and the Making of the Wild Frontier

> We did not know which direction to go in the beginning. Where should SEZ be placed? Ministry or Province? We have done trial and error for a while. In 2010, ADB has developed a capacity building project for SEZ which has helped make the direction more clear. We have also learned from China, Vietnam and Thailand. Now we have improved our legal system tailored to a more efficient process of SEZ management. (Director of Planning and Evaluation Division, the Secretariat to NCSEZ)[30]

As instruments of neoliberalism, SEZs not only enhance economic liberalism but also partner the state to create what Aihwa Ong (2006, p. 5) calls 'the Zone of Exception'—that is, "an extraordinary departure in policy that can be deployed to include as well as exclude". The 'exception' allows the developer to seize private property in the name of the state while being inclusive of economically productive citizens and excluding those who are not. As such, SEZs, according to Ong, allow neoliberal logic to reconfigure the relationship between the state and its citizens, distributing basic rights according to their market skills and not according to their membership to the nation-state.

Border SEZs such as the GT SEZ also represent an interesting "out of control interstitial capitalist expansion" (Tsing 2005, p. 28). It is often claimed that the ultimate goal of the border SEZ is to transform border areas into a developed trade zone that would help in the reduction of illicit frontier activities. The establishment of the GT SEZ, however, has had the opposite effect, where national governance has been replaced by trade deregulation and economic control. As such, a new frontier has arisen in the interstitial space of exception made possible by the Lao state and its developer, where the boundary between legality and illegality is blurred. The GT SEZ has consequently witnessed the emergence of shadow economies that are prohibited outside the zone. Gambling, prostitution, drug and wildlife trades, all of which are illegal economic activities in Laos and neighbouring countries, are now fundamental economic activities in the zone, with the casino at its inner core (內围). As a regional hub for tourism, the GT SEZ serves to link up with existing nodes of sex and wildlife trade in Laos and its neighbouring countries, catering to Chinese tourists in search of exotic wildlife and sex.

Lauren Hilgers offers two reasons why border casinos are attractive to Chinese investors. First, there has always been a high demand for gambling among Chinese in mainland China. While traveling to Macau requires a special visa to visit, it is far easier for Chinese gamblers to access border casinos. Second, because China restricts the amount of currency that can be brought across the border, these border casinos are useful in moving money out of the country. Casinos across the border issue gambling chips for Chinese currency that is deposited in banks in China, thus allowing gamblers to cash in these chips outside China after a few games.[31] Although it is difficult to estimate the annual profit generated by the GT SEZ casino, as such information has never been disclosed, it was profitable enough to allow the developer to invest US$2.25 billion by 2020 to fully develop the zone.[32] It is rumoured that Zhao Wei stores his enormous amounts of money in his many apartments. One interviewee tells a story of how, in 2012, the rainy season in northern Laos caused all his bank notes to become mouldy such that Zhao laid his money out to dry in front of his apartment whilst guarded by armed men.[33]

One of the casino's strategies to bring in gamblers is to hire several groups of mostly male brokers (经纪人) who would coordinate casino trips, which usually start from Yunnan and go to Myanmar's Tachilek via a passenger ship and cross the border to Ton Phueng from Chiang Rai's Chiang Saen. Gambling is the highlight of the packaged tour. Brokers are responsible for taking care of the customers' needs while in the zone, including arranging accommodation, providing a female escort, assisting in currency exchange and lending money to clients at unique interest rates. Different groups of brokers often compete with each other for customers, sometimes leading to confrontation and violent conflict. Incidents involving assault and the use of physical force against customers who fail to repay loans from brokers and the casino are common.[34]

The GT SEZ is also notorious as a hub for commercial sex. Women of various ethnic backgrounds, including Chinese, Lao and Thai, but not Burmese, travel to the SEZ for sex work. Sex trade and commercial sex are illegal in both Laos and China but are conducted openly in the GT SEZ either directly in brothels or indirectly in massage parlours. Casino hotels usually offer commercial sex as part of their services, with male guests often asked if they would like the company of a young woman during their stay when they check in.[35] Advertising cards of women and their contact numbers are usually placed on the dressing table in the hotel rooms or slipped under the door at night. Most sex workers in the zone have male procurers who bring in customers through their network with the casino's brokers. Procurers are also the ones who arrange accommodation, negotiate prices and provide 'protection' for their sex worker. In return, the sex worker pays her procurer 250 yuan (US$38) per day regardless of whether she has any customers. The sex worker usually charges 400 yuan (US$60) for two hours and 1,800 yuan (US$274) for the entire night. During the low season months, especially the rainy season, some of these women would move to China or Thailand for prospective customers before returning to the GT SEZ again.

Nevertheless, what characterizes the GT SEZ most as a wild frontier is perhaps its robust industry of trafficking endangered wildlife. Known as a hub for the trade of animal parts and products, GT SEZ has no shortage of exotic meats from tigers, pangolins, bear cubs and pythons served in restaurants, while tiger bone wine is favoured by Chinese tourists. Stuffed animals, ivory and tiger skins from across Asia are on display and ready for sale by Chinese shops in the zone, as confirmed by undercover investigations by the Environmental Investigation Agency (EIA) and Education for Nature Vietnam (ENV) in January 2014.[36] Tiger products and meat are the most profitable in several shops and restaurants. According to the EIA/ENV report, tiger products come from various places: stuffed tigers were processed in Yunnan and Laos and tiger skins are trafficked from Myanmar's Mong La, Thailand and Malaysia as well as those raised in captivity in the GT SEZ's own zoo. The zoo, located not far from the casino, has twenty-six tigers and thirty-eight Asiatic black bears, among others, under the supervision of a head keeper claimed to be an experienced tiger breeder.[37] It is evident that the GT SEZ is planning to adopt the Chinese model of industrial tiger farming in order to meet the rising demand from Chinese consumers for medicine made from tiger parts even though the zoo has not applied for permission to breed and trade live tigers and bears.[38] The fact that Laos is a party to CITES does not seem to have any impact on the GT SEZ's ongoing wildlife trade and trafficking.

Conclusion

In "The Chinese Axis: Zoning Technologies and Variegate Sovereignty", Aihwa Ong (2004) proposes to look at Special Economic Zones as a form of zoning technology made successful by the Chinese state. As Ong contends, such technology has been employed to integrate distinct political entities such as Hong Kong and Macao, and even Taiwan and

Singapore, into a conglomerated Chinese axis. In creating zones of political exception, sovereignty has been reconfigured into a variety of economic and administrative strategies to mobilize resources, improve economic competitiveness and facilitate the flow of foreign investment—the process that led to an emergence of what Ong calls the 'system of variegated sovereignty'.

Following in China's footsteps, the Lao state made SEZs an integral part of its economic development. For a small country with only a total of 1.5 million hectares of cultivated agricultural area (in 2010),[39] it has already created 14,000 hectares of SEZs, mostly in fertile agricultural areas, and is planning to quadruple it in the next decade. I have argued in this chapter that SEZs have taken Laos beyond its previous land concession policy. The case of GT SEZ has shown that SEZs may not only reconfigure industries and the way people live, but also problematize the notion of sovereignty when foreign investors and developers can operate autonomously. In this context, the Lao state has become a subservient service provider, catering to the economic interests of a foreign patron, while leaving the planning, establishment and management of the SEZ to the developer. As a result, instead of generating domestic economic growth or skills development among rural farmers, the casino capitalism at the GT SEZ has become a stand-alone business that has contributed very little to the betterment of Lao communities. Forced relocation, displacement, failed development schemes and conditional job provision have left the Lao population living in the zone in a state of suspension. Struggling to survive outside the interstice, migration and protests are among the remaining strategies local villagers employ to negotiate the uncertainty of their livelihood and their rights as citizens.

Postscript

In recent decades the Golden Triangle SEZ has come to worldwide attention for its notorious illegal industries. In 2018, the Office of Foreign Assets Control (OFAC) of the US Treasury Department imposed sanctions on the Zhao Wei transnational criminal organization (Zhao Wei TCO) for its engagement in laundering money and facilitating the storage and distribution of heroin, methamphetamines and other narcotics for illicit networks. A group of four individuals and three entities in Laos, Thailand and Hong Kong have also been designated by OFAC as supporting the

Zhao Wei TCO. As a result, all the assets so designated that were under US jurisdiction have been confiscated. Engagement in business between US citizens and the Zhao Wei TCO has also been prohibited (US Department of the Treasury 2018). Director of research at the Adrianople Group, a corporate intelligence consultancy that focuses on special economic zones and master-planned cities, describes the GT SEZ as "The world's worst special economic zone" and calls for the international SEZ organization to issue statements publicly condemning the GT SEZ (Serlet 2022). Despite the international intervention, however, criminal activities within the GT SEZ have continued to proliferate. These include human trafficking, forced prostitution and drug smuggling. In early February 2022, Laotian police rescued six women—victims of human trafficking and labour abuse—who had escaped from the Kings Romans Casino. But there are still many women who are confined inside the GT SEZ as Lao authorities are not authorized to enter the Chinese-run zone (Radio Free Asia 2022). While the zone continually captures headlines for abusive labour conditions, neighbouring countries such as Thailand and Malaysia issue warnings to their citizens about traveling to work in the GT SEZ (Latsamy 2022).

Zhao Wei, however, has declared the designation by the United States of the SEZ as a "transnational criminal organization" as a "unilateral, extraterritorial, unreasonable and hegemonic act of ulterior motives and malicious rumor-mongering" (Radio Free Asia 2018). This denial was supported by the local Lao authority at Bokeo Province, who claimed the zone was well managed and operated (ibid.). Regardless of the sanctions by the United States, development in the GT SEZ has expanded rapidly. In July 2022, a new road connecting the GT SEZ with Bokeo international airport was completed, and the airport itself is planned to open for business at the end of the year. A celebration was held in the zone in March 2022 to mark the fifteenth anniversary of the Chinese GT SEZ in northwestern Laos. In October 2020, a US$50 million port construction project on the Mekong river upstream of the GT SEZ was inaugurated (Radio Free Asia 2020). This is a larger port than the one Kings Romans has already operated. It is expected that this international port, if completed, will facilitate more sizeable shipments from China to the GT SEZ. Moreover, it was reported that Zhao has also been exploring new development possibilities in other rural areas of Laos such as in Saravan province in the south and in Pek district near the Plain of Jars, a major archaeological landscape and UNESCO World Heritage Site (Radio Free Asia 2021). The Lao

Casino Capitalism in Northern Laos

government has already granted permission to Zhao Wei to undertake a feasibility study on a 150-hectare plot of land to develop a tourist attraction complex, along with a traditional medicine factory and a golf course. With the GT SEZ as a stepping stone, Zhao's casino empire will undoubtedly penetrate further into the frontier of the Lao economy.

Notes

1. See full interview at http://fangtan.china.com.cn/2011-05/04/content_22492727.htm (accessed 7 November 2011).
2. See http://www.rfa.org/english/news/laos/farmers-04112014180934.html (accessed 5 November 2014). Although Khammane Souvileunt, Governor of Bokeo province, stated that the compensation to the people affected by the airport project had already been made, the construction has yet to be completed. See http://englishnews.thaipbs.or.th/content/64541 (accessed 5 November 2014).
3. http://webcache.googleusercontent.com/search?q=cache:FsB3rHRhqHMJ:www.vientianetimes.org.la/FreeContent/FreeConten_Revenue%2520from.htm+&cd=2&hl=th&ct=clnk (accessed 13 December 2015).
4. The chaotic system of land concessions led to the decision of the Prime Minister to declare a moratorium on new economic land concessions in May 2007. However, the moratorium was revoked in mid-2009 and then a four-year moratorium was again announced in July 2012. The July 2012 moratorium had suspended approvals for all investment proposals for the exploration and survey of a range of mineral ores and the export of raw minerals, rubber and eucalyptus plantations until the end of 2015. See http://www.usaidlandtenure.net/sites/default/files/country-profiles/full-reports/USAID_Land_Tenure_Laos_Profile.pdf (accessed 12 January 2016).
5. SEZs in the Lao PDR are classified into three different spatial characteristics with different purposes for investment: Industrial Zones; Tourism and New Urban Centres; and Trade and Logistics. Accordingly, different government agencies have been assigned to supervise different zones: the Savan-SENO SEZ (trading and logistics) is under the direct supervision of the Prime Minister's Office; the Golden Triangle SEZ and Boten-Daenkham SEZ (tourism and new urban centres) are under the direct supervision of the Ministry of Planning and Investment; and Vientiane–Nonthong Industry–Trade is under the direct supervision of the Ministry of Industry and Commerce. See http://lao-vita.com/upfiles/20158520517__DevelopmentStrategyeng.pdf (accessed 12 January 2016).
6. See similar historical process in the case of India in Levien (2013).

7. See http://qz.com/172350/china-just-became-the-biggest-investor-in-laos-and-laoss-neighbors-are-worried/ (accessed 5 March 2016).
8. See Ng and Tang, "The Role of Planning in the Development of Shenzhen, China: Rhetoric and Realities", http://scripts.mit.edu/~11.306/wiki/images/archive/20080108222452!NgTang_2004.pdf.
9. http://fangtan.china.com.cn/2011-05/04/content_22492727.htm?show=t (accessed 12 March 2012).
10. "Development Strategy for Special and Specific Economic Zone (SEZ) in the Lao PDR, 2011–2020", http://lao-vita.com/upfiles/20158520517__DevelopmentStrategyeng.pdf (accessed 5 January 2016).
11. Apart from the casino-oriented SEZ, other Chinese impacts in this area could be seen in commercial plantations. It was reported by the *Vientiane Times* and the Lao Cultural Heritage Forum that the actual site of the Souvanna Khomkham ancient city, which is forty kilometres away from Ton Phueng district, had been threatened by the Chinese banana plantation concession. See https://groups.google.com/forum/?hl=zh-TW#!topic/laochf/uTAKRBeBZ40, https://groups.google.com/forum/?hl=zh-TW#!topic/laochf/e31-PiR0_K0 (accessed 5 January 2016).
12. Indeed, as a Bokeo Information, Culture and Tourism official lamented, "There is not enough funding available to preserve and renovate the site, particularly given the area [Souvanna Khomkham] is so large". See https://groups.google.com/forum/?hl=zh-TW#!topic/laochf/uTAKRBeBZ40 (accessed 5 January 2016).
13. JICA funded a feasibility study of the Special Economic Zone in Laos in Savannaket province (along the route no. 9) in 2000, while from 2007 onwards the ADB has actively provided technical assistance, special funds for the improvement in management, and offered assistance for legal and regulatory frameworks and improving institutional capacity, as well as identifying chain production business opportunities.
14. http://lao-vita.com/upfiles/20158520517__DevelopmentStrategyeng.pdf (accessed 5 January 2016).
15. In my interview with a government official at the NCSEZ office, he made the observation that Thai investors tend to be less serious about investments but are rather speculative. Similar to the Ton Phueng project, the Savan-seno that started with a commitment by Thai investors has never materialized. On the contrary, Chinese were considered as more genuine and "really have money" (interview, 2 October 2012).
16. http://lao-vita.com/upfiles/20158520517__DevelopmentStrategyeng.pdf (accessed 5 January 2016).
17. http://treasuresoflaos.blogspot.com/2013/02/macao-on-mekong-how-chinese-money-flows.html (accessed 10 November 2016).

18. http://fangtan.china.com.cn/2011-05/04/content_22492727.htm?show=t (accessed 12 March 2012).
19. *Asian Commerce Magazine*. Bilingual Magazine for Traders and Investors in Thailand–China–ASEAN, 2010.
20. Prior to Zhao's arrival, there was a casino established in Boten border town located in the Boten Special Economic Zone. Also owned by a Chinese company, the casino was generally successful in attracting a large number of Chinese gamblers from across the border in Yunnan Province. But as it developed, news of violent and abusive incidents against customers who failed to pay their debts started to circulate widely. In March 2011, China closed down the border and cut off its supply of electricity. Subsequently, the Lao authorities terminated the contract with the Chinese investor and that brought an end to the first casino SEZ in Laos.
21. http://fangtan.china.com.cn/2011-05/04/content_22492727.htm?show=t (accessed 12 March 2012).
22. http://fangtan.china.com.cn/2011-05/04/content_22492727.htm?show=t (accessed 12 March 2012).
23. Baird et al., "International Resettlement in Laos: Reading too much into aspirations: More explorations of the space between coerced and voluntary resettlement in Laos", *Critical Asian Studies* 41 (2009): 4, 6054d e.
24. Other villages include Ban Ponehom, Ban Don Mun, Ban Vieng Savang, Ban Piang Ngam, Ban Mok Kajok, Ban Long Khone, Ban Si Bunhueng, and Ban Muang Kham. The total area to be lost to the company is 3,000 hectares.
25. Ban Kwan was an old village with a history of settlement dating back to the nineteenth century. The majority of the villagers were descendants of Yuan and Lue people who migrated from Lampoon in northern Thailand due to land shortage and to escape from the oppression by the Burmese and Lanna States. There were also other ethnic groups such as the Tai Dam, Lao, and Khmu living in the village.
26. Interview, 2 February 2012.
27. It is estimated that the total number of casino employees was around 4,000 people, of which 1,800 are card dealers. The ages of the employees are between 20 and 25 years old, the majority of which were Chinese. Priority is given to those who can speak Chinese, Thai and English. Some young Chinese are students who have learned the Thai language from Mae Fa Luang or Ratchabhat universities in Chiang Rai province. The salary ranges from 2,000 to 3,000 yuan (US$300–450). The casino has strict regulations and punishment against cheating. Ex-employees are not allowed to be rehired. Any fraudulence or stealing will be heavily punished, which sometimes involves the use of force.
28. Souksamone Sengchanh (2013, p. 75).

29. Ibid.
30. Interview, 4 February 2012.
31. Hilgers, "Laos Vegas: A Chinese Entrepreneur Crosses the Border to Build His Gambling Empire", https://www.good.is/articles/laos-vegas (accessed 3 February 2016).
32. The national budget of Laos in 2009 was US$1.13 billion. http://www.scmp.com/article/736471/high-stakes-laos-turns-casinos (accessed 2 May 2012).
33. This story was told by a Chinese shop owner near the casino. Interview on 4 May 2012.
34. Interview with a Chinese shop owner, 5 April 2012.
35. http://www.independent.co.uk/news/world/asia/chinese-take-a-gamble-on-the-pleasures-of-sin-city-2312139.html (accessed 5 January 2016).
36. EIA, 2015, "Sin City: Illegal Wildlife Trade", https://eia-international.org/wp-content/uploads/EIA-Sin-City-FINAL-med-res.pdf (accessed 1 April 2016).
37. Ibid., p. 6.
38. Ibid., p. 11.
39. http://www.pecad.fas.usda.gov/highlights/2011/12/Laos_13Dec2011/ (accessed 10 January 2016).

References

Agamben, Giorgio. 2003. *State of Exception. Homo Sacer II, 1*. Chicago: University of Chicago Press.

Baird, Ian, Keith Barney, Per Vandergeest, and Bruce Shoemaker. 2009. "Internal Resettlement in Laos: Reading Too Much into Aspirations, A Reply to Holly High". *Critical Asian Studies* 41, no. 4: 605–20.

Farole, T., and G. Akinci, eds. 2011. *Special Economic Zones Progress, Emerging Challenges, and Future Directions.* Washington, DC: The World Bank. https://openknowledge.worldbank.org/bitstream/handle/10986/2341/638440PUB0Exto00Box0361527B0PUBLIC0.pdf? sequence=1 (accessed 2 April 2016).

Ferguson, James. 1994. *The Anti-Politics Machine Development, Depoliticization, and Bureaucratic Power in Lesotho*. University of Minnesota Press.

Foucault, Michel. 1979. *Discipline and Punish: The Birth of the Prison*. New York: Vintage.

High, Holly. 2008. "The Implications of Aspirations: Reconsidering Resettlement in Laos". *Critical Asian Studies* 40, no. 4: 531–50.

Kenney-Lazar, Miles. 2010. *Land Concessions, Land Tenure, and Livelihood Change: Plantation Development in Attapeu Province, Southern Laos. Vientiane.* Faculty of Forestry, National University of Laos.

Latsamy Phonevilay. 2022. "Golden Triangle Special Economic Zone Celebrates 15th Anniversary". *Laotian Times*. https://laotiantimes.com/2022/04/28/golden-triangle-special-economic-zone-celebrates-15th-anniversary/ (accessed 12 July 2022).

Levien, Michael. 2013. "Regimes of Dispossession: From Steel Towns to Special Economic Zones". *Development and Change* 44, no. 2: 381–407.

Li, Tania. 2007. *The Will to Improve: Governmentality, Development, and the Practice of Politics*. Durham, NC: Duke University Press.

Littleton, Chris, and Pal Nyiri. 2011. "Dams, Casinos, and Concessions: Chinese Mega-Projects in Laos and Cambodia". In *Engineering Earth: The Impacts of Megaengineering Projects*, edited by Stanley D. Brunn, pp. 1243–266. London: Springer-Verlag.

Litwack, John M., and Yingyi Qian. 1998. "Balanced or Unbalanced Development: Special Economic Zones as Catalysts for Transition". *Journal of Comparative Economics* 26, no. 1: 117–41.

Nyiri, Pal. 2012. "Enclaves of Improvement: Sovereignty and Developmentalism in the Special Zones of the China-Lao Borderlands". *Comparative Studies in Society and History* 54, no. 3: 533–62.

Ong, Aihwa. 2004. "The Chinese Axis: Zoning Technologies and Variegated Sovereignty". *Journal of East Asian Studies* 4: 69–96.

———. 2006. *Neoliberalism as Exception: Mutations in Citizenship and Sovereignty*. Duke University Press.

Radio Free Asia. 2018. "Lao Casino Operator Rejects U.S. 'Transnational Criminal Organization' Designation". https://www.rfa.org/english/news/laos/lao-zhaowei-02052018145742.html (accessed 10 October 2019).

———. 2020. "Chinese Casino Kingpin behind New Mekong Port to Serve Golden Triangle SEZ in Laos". https://www.rfa.org/english/news/laos/port-10072020195319.html (accessed 11 July 2022).

———. 2021. "Chinese Casino Mogul Zhao Wei Explores Expansion out of Laos' Golden Triangle SEZ". https://www.rfa.org/english/news/laos/zhao-04072021142653.html (accessed 11 July 2022).

———. 2022. "Lao Authorities Rescue Women Trapped in Chinese-Run Economic Zone". https://www.rfa.org/english/news/laos/rescues-escapes-02082022170241.html (accessed 12 July 2022).

Serlet, Thibault. 2022. "Golden Triangle: The World's Worst Special Economic Zone". Investmentmonitor. https://www.investmentmonitor.ai/comment/golden-triangle-special-economic-zone-laos-worst (accessed 11 July 2022).

Strangio, Sebastian. 2020. "Golden Triangle Casino Baron Bankrolls New Mekong River Port". *The Diplomat*. https://thediplomat.com/2020/10/golden-triangle-casino-baron-bankrolls-new-mekong-river-port/ (accessed 11 July 2022).

Souksamone Sengchanh. 2013. "Border Development, Resettlement and

Adaptation in a Special Economic Zone: A Case Study of Khuan Village, Tonpheung District, Bo Kaeo Province in Lao PDR". MA Thesis, Faculty of Social Sciences, Chiang Mai University.

Tsing, Anna Lowenhaupt. 2005. *Friction: An Ethnography of Global Connection*. Princeton: Princeton University Press.

15

'Old' and 'New' Chinese Business in Cambodia's Capital

Michiel Verver

Ever since Hun Sen's state visit to Beijing in 1996, ties between Cambodia and China—or more accurately, between Hun Sen's ruling Cambodian People's Party (CPP) and the Chinese Communist Party (CCP)—have only grown stronger. The state visit was a watershed moment. The Chinese had supported the Khmer Rouge regime (1975–78), while Hun Sen came to power under the auspices of China's rival, the Vietnamese, who had pushed the Khmer Rouge forces towards the Thai border, and founded the People's Republic of Kampuchea (PRK) (1979–89). The 1996 state visit not only signalled a rapprochement between China and Cambodia, but also China's confidence that Hun Sen was Cambodia's strongman in the making. The Chinese had invited Hun Sen but not Prince Rannaridh, whose *Front Uni National pour un Cambodge Indépendant, Neutre, Pacifique, et Coopératif* (FUNCINPEC) had formed an unstable coalition government with the CPP after the 1993 elections organized by the United Nations Transitional Authority in Cambodia (UNTAC). Perhaps encouraged by China's backing, Hun Sen ousted Rannaridh in a *coup de force* in 1997. In June 2016, roughly two decades after Hun Sen's state visit and around

US$3 billion in Chinese loans and grants later (Veasna 2016), warm ties were once again reaffirmed. Reportedly, as it had done in 2012, Cambodia demanded that ASEAN tone down its statement on China's disputed claim over the South China Sea, and a few days later China pledged another US$600 million in loans and grants (Hutt 2016a).

Political interdependencies have emerged alongside the influx of Chinese investments, businesses and economic migrants since the 1990s. Cambodia's infrastructure development, including the construction of bridges, roads and hydropower dams, is largely undertaken by Chinese state-owned companies and financed by Chinese banks (Sullivan 2011). The majority of Cambodia's garment factories, which account for over three quarters of total exports, are owned and managed by Chinese from 'Greater China' (i.e., mainland China, Hong Kong, Taiwan and Macau) (Ear 2016). China is the biggest investor in Cambodia, adding nearly US$5.3 billion between 2013 and 2017 (Hin 2019), and Chinese firms currently hold over forty Economic Land Concessions (ELCs) allocated for tourism development or the cultivation of crops such as rubber, sugar and cassava (LICADHO 2019). Officials hope that annual bilateral trade between the two countries will reach US$10 billion in 2023 (Prak 2019). China's influence over economic and political affairs in Cambodia is undisputed, which leads Percival to argue that "[i]f any modern relationship between China and a Southeast Asian country smacks of the old 'tributary system,' it is the one between Beijing and Phnom Penh" (2007, p. 41).

Extant studies that examine China's recent re-engagement with Cambodia consider the perspective of either the political elite or of Cambodia's poor. Political scientists and observers are particularly interested in what the CPP gains from China's patronage in terms of power consolidation and financial rewards, and, vice versa, what is behind Beijing's rhetoric of unconditional aid and 'Principles of Peaceful Coexistence', suggesting that China strives for a bigger say in ASEAN via Cambodia, access to Cambodian oil and gas reserves, or even a naval base at the Sihanoukville port (see, for example, Burgos and Ear 2010; Chanda 2002; Ciorciari 2015; Dahles 2013; Sullivan 2011). In addition, a number of sector-specific studies, including garments (Arnold and Toh 2010), hydropower (Heng 2015), and logging (Milne 2015), have revealed the ways in which Chinese investments and demand for natural resources affect Cambodia's rural and urban poor. These studies, as well as a steady stream of reports by international watchdog Global Witness (2007 and 2015), expose opaque alliances between Cambodian and Chinese elites, and highlight resultant human rights abuses and environmental degradation.

In considering ways in which China's newfound assertiveness affects Cambodian society, the perspective of the domestic private sector is largely overlooked (for an exception, see Nyíri 2012). Yet, this perspective is intriguing for at least two reasons. First, the domestic private sector, especially in the capital Phnom Penh, reveals an internal division between the politically connected and the bereft. An exclusive group of tycoons enjoys privileges and protection from top CPP officials and own the country's large and diversified business groups, while the majority of the private sector comprises small and medium-sized enterprises (SMEs) that cope without political backing (Verver and Dahles 2015). Second, most entrepreneurs in Phnom Penh, tycoons and SME owners are children or grandchildren of Chinese migrants who came to Cambodia especially during the French colonial period (1863–1953). Overlaying the two is the question of how different local entrepreneurs are differently embedded 'in between' Chinese ethnicity and Cambodia's political economy, and how this position of "mixed embeddedness" (Kloosterman and Rath 2001) enables or constrains them to link up with and benefit from 'new' Chinese investments and commerce in Cambodia.

In this analysis, I explore the relationship between the local business community in Phnom Penh, which is historically dominated by 'old' Chinese immigrants and their descendants, and 'new' Chinese migration, business and investments. I do so from the perspective of the 'old' Chinese, drawing on ethnographic fieldwork conducted in Phnom Penh between October 2010 and December 2011, and more recent secondary sources and updates on the topic. During this period, I interviewed entrepreneurs, their family members, employees and business partners; I talked to people working for the government, media, NGOs, research institutes and other civil society representatives knowledgeable on Phnom Penh's private sector dynamics or Cambodian society more broadly; and I visited individual businesses and business-related events (Verver 2015).

The next section provides a history of the business activities and societal position of 'old' Chinese migrants in Cambodia, while the ensuing empirical sections examine, for Phnom Penh's SMEs and big business groups respectively, how 'new' Chinese migration and capital have affected the business endeavours of the 'old' Chinese. The last section discusses the implications for Phnom Penh's ethnic Chinese and Cambodian society more broadly.

Context: The 'Old' Chinese in Cambodian Society

Most Chinese migrated to Cambodia during the French colonial period (1863–1953), although in the pre-colonial era, a symbiosis had already emerged between the mainly agrarian Khmer and the trade- and commerce-oriented Chinese (Kuhn 2008). This "plural society" (Willmott 1967, p. 9) was further perpetuated by the French colonial administration, who actively promoted occupational and spatial separation of the Khmer, Chinese and Vietnamese residing in Phnom Penh. The French organized the Chinese through *congrégations* that represented the five dialect groups in Phnom Penh—Teochew, Cantonese, Hakka, Hokkien and Hainanese—and that formed the basis for Chinese communal, economic and political life (see Edwards 2007; Willmott 1967).

The ethnic Chinese retained their dominance over the Cambodian economy during the post-independence rule of King Sihanouk (1953–70). In Phnom Penh lived some 135,000 Chinese in the early 1960s, or one third of the population (Willmott 1967). The majority of Chinese families were not especially wealthy. They owned small boutiques or worked as shoemakers, carpenters, dentists, cinema owners, barbers or bakers, and relied heavily on informal familial and ethnic ties for labour and capital. Chinese small business owners carved out economic niches largely along dialect lines. Hainanese ran restaurants and hotels, Hokkien controlled hardware, Hakka owned bakeries, and Cantonese concentrated on carpentry and mechanics, while Teochew were found in most other economic niches (Willmott 1970). In the countryside, Chinese grew cash crops such as vegetables and pepper, and Chinese merchants bought surplus rice, sold commodities and lent money to Khmer peasants (Willmott 1981).

A smaller group of wealthy Chinese business magnates was either active in trade or engaged in revenue farming. The latter was exceptionally profitable. Activities like gambling, opium farming, prawning and fisheries were subcontracted by the royal family to business people at an annual fee (Osborne 2004). These contracts almost entirely went into the hands of Chinese entrepreneurs, who had strong connections to the Khmer throne, access to extensive regional kinship networks to round up capital and credit, and a local network of sub-farmers and agents—again mostly Chinese—to manage the revenue farming operations (Cooke 2011; Muller 2006). Cantonese traders in Phnom Penh, who were linked to fellow Cantonese in the Vietnamese twin-city of Saigon-Cholon, controlled the rice, pepper and salt trade (Willmott 2012). The Teochew, however, gradually erected a network of wholesalers and retailers that spanned Cambodia's cities and villages. The Teochew outnumbered the earlier Hokkien and Cantonese settlers, and came to dominate the Cambodian economy in the post-colonial period (Willmott 1967).

The civil war and the subsequent Khmer Rouge regime of the 1970s left Cambodia in a state of destruction. After the Khmer Rouge overtook Phnom Penh—which had swollen to approximately two million people during the civil war—on 17 April 1975, they emptied the city overnight and forced people into rural labour camps. In less than four years, an estimated 1.5 to 2 million Cambodians died from starvation, exhaustion, diseases and execution (Heuveline 1998). The ethnic Chinese were hit particularly hard as they were persecuted for being urban dwellers, capitalists or Chinese, labels which were often conflated (Edwards 2012). Many ethnic Chinese fled Cambodia through Thai border camps and found final refuge in France, Australia or North America (Wijers 2011), while those who stayed behind were forced to "become Khmer" in terms of housing, dress, language and food (Edwards 2009). When the Vietnamese army invaded Cambodia late in 1978, Kiernan (1986) estimated, half of Cambodia's ethnic Chinese population had died.

The Vietnamese restored basic state institutions and assured relative political stability from 1979 to 1989. Vietnamese antagonism towards China as well as ethnic Chinese capitalist activity led to repression and discrimination, and Chinese culture and language were forced underground (Gottesman 2003). Businesses were initially repressed, but because state enterprises failed and as Hun Sen—a pragmatist more than a devoted communist—became prime minister in 1985, Chinese small-scale businesses were increasingly tolerated (ibid.). Markets were unregulated, and the petty trade that emerged at the Thai border between Teochew from Phnom Penh and Bangkok effectively "amounted to state-sanctioned smuggling" (Slocomb 2003, p. 113). In the final analysis, the Vietnamese left Cambodia a small but functioning economy.

The 1990s onwards have seen the steady ascent of Hun Sen's CPP, which grew out of the Vietnamese-backed regime. Under Hun Sen, the economy was liberalized, state enterprises privatized, and ethnic and religious freedom of expression constitutionally assured. At the same time, by placing loyal individuals in key state, military and business positions, and by distributing favours to reinforce this loyalty, the upper echelon of the CPP erected an all-pervasive patronage-based political economy (Hughes and Un 2011; Springer 2010; Verver and Dahles 2015). Hun Sen has been manoeuvring the international stage in a similarly pragmatist fashion. Benefitting from foreign investments and donor money from Asia and the West, he has managed to curb Western demands for democratization, transparency and 'good governance', while exploiting increasing economic opportunities and 'unconditional' aid extended from China.

Hun Sen's rise has paralleled the revitalization of Chinese enterprise and cultural life. Since the 1990s, the Teochew trading networks of the 1980s expanded, ethnic Chinese from around Asia came in to trade or invest, and Phnom Penh's ethnic Chinese ventured into a wide range of economic niches. Chinese New Year was celebrated again for the first time in 1991, and the famous Duanhua School in Phnom Penh re-opened its doors in 1992 (Willmott 1998). At the same time, almost all ethnic Chinese in contemporary Phnom Penh speak Khmer, and most self-identify as Khmer more than Chinese. Arguably, Chinese business and culture "has become disembedded from a definable Chinese community and, over the last two to three decades, reembedded in Phnom Penh's socio-economic sphere, which is largely made up of Cambodian Chinese entrepreneurs" (Verver 2012, p. 319).

Hun Sen's rise also witnessed a re-emergent divide between small and big business. Cambodia was deprived of human capital after the Khmer Rouge, and material and financial resources have been similarly scarce. Corruption permeates society, and so SME owners shun state institutions in general and rent-seeking officials in particular. The modal firm is small, family owned and operated, financially self-reliant and technologically ill-equipped (Slocomb 2010). At the same time, a small group of tycoons has been co-opted by Hun Sen and other CPP top officials, and they run large and diversified business groups active in the most lucrative economic niches. These tycoons carry the title of *oknha*, which was once bestowed upon prominent officials surrounding the king but is now awarded to business people who make financial contributions in excess of US$100,000 to national development projects. The *oknha* receive benefits in business—including import monopolies, public contracts and land concessions—in return for loyalty and financial contributions to individual officials and the CPP party as a whole (Verver and Dahles 2015).

Migration from China to Cambodia largely ceased after decolonization in 1953, and only resumed towards the end of the twentieth century. Aside from tourists, 'new' Chinese migration since the 1990s includes petty traders and service entrepreneurs, private investors, garment factory managers, teachers, journalists and sub-contractors to infrastructural projects financed by the Chinese state (Nyíri 2014). The differences between the 'old' and the 'new' Chinese are vast. The 'old' Chinese trace their roots to the coastal provinces of South China, while the 'new' Chinese are largely from the Shanghai region, Hong Kong and Taiwan. The 'old' Chinese originally spoke one of the southern Chinese dialects (mainly Teochew), while Mandarin is the mother tongue of most 'new' Chinese. Most fundamentally, the 'new' Chinese have not been subjected to the turbulent history of Cambodian society, which fundamentally changed the 'old' Chinese community. These differences are also reflected in Cambodian popular lexicon. The 'new' Chinese are labelled *cendaekook*, which translates into 'dry land Chinese' but broadly refers to recent migrants and temporary residents from Greater China, whereas the 'old' Chinese are referred to as *kmae-cen* (Khmer–Chinese), *coul kmae* (literally 'entered the Khmers') and *kmae yeung* ('we Khmer', indicating attachment to the nation) (see also Edwards 2009). In the following sections, I use the broad label of 'Cambodian Chinese' to refer to the 'old' Chinese.

Findings: 'Old' and 'New' Chinese Business in Phnom Penh

Looking at SMEs and the *oknha* business groups, respectively, the ensuing sections explore linkages, collaboration and competition between Phnom Penh's Cambodian Chinese entrepreneurs and 'new' Chinese traders and investors.

Small- and Medium-Sized Enterprises

For SMEs in Phnom Penh, 'new' Chinese engagement with the Cambodian economy has been instrumental in a number of ways. To begin with, the 'new' Chinese migrants represent an important clientele for service providers and retailers in Phnom Penh. Many 'new' Chinese in Cambodia work as managers, technical staff and foremen in garment factories, and many others work for Chinese (state-owned) companies that build roads, bridges or hydropower dams in the Cambodian provinces. These professionals come to Phnom Penh on weekends, and settle in areas such as around Preah Monivong Boulevard, a main boulevard in Phnom Penh's city centre. The area houses Chinese restaurants that, according to a Chinese community insider, are owned and visited by 'new' Chinese, but shunned by most Cambodian Chinese, who are used to a different cuisine and hardly mingle with the 'new' Chinese migrants. Yet, Cambodian Chinese have opened up stores and hotels in the area that cater to the 'new' Chinese. As a hotel manager, who speaks Mandarin because he spent his youth in Beijing where his father worked for the Cambodian embassy, explains: "Mandarin is becoming popular because there is so much investment coming in from China, a lot. Chinese come to invest in garment, real-estate, import-export, shipping. That's why we should learn the Chinese language. That's why I joined here, why they hired me in sales and marketing."

Another interviewee, Kimsun,[1] owns a computer shop in the Preah Monivong Boulevard area and has benefited from 'new' Chinese who come to buy or have computers repaired in his shop. Growing up in the anti-Chinese climate of the 1980s, Kimsun never learned Mandarin. He elaborates:

> In the beginning, I didn't speak Chinese at all, but some years ago a lot of Chinese customers started coming here. Every weekend my shop is full of Chinese people. They work for the garment factories and come to this area to buy food or computers. They stay in the hotels and apartments here, upstairs [from his shop] also. Now I can speak a little Mandarin, not much, and one of my guys [his staff] also. I did not go to Chinese school. This is my school.

Kimsun displays his company's name in Khmer, English and Chinese on his storefront, and he has a Chinese shrine in the corner of his shop to ensure good luck in business. Some interviewees argue that such Chinese paraphernalia, as well as Chinese appearance and language-use, attract customers. Popular understanding in Phnom Penh, as expressed here by a younger generation of Cambodian Chinese, is that "Chinese work hard and sell goods for a small profit margin. That's why people want to buy at Chinese shops". Kimsun, however, downplays the relevance of his Chinese background. It is customary to display the company name in Chinese next to Khmer and English, he argues, and concerning the Chinese shrine:

> You see it in every shop, even if the owner is 100 per cent Khmer, and most business people in Phnom Penh are *kmae-cen* anyway. It's decoration that we copy from each other. Actually, I don't know the meaning of the little shrine. I never pray in the morning; I cannot fix a computer by praying.

Recreated economic links between Cambodia and China have not only generated a clientele of 'new' Chinese customers for local service providers and retailers, but also allow Cambodian Chinese entrepreneurs to establish new trading connections with China, especially in import. Kimsun, for example, imports his computers from Singapore and Hong Kong. In line with the above, Kimsun argues that shared Chinese background is of minor importance in these trading partnerships:

> They are traders who secure themselves. They don't feel like I am Chinese and then they trust me, they think whether I am a real businessman or not [*sic*]. My suppliers in Singapore and Hong Kong, they sometimes send me goods first [before payment]. They trust me, not because I am Chinese, but because I import from them for a long time already.

In contrast to Kimsun, many other entrepreneurs who have experience importing from Chinese-speaking countries do highlight the significance of 'being Chinese', and especially of speaking Chinese. One interviewee, for example, imports children's toys from China, and whenever he goes there he brings along his wife, who studied Mandarin and speaks it fluently. When she bargains in Mandarin, he ascertains, the price for a shipment of toys is much lower than for those who "just press the calculator" to negotiate the price.

While retailers and wholesalers import products such as computers and toys from China, production firms in Phnom Penh depend on Chinese raw materials and packaging material (the latter of which, due to high electricity costs, is hardly produced in Cambodia itself). Lina and Dara, a brother and sister who own and manage a rice cracker factory and a jelly sweets factory together with their elder brother, import packaging material, machinery and raw materials from China. While rice and corn, the main ingredients for the rice crackers, are grown domestically, Dara estimates that they import ninety per cent of the raw materials for the jelly sweets from China. "I would like to buy more here so we can make the Cambodian economy stronger, but it's really hard to find." Lina and Dara are from a Teochew background and speak both Teochew and Mandarin. They learned both languages secretly at home in the 1980s; Teochew from their parents and Mandarin from a private teacher. In the 1990s, Dara, the youngest among the siblings, studied Mandarin in China for one and a half years while living with relatives there. His parents wanted him to, not because of business opportunities per se, but because "my grandparents are Chinese people so they want the next generation to speak Chinese. In my generation there are a lot of Cambodians who studied in China."

Lina and Dara go to China regularly to do business and visit family members, who produce cutlery for the US and European markets. Their family members have introduced them to entrepreneurs in China over the years, which provided them a strong partnership with a company that makes their machines as well as provides strong connections to suppliers of raw materials. "All around the world", Lina argues, "Chinese are successful business people. They work hard and keep their mind on the business. In China, I got to know many of them and we get on well with each other." Dara adds:

> Chinese think that if you have the same background you can help each other. Every time we go to China for business, we visit the family also. If we don't visit for a long time, we will lose them, but we are still close.... Chinese are smart to keep good relationships; they go out and know more people for doing business and sharing experience.

To a large extent, whether SMEs in Phnom Penh are able to develop trading partnerships with China depends on existing connections in China, and particularly family connections. This is the case for the import of machinery and raw materials as much as consumer goods. The bulk of consumer goods from China enter the Cambodian market via 'new' Chinese traders, but by employing family connections, Cambodian Chinese families also import Chinese goods. Three brothers, for example, have teamed up with their niece in Hong Kong, who is a representative for a Chinese food company, to import food products such as bottled sauce. She sends samples of products to them, and if the brothers think there is a market for the products in Cambodia, she sends larger shipments. One of the brothers explains:

> I think it is important for Cambodian businesses to look at Chinese products. The whole world uses Chinese products and if we look at the price and their resources, we cannot compete so we have to import. It's easy to trust our family and she knows about the products, so she can arrange it for us.

While it is not uncommon for Cambodian Chinese to import from China, the experience of the typical entrepreneur is better represented in the following quote, by an interviewee who owns two small guesthouses and imports detergents that he resells to local hotels and catering firms:

> More and more Chinese from the mainland are doing business here. They have family here, associations, the embassy, so there is communication. It is beneficial for those [local entrepreneurs] who have relationships and can do business with them, but not for us. We don't have any connection to China, and we import from Singapore, Malaysia and Thailand, not China. We are the young generation of Chinese who settled in Cambodia, and we think of ourselves as Khmer, not Chinese. The only thing is that we can still speak the language.

Clearly, then, as a journalist observes, due to the disruptive Khmer Rouge regime and its aftermath, "most connections that were once there haven't been passed on from one generation to the next".

While some local entrepreneurs benefit from 'new' Chinese customers and import connections, and while for many others the 'rise of China' has largely gone unnoticed, yet others face new competition from the 'new' Chinese. Take the case of Mr Lok, who imports and sells the two kinds of textile—silk and embroidery—needed to make traditional Cambodian wedding dresses. The silk is produced in Cambodian provinces, mostly by women who weave silk as a side activity to farming, whereas the embroidery textile is imported from around Asia and from Europe. Mr Lok is a prominent wholesaler for the two kinds of textiles. Together with his wife and two children, he runs a business with two locations near Phnom Penh's two largest indoor markets, *Psar Olympic* and *Psar Orrusey*. The family has a vast stock of textiles, which they sell to market vendors that run small booths in the two markets. Mr Lok is in his late fifties and of full Teochew descent, but he never learned Teochew or Mandarin. He does speak Thai, however, which he picked up in the early 1980s when, like so many entrepreneurs of his generation, he was active in petty trade along the porous Thai-Cambodian border. After importing a variety of cheap goods for a few years, which his wife sold in Phnom Penh, Mr Lok befriended a Thai Teochew supplier, who offered to supply him the more expensive embroidery textile on credit.

The family built their business from there, which required two things. First, they established themselves within the domestic silk trade, which is characterized by reciprocal relationships within a pyramid structure of weavers, middlemen, wholesalers and market vendors (Dahles and Horst 2012). Second, to assure a diversified supply of embroidery textiles, which is vital as the quality and price of embroidery textiles differ greatly between producing countries, they forged trading partnerships abroad, beyond their existing connections with the Thai. On the invitation of a distant family member who had fled the Khmer Rouge to France, Mr Lok started visiting French and Italian factories to purchase up-market textiles. Since the 2000s, he also imports cheaper embroidery textiles from China, and has been to exhibitions in China a number of times. Due to language barriers, however, Mr Lok had a hard time bargaining and settling transactions with potential Chinese suppliers. He brought along his son-in-law, who speaks English, when visiting exhibitions or factories abroad, but in China he could not be of much assistance as people expected them to speak Mandarin.

Since the 2000s, middlemen from China have been coming to Cambodia to sell embroidery textiles themselves. On the one hand, this is a blessing as Mr Lok can now stay in Phnom Penh and buy directly from the middlemen. His daughter Theary explains: "There are many factories in China. They [the Chinese middlemen] come to us with samples so we can see and order with them. We can order what we need, and if we want to change the pattern or colour, we inform them." On the other hand, the 'new' Chinese also mean new competition. After all, individual market vendors can now buy directly from the middlemen from China rather than having to go through Mr Lok. "Cambodia is now a free market. The Chinese can also come to our country and bring in their products." The family, however, is not anxious about their competitors. The Chinese only have cheap embroidery on offer while their assortment is very diverse as they import from a range of countries. More importantly, Mr Lok has co-opted a lot of market vendors by means of an informal yet effective arrangement; he rents out market booths, which he bought over the years, or provides credit to individual market vendors, compelling these vendors to purchase the textiles from him.

In two respects, the story of Mr Lok and his family is illustrative of Cambodian Chinese entrepreneurs active in Phnom Penh's SME sector. First, a localized Teochew identity is considered more important than a supposed pan-Chinese regional identity in doing business (Verver and Koning, 2018). Mr Lok acknowledges that his Teochew background has been crucial in his friendship with the Thai Teochew in the 1980s, but he downplays his Chinese background: "I think my business has grown not because I have Chinese blood, but because of my luck, smartness and hard work." Daughter Theary adds: "In my family we cannot speak Chinese anymore. Our kinship seems to be lost, so we speak Khmer." At the same time, Theary does take pride in her family's Chinese roots: "Chinese in Cambodia never become beggars, they are hardworking. Chinese are patient with their business even though they face many problems, and they run small businesses even if they make little profit." While talking to Theary in her market store, her mother was attending to the conversation, and she interjected by saying that "these days, the Chinese are much more appreciated than before. Cambodians all want to marry a Chinese because then they marry into a business family." Accounts like these illustrate that 'Chineseness' takes on a specific meaning within the Cambodian context, and in a manner that does not necessarily imply a pan-Chinese ethnic affinity being extended to 'new' Chinese migrants from Northeast Asia.

Second, the story of Mr Lok and his family indicates that, despite the inflow of 'new' Chinese migrants and investments, the Cambodian Chinese have reclaimed their dominance over Phnom Penh's SME sector. A younger-generation entrepreneur named Kosal, who manages a mattress production, retail and wholesale business owned by his parents, for example, said: "so far there are only a few companies that produce mattresses, all Cambodians, but we'll wait and see. There were a couple of companies that came in from China, but it didn't work out for them. In the end they quit and we bought their machines." As is the case for Mr Lok, Kosal's parents have developed their international network through connections with family members and Southeast Asian Chinese more than 'new' Chinese from Northeast Asia. Kosal has a granduncle in South China who supplies the raw materials. "All my dad does is be on the phone with my granduncle in China. And once a year we visit him and he takes us to exhibitions to look for new material." While Kosal's granduncle supplies the raw materials, they buy machines and chemicals from a Singaporean businessman, who visited Phnom Penh in 1997 looking for investment opportunities and trading partnerships. Domestically, Kosal's family has secured their market position by building up a steady clientele of local buyers. These include individual customers who come to their store, but the bulk of the mattresses are either sold to middlemen who resell in the provinces or to hotel and condominium developers in Cambodia's urban areas. Like Kosal's family, both the middlemen and developers are mostly Cambodian Teochew.

It seems that for many local Cambodian Chinese entrepreneurs, the 'new' Chinese active in trade, service or production in Phnom Penh since the 1990s do not pose a substantive threat. When the Vietnamese left Cambodia in 1989, the Cambodian Chinese were slowly recovering, while hampered by resource scarcity, a lack of capital and political insecurity. They had set up home-based businesses that required little investment, including grocery stores, bakeries, cafés and mechanics' workshops, or produced rice wine and sausage rolls, while trade was largely restricted to the Thai–Cambodian border area. Petty traders from China were quick to exploit the demand for cheap, Chinese-made consumer goods and, to a lesser extent, tried their luck in the service and production sectors. It was only gradually that Cambodian Chinese accumulated the material, financial and social capital to embark on more capital-intensive and durable business ventures. As the cases of the textile and mattress businesses indicate, the Cambodian Teochew developed their own connections to Chinese suppliers—often through family links—and forged a tight-knit local network of traders and both urban and rural shopkeepers that now controls a wide range of sectors. As Pál Nyíri (2014) points out, many 'new' Chinese traders and service entrepreneurs have returned to China since the 2000s, both because living standards in China increased and because the Cambodian Chinese reasserted their dominance over the Cambodian economy.

At the same time, more recent evidence (albeit largely anecdotal) suggests that local entrepreneurs are increasingly experiencing competition from the 'new' Chinese (Cheng 2018). This is especially so in the coastal town of Sihanoukville, which is turning into a Chinese enclave comprising Chinese tourists and Chinese-owned tourism businesses such as casinos, restaurants and shops (Po and Heng 2019; Sim 2019). Yet, 'new' Chinese influences are also felt in Phnom Penh. In what seemed an attempt to protect local SMEs against the 'new' Chinese, in August 2019 the government signed a decree stating that ten categories of jobs (including hairdresser, tuk-tuk driver and mechanic) were off limits for foreigners. Remarkably, the ban was lifted two months later (Soth 2019). In any case, there certainly is a substantial number of 'new' Chinese active in Phnom Penh's SME sector. As a journalist for a local Chinese newspaper notes:

> The newcomers are not just in garments, this is a misunderstanding. Many of them import all kinds of things from the mainland, and once they have set something up, they invite more people or bring their families from the mainland. Some also marry Cambodians and speak Khmer already. Although Cambodia is poor, some of them still prefer Phnom Penh because it's so easy to do business. There are few restrictions here, they can start right away, and they have connections in China.

Oknha Business Groups

The most prominent among Phnom Penh's *oknha* also benefit most from 'new' Chinese investments. For example, Oknha Lao Meng Khin, a CPP senator, and his wife Choeung Sopheap, reportedly a close friend of Hun Sen's wife Bun Rany, have a reputation of bringing in Chinese investment (Bahree 2014). Their business portfolio includes a Special Economic Zone (SEZ), the highly controversial Boeung Kak Lake development project in Phnom Penh, which was implicated in the eviction of thousands living along the lake, as well as mining activities, power plants and ELCs. In all of these they collaborate with Chinese investors. Lao Meng Khin and Choeung Sopheap—dubbed the 'power couple' in a 2007 WikiLeaks cable from the US embassy in Phnom Penh—speak Mandarin and several Chinese dialects (WikiLeaks, 9 August 2007).

Another prominent *oknha*, Ly Yong Phat, has similarly strong connections with the regional Chinese. He is especially active in his home province of Koh Kong—Ly Yong Phat is locally known as the 'king of Koh Kong'—in western Cambodia, where he owns hotels, casinos, a SEZ, vital infrastructure including a 1.9-kilometre bridge that links Koh Kong and Thailand, facilities for water and electricity supply, and a disputed sand-dredging business. His sugar plantation in Koh Kong, which he co-owned with a Taiwanese company before selling his shares to a befriended Thai Chinese sugar mogul in 2010, is notorious for human rights abuses and land grabs taking place in and outside the concessionary land (Pellechi 2012). A CPP senator and special economic advisor to Hun Sen, he "boasts to visitors that he was personally appointed to develop his home province" (WikiLeaks, 9 August 2007). As such, Ly Yong Phat is also linked to plans, which have yet to materialize, by Chinese firms to develop a 400-kilometre railway linking iron ore mining operations in western Cambodia to a new port in Koh Kong (Hunt 2013). He was also granted the contract to build a massive new sports and entertainment complex on the Chroy Changvar peninsula outside Phnom Penh, meant to host the 2023 Southeast Asian Games and financed by the Chinese government. Ly Yong Phat presumably holds dual Cambodian and Thai citizenship, and he speaks Khmer, Thai and Chinese dialects. He seems to cherish his Chinese roots. According to a company brochure, he became president of Cambodia's Chinese Hainanese Association in 1992, and senior advisor of the Ly Chinese Family Association in 2005 (L.Y.P. Group n.d.). He even has plans to build a Chinatown as part of a satellite city he is currently developing outside Phnom Penh (Khy 2013), perhaps in an attempt to revive the capital's *Quartier Chinois* of the colonial period.

Tycoons like Lao Meng Khin and Ly Yong Phat keenly manoeuvre their Cambodian and Chinese identities. On the one hand, they rely on their ties to Hun Sen and top CPP and military officials for preferential treatment and to secure their business ventures. On the other hand, they employ their Chinese background, language abilities and established connections in China, Taiwan and Hong Kong to attract investments. The *oknha* thus bridge regional ethnic Chinese business networks and Phnom Penh's highly politicized business sphere, while pocketing large sums of money in the process (no small part of which, of course, flows back to their political patrons).

Although, according to the son of an *oknha*, 'new' Chinese investors "definitely give priority to the local ethnic Chinese", the role of shared Chinese background must not be overstated. Many prominent *oknha*, most of whom grew up in the 1970s and 80s and are now in their sixties, hardly speak Chinese, have no established network in China, Taiwan or Hong Kong, and self-identify as Khmer. One *oknha* interviewee, for example, said that, although Cambodians tend to assign officialdom to Khmer and business to Chinese, "actually it is the same. In government people also have Chinese blood, in business people also have Khmer blood.... I don't know much about my Chinese background. I'm Cambodian, not Chinese anymore. I feel *kmae*, not *cen*." Partly, such statements reflect the actual blurring of ethnic boundaries in Phnom Penh. Partly, perhaps, the fact that the *oknha* owe their wealth to privileges and protection provided by 'Khmer' political patrons urges the *oknha* to foreground their Khmer identity and downplay Chinese identity. As a Phnom Penh–based historian argues, "they have no stake in displaying Chineseness, on the contrary. And they grew up in a time when Chinese were discriminated."

Irrespective of Chinese language abilities and identification, the *oknha* manage to attract Chinese investments and joint-ventures with Chinese companies. In some cases, it is all too evident that business deals between Cambodian Chinese *oknha* and 'new' Chinese investors spring from CPP patronage more than shared ethnic background. A deal between Pheapimex—owned by the earlier-mentioned Lao Meng Khin and Choeung Sopheap—and the Chinese firm Jiangsu Taihu International, who joint-ventured to develop a SEZ, was purportedly sealed on one of Hun Sen's visits to China (Global Witness 2007, p. 77). Indeed, a number of *oknha* who are also CPP senators, including Lao Meng Khin, have joined Hun Sen on trips to China. Another example is a US$8 million loan to build a palm oil processing plant, which was obtained by Oknha Mong Reththy, who lived in the same Buddhist pagoda as Hun Sen in their teenage years and who now owns a wide range of agri-businesses. The US$8 million was borrowed by the Cambodian government from a state-owned Chinese bank, and in turn lent to Mong Reththy, who argued this was "to save the company paperwork" (Kimsong 2001). A last noteworthy example is Oknha Try Pheap, who owns a logging syndicate that exports timber to Hong Kong, catering to Chinese demands for luxury *Hongmu* furniture. In return for exclusive logging rights and export permits, and even the rights to all 'illegally' logged timber confiscated by the Forestry Administration, Try Pheap allegedly pays a US$1 million monthly 'tax' to Hun Sen's family (Milne 2015). Unsurprisingly, instances like these only reinforce notions in Phnom Penh that the *oknha* are mere proxies of Hun Sen. Moreover, these instances suggest that connections to the CPP are more vital than 'new' Chinese connections for the *oknha*, and that, in fact, the CPP orchestrates the link between *oknha* and 'new' Chinese investors.

Well-aware of the importance of local political embeddedness (O'Neill 2014), 'new' Chinese investors who lack established connections often turn to the various chambers of commerce. These include the Chinese Chamber of Commerce in Cambodia (which is closely tied to the Chinese Embassy), the China, Hong Kong and Macau Expatriate & Business Association of Cambodia (the name of which, due to Cambodia's official support for the One-China Policy, conceals the de facto inclusion of Taiwanese in the association), and the Cambodian Chamber of Commerce (which is also referred to as the '*oknha* club' in Phnom Penh). A representative of the latter explains that many investors do not approach the chamber but pick 'the wrong partners' for collaboration: "Especially the Chinese, they have connections, but the wrong ones. They know some three- or four-star generals and they think they can invest in whatever they want. They invest a lot but it's all wasted on drinks and karaoke bars, and then they go back home with nothing." Members of the chamber, contrarily, are "good partners for investors" as they are "straightforward" and "have proven themselves", according to the representative. He holds that the chamber redirects foreign investors to local *oknha* "in a fair manner", depending on what the investor is looking for and "without benefitting anyone". Other interviewees disagree, including a businesswoman whose father is an *oknha* and used to be a member of the chamber: "He stopped because he didn't like it; they're not really helpful actually. Mostly they [the board, which is made up of the most prominent *oknha*] share whatever investment comes in. Often the president takes it all."

Successful collaborations between *oknha* tycoons and regional investors, whether established via the CPP, the chambers of commerce, or other connections, reveal a basic arrangement. The foreign partner brings in investment, technical expertise and skilled labour, while the *oknha* provides the land—which foreigners are not allowed to own in Cambodia—and political *khnorng* ('backing'). An elite insider adds:

> The Chinese want to joint-venture with us because we know how to process documents, deal with tax, find the location. It should be a joint-venture, otherwise it's not a success for them. They look for the right person, and normally they look for someone who speaks Chinese.

It is through this arrangement that plantations and production facilities have been set up, and—as an employee of a logistics company ascertained—that cargo is unloaded at the Sihanoukville and Phnom Penh ports while customs turn a blind eye. It is also this arrangement that has fuelled much of Cambodia's real-estate boom over the last decade. Condominium complexes, office towers and satellite city megaprojects have mushroomed in and around Phnom Penh (see, for example, Percival 2012) despite warnings of a real-estate bubble caused by the discrepancy between the construction frenzy and the limited growth of the private sector and middle class. 'New' Chinese prove especially eager to invest in Cambodian real-estate, allegedly more so as a result of Xi Jinping's corruption crackdown in China coupled with Cambodia's reputation as a safe-haven for money laundering (Hutt 2016a).

The number of *oknha* has mushroomed, from an estimated 20 in 2004 to more than 700 in 2014 (Odom and Henderson 2014). Less prominent *oknha*, who do not rely on such strong political backing as the *oknha* mentioned above, often manage to link up with 'new' Chinese investors because of their expertise in particular sectors. The family of Vuthy, which is "one of the biggest families" in Cambodia, is among them. When Cambodia opened up in the 1990s, the family started focusing on the construction sector. They made sure to set up complementary businesses that cater to the construction of warehouses and factory buildings. In Vuthy's words:

> Most of them are in construction; trading materials and construction itself. One of my uncles is in steel, my father is in construction, another aunt and uncle are the importer and sole distributor for [a renowned brand of] paint. So our parents do steel, coating, roofing, construction, different things.

Vuthy and his cousins are currently being prepared to take over their parents' businesses, while they have also set up novel businesses themselves using their parents' capital.

Throughout the 1990s, the family mainly acquired construction contracts from local, mostly Cambodian Teochew, business people. The family built warehouses and factories for local tycoons who, for example, own sugar or rubber plantations or are active in logging or petrol and gas. New business opportunities arose when, around the turn of the century, Northeast Asian garment manufacturers came to Cambodia to exploit the low duties imposed by the United States and European Union on imports from Cambodia. Cambodia, in the words of a garment sector representative, effectively became "one big processing zone" for manufacturers. Drawing on their established expertise and network, Vuthy's family acquired contracts from foreign manufacturers—mostly from Greater China—who came looking for reliable local construction firms. They built many of the garment factories located at the outskirts of Phnom Penh and along the highway to the Sihanoukville port. Because the 'new' Chinese often have factories built within SEZs or on concessionary land owned by Cambodian tycoons or CPP officials, acquiring construction contracts also required them to reinforce their position within Phnom Penh's business-state elite. One of Vuthy's uncles carries the title of *oknha*, indicating that he is indeed part of this elite. On the supply side, 'new' Chinese involvement has similarly led them to embark on new projects. The family previously imported steel from China and Vietnam, but more recently started importing from Taiwan, and joint-ventured with a Taiwanese company to set up a facility in Cambodia specializing in steel structures, as such assuring the quality of raw materials and the transfer of technology in fabrication and design.

Vuthy's family nurtures its Chinese background because Chinese identity and language facilitate business arrangements locally and regionally. Vuthy considers his Chinese background "pretty much a push for starting up your own business". Before they attended renowned universities abroad to study engineering, architecture and business management, Vuthy and his cousins went to the Duanhua Chinese school in Phnom Penh.

> At home all our parents spoke Khmer or Teochiu with us, but I have a broken Teochiu now, very basic. Some of our parents speak Mandarin also, but not so well because during the Vietnamese [period] they didn't have a chance to speak it.... Most Chinese parents in Cambodia would send their children to Chinese school to learn Mandarin. At school they never teach Teochiu in Cambodia, always Mandarin. It's Chinese in the morning and general [Cambodian curricular] education in the afternoon.

The school belongs to the Teochew dialect association, and the school compound also houses a Teochew temple. Every year during Chinese New Year, Vuthy's father and uncles invite Duanhua's dancing squad, which performs lion and sword dances. "We invite them to bless the business. It's pretty expensive, but all the money goes to the association."

The case of Vuthy's family illustrates that the *oknha* benefit greatly from 'new' Chinese investments and industry in Cambodia, especially if they cater to the garment and real-estate sectors where much of this investment is concentrated. At the same time, families who do not speak Mandarin face more barriers (as was also observed for SMEs in the previous section). In the family of Phally, who is also in construction and whose father carries the *oknha* title, they do not speak Mandarin. The family fled to Canada before the Khmer Rouge takeover of 1975, and growing up in Montréal, Phally and her siblings learned Khmer, French and English, but not Mandarin. Since her father came back to Cambodia in 1990 to establish a construction company, they have largely relied on public contracts for the construction of roads, bridges, drainage systems, and railroads, which are issued by Cambodian ministries or municipalities, but financed and overseen by the Asia Development Bank, World Bank or Agence Française de Développement. They have secured these public contracts through their father's ties to officialdom, which he cements on the golf course, and his children's knowledge needed to meet the donors' demands, including formal contracting, tendering procedures and the French and English languages. The family has hardly done business with 'new' Chinese—only "some import"—and Phally feels that although "we came from China also, the mentality is not the same; we have been educated in different ways". As Western donor money is increasingly replaced by Chinese investments and aid, however, Phally is considering learning Mandarin, if only because Chinese investments represent a "huge" opportunity.

Discussion: Impacts of the 'New' Chinese on Cambodian Society

Phnom Penh's SME owners and *oknha* have engaged with 'new' Chinese investments and economic migrants in different ways. For SME owners, 'new' Chinese migrants are an increasingly important clientele, and raw materials, machinery, consumer goods and capital from Greater China have been vital resources for many of their business ventures. For the *oknha*, China is an export destination for Cambodian timber and cash crops, and 'new' Chinese investments provide business opportunities in the form of construction contracts and joint-ventures in real-estate development, industrial parks or the energy sector. Arguably, then, the 'old' Chinese play an important role in facilitating the inflow of 'new' Chinese capital and goods. For Phnom Penh's 'old' Chinese business community, the economic rewards of comprador capitalism (Yoshihara 1988)—that is, of bridging 'new' Chinese capital and the Cambodian economy—is substantial, which has also spurred the revitalization of Chinese language and cultural expression in the city.

This conclusion merits a few caveats. First, under the broad umbrella of 'Chineseness', actual business exchanges among 'old' and 'new' Chinese often rely on family connections (among SMEs) or CPP matchmaking (among the *oknha*) more than shared Chinese ethnicity per se. Second, many local firms, big and small, have hardly been affected by the 'new' Chinese presence. Most entrepreneurs do not have the connections to benefit from 'new' Chinese investment and trade, nor do the 'new' Chinese pose a threat to the competitiveness of many local businesses. Third, the 'new' Chinese frequently bypass the 'old' Chinese. Petty traders from China go at it alone selling their products in Phnom Penh, and large-scale infrastructural projects are wholly financed and executed by Chinese state enterprises.

That being said, the impacts of 'new' Chinese investments, businesses and migration on Cambodian society are undisputed, and Phnom Penh's business community offers a valuable window into these impacts. It can be argued that 'new' Chinese involvement reinforces Cambodia's established politico-economic order, which is characterized by ethnic Chinese economic dominance as well as a divide between the business-state elite and the general population. This order existed during Sihanouk's rule and rapidly re-emerged in the post-conflict 1980s and 1990s. Indeed, as pointed out by Slocomb, in the early 1990s "the traditional patterns and inequalities of Cambodian society had largely reasserted themselves" (2003, p. ix). Cambodian Chinese—mostly of Teochew descent—were quick to reclaim economic control over the SME sector as well as within the elite, and in doing so, built legacies of Chinese language, business culture, and ethnic, kinship and political ties. Although not fundamentally altering Cambodia's political economy, in two ways the 'new' Chinese have further perpetuated it.

First, 'new' Chinese involvement propels the revival of ethnic Chinese economic dominance, culture and language in Cambodia. By sending teachers and donating books and money, China supports Chinese schools in Cambodia (Marks 2000), including the earlier-mentioned Duanhua school, which is now the largest overseas Chinese school, with 15,000 students (Strangio 2014). Chinese investors, white-collar workers and tourists are omnipresent, Chinese identity has come to stand for business success and prosperity, Phnom Penh's otherwise bustling markets come to a standstill during Chinese New Year, and even Hun Sen has encouraged Cambodians to emulate Chinese-style wealth (Phorn 2012). A newfound cultural confidence holds sway especially over younger-generation Cambodian Chinese, many of whom speak Mandarin and have been spared the discrimination and atrocities of the Cold War. Without doubt, 'new' Chinese migration, investment and Sino-Cambodian political amity have contributed to this "*identité recomposée*" (Tan 2006).

Second, 'new' Chinese involvement in Cambodia has augmented the divide between the elite and the general population. By channelling aid and investment into Cambodia via the *oknha* and in accordance with Hun Sen's development agenda, Chinese private and public investors have provided Hun Sen the resources to oil the patronage system. Although a portion of Chinese investments and goods enter Cambodia through the effort of small-scale entrepreneurs—either 'old' or 'new' Chinese—without ties to the elite, these efforts are dwarfed by large-scale infrastructural and real-estate projects, ELCs and mining concessions, and garment or tourism sector investments. Phnom Penh's business-state elite benefits from these investments by way of financial rewards, political consolidation and expanded business portfolios, while for the majority of Cambodians these investments entail land evictions, the loss of rural livelihood, or low-paid jobs in the garment or construction sectors. The private sector divide between the *oknha* and SME owners, then, is symptomatic of a society-wide divide between the elite and ordinary Cambodians.

In conclusion, it is worthwhile considering the societal challenges posed by these developments. To begin with, it remains to be seen what the effect of 'new' Chinese commercial influence on the position of Chinese culture and identity in Cambodia will be. On the one hand, the relentless exploitation of Cambodia's natural and human resources is generally blamed on Hun Sen's government and only sporadically on China or Chinese companies (Ciorciara 2015). Indeed, especially when compared to other countries in Southeast Asia, anti-Chinese sentiments have historically been limited in Cambodia (Willmott 1981). On the other hand, it is reported that such anti-Chinese sentiments are on the rise due to alleged unethical behaviour of Chinese tourists and the 'takeover' of Sihanoukville (Wright 2018). It is unlikely, however, that negative sentiments directed at the 'new' Chinese will also affect the 'old' Chinese. Ethnic boundaries between Khmer and the 'old' Chinese have blurred due to intermarriage, cultural and religious exchange, and the assimilation policies of the 1970s and 1980s. Moreover, despite popular notions that business is the preserve of the Chinese, Cambodians of Chinese descent are also represented in government and civil society. For these and other reasons, it is unlikely that 'new' and 'old' Chinese identities will be conflated in public discourse.

The growing divide between chiefly exploitative elites and exploited local communities certainly is problematic, and may indeed backfire on members of this elite, including the *oknha*. In 2013, the CPP faced its worst electoral performance since 1998. It fell back from 90 to 68 seats in the

National Assembly, whereas the opposition—united under the leadership of Sam Rainsy and his Cambodia National Rescue Party (CNRP)—won fifty-five seats despite electoral 'irregularities' and a CPP-dominated National Election Committee. In the aftermath of the elections the CNRP boycotted parliament and protesters took to the streets, but the storm settled. In the run-up to the 2018 elections, Hun Sen turned increasingly authoritarian, banning the CNRP and forcing critical media to close. The CPP eventually claimed all national assembly seats in what were widely considered sham elections. Observers of Cambodia are worried as few reassuring scenarios are available (Hutt 2016b). It is unlikely that the SME owners of this study will instigate political change. Although they have to put up with rent-seeking officials and are excluded from the get-rich-quick opportunities enjoyed by the *oknha*, they are served by political stability and are relatively well-off. Cambodia's rural and urban poor, however, are increasingly disillusioned as a result of displacement and indebtedness, persistent corruption, poor education and health care, and few opportunities for upward socio-economic mobility. As the excesses of Hun Sen–style authoritarianism spread across Cambodia and with generational succession changing the demographics of the electorate (Eng and Hughes 2017), people seem "no longer willing to accept Pol Pot's nightmare as a benchmark" (Strangio 2014, p. 259) for CPP legitimacy.

Note

1. Names of interviewees have been changed to ensure anonymity. Actual names of business people do appear throughout this article (in the next section), but only where information is derived from publicly accessible sources such as newspapers or websites, not where information is derived from fieldwork.

References

Arnold, Dennis, and Toh Han Shih. 2010. "A Fair Model of Globalisation? Labour and Global Production in Cambodia". *Journal of Contemporary Asia* 40, no. 3: 401–24.

Bahree, Megha. 2014. "Gateway to Cambodia: The Mysterious Couple Who Bring Investments in to Cambodia". *Forbes*, 24 September 2014. http://www.forbes.com/sites/meghabahree/2014/09/24/gateway-to-cambodia-the-mysterious-couple-who-bring-investments-in-to-cambodia/#32f5ce97a3bc.

Burgos, Sigfrido, and Sophal Ear. 2010. China's Strategic Interests in Cambodia. *Asian Survey* 50, no. 3: 615–39.

Chanda, Nayan. 2002. "China and Cambodia: In the Mirror of History". *Asia-Pacific Review* 9, no. 2: 1–11.
Cheng Sokhorn. 2018. "Business Insider: China Investment Boon Comes with a Price". *Phnom Penh Post*, 5 February 2018. https://www.phnompenhpost.com/business/business-insider-china-investment-boon-comes-price?utm_source=Phnompenh+Post+Main+List&utm_campaign=1cdbcbf00f-20180109&utm_medium=email&utm_term=0_690109a91f-1cdbcbf00f-62156065.
Ciorciari, John D. 2015. "A Chinese Model for Patron-Client Relations? The Sino-Cambodian Partnership". *International Relations of the Asia-Pacific* 15, no. 2: 245–78.
Cooke, Nola. 2011. "Tonle Sap Processed Fish: From Khmer Subsistence Staple to Colonial Export Commodity". In *Chinese Circulations: Capital, Commodities and Networks in Southeast Asia*, edited by Eric Tagliacozzo and Wen-chin Chang, pp. 360–79. Durham: Duke University Press.
Dahles, Heidi. 2013. "Why China Charms Cambodia". *East Asia Forum*, 24 August 2013. https://www.eastasiaforum.org/2013/08/24/why-china-charms-cambodia/.
Dahles, Heidi, and John Ter Horst. 2012. "Institutionalising Chineseness: Legacies of Chinese Commercial Hegemony in the Cambodian Silk Industry". *Journal of Contemporary Asia* 42, no. 2: 210–29.
Ear, Sophal. 2009. "The Political Economy of Aid and Regime Legitimacy in Cambodia". In *Beyond Democracy in Cambodia: Political Reconstruction in a Post-Conflict Society*, edited by Joakim Öjendal and Mona Lilja, pp. 151–88. Copenhagen: NIAS Press.
———. 2016. "Greater China, Cambodia, and the Garment Industry". In *Chinese Global Production Networks in ASEAN*, edited by Young-Chan Kim, pp. 119–35. Heidelberg: Springer.
Edwards, Penny. 2007. *Cambodge: The Cultivation of a Nation, 1860–1945*. Chiang Mai: Silkworm Books.
———. 2009. "Ethnic Chinese in Cambodia". In *Ethnic Groups in Cambodia*, edited by Hean Sokhom, pp. 174–234. Phnom Penh: Center for Advanced Studies.
———. 2012. "Sojourns across Sources: Unbraiding Sino-Cambodian Histories". *Cross-Currents: East Asian History and Culture Review* 1, no. 2: 398–418.
Eng, Netra, and Carolina Hughes. 2017. "Coming of Age in Peace, Prosperity, and Connectivity: Cambodia's Young Electorate and its Impact on the Ruling Party's Political Strategies". *Critical Asian Studies* 49, no. 3: 396–410.
Filippi, Jean-Michel. 2010. "Cambodia: The Swing of the Pendulum". *Phnom Penh Post*, 26 November 2010. http://www.phnompenhpost.com/post-plus/cambodia-swing-pendulum.
Global Witness. 2007. *Cambodia's Family Trees: Illegal Logging and the Stripping of Public Assets by Cambodia's Elite*. London: Global Witness.

———. 2015. *The Cost of Luxury: Cambodia's Illegal Trade in Precious Wood with China*. London: Global Witness.

Gottesman, Evan R. 2003. *Cambodia after the Khmer Rouge: Inside the Politics of Nation Building*. New Haven: Yale University Press.

Heng Pheakdey. 2015. "China's Role in the Cambodian Energy Sector: Catalyst or Antagonist for Development?" *South East Asia Research* 23, no. 3: 405–22.

Heuveline, Patrick H. 1998. "'Between One and Three Million': Towards the Demographic Reconstruction of a Decade of Cambodian History (1970–79)". *Population Studies* 52, no. 1: 49–65.

Hin Pisei. 2019. "China Still No1 Source of FDI". *Phnom Penh Post*, 23 September 2019. https://www.phnompenhpost.com/business/china-still-no1-source-fdi.

Hughes, Caroline, and Kheang Un, eds. 2011. *Cambodia's Economic Transformation*. Copenhagen: Nordic Institute of Asian Studies Press.

Hunt, Luke. 2013. "Ly Yong Phat, the King of Koh Kong". *Bangkok Post*, 3 February 2013. http://www.bangkokpost.com/print/334020/.

Hutt, David. 2016a. "How China Came to Dominate Cambodia". *The Diplomat*, 1 September 2016. http://thediplomat.com/2016/09/how-china-came-to-dominate-cambodia/.

———. 2016b. "The State and the CPP: Cambodia's Social Contract". *The Diplomat*, 19 August 2016. http://thediplomat.com/2016/08/the-state-and-the-cpp-cambodias-social-contract/.

Khy Sovuthy. 2013. "CCP Senator Starts Work on SEA Games Sports Complex". *Cambodia Daily*, 14 April 2013. https://www.cambodiadaily.com/archives/cpp-senator-starts-work-on-sea-games-sports-complex-18748/.

Kiernan, Ben. 1986. "Kampuchea's Ethnic Chinese under Pol Pot: A Case of Systematic Social Discrimination". *Journal of Contemporary Asia* 16, no. 1: 18–29.

Kimsong, Kay. 2001. "Cambodia to Build First-Ever Palm Oil Processing Plant". *Cambodia Daily*, 20 December 2001. https://www.cambodiadaily.com/archives/cambodia-to-build-first-ever-palm-oil-processing-plant-28224/.

Kloosterman, Robert, and Jan Rath. 2001. "Immigrant Entrepreneurs in Advanced Economies: Mixed Embeddedness Further Explored". *Journal of Ethnic and Migration Studies* 27, no. 2: 189–201.

Kuhn, Philip A. 2008. *Chinese among Others: Emigration in Modern Times*. Singapore: National University of Singapore Press.

LICADHO. 2019. "Cambodia's Concessions". http://www.licadho-cambodia.org/land_concessions/ (accessed 5 December 2019).

L.Y.P. Group. n.d. "Home". http://www.lypgroup.com (accessed 13 September 2017).

Marks, Paul. 2000. "China's Cambodia Strategy". *Parameters* 30, no. 3: 92–108.

Mertha, A. 2012. "Surrealpolitik: The Experience of Chinese Experts in Democratic

Kampuchea, 1975–79". *Cross-Currents: East Asian History and Culture Review* 4, no. 4: 65–88.
Milne, Sarah. 2015. "Cambodia's Unofficial Regime of Extraction: Illicit Logging in the Shadow of Transnational Governance and Investment". *Critical Asian Studies* 47, no. 2: 200–28.
Muller, George. 2006. *Colonial Cambodia's "Bad Frenchmen": The Rise of French Rule and the Life of Thomas Caraman*. London: Routledge.
Nyíri, Pal. 2012. "Investors, Managers, Brokers, and Culture Workers: How the "New" Chinese are Changing the Meaning of Chineseness in Cambodia". *Cross-Currents: East Asian History and Culture Review* 1, no. 2: 369–97.
———. 2014. *New Chinese Migration and Capital in Cambodia*. Trends in Southeast Asia, no. 3/2014, pp. 1–20. Singapore: ISEAS – Yusof Ishak Institute.
Odom, Sek, and Simon Henderson. 2014. "As Oknha Ranks Grow, Honorific Loses Meaning". *Cambodia Daily*, 21 June 2014. https://www.cambodiadaily.com/archives/as-oknha-ranks-grow-honorific-loses-meaning-62057/.
O'Neill, Daniel. 2014. "Playing Risk: Chinese Foreign Direct Investment in Cambodia". *Contemporary Southeast Asia* 36, no. 2: 173–205.
Osborne, Milton. 2004. *Before Kampuchea: Preludes to Tragedy*. Bangkok: Orchid Press.
Pellechi, Gregory. 2012. "Koh Kong King Bowed Out of 'Blood Sugar' Firm". *Phnom Penh Post*, 3 August 2012. http://www.phnompenhpost.com/national/koh-kong-king-bowed-out-%E2%80%98blood-sugar%E2%80%99-firm.
Percival, Bronson. 2007. *The Dragon Looks South: China and Southeast Asia in the New Century*. Westport: Praeger Security International.
Percival, Thomas. 2012. *Articulating Intra-Asian Urbanism: The Production of Satellite City Megaprojects in Phnom Penh*. PhD dissertation, University of Leeds.
Phorn Bopha. 2012. "Hun Sen Encourages Cambodians to Emulate Chinese-Style Wealth". *Cambodia Daily*, 30 December 2012. https://www.cambodiadaily.com/archives/hun-sen-encourages-cambodians-to-emulate-chinese-style-wealth-7028/.
Po, Sovinda, and Kimkong Heng. 2019. "Assessing the Impacts of Chinese Investments in Cambodia: The Case of Preah Sihanoukville Province". *Pacific Forum Issues & Insights* 19: 1–19.
Prak Chan Thul. 2019. "Cambodian Leader, in Beijing, Says China Pledges Nearly $600 Million in Aid". Reuters, 22 January 2019. https://www.reuters.com/article/us-cambodia-china/cambodian-leader-in-beijing-says-china-pledges-nearly-600-million-in-aid-idUSKCN1PG0CZ.
Sim Vireak. 2019. "Sihanoukville: A Cambodian City Losing Its 'Cambodian-ness'". *The Diplomat*, 20 April 2019. https://thediplomat.com/2019/04/sihanoukville-a-cambodian-city-losing-its-cambodian-ness/.

Slocomb, Margaret. 2003. *The People's Republic of Kampuchea, 1979–1989: The Revolution After Pol Pot*. Chiang Mai: Silkworm Books.

———. 2010. *An Economic History of Cambodia in the Twentieth Century*. Singapore: National University of Singapore Press.

Soth Koemsoeun. 2019. "Gov't Backtracks on Ban on Self-Employed Foreigners". *Phnom Penh Post*, 6 October 2019. https://www.phnompenhpost.com/national/govt-backtracks-ban-self-employed-foreigners.

Springer, Simon. 2010. *Cambodia's Neoliberal Order: Violence, Authoritarianism, and the Contestation of Public Space*. London: Routledge.

Strangio, Sebastian. 2014. *Hun Sen's Cambodia*. Chiang Mai: Silkworm Books.

Sullivan, Michael. 2011. "China's Aid to Cambodia". In *Cambodia's Economic Transformation*, edited by Caroline Hughes and Kheang Un, pp. 50–69. Copenhagen: Nordic Institute of Asian Studies Press.

Tan, Danielle. 2006. *La diaspora chinoise du Cambodge: Histoire d'une identité recomposée*. Master's thesis, Institut d'Etudes Politiques.

Veasna Var. 2016. "Cambodia Should be Cautious When It Comes to Chinese Aid". *East Asia Forum*, 9 July 2016. http://www.eastasiaforum.org/2016/07/09/cambodia-should-be-cautious-when-it-comes-to-chinese-aid/.

Verver, Michiel. 2012. "Templates of 'Chineseness' and Trajectories of Cambodian Chinese Entrepreneurship in Phnom Penh". *Cross-Currents: East Asian History and Culture Review* 4, no. 4: 23–51.

———. 2015. *Chinese Capitalism in Cambodia: An Anthropological-Institutional Approach to Embedded Entrepreneurship*. Zutphen: CPI Koninklijke Wöhrmann.

Verver, Michiel, and Heidi Dahles. 2015. "The Institutionalisation of Oknha: Cambodian Entrepreneurship at the Interface of Business and Politics". *Journal of Contemporary Asia* 45, no. 1: 48–70.

Verver, Michiel, and Juliette Koning. 2018. "Toward a Kinship Perspective on Entrepreneurship". *Entrepreneurship Theory and Practice* 42, no. 4: 631–66.

Wijers, Gea D. 2011. "The Reception of Cambodian Refugees in France". *Journal of Refugee Studies* 24, no. 2: 239–55.

WikiLeaks. 2017. "Cambodia's Top Ten Tycoons". 9 August 2007. https://wikileaks.org/plusd/cables/07PHNOMPENH1034_a.html.

Willmott, William E. 1967. *The Chinese in Cambodia*. Vancouver: University of British Columbia Press.

———. 1970. *The Political Structure of the Chinese Community in Cambodia*. London: Athlone.

———. 1981. "Analytical Errors of the Kampuchean Communist Party". *Pacific Affairs* 54, no. 3: 209–27.

———. 1998. "Cambodia". In *The Encyclopedia of the Chinese Overseas*, edited by Lynn Pan, pp. 144–50. Randwick: Archipelago Press.

———. 2012. "Reflections on Research in Cambodia, Half a Century Ago: An Address to the Thailand, Laos, Cambodia Studies Group". *Cross-Currents: East Asian History and Culture Review* 1, no. 2: 279–90.
Wright, George. 2018. "Anti-Chinese Sentiment on the Rise in Cambodia". *The Diplomat*, 7 November 2018. https://thediplomat.com/2018/11/anti-chinese-sentiment-on-the-rise-in-cambodia/.
Yoshihara, Kunio. 1988. *The Rise of Ersatz Capitalism in South East Asia*. Singapore: Oxford University Press.
Zhou Daguan. 2007. *A Record of Cambodia: The Land and Its People*. Chiang Mai: Silkworm Books.

16

Entrepreneurial Excursions: Short-Hop Chinese Migration at the Peripheries of Myanmar

Andrew Ong

The boatman perches precariously on one end of a long bamboo raft, his hands clutching the long pole that guides the raft to the opposite bank. A traveller hops gingerly from the bank on to the other end of the raft, his right arm stretched out by his side to balance the weight of a heavy suitcase in the other. Stabilized, the boatman pushes off from the edge with his pole, artfully drifting across the river eddies and edging carefully to the other bank. It is dry season, the river is barely thirty metres wide, and the currents are gentle. The traveller strolls from one end of the raft to the other, hands the boatman some money, and hops off at the other end. This crossing of an international boundary has taken all of forty seconds.

This river is the international border between Yunnan Province, China and Shan State of Myanmar. And this illicit crossing has taken place in full view of the official border bridge just 200 metres upstream. The Chinese banks of the river are filled with gravel and larger rocks, dumped here as part of ongoing construction to build up its embankments. On the other side, sits Myanmar, but not really. It is a place called Wa Region, territorially part of Myanmar, but almost completely de facto autonomous, governed by the United Wa State Army (UWSA), an Ethnic Armed Organization (EAO) at odds with the Myanmar military (Tatmadaw) and Myanmar state. A ceasefire signed in 1989 when the UWSA was formed has never been broken, and an uneasy truce has held for thirty years. There are no Myanmar government representatives on the border; movement is regulated by the Chinese state and the UWSA.

Dozens of crossing points like this exist along the China–Myanmar border, perhaps somewhat surprising for two states which so jealously guard their national sovereignty. But such crossings are the sustenance of the borderland economy integral to China's 'going out' policy: it circumvents the bureaucratic hassle of passports and documents; it provides commercial opportunities and livelihoods for border crossers, and eases pressures on the Chinese labour market. The Chinese state closes an eye to such movements; it sets up larger checkpoints further inland to stop narcotics smuggling and other criminal activity, but flexibility on the border is integral to economic activity. Hundreds of thousands of border crossers move illegally from China to autonomous regions on Myanmar's peripheries and vice versa every year. This is the unseen dimension of Chinese migration to Myanmar—an issue of increasing concern to the Myanmar government, especially in light of the Chinese Belt and Road Initiative (BRI), which has seen the influx of Chinese capital and investment in infrastructural projects and Special Economic Zones.

Several hundred kilometres along the border to the North is the Ruili–Muse crossing, the only official full international crossing from China to Myanmar. Most official traffic crosses here and on to the Burma Road down south towards the cities of Lashio and Mandalay. Other Chinese travellers fly directly from Chinese cities to Yangon and Mandalay. These crossings have seen millions of arrivals of People's Republic of China (PRC) nationals in Myanmar over the last three decades, along with their investments in real estate, infrastructure and resource extraction.[1] Farrelly and Olinga-Shannon estimate nearly two million migrants moving from China to Myanmar during the period from the late 1980s to 2010.[2] This influx has led to macro-level anxieties over China's increasingly overt influence in Myanmar in foreign policy,[3] its high-profile 2010s investments associated with the BRI, and the cultural impact on Myanmar's nation-building processes.

This chapter, however, looks away from Chinese influx to Myanmar's big cities, and turns its attention to entrepreneurial excursions, a lesser-known short-hop migration of Chinese citizens to autonomous zones at the peripheries of Myanmar. Such movement, I argue, is characterized by three things: low barriers to entry, ambivalence about the permanence of stay, and the prospects for further movement onward into lower Myanmar.

In this chapter, I first lay out four different waves of Chinese migration into Myanmar, along with the historical complexities of the Chinese communities in Myanmar. I situate short-hop Chinese migration as but one subgroup of this wider milieu. I briefly describe the different autonomous zones, then explore the nature of this short-hop migration—the ease of movement due to alternative legal regimes, the benefits of remaining close to the Chinese border through a 'short-hop', and the networks that give rise to potential further movement into Myanmar. Finally, I conclude with the implications of this form of new Chinese migrants (*xin yimin*) to Myanmar, primarily the ambivalent role that their opportunism has in either fragmenting or consolidating Myanmar's national sovereignty and impacting its nation-building processes.

Context: Chinese Migration into Myanmar

To be sure, short-hop cross-border movement is no new phenomenon—borders have long been porous, especially during the post–World War II period, when instability on both sides of the border saw migrants moving to seek safety and livelihoods in whatever havens they could manage. In this immediate post-war period, newly independent Burma (1948) and the fledgling PRC (1949) were accosted by the nationalist (Kuomintang, KMT) remnants, who, defeated in the Chinese Civil War, fled to the Burmese border to wage counter-attacks against the Chinese Communist Party. The 1950s chaos saw the movement of thousands of Chinese along with the KMT into North and Eastern Burma.[4] In the late-1960s, the Communist Party of Burma (CPB) moved into the same borderlands seeking a stronghold and recruitment pool for its revolutionary war against the Burmese state.[5] With them came Chinese support in the form of weapons, equipment, volunteers and advisors.

The CPB was ultimately unsuccessful in overthrowing the Burmese military junta during the 1970s, and by the 1980s had lost its Chinese support. In 1989 it splintered into various ethnic-based armed groups, several of which formed the EAOs that are at loggerheads with the Myanmar state today. Many of these groups were co-opted by the Tatmadaw over the years as militias, while others signed bilateral ceasefire agreements in the early 1990s. This created a "ceasefire capitalism"[6] that produced autonomous zones controlled by EAOs—militias signing ceasefires with the Myanmar state in return for concessions to tax trade, produce and traffic narcotics, and to extract natural resources such as minerals, timber and gems. The EAOs administered their own autonomous zones of control, with capital to run services and maintain standing armies of anywhere between 500 and 30,000. A map of Myanmar's zones of control is a patchwork of different colours and an alphabet soup of insurgent groups.[7] Throughout this period of fractured sovereignties and overlapping zones of control at the edges of Myanmar, Chinese migrants were present, brokering commercial deals, investing in industry or operating businesses from restaurants and hotels to mining and gemstone companies.

Scholars have largely distinguished four waves of Chinese migration into Myanmar. First, the colonial and pre-colonial migration up to the 1950s. These were mainly maritime ('overseas') networks of Cantonese and Hokkien from Guangdong and Fujian provinces who settled in Yangon, and some upriver to Mandalay.[8] Other Yunnanese came over the land border to Northern Myanmar, but fewer in number compared to the maritime route. Second, the 1950s–1970s influx of Yunnanese migrants who came overland with the KMT troops, or fled the disorder and hardships of the Great Leap Forward (1958–62) and Cultural Revolution (1966–76).[9] These migrants settled in Northern Myanmar, either in Shan State or in Mandalay, and were quickly involved in all forms of commercial activity.

Third, another wave of Yunnanese overland migration following the 'opening up' of China with Deng Xiaoping's economic reforms of the late 1980s. It became possible after 1986 for Chinese nationals to leave China legally without needing government permission with the passing of the Control of the Exit and Entry of Citizens Law.[10] Ceasefires with the EAOs at the peripheries of Myanmar in the early 1990s also led to stability that encouraged economic development and movement.[11] These Yunnanese migrants moved mainly to Mandalay in great numbers (an estimated 200,000 Chinese arriving in the 1990s, out of a city population of 1,000,000[12]), leading to an outcry from the local Burmese population. By the late 2010s, the population of ethnic Chinese in Mandalay was estimated to be around 1.5 million.[13]

Fourth was the 2000s and 2010s wave of what might be described as *xin yimin* or New Migrants. This corresponded with Myanmar's geopolitical turn towards China following US sanctions in 2003, and the easing of travel restrictions when President Thein Sein's quasi-civilian government came to power in 2010.[14] With frequent flights from big cities all over China, Chinese movement to Yangon and Mandalay was no longer limited to Yunnanese, Hokkiens and Cantonese. While some observers tend to lump the new migrants of the 2010s in together with the Yunnanese moving across the border in the 1990s, the linguistic and cultural differences between the Yunnanese and the Chinese from the eastern coast make the latter far more conspicuous in terms of consumption, wealth and business practices. This final wave has been associated with a rapid pace of Chinese migration, infrastructural mega-projects altering physical landscapes across the country, commercial takeovers and rising prices, and increasingly overt political engagement by the Chinese state.[15] Consequently, contemporary Chinese identities in Myanmar are an overlapping mosaic of origins and subjectivities: Sino-Burmese, Kokang Chinese,[16] PRC nationals and Yunnanese borderlanders complicate any conception of a monolithic Chinese community.

Three Autonomous Regions and Changing Notions of 'Illegality'

The peripheries of Myanmar are peppered with zones controlled by autonomous and semi-autonomous armed actors that exhibit varying degrees of state control and integration into the Myanmar economy. Twenty or so EAOs are currently involved in an ongoing peace process with the Myanmar state, marked by the partial success of the 2015 Nationwide Ceasefire Agreement (NCA). The 2015 NCA, however, excludes most of the northern EAOs, who refused to sign the agreement, forming instead a political alliance to negotiate with the government as a bloc. Most of these groups have bilateral ceasefires with the Tatmadaw, but others, like the Arakan Army, are still engaged in ongoing armed conflict.

I focus on contemporary Chinese migration to three of these non-government controlled 'special regions' at the edges of northeastern Myanmar—Kokang Region, Wa Region and Mongla Region. The regions have long-standing ties with China by virtue of their border location and being governed by groups that emerged from the fragments of the CPB.

While this patchwork of overlapping control poses challenges to the sovereignty and nation-building project of the Myanmar state, the overall stability of these regions has made them particularly attractive to Chinese migrants and investment—ranging from labourers to businessmen to gamblers to traders and investors.

Kokang Self-Administered Zone is largely controlled by the Myanmar government, the Tatmadaw having driven out the Kokang insurgent group (the MNDAA) in 2009 and installing a friendly militia commander in its stead. Nonetheless, its main town of Laukkai, which sits directly on the Chinese border, is largely Chinese in appearance and activity. Granted the status of Shan State Special Region 1 (Kokang) in 1989, it has a population of about 200,000.[17] A total of 25,000 people live in Laukkai, and the area is estimated to be 90 per cent ethnically Chinese.[18] Chinese, Yunnanese and the Kokang dialect (similar to Yunnanese) are widely spoken across town; the majority of its schools follow the Chinese curriculum across the border.[19] Laukkai's economy includes rubber, tea, walnut and sugarcane plantations in the rural hills, but mainly relies on the glitzy casinos, which provide employment to locals and attracts visitors from China.

Further to the south of Kokang region is Wa Region, formerly Special Region 2 and now the Wa Self-Administered Division. This region is by far the most autonomous of all zones across Myanmar, and is controlled by the UWSA, with 30,000 troops, the strongest of Myanmar's EAOs.[20] The Myanmar state has only a small presence of healthcare and education officials in Wa Region. The UWSA made its capital in the narcotics trade in the 1990s and has since diversified its income into a variety of hotels, airlines, properties, mines and plantations across the country. Its main town of Pangkham, like Laukkai, resembles a Chinese lower-tier town and operates almost completely in the Chinese language, using Chinese mobile networks and Chinese currency. As with Kokang Region, rubber, sugarcane and some tea plantations provide a cash crop for the Wa economy, and commercial opportunities are created around Chinese visitors to its main casinos. Wa Region has large tin mines in its highlands, which accounted for more than 95 per cent of Myanmar's total tin output in 2015. It maintains its military and administration with revenue from these sources, providing for its people in a haphazard fashion. While the population of Wa Region is more than 70 per cent ethnically Wa, the town of Pangkham itself has a large Chinese community of new PRC migrants who work in the hotels, casinos and other businesses.

Mongla region, formerly Special Region 4 and now the Mongla Self-Administered Zone, is located just east of Wa Region. Run by the National Democratic Alliance Army (NDAA), a close ally of the UWSA, the town of Mongla has been sensationally described as a "Sin City" at the "edge of the law".[21] Known for its glitzy casinos, availability of wildlife products, sex industry and narcotics production, Mongla's NDAA seems happy to rely on the protection of the UWSA and take a backseat in national politics. Its economy relies heavily on taxes from the gambling industry, which has recently moved online catering to Chinese gamblers (Than 2016). Casinos provide higher paying jobs to locals as card dealers and hostesses. The town is filled with hotels, shops and restaurants banking on the tourism industry of visitors mainly from China. Smaller areas of rubber plantations exist, but given the low prices of rubber, these are not the mainstay of the economy. More so than Pangkham and Laukkai, Mongla town itself is highly transitory—gamblers, traders and sex workers make it a region that relies more on tapping on transactions and flows than on resource extraction.

Chinese migrants moving into all these three areas from China require a border pass to cross from China. Chinese citizens who have household registrations (*hukou*) from counties adjacent to the border can apply for a 'border citizen's pass' (*bianmin tongxingzheng*). Other Chinese citizens from across China can register for a border entry pass (*churujingzheng*), which will allow them to cross legally at the official provincial-level border gateways at Zhenkang, Menga and Daluo. The criteria for receiving this border entry from the administration is unclear and perhaps discretionary. There are several other district-level crossings along the borders of these regions that accept these passes as well. But many other travellers from China simply cross illegally across rivers or by motorbike on small paths along the porous border.

All these forms of 'neighbourhood' movement challenge the definitions of legal, illegal and illicit. The Chinese government, at least at the provincial level and below, seems to permit informal crossings by its citizens, allowing them to venture out in search of livelihoods. With the exception of the crossing at Kokang region (Laukkai), none of these movements are marked or registered by the Myanmar state since it does not control Wa or Mongla Regions. Official checkpoint movements departing China are presumably recorded by the Chinese government, but not made publicly available. The illegal crossings are not captured by government statistics.

Abraham and van Schendel make a distinction between the il/legal and the il/licit: where "[the 'legal' is] what states consider to be legitimate and [the 'licit' is] what people involved in transnational networks consider to be legitimate".[22] Borderland economic flows and practices, according to them, often fall into the category of being illegal yet licit; that is, "legally banned but socially sanctioned and protected",[23] deemed morally acceptable within the borderland milieu. The notion of what qualifies as il/licit, they note, invariably changes over time.[24]

The borderland commercial dealings of the special regions fall into the grey zone of illegal yet licit economies, offering extremely attractive opportunities for Chinese migrants to exploit. Gambling, for instance, is illegal under Myanmar law, yet a special dispensation is applied to the Kokang region, while Wa and Mongla regions fall outside of Myanmar state control. Casino capitalism is rife in these borderlands, allowing joint ventures between Chinese entrepreneurs and local businessmen to profit off Chinese tourists coming across the border to gamble in the autonomous zones. Online gambling catering to Chinese customers is extremely profitable. With the increased flows of capital and commercial activity, business opportunities are numerous—hotels, restaurants, prostitution, the sale of wildlife parts and other petty trade. Here, the increased cost of living in the casino towns allows for higher profit margins to be extracted from the economic disparities of moving across the border—a bowl of noodles can draw a 50 per cent higher price than on the Chinese side. Most of these businesses are set up by Chinese businessmen and entrepreneurs, operating hotels, working as dealers at the casinos, motorcycle taxi drivers or hawker. In Laukkai, for instance, 90 per cent of the businesses are run by new Chinese migrants, with the remainder being local descendants of earlier Chinese migrants.[25] A similar figure applies to Pangkham and Mongla, though larger businesses in Wa Region are often owned by ruling families from the UWSA.

Commercial opportunities—business permits, extractive concessions, building and land leases—are run through agreement with leaders of the armed groups in the autonomous zones where laws and regulations are not always clearly defined. Money and connections are the de facto mode of operation. Mining concessions were bought by groups of investors in the Wa Region, with ore taxed upon export to China. The jade industry in Kachin State, worth an estimated $31 billion in 2014, was part of these extractive endeavours.[26] Migrant workers from China provide skilled and unskilled labour in the mines, as well as on construction projects. Chinese investors hired Chinese contractors and construction companies, who hired Chinese transportation companies and labourers. Timber, too, was extracted for sale into China, with concessions granted by military commanders of the autonomous areas for the right price. The narcotics industry, while statistics are unreliable, was both an illicit and illegal good that created profit by its movement across legal regimes. Finally, in the plantation sector, Chinese businessmen moving across to Myanmar territory utilized the subsidies and tax cuts offered by China's Opium Reduction Fund to set up plantations in the autonomous zones.[27] They pay local Kokang, Wa and Akha villagers to work the rubber plantations, or provide the fertilizers and inputs for villagers to grow sugarcane and tea. Opportunities exist across all levels—investors, bosses, entrepreneurs and labourers.

Short-Hop Migration to the Autonomous Regions

Because of affinity and proximity to China, and the nature of economic opportunities available, these autonomous zones are particularly suitable for short-hop migration. This is a short-term movement across the Myanmar–China border which demonstrates three characteristics.

First, such movement has *low barriers to entry*. Stealing illegally across the border in Wa Region requires little more than the 100 yuan (US$16) fee for the boatman, and a registration charge of 30 yuan (US$5) upon arrival. Along the Kokang and Mongla borders, it is a quick motorcycle ride through rubber plantations. No passports or passes were required for this route. Upon arrival, the registration of a temporary resident pass would allow a Chinese migrant to stay for renewable periods in Wa Region. Similar arrangements and registrations were possible in the Mongla areas for a price, and yet many others were unregistered under the radar. In Mongla and Pangkham, cracking down on visitors and spot-checks were bad for the business of the town in general, and authorities were willing to keep regulation lax.

Networks of kin and compatriots also made the movement easier. In Pangkham, Chinese migrants from the different provinces often grouped together. Those from Hunan were traders of household items in the market; Sichuanese set up restaurants, ran hotels and drove motorized three-wheeler taxis; investors from the coastal cities pooled money in groups to run mining enterprises. In certain more sensitive and controversial industries like mining and timber, and even smuggling, Chinese migrants were more trusted and valued by Chinese companies for their 'diligence', technical skill and ethnic affinity. Local Wa, Shan or Burmese living in these areas were less frequently employed in these sectors, except to perform more menial tasks like washing. 'Outsiders' were less likely to be trusted. Chang Wen-Chin records a form of this sentiment in the Burmese state-sponsored contraband trade caravans utilized by the Yunnanese Chinese in Burma in the 1980s: "we didn't let strangers join our group. Strangers might steal."[28] In Wa Region in 2015, Wa authorities estimated up to 20,000 Chinese workers in the tin mines of Man Maw during the peak season. Chinese companies often hired Chinese migrant labour rather than turning to local populations in Myanmar: in 2015 there were reports of more than 150 Chinese loggers arrested in Kachin state for illegal logging,[29] and in the Shwe Kokko New City on the Thai–Myanmar border, thousands of Chinese workers were brought in for construction.[30] Low barriers to entry also include the lax regulations in mining, plantation and logging industries. For instance, rubber, sugarcane, watermelon and banana plantations at the peripheries of Myanmar involve unregulated contract farming and land leases that often fall within the areas controlled by armed groups and militias.[31]

Furthermore, the cultural proximity of Kokang, Wa and Mongla regions mean that commercial practices are far more accessible to arriving Chinese migrants. Because bureaucratic structures were adopted from the CPB-era, administrative regulations not only operated in Mandarin Chinese, but political structures were similar to those in China (policing, justice or registries). Informal rules of gift-giving and *guanxi* made it easier for Chinese migrants to navigate the local business communities, and formal permissions were often not required as long as one cultivated the right patrons and connections. The use of Chinese currency and language, mobile networks and internet services in these border towns also reduces the friction for Chinese migrants. WeChat and Alipay are Chinese mobile and online payment platforms readily in use in the regions. This infrastructure keeps transaction costs of time and capital low.

Second, short-hop migration is *exploratory and ambivalent* in the sense that it requires no firm decision and commitment to stay in Myanmar. Hu and Konrad write of Chinese businessmen in Kokang:

[Li] and one of his brothers moved to Kokang from China to establish businesses because of recently enabled benefits of being Chinese and living in Myanmar. Chinese businessmen who become Burmese nationals enjoy privileges by investing in China from the outside, and they are more successful than Burmese businessmen in Myanmar. Meanwhile, Li and his immediate family are close to his extended family across the border, and his children study in China where school costs are lower than in Myanmar and the children are eligible for Chinese local and national scholarships.... Another businessman, also named Li, originally from Sichuan Province, had migrated to Kokang three years ago because Kokang was a better place to do business than his region of China.[32]

Others can leave their families across the border in Yunnan and make short trips back and forth to see relatives. They can wait to see if businesses such as restaurants flourish before deciding to make moves more permanent.[33]

A single male hairdresser I met, Wen, from a Chinese town outside Kunming, Yunnan, moved to Wa Region at the age of twenty. He has been there four years, and though his Temporary Residence Permit has expired, he remained relaxed about renewing it. Working in an up-market hair salon in town, he earned 8,000 yuan a month (US$1,333) compared to 5,000 yuan (US$833) back in China. The narcotics and casino industries in Wa Region created higher costs of living. Wen admits that he moved out of pure curiosity, having read about the Golden Triangle in books. He has never been outside Wa Region to the rest of Myanmar, and has no intention to do so.

Third, short-hop migration holds within it the possibility of becoming a *stepping stone* for further movement into Myanmar. In particular, the towns of Lashio and Mandalay were easier secondary destinations, and "other border towns in the Shan State and Kachin State were obvious places to develop familiarity with the new country".[34] More than half of Lashio's population is said to be Sino-Burmese or Yunnanese in origin.[35] As Hu and Konrad note, Kokang (and the other autonomous regions) have a potentially transitory nature as "an interlocutor and a buffer zone between China and Myanmar."[36]

Business and industry networks create movement between the autonomous zones and across the borderlands. Entering into a particular industry, for instance tin mining in Wa Region, often entails travel to other parts of Shan State in search of further mines. Others make contacts in the jade industry and wind up travelling to the markets in Mandalay or Myitkyina of Kachin State. Hoteliers, plantation investors and traders follow routes and move further south. This movement pattern is widespread across Shan State's history. Chang Wen-Chin records the life history of an informant whose parents were from Longling in Yunnan, escaping to Shan State in Burma with the KMT in the 1950s, then to Taunggyi, Lashio, on to Northern Thailand and finally to Taiwan.[37] Many purchased Burmese nationality on the black market, especially in Mandalay.

Conclusion: Short-Hop Migration, *Xin Yimin* and Nation-Building

This recent Chinese migration to the autonomous zones of Myanmar, especially Kokang, Wa and Mongla regions, all of which bear great social resemblances to China, offers us three different insights into *xin yimin* across Myanmar, and their implications for nation-building. First, they highlight the wide diversity of social experience amongst Chinese migrants in Myanmar. Many do not simply live in government-controlled cities or townships, but have chosen to search for livelihoods and fortunes in the supposedly less-stable peripheries of Myanmar, in areas controlled by insurgent groups at odds with the state. Here they take on a large variety of roles—investors, traders, businessmen, labourers or managers—a demonstration of how different the experience and possibilities of mobility are for people of different classes and backgrounds. Many have different temporal horizons; some seeing the movement as a temporary excursion to make money, while others hope for a longer-term stay.

Second, *xin yimin* and the forms of capital and brokerage they bring with them have an ambiguous relationship with Myanmar's national sovereignty. On the one hand, it is tempting to see their role and their domination of certain industries as part of Chinese colonization of Myanmar, eroding its national sovereignty, as several Burmese observers have.[38] They extract natural resources without providing much employment for ordinary people or investment in local capacities. The capital they spend in obtaining extractive concessions go largely to Myanmar military commanders and political leaders. At the same time, their roles in the conflict economies of the autonomous zones, such as jade, copper and tin, narcotics and the casino economy, have arguably provided insurgents with sources of revenue that have strengthened their opposition to the state,[39] further undermining its sovereignty over its peripheries.

Yet scholars, while acknowledging how armed groups pose a challenge to the state, have simultaneously argued that "armed sovereignties"[40] and the "entrepreneurial turn"[41] have also served to extend the reach of the Myanmar state into its peripheries by co-opting or establishing good relations with insurgent rulers. Insurgents perform rule on behalf of the state. In a sense, the business ties and economic channels established and brokered by Chinese traders and entrepreneurs have actually served to integrate the illegal yet licit economies of these regions into wider spheres of influence. For instance, joint-ventures such as road construction and plantations by Kokang and Wa companies (Asia World and Hong Pang), made possible by Chinese companies providing labour, technology and machinery, actually end up building economic ties between the Myanmar government and armed groups like the UWSA.

While the peace process remains in apparent deadlock, military commanders on both sides are collaborating on business ventures, including in hotels and real estate. Jade and mining industries, again made possible by Chinese investment and technology, open channels of communication through personal ties between state and insurgent leaders. While this seems a perverse form of national integration, with a wide range of adverse consequences, it does open up common ground for collaboration and extends the reach of the state. Chinese investment in the country should not be simply dismissed as fragmenting nation-building projects, but are also an opportunity for brokering integration.

Finally, the movement of *xin yimin* to the autonomous zones brings into relief the complex and changing notions of what it means to be Sino-Burmese—both ethnic Chinese and inhabitants or citizens of Myanmar. Many ethnic Chinese born in Myanmar may not have a national registration card, while PRC Chinese who have only arrived in the 2010s have already purchased these identity documents on the black market. They may not in fact have any long-term interest in staying in the country. Given the sheer difficulty of obtaining statistical information on such movements, aggregate data is almost impossible to compile. Other *xin yimin* have adopted borderland identities, such as the Kokang identity, in order to make claims to indigeneity and move to other parts of Myanmar.[42]

Research should pay attention to their roles in creating conduits drawing the ethnic minority peripheries closer to the centre, rather than simply fuelling conflict and insurgency. Many Chinese migrants are pragmatists with flexible loyalties, seeking a livelihood and form of belonging. They owe no necessary allegiance to China and have a wide potential for assimilation, depending on the Myanmar state's willingness to integrate new migrants. Future directions for inquiry include the relations between the different cohorts of ethnic Chinese migrants to Myanmar—for instance how Sino-Burmese either resist or broker the influx of Chinese investments and capital; how they feel anxious about being caught up in 'anti-Chinese' sentiment triggered by the conspicuous consumption of PRC nationals; or the networks between these cohorts that create pathways from the autonomous zones as stepping stones into the rest of Myanmar. Chinese identity as lived and performed in Myanmar remains an ambivalent mode of belonging.

Notes

1. Tin Maung Maung Than, "Myanmar and China: A Special Relationship?", *Southeast Asian Affairs* (2003): 189–210; TNI (Transnational Institute), "China's Engagement in Myanmar: From Malacca Dilemma to Transition Dilemma", *Myanmar Policy Briefing*, no. 19, July 2016.
2. Nicholas Farrelly and Stephanie Olinga-Shannon, *Establishing Contemporary Chinese Life in Myanmar*, Trends in Southeast Asia, no. 2015/15 (Singapore: ISEAS – Yusof Ishak Institute, 2015), p. 3.
3. Maung Aung Myoe, *In the Name of Pauk-Phaw: Myanmar's China Policy Since 1948* (Singapore: Institute of Southeast Asian Studies, 2011); David I Steinberg, and Hongwei Fan, *Modern China–Myanmar Relations: Dilemmas of Mutual Dependence* (Copenhagen: NIAS Press, 2012).
4. Wen-chin Chang, *Beyond Borders: Stories of Yunnanese Chinese Migrants of Burma* (Ithaca: Cornell University Press, 2014).
5. Bertil Lintner, *Burma in Revolt: Opium and Insurgency Since 1948* (Boulder: Westview Press, 1994).
6. Kevin Woods, "Ceasefire Capitalism: Military–Private Partnerships, Resource Concessions and Military–State Building in the Burma–China Borderlands", *Journal of Peasant Studies* 38, no. 4 (2011): 747–70.
7. BNI (Burma News International), *Deciphering Myanmar's Peace Process: A Reference Guide 2016* (Chiang Mai: BNI, 2017), p. 7.
8. Li Yi, *Chinese in Colonial Burma: A Migrant Community in A Multiethnic State* (Cambridge: Cambridge University Press, 2017); Jayde Lin Roberts, *Mapping Chinese Rangoon: Place and Nation among the Sino-Burmese* (Seattle: University of Washington Press, 2016).
9. Li Yi, *Yunnanese Chinese in Myanmar: Past and Present*, Trends in Southeast Asia, no. 12/2015 (Singapore: ISEAS – Yusof Ishak Institute, 2015), p. 6; Chang, *Beyond Borders*.

10. Pál Nyíri, "Chinese Entrepreneurs in Poor Countries: A Transnational 'Middleman Minority' and Its Futures", *Inter-Asia Cultural Studies* 12, no. 1 (2011): 145–53.
11. Li Yi, *Yunnanese Chinese in Myanmar*, p. 9.
12. Tin Maung Maung Than, "Myanmar and China", p. 206.
13. TNI, "China's Engagement in Myanmar", p. 5.
14. Li Yi, *Yunnanese Chinese in Myanmar*.
15. TNI, "Selling the Silk Road Spirit: China's Belt and Road Initiative in Myanmar", *Myanmar Policy Briefing*, no. 22, November 2019; ICG (International Crisis Group), "Commerce and Conflict: Navigating Myanmar's China Relationship", *Asia Report*, no. 305, 30 March 2020.
16. Myint Myint Kyu, *Spaces of Exception and Shifting Strategies of the Kokang Chinese along the Myanmar/China Border* (Chiang Mai: Chiang Mai University Press, 2018).
17. Ibid. p. 29.
18. Zhiding Hu and Victor Konrad, "In the Space between Exception and Integration: the Kokang Borderlands on the Periphery of China and Myanmar", *Geopolitics* 23, no. 1 (2018): 156.
19. Myint Myint Kyu, *Spaces of Exception*, p. 78.
20. Andrew Ong, "Producing Intransigence: (Mis)Understanding the United Wa State Army in Myanmar", *Contemporary Southeast Asia* 40, no. 3 (2018): 449–74.
21. Charlotte Rose, "Mong La: Myanmar's Sin City", *Myanmar Times*, 31 July 2015, https://www.mmtimes.com/lifestyle/travel/15777-sin-city.html; Andrew Jacobs, "A Border City on the Edge of the Law", *New York Times*, 24 February 2014, https://www.nytimes.com/2014/02/25/world/asia/a-border-city-on-the-edge-of-the-law.html.
22. Itty Abraham and Willem van Schendel, "Introduction: The Making of Illicitness", in *Illicit Flows and Criminal Things: States, Borders, and the Other Side of Globalization*, edited by Willem van Schendel and Itty Abraham (Bloomington: Indiana University Press, 2005), p. 4.
23. Ibid., p. 22.
24. Abraham and van Schendel also contrast borderland flows to crony capitalism, which is the opposite—illicit yet legal—where corrupt state actors legalize for its cronies what everyday people find unethical; see Ibid., p. 20.
25. Myint Myint Kyu, *Spaces of Exception*, pp. 109–10.
26. Global Witness, *Jade: Myanmar's "Big State Secret"*, October 2015.
27. TNI, *Financing Dispossession: China's Opium Substitution Programme in Northern Burma* (Amsterdam: TNI, 2012).
28. Wen-chin Chang, "The Everyday Politics of the Underground Trade in Burma by the Yunnanese Chinese Since the Burmese Socialist Era", *Journal of Southeast Asian Studies* 44, no. 2 (2013): 303.

29. BBC, "Myanmar Jails 153 Chinese Illegal Loggers for Life", BBC, 23 July 2015, https://www.bbc.com/news/world-asia-33632291.
30. Bertil Lintner, "A Chinatown Mysteriously Emerges in Backwoods Myanmar", *Asia Times*, 1 March 2019, https://asiatimes.com/2019/03/a-chinatown-mysteriously-emerges-in-backwoods-myanmar/.
31. ICG, "Commerce and Conflict", p. 18.
32. Hu and Konrad, "In the Space between Exception and Integration", p. 167.
33. A Channel News Asia documentary on Boten, the border town between Laos and China, interviewed a restaurant owner whose family remains in Yunnan for healthcare and education. Using Chinese mobile networks to stay in touch with his family, he runs his restaurant full-time in Boten, where he feels there is less competition in business. See CNA Insider, "The Rebirth of Casino Town Boten, Laos", CNA, February 2020, https://www.youtube.com/watch?v=p9E0NVroum0&ab; Other stories of Chinese migrants include hotel managers and a manager of a 'ladyboy' performing theatre.
34. Farrelly and Olinga-Shannon, *Establishing Contemporary Chinese Life*, p. 7.
35. Helene Le Bail and Abel Tournier, "From Kunming to Mandalay: The New 'Burma Road'", *Centre Asia IFRI, Asie Visions* 25 (2010): 35; Farrelly and Olinga-Shannon's *Establishing Contemporary Chinese Life* have this figure at 30–35 per cent (see p. 8).
36. Hu and Konrad, "In the Space between Exception and Integration", p. 158.
37. Chang, *Beyond Borders*, Ch. 1.
38. Mya Maung, "On the Road to Mandalay: A Case Study of the Sinonization of Upper Burma", *Asian Survey* 34, no. 5 (1994): 447–59.
39. ICG, "Commerce and Conflict".
40. Kevin Woods, "Rubber Out of the Ashes: Locating Chinese Agribusiness Investments in 'Armed Sovereignties' in the Myanmar–China Borderlands", *Territory, Politics, Governance* 7, no. 1 (2019): 79–95.
41. Ken MacLean, "Sovereignty in Burma after the Entrepreneurial Turn: Mosaics of Control, Commodified Spaces, and Regulated Violence in Contemporary Burma", in *Taking Southeast Asia to Market: Commodities, Nature, and People in the Neoliberal Age*, edited by Joseph Nevins and Nancy Lee Peluso (Ithaca: Cornell University Press, 2008), pp. 140–57.
42. Myint Myint Kyu, *Spaces of Exception*, p. 44.

Index

A
Abdullah Badawi, 104
Abdul Razak, 94, 162, 166
Abdurrahman Wahid, 194
accommodationist policy, 74
Aceveda Institute of Business, 72
Adrianople Group, 286
Afro-Asian Conference, 20
Agence Française de Développement, 313
"Agreement on Cultivating Indonesian Chinese Language Teachers", 54
Air America, 247
alien employment permit (AEP), 145–46
Alipay, 331
All-China Federation of Trade Unions, 150
Alliance Party, 166
American War, 216, 256
Amoy University, 99
ancestral land, 3, 23, 94, 100, 102
Angeles University Foundation, 54, 60
Angkor High School, 72
anti-Chinese sentiment, 23, 85, 128, 138, 142, 185, 190, 204, 300, 315, 335
Anti-Money Laundering Council (AMLAC), 152–53
see also money laundering

APTK (*Asosiasi Pengusaha Tiongkok di Kepri*), 187–88
Aquino, Cory Cojuangco, 26
Arakan Army, 326
Army Institute, Cambodia, 72
ASEAN (Association of Southeast Asian Nations), 33, 35, 38, 56, 94, 97, 101, 110, 127, 168, 248, 294
Asia-Europe University, 72
Asian Development Bank (ADB), 12, 127, 262–63, 265, 288, 313
Asian Infrastructure Investment Bank (AIIB), 169, 263
assimilation policy, 4–5, 15, 23, 26, 29, 214, 236, 315
Association for Philippines–China Understanding, 147
Assumption University, 59
Ateneo de Davao University, 60
Ateneo de Manila University, 60
authoritarianism, 93, 316

B
Bahasa Indonesia, 197, 200–201
'bamboo network', 129
Bandung Conference, 20
Bandung–Jakarta high-speed railway project, 197, 202–3
Bangladesh Bank, 153
Bank of China, 169

Banphai Industrial and Community Education College, 55
Bansomdejchaopraya Rajabhat University, 59
Barisan National (National Front) coalition, 166
Basuki Tjahaja Purnama (Ahok), 185, 191, 203–4
Bauxite Nhân Cơ, 226
BECAMEX Bình Dương Corporation, 237
Beijing Foreign Studies University (BFSU), 58, 95
Beijing Olympics, 6, 20, 23, 34, 42
Bello, Silvestre, 145
Belt and Road Initiative (BRI), 4, 6, 10–11, 24, 34, 37–40, 42, 83–84, 94, 96, 129, 142, 148, 158, 163, 167–69, 171, 173, 180, 186, 236, 243, 323
Betong Municipality, 59
Bian Huibin, 112
"Blossoms of Vitality, Colours of Life", exhibition, 108, 115, 117, 121
Boediono, 198
Boeung Kak Lake development project, 307
border SEZ (Special Economic Zone), 282–84
  see also Golden Triangle Special Economic Zone (GT SEZ); Special Economic Zone
Brigade 70, Cambodia, 72
British Malaya, 62, 99, 165
British Virgin Islands, 262
Buddhism, 26
Bulacan State University, 60
Bumiputra, 100
Bun Rany, 307
Burapha University, 59

Burma-Macaolandou Co., Ltd., 275
Burmese Communist Party, *see* Communist Party of Burma (CPB)

C
Cambodia
  Chinese businesses in, 299–313
  Chinese investments in, 79–82
  civil war, 297
  'new' Chinese in, 76–79, 86, 313–16
  'old' Chinese in, 296–99
  partnership, with China, 68, 84
  perceptions towards China, 82–84
Cambodia-China bilateral relationship, 84–86
Cambodia-China Friendship Radio Station, 72
Cambodia National Rescue Party (CNRP), 316
Cambodian Chamber of Commerce, 310
Cambodian People's Party (CPP), 41, 293, 297–99, 307–11, 313, 315–16
Canadia Bank, 72
Cantonese, ethnic group, 74, 215, 296–97, 325–26
Cantonese Opera, 113
caravan trade, 12, 244–45, 331
cash crop, 255, 296, 313, 327
casino, 12, 145, 152–53, 155, 247, 251, 258–61, 275–77, 279–82, 287–89, 306–7, 327–29, 332–33
casino brokers, 283–84
casino capitalism, 12, 273, 285, 329
casino city, 258
"catalytic state", 252
Catholicism, 26
"ceasefire capitalism", 325

Index   341

Center for Migrant Advocacy, 150
Central China Normal University, 57
Central Intelligence Agency (CIA), 247
Chalieco Company (Chinalco Corporation), 226
Chamber of Commerce of China's Enterprises in the Riau Archipelago of Indonesia, 188
Changsha University of Science and Technology, 58
Chan Heng Chee, 111
Chea Sim High School Tbeng Meanchey, 72
Cheng Ho, *see* Zheng He
Chen Xiaodong, 110
Cheongsam Cultural Association, 149
Chiang Mai University, 59
China
    '100 years of humiliation', 32, 34
    Cambodian perceptions towards, 82–84
    economic aid, 37–38, 222–23
    Indonesian perception towards, 198–206
    partnership, with Cambodia, 68, 84
    soft power, 6–8, 25, 50, 62, 68–71, 83, 91–95, 98–100, 102–3, 111, 114, 118, 157, 248
    trading partner, as, 56, 122, 162, 168
    Vietnam, economic relations with, 217–23
China Aluminium Intl. Engineering Company, 218
China Bank, 187
China Brief, 114
China Chamber of Commerce in Indonesia (CCCI), 186–88
China Cultural Centre (CCC), 8–9
    Singapore, in, 107–21

China Donfang Electric Co (DEC), 218
'China Dream', The, 8, 20, 114, 118
China Hongkong and Bay Areas Enterprise, 188
China, Hong Kong and Macau Expatriate & Business Association of Cambodia, 309
China Huanqiu Group, 218
China–Lao Ruifeng Rubber, 256
China–Laos railway, 242, 262
China-Malaysia relationship, formalization of, 94
China–Malaysia Students and Alumni Association, 172
China National Peking Opera Company, 113
China Pacific Insurance, 187
China Railways Corporation, 187
China's Businessmen Association in Riau, *see* APTK
China's Footprints in Southeast Asia, 114
China State Oil Company, 187
Chinatown, 24, 26, 109, 115, 235, 237, 251, 260, 308
Chinese Alumni Associations in the Philippines, 148
Chinese Association of Vientiane, 138
Chinese BPOS IT (Business Processing Outsource Services Information Technology), 151
Chinese capital, impact of, 37–42
Chinese Chamber of Commerce, 23, 216, 309
Chinese Civil War, 324
Chinese Communist Party (CCP), 39, 162, 165, 219, 236, 293–95, 324
"Chinese Culture and I", competition, 113

Chinese Enterprises Philippine
    Association, 144
Chinese Filipino Disaster Relief
    Fund, 149
Chinese Hainanese Association, 308
Chinese Heritage Centre, 108
Chinese identity, 6–8, 27, 41
Chinese International Education
    Foundation, 63
Chinese Language Training
    Institutions, 72–73
Chinese migrants
    anti-Chinese sentiment, 23, 85,
        128, 138, 142, 185, 190, 204,
        300, 315, 335
    organizations of, 147–50
    Philippines, in, 25–26, 141–57
    Southeast Asia, in, 2–5, 19–27
    Vietnam, in, 223–30
    see also migrant workers; overseas
        Chinese; xin yimin
Chinese migration, 1–3, 7
    Beijing's policy on, 20–21, 27
    characteristics, 4–5
    impact of, 37–42
    local communities, and, 9–11
    local economy, and, 11–14
    waves of, 34–37, 39, 42, 196
Chinese Muslims, 163, 171, 177,
    178, 244
Chinese National Office for Teaching
    Chinese as a Foreign Language
    (NOTCFL), 135
'Chinese Nation' (Zhonghua Minzu),
    20
Chinese Opera and Drama Society, 112
"Chinese Overseas", see overseas
    Chinese
Chinese Partner Universities, 57–60
Chinese Power Investments
    Company, 40

Chinese Privilege, mindset of, 117
Chinese proxy, 38
'Chinese–Singaporean culture', 109
Chinese Training Workshop, 53
"Chinese villages", 229
Choeung Sopheap, 307, 309
Chong, Jun, 116
Chongqing University, 59
Chongqing Vocational Institute of
    Engineering, 55
Chua Thian Poh, 108
Chulalongkorn University, 58, 61
citizenship, 6, 9, 20, 129, 131–33,
    137, 164, 175, 178, 214, 217,
    230, 236, 272, 308
'civilization state', 70
civil society, 82, 295, 315
CLMV countries (Cambodia, Laos,
    Myanmar and Vietnam), 6, 11
Cold War, 4, 162, 166, 248, 314
colonization, 39, 128, 263, 299, 333
Command Headquarters of Special
    Forces Paratroopers Brigade
    911, Cambodia, 72
Communist Party of Burma (CPB),
    260, 324, 326, 331
concessional loan, 218, 221–23
Confucius Institute (CI), 7–8, 11, 26,
    49, 63, 68, 70–71, 75, 78, 92,
    95–96, 99, 103, 114
    growth of, 50
    host universities, and, 57–60
    locations in Southeast Asia, 51–52,
        57–60
    Malaysia, in, 95–96, 103–4
    roles of, 52–56
Confucius Institute Headquarters
    (Hanban), 50–51, 54–56, 63, 71,
    95–96, 135, 197
congregations system, 216, 245, 263,
    296

contract farming, 256
Control of the Exit and Entry of Citizens Law, 325
"coolie pattern", 31–32
corruption, 6, 21, 31, 79, 81–82, 86, 133, 153, 242, 246–47, 298, 311, 316
cost of living, 7, 39, 80, 86, 171, 280–81, 329
Council of Ministers, Cambodia, 71–72
Country Garden Holdings, 176
Covid-19 pandemic, 147, 149, 155–56, 185
"Creativity in Pulses" Special Exhibition, 116
crime rate, 70, 80, 85–86, 142, 152–53, 155
"cultural assimilation", 29
cultural diplomacy, 70, 93
cultural identity, 4, 24, 76, 111, 123
Cultural Revolution, 34, 139, 260, 325

D
Dali University, 60
Deng Xiaoping, 1, 4, 19–20, 32–33, 94, 142, 183, 186, 325
Dewi Fortuna Anwar, 203–5
dialect, as identification, 165, 245, 296
dialect-based schools, 134
Ding Yi Music Company, 118, 120
Dok Ngiou Kham Group, 275
DP Architects, 110
Drilon, Franklin, 152
drug trade, 202, 206, 233–34, 247, 258, 260–61, 273–75, 277, 282, 286
  see also narcotics industry
Duterte, Rodrigo, 9, 141–42, 151, 157

E
East Coast Rail Link, 168
Economic Land Concessions (ELCs), 294, 307, 315
Education for Nature Vietnam (ENV), 284
environmental degradation, 7, 80–82, 86
Environmental Investigation Agency (EIA), 284
Ethnic Armed Organization (EAO), 323, 325–27
ethno-nationalism, 27,185
European Union, 5, 56, 311
Excalibur Group Pte Ltd, 40
EXIM Bank, 222, 262
'Exportation of (Communist) Revolution', 135

F
Facebook, 113
Federation of Filipino–Chinese Associations, 147–48
Federation of Filipino–Chinese Chambers of Commerce and Industry, Inc. (FFCCCII), 148, 156
Feihua Xinlian Gong Hui, 148
feudal economy, 1–3
Filipino–Chinese Amity Club, 147–48
Five-Eyes alliance, 98
'flexible citizenship', 272
"floating population", 213, 227
foreign direct investment (FDI), 168, 187, 219–22, 251–52
foreign intervention, 12, 273
foreign workers, 21, 23, 145, 173–74, 185, 191, 237, 262
Forest City project, 24, 176–78
Four Modernizations project, 32

Free Trade Agreement (FTA), 79, 84
Fujian Association, 216
Fujian Normal University, 54, 57, 60, 197
Fujian Province Overseas Association, 148
Fujian Youth Association, 149
FUNCINPEC (*Front Uni National pour un Cambodge Indépendant, Neutre, Pacifique, et Coopératif*), 293

G
gambling industry, 7, 36, 70, 80, 85–86, 142, 145, 147, 152, 154–55, 229, 234, 250–51, 258–61, 273, 276–77, 282–83, 296, 328–29
  see also online gambling, 70, 142, 145, 147, 152, 154, 329
gaming industry, 9, 26, 142, 150, 152–55
Gaokao (University Entrance Examination), 176
Gatot Nurmantyo, 185
General Commissariat of National Police, Cambodia, 72
General History of the Chinese in Singapore, A, 117
General Secretariat of the Senate, Cambodia, 72
Geneva Accords, 215
Gerakan, 166
Giant Consolidated Limited (GCL), 262
global financial crisis, 37
globalization, 4, 12, 27, 213, 243, 252, 255, 262
Global Machinery Company in Indonesia, 187
Global United Chinese Organizations, 134

Global Witness, 295
Goh Chok Tong, 108
Golden Boten City, 257–61
Golden Triangle, 245, 247, 255, 257, 259, 261, 332
Golden Triangle Special Economic Zone (GT SEZ), 12, 270, 273–77, 279–87
  see also border SEZ; Special Economic Zone
Gong Bencai, 187
government-linked companies (GLC), 173
"graduated sovereignty", 257
'Great ChinaTown', 237
Great Depression, 3
Greater Mekong Subregion (GMS), 12, 127, 243, 250, 261, 265
'Greater Southwestern China', 127
Great Famine, 34
Great Leap Forward, 325
Green, Marshall, 274
Groupements administratifs chinois régionaux (Chinese Regional Administration Grouping), 216
Guangtung Association, 216
Guangxi Normal University, 57, 59–60
Guangxi University for Nationalities, 57–59
guanxi, 251, 331
Guilin University of Electronic Technology, 57

H
Hainan Association, 216
Hainanese, ethnic group, 74, 215, 296, 308
Hainan Normal University, 58
Hải Phòng Thermal Power Plant, 228, 238

Hakka, ethnic group, 74, 132, 139, 214–16, 296
Han dynasty, 1
Han language (Hanyu), 23
Hanoi University, 60
Harvard University, 93
Hasanuddin University, 57
Hebei Normal University, 57–58
He (Hakka) Association, 216
Heng Samrin Tboung Khmum University, 72
High, Holy, 278
"High-Speed Rails China-Thailand Chinese Language Training Programme", 55
Hilgers, Lauren, 282
Hokkien, ethnic group, 74, 215, 296–97, 325–26
Hong Kong Fuk Hing Travel Entertainment Group Ltd., 258
Hontiveros, Risa, 153
HSK test, 71–72
HSKK test, 71
Huachiew Chalermprakiet, 60
Huang Huikang, 24
Huang Minxuan, 258
huaqiao (Chinese citizens overseas), 6, 20, 23–24, 27, 190, 214, 217, 245–46, 248, 251
Huaqiao School of Pakse, 136
Huaqiao University, 58, 60
huaren (foreigners of Chinese descent), 6, 20, 23–24, 27, 214
Huawei, 97
Hui Chinese, 10, 163, 178–80
Hu Jintao, 34, 69, 93, 108, 186, 194
human capital, 39, 248, 298
human rights, 38, 93, 180, 295
human trafficking, 142, 152–53, 286
Hun Sen, 38, 73, 293, 297–98, 307, 309, 314–16
hybrid community, 164
hydropower, 40, 82, 170, 251, 253, 262, 294, 300

I

identity politics, 185, 191
"imagined community", 35
IMPART Collectors' Show, 116, 121
indigenization, 74, 158
'indigenous Indonesians', 185
Indonesia
  China Chamber of Commerce in Indonesia (CCCI), 186–88
  Chinese in, 22–24
  "migrant workers", as defined in, 191
  perception of China, and, 198–206
  xin yimin in, 185–90, 196–203
Indonesian Air Force, 200
Indonesian House of Representatives (DPR), 202
Indonesian Institute of Science (LIPI), 203
Industrial and Commercial Bank of China (ICBC), 169, 187–88
Institute of China Studies, 104
Institute of Malaysian Studies, 100, 104
inter-marriage, 3, 35
international higher education, 97–99, 103
International Islamic University of Malaya (IIUM), 167, 179
International Organization for Migration of the United Nations (UN), 183
international students, 8, 61, 70, 98–99, 104, 136, 171–72
inflation, 79–80, 86
Irrawaddy, The, 40
Islam, 179

J

Jaime, Sin, 26
Jakarta Post, The, 199
Jamestown Foundation, 114
Jiangsu Taihu International, 309
Jiujiang University, 57, 71–72
John Hopkins University, 98
Joko "Jokowi" Widodo, 11, 190, 199–200, 204–5
Junior Chinese Chamber of Commerce, 148

K

Kabalikat ng Migranteng Pilipino, 150
Kasetsart University, 53, 58
Kaun Chao Chen (Cambodians of Chinese descent), 69, 74
Khemarak University, 72
Khmer culture, 74, 76
Khmer identity, 85
Khmer Rouge, 4, 74, 293, 297, 303–4, 312
Khon Kaen University, 55, 59
Kings Romans Casino, 259, 265, 286
Kings Romans Co., Ltd., 275
Kings Romans Company, 270–71, 275–76, 281
Kings Romans Group, 259–61, 265
Ko Ko Thett, 40
Kompas, news agency, 199
Kong Zi Institute for the Teaching of Chinese Language, 53, 55, 58, 104
Koran Tempo.co, news agency, 199
Kuantan–Qingzhou Industrial Parks, 168
Kunming–Bangkok high-speed railway, 127
Kunming University of Science and Technology, 58
Kuomintang (KMT), 20, 245, 247, 324–25, 333
Kwa Chong Guan, 109
Kwok Kian Woon, 117
Kyaukpyu, port of, 38

L

labour union, 200–201, 228
Lagunzad III, Ciriaco A., 145
land concession, 41, 254, 255–56, 271–72, 279, 285, 287, 294, 298
land-grabbing, 81
language acquisition, 68–70, 87
language diplomacy, 70–71
language education, 68–69, 135, 150
language training, 7, 53, 72, 234
Lao Airlines, 247
Lao Army, 256
Lao Cultural Heritage Forum, 288
Lao Kingdom of Lan Xang, 244–45, 263
Lao Meng Khin, 307–9
Laos
   caravan trade in, 244–45
   Chinese alliance, and elites, 246–47
   Chinese middlemen, and, 244–52
   Chinese schools in, 136
   Northern Master Plan, 254–55
   "Old" and "New" Chinese in, 129–34, 137–39
   population density, 128
   resettlement in, 277–81
   "turning land into capital" strategy, 252–61, 271, 278
'*lao yimin*' (old migrants), 195
Leechiu, David, 151
Leechiu Property Consultants, 151
Lee Hsien Loong, 25, 29, 108, 116–17
liberal values, 93

Index   347

Li Keqiang, 95
Lin Mingxian, 260
Li, Tania, 274
Liu Cheng, 187
Liu Peng, 144, 158, 248
Liu Thai Ker, 109–11
Liu Yandong, 199
Li Wenguang, 188
Li Yinze, 23
Low Sin Leng, 111
Low Tze Wee, 116
Luhut Pandjaitan, 187
Lukchin, 3
luodi shenggen, policy, 5–6, 20
'luoye guigen' (return to original roots), 5–6, 14, 20
lychees trade, 231
Ly Chinese Family Association, 308
Ly Yong Phat, 307–8

M
Mae Fah Luang University, 59
Mahasarakham University, 59
Mahathir Mohamad, 24, 38, 166, 178, 180
Ma Jianfei, 63
Malang State University, 57
Malayan Communist Party, 162, 165–66
Malay Archipelago, 3
Malaysia
  China's soft power in, 94–95
  Chinese in, 24, 163–66
  Chinese students in, 171–72
  Chinese workers in, 173–74
  Confucius Institute (CI), in, 95–96, 103–4
  Emergency, the, 165
  foreign workers in, 173
  General Election, 24, 39, 174, 178
  new Chinese nationals in, 166–81

  projects by Chinese companies in, 170
  trading partner, 162, 168
Malaysia, Federation of, 181
Malaysia My Second Home Programme (MM2H), 163, 171, 175–78
Malaysian Chinese Association, 38–39
Malaysia Studies Programme, 8
Malay Studies programme, 100
"Mandarin +", 55
Mandarin Center, 53
Mandarin language, 23, 35, 49, 53, 73–76, 150, 188–89, 197
Maranatha Christian University, 57
Maritime Silk Road Confucius Institute, 60
market economy, 253, 255
Mason, Frederic, 61–62
Mass Rapid Transit System, 168
MCA, 166
McCarthyism, 101
Melaka Gateway, 38
Melaka Sultanate, 94
'Memoirs of Nanyang', 116
mestizo Chinese, 3, 25–26
MIC, 166
middle class, 33
Migrant Chinese Chamber of Commerce and Industry of the Philippines, 148
'migrant', definition, 183
migrant workers, 10, 21, 150, 185, 191, 198, 200–201, 203, 205, 209, 223, 227, 236–37, 329
  see also Chinese migrants
'migration strategy', 201–2
Ming dynasty, 1, 94, 164
Minh Huong, 3
Ministry of Agriculture and Forestry, Laos, 254

Ministry of Culture and Fine Arts, Cambodia, 72
Ministry of Culture, China, 73
Ministry of Culture, Community and Youth (MCCY), Singapore, 108
Ministry of Education, China, 95, 100
Ministry of Foreign Affairs and International Cooperation (MOFAIC), Cambodia, 72, 74, 78, 80, 83, 85
Ministry of Health, Vietnam, 233
Ministry of Industries and Commerce, Vietnam, 219
Ministry of Justice, Cambodia, 72
Ministry of Labour, Invalids and Social Affairs (MOLISA), Vietnam, 223–24, 226
Ministry of Manpower, Indonesia, 23
Ministry of National Assembly–Senate Relations and Inspections, Cambodia, 72
Ministry of National Defence, Cambodia, 72
Ministry of Planning and Investment, Laos, 252
Ministry of Public Security, China, 155
Ministry of Tourism, Malaysia, 175
'modern slavery', 155
Monash University, 99, 172
money laundering, 142, 154, 261, 276–77, 285, 311
   see also Anti-Money Laundering Council (AMLAC)
Mong Reththy, 309
Morrow Architects & Planners, 111
"motherland", 39, 131, 217
multiculturalism, 92, 181
multilateralism, 93
Muslim Chinese, see Chinese Muslims

Myanmar
   autonomous regions, and, 326–33
   Chinese migration into, 324–26
   Kokang Region, 326–27, 329–34
   military (Tatmadaw), 323, 325, 327
   Mongla Region, 326, 328–31, 333
   Nationwide Ceasefire Agreement (NCA), 326
   short-hop migration, 13–14, 324, 330–33
   Wa Region, 323, 326–27, 329–34
Myitsone Dam, 38, 40, 138

N
Najib Razak, 24, 96
Nanchang University, 57
Nanyang Academy of Fine Arts, 109, 111
Nanyang Technological University, 58, 108
narcotics industry, 261, 285, 323, 325, 327–28, 330, 332–33
   see also drug trade
National Arts Council, 111
National Democratic Alliance Army (NDAA), 260, 328
national identity, 25, 96, 117–19
national language, 62, 74
National Library, 109
nationalism, 2, 14, 27, 34, 74, 185
nationality law, 20
National University of Laos, 53, 55, 58
National University of Singapore, 117
nation-building, 2, 4, 14, 19, 36, 62, 70, 74, 164, 324, 327, 333–34
Nationwide Ceasefire Agreement (NCA), 326

natural resources, extraction of, 4, 40, 127, 187, 243, 253, 270, 272, 276, 294, 325, 333
neo-colonialism, 243, 262
neoliberalism, 13, 273, 282
Neo Peng Fu, 118
network building, 55–56
'New Chinese Migration', 32
New Economic Policy, 166
New Order, 189, 194, 204
New York University, 98
NGOs (non-government organizations), 40, 69, 82, 150, 180, 195, 200, 295
Nhất An Company, 228
nine-dash-line claim, 94
North China University of Water Resources and Electric Power, 58
North–South Economic Corridor (NSEC), 12, 243, 249–50, 263
Northwest University, 60
Nottingham University, 98, 172
Nye, Joseph, 93

O

Office of Chinese Language Council International, 50
Office of Foreign Assets Control (OFAC), 285
oknha business groups, 307–15
'*oknha* club', 310
oknha, title, 41, 298–99
Olympic Games, *see* Beijing Olympics
One Belt One Road, *see* Belt and Road Initiative (BRI)
One-China Policy, 310
online gambling, 70, 142, 145, 147, 152, 154, 329
  see also gambling industry

'Open and Reform' policy, 9, 129, 163, 252, 255, 323
open-door policy, 2, 4, 32, 94, 98, 180, 186, 325
opium, 128, 247, 255, 260
Opium Reduction Fund, 330
Opium Replacement Policy, 255, 260
Opium Replacement Special Fund, 256
Opium War, 2
Organisation of Islamic Cooperation (OIC), 179
overpopulation, 2
overseas Chinese, 20, 22–23, 26, 32, 34–36, 39, 91–92, 94, 102–3, 119, 132, 135–36, 139, 158, 190, 214, 216–17, 236, 245, 250, 264, 314
  effect of, 99–101
  see also Chinese migrants; *xin yimin*
Overseas Chinese Affairs Office (OCAO), 23, 26, 39
Overseas Chinese Associations, 216
Overseas Chinese Enterprise and Employee Survey (OCEES), 158
"Overseas Chinese wealth", 32
Overseas Community Council, 135, 138
overseas Filipino workers (OFWs), 150

P

PAGCOR, 151–52, 154
Panin Group, 188
Panthay Rebellion, 245
passports, revocation of, 155
"*pastillas* scheme", 153
patriotism, 34

patronage system, 53, 246, 294, 298, 309, 315
Peidu Mama (Mother Who Accompanies Children for Education), 176
Peking University, 58, 61
People's Liberation Army (PLA), 247
People's Republic of China (PRC), see China
Peranakan Chinese, 3, 22–25, 117, 137, 190
Peranakan Museum, 117
Perng Peck Seng, 108, 111
Pheapimex, 309
Philippine Chinese Chamber of Commerce and Economics, 148
Philippine Council for the Peaceful Unification of China, 148
Philippine Migrants Rights Watch, 150
Philippine National Police, 153
Philippine offshore gaming operations (POGO), 9–10, 142, 145, 151–56
Philippine Retail Trade Nationalization Law, 147
Philippines
  Bureau of Immigration (BI), 143, 145, 153–54
  Chinese migrants in, 25–26, 141–57
  Department of Foreign Affairs, 155
  Department of Labor and Employment (DOLE), 145–47
  Department of Tourism (DOT), 143–44
  dualism in, 10
  National Bureau of Investigation (NBI), 153
  population, 142–43
Philippines China Chamber of Commerce, 142, 148
Philippines–China Friendship Association, 147
Philippines–China Friendship Foundations, 148
Philippines East China Amity Club, 148
Philippines Soong Ching Ling Foundation, 148
Phnom Penh China Cultural Centre, 72–73
Phranakhon Rajabhat University, 60
Ping Sheh Singapore, 112–13
pluralism, 29, 111
pollution, 70, 85, 276
Pol Pot, 316
poverty, 2, 32, 78, 82, 156, 185, 213, 261, 274, 279–80
Powell, Colin, 98
PP Group Co., Ltd (Thailand), 275
Prabowo Subianto, 190
President University (Universitas Presiden), 188, 197
'pribumi', 195, 201, 203, 205, 207
Prince of Songkla University, 59
'Principles of Peaceful Coexistence', 294
pro-China organizations, 147–50
Promotion of Peaceful Development, Philippine Chapter, 148
property prices, rising, 7, 39
PT Bank ICBC Indonesia, 188
PT China Communications Construction Industry Indonesia, 188
PT Cindo International Marine Trading, 188

Index   351

PT Damai Indo Pertama Sukses, 188
PT Indah Kiat Pulp & Paper, 197
PT TJK Power 188
'pure' Chinese, 3
Pusat Bahasa Mandarin, 53, 57

Q
Qianqian Luli, 197
qiaoju, 3
Qing Dynasty, 138, 165, 215
Quảng Ninh Thermo-Power Plant, 226

R
race politics, 178
racial riot, 166
racism, 24, 156
Rannaridh, Prince, 293
Rattikone, Ouane, 247
Reading University, 172
'Reform and Open' policy, 135
"resource frontiers", 257
Rich Banco Berhad, 262
Rise of China and the Chinese Overseas: A Study of Beijing's Changing Policy in Southeast Asia and Beyond, The, 114
'rootless' migrants, 5
Royal Academy of Cambodia, 53, 57, 71, 73
Royal Cambodian Armed Forces, 72
Royal University of Phnom Penh (RUPP), 72–76, 78, 80, 83, 85

S
Sam Rainsy, 316
'satellite Chinese', 6
Scalabrini Migration Center, 150
scholarship, 7, 55–56, 61, 72, 92, 100–101, 136, 188, 197, 332

School of Chinese Language and Culture, 100
sea embargo, 2
Second Penang Bridge, 168
Secret War, 247
SEGI University, 58, 96
shadow economies, 272–73, 282
"shadow state", 12, 252
Shandong University, 58
Shanghai Electric Group Co Ltd. (SEC), 218
Shanghai University, 59
'shared sovereignty', 272
shared values, 25
Shen Xiaoqi, 188
short-hop migration, 13–14, 324, 330–33
Sihanouk, King, 296, 314
Sihanoukville, 38, 70, 77–79, 85, 294, 306, 310–11, 315
Silk Road, 243, 263
Silk Road Fund, 263
Sindonews.com, 199
Singapore
    China Cultural Centre (CCC) in, 107–21
    Chinese in, 25
    General Election, 25, 29
    identity, 117
'Singaporean Chinese identity', 8
Singapore Art Museum, 109
Singapore Arts Federation, 112
Singapore Chinese Arts & Cultural Group Directory, 113
Singapore Chinese Cultural Centre (SCCC), 8–9, 25, 107–11, 113, 115–18
'Singapore Chinese culture', 109, 115, 117
'Singapore Chineseness', 111
Singapore Chinese Orchestra, 109

Singapore Conference Hall, 109
Singapore Federation of Chinese Clan Associations (SFCCA), 108
'Singapore Heart', 8
Singapore Press Holdings, 111
Sino-Japanese War, 100
Sino-Native communities, 164
Sino-Vietnamese war, 264
slaves, indentured, 32
small and medium enterprises (SMEs), 129, 186, 295, 298–99, 302, 305, 312–16
Social Weather Station (SWS), 147
soft power, definition of, 93
  see also soft power *under* China
Sok An, 71
Song dynasty, 1–2, 164
Souphanouvong University, 58
Southampton University, 99
South China Sea dispute, 26, 34, 36, 94, 294
Southeast Asia
  immigration waves, 31–33, 137, 196, 264
  indigenous populations, and, 19–20
  migration to, 2–5, 19–20
Southeast Asian Affairs, 143
Southeast Asian Games, 308
'Southeast-Asianized', 4
Southwest University, 59
Souvanna Khomkham, ancient city, 274, 288
Special Economic Zone (SEZ), 257–61, 265, 271–73, 284–85, 287–88, 307, 309, 311, 323
  see also border SEZ; Golden Triangle Special Economic Zone (GT SEZ)
Special Edition, 116

special working permits (SWP), 145–46, 153
  see also work permit
state-owned enterprises (SOEs), 33, 39, 166–67, 173
Suan Dusit Rajabhat University, 59
Suharto, 4, 22
Sun Tzu, 92
Sun Yat-sen, 135
Sun Yat Sen Nanyang Memorial Hall, 108
Sun Yat-Sen University, 60
supply chain, 40
Surabaya–Madura Bridge (Suramadu bridge), 197–99
Susilo Bambang Yudhoyono (SBY), 11, 194, 198, 202, 204
Swinburne University, 172

T

Tai kingdoms, 244
Taiping Rebellion, 215, 245
Talat Sao Mall, 40
Tan, Anthony, 111
Tan, Eugene K.B., 107
Tanjungpura University, 57
Tan Kah Kee, 99–100
Tan, Kevin, 115
Tân Rai Bauxite Mining, 226
teacher training programme, 7, 54
"Teaching Chinese to Speakers of Other Languages", 72
'tea money', 264
telecom fraud, 155
Teochew Association, 216
Teochew, ethnic group, 74–75, 130, 139, 215, 296–99, 302–6, 311–12, 314
Teochew Opera, 113, 120
TGIF Music Station, 115, 116, 121
Thailand, Chinese in, 26–27

Index

Thein Sein, 326
Thongloun Sisoulith, 134
Tiananmen, 34
Tianjin Normal University, 59–60
Tianjin University of Science and Technology, 59
Tianjin University of Traditional Chinese Medicine, 60
Tian Tian Xiang Shang Exhibition, 116, 121
Toh Lam Huat, 115
totok Chinese, 22, 137, 190
tourism, 73, 78–79, 95, 143–44, 174–75, 195, 223, 235, 251, 253, 259, 261, 273, 276, 279, 282, 287, 294, 306, 315, 328
traditional medicine, 232–34
Traditional Medicine Association, 149
"transnational Chinese", 21, 164, 181
'tributary system', 294
Trump administration, 93
Try Pheap, 309
Tsinoy (Chinese Filipino), 26, 142, 150, 156–57

U

Udayana University, 57
Uighur, 10, 180
UMNO, 24, 166
"Understanding the Internet-Based Casino Sector in the Philippines: A Risk Assessment", 152
unemployment, 2, 147, 201, 213
UNESCO, 274
UNESCO World Heritage Site, 286
Union Youth Federations of Cambodia, 72
United Front strategy, 9
United Front Work Department, 39

United Wa State Army (UWSA), 323, 327–29, 334
Universitas Negeri Surabaya, 57
Universitas Sebelas Maret, 57
Universiti Malaysia Pahang, 58, 96
Universiti Malaysia Sabah, 58, 96
University College of Technology Sarawak, 58
University of Al Azhar, 53, 57
University of Battambang, 54, 57
University of Indonesia, 197
University of Malaya (UM), 53, 55, 61, 92, 95, 104, 172
University of the Philippines, 53, 60
University Sarawak, 96
UNTAC (United Nations Transitional Authority in Cambodia), 293
U Sai Lin, 260
US-China rivalry (Sino-US rivalry), 91–92, 101–2, 222
US Treasury Department, 285
Uyghur, *see* Uighur

V

vaccination programme, 95
Vientiane Times, 288
'vice economy', 261
Vietnam
　China, economic relations with, 217–23
　Chinese traders in, 230–32
　Chinese traditional healers in, 232–34
　engineering, procurement and construction sector (EPC), 218–19, 221, 223
　ethnic Chinese in, 214–17
　General Statistical Office, 214, 223
　Law of Personal Income Tax (PIT), 237
　new Chinese migrants in, 223–30

Vietnam Labour Law, 237
Vietnam War, 246
Villanueva, Joel, 145
visa-upon-landing (VUA), 144, 153
vocational training, 7, 55

W
Wang Gungwu, 3
Wan Qing Yuan, 108
WeChat, 114, 154, 331
Wen Jiabao, 96
Wenzhou University, 59
West Ocean, 1
'Whispers from the Dragon's Teeth Gate', dance, 116
wildlife trade, 260–61, 273, 277, 282, 284, 328–29
Will to Improve: Governmentality, Development, and the Practice of Politics, The, 274
Wine or Spirits Culture, 149
'wolf-warrior' diplomacy, 70
Wollongong University, 172
Wong Man Suen, 258
work permit, 143, 145–46, 154, 185, 200, 226–27, 229, 235
    see also special working permits (SWP)
World Bank, 128, 262–63, 313
World Federation of Huaqiao and Huaren Associations, 20
World Population Review, 128
World Trade Organization (WTO), 34, 42
World War II, 4, 9, 129, 136, 324
World Youth Federation, Philippine Chapter, 148
Wuhan Engineering Co (WEC), 218
Wuhan Kadi Power Chemicals Co Ltd. China, 218
Wuhan Railway Vocational and Technical College, 55
Wu Yi, 256

X
Xiamen Chamber of Commerce, 149
Xiamen University, 5, 8, 59–60, 92, 96, 99–100, 104, 138
Xiamen University in Malaysia (XMUM), 91–92, 96–103, 171
Xihua University, 57
Xi Jinping, 4, 20, 33–34, 42, 69, 71, 73, 83, 94, 101, 108, 117, 133, 168, 186, 194, 263, 311
xin yimin (new Chinese migrants), 1, 9–12, 14, 19, 22, 25–27, 34, 92, 102–3, 113–16, 141–43, 145, 183, 195, 251, 324, 326, 333–34
    Indonesia, in, 185–90, 196–203
    worldwide estimate, 184
    see also Chinese migrants; overseas Chinese
Xinzhi Group, 73
Xue Baohua, 187

Y
Yang Wei, 63
Yeo Huai-seng, 112
Yunnanese, ethnic group, 35, 139, 245, 247, 250–51, 325–27, 331–32
Yunnan Hai Chang Industrial Group Stock Co., 259
Yunnan Normal University, 59
Yunnan Rubber Company, 256
Yunnan University, 144

Z
Zahid Hamidi, 180
Zhang Chaoyang, 187
Zhang Jinxing, 187

Zhang Min, 187
Zhang Wei, 187
Zhao Wei, 270, 274, 276–77, 283, 285–87, 289
Zheng He, 1, 94
Zhou Enlai, 20
Zhuang Guotu, 5, 138
ZTE Corporation Shanghai, 218–19

www.ingramcontent.com/pod-product-compliance
Lightning Source LLC
Chambersburg PA
CBHW072119290426
44111CB00012B/1713